The Unitarian Conscience

The Unitarian Conscience

Harvard Moral Philosophy, 1805-1861

Daniel Walker Howe

Harvard University Press
Cambridge, Massachusetts
1970

© Copyright 1970 by the President and Fellows of Harvard College
All rights reserved
Distributed in Great Britain by Oxford University Press, London
Library of Congress Catalog Card Number 75–11673–6
SBN 674–921–216
Printed in the United States of America

To my mother, Lucie Walker Howe,
and to the memory of my father,
Maurice Langdon Howe

Acknowledgments

I began my study of the New England Unitarians in a seminar taught by John C. Green, from whom I learned much. While the project was in a formative state, Conrad Wright was kind enough to talk it over with me and give me a number of helpful leads. The major portion of this book was presented as a doctoral dissertation to the University of California at Berkeley in 1966. During the process of revision, it has been read by Sydney Ahlstrom, David Hall, Bruce Kuklick, James McLachlan, Robert Middlekauff, Edmund Morgan, Kenneth Stampp, and Ernest Tuveson, each of whom gave me useful advice. I must thank Professor Stampp especially, for his reassuring encouragement when it was most needed. Among the others who have favored my study with their interest and informed suggestions are Robert Archer, Beverly Kelsey, William Moore, Donald Harvey Meyer, and David Tyack.

My work has been generously supported by grants from the Kent Fellowship Program of the Danforth Foundation, the University of California, and Yale University. The staffs of the Harvard College Library (especially those of the University Archives and the Houghton Library), the Andover-Harvard Theological Library, the Boston Athenaeum, the Massachusetts Historical Society, the University Library in Berkeley, California, Starr King Seminary, the State University of Iowa Library, and the Yale University Library went out of their way to be helpful when I was using their facilities. I also thank them for permission to quote from their relevant manuscript collections.

Sandra Shumway Howe has combined wifely attentiveness and loving care with professional skill in assisting me at many points.

I am grateful to the American Society of Church History for awarding the manuscript of this book the Frank S. and Elizabeth D. Brewer Prize for 1970, and for the material assistance that Prize entails.

Finally, I thank Henry F. May, who directed my work through the dissertation stage, for his open-mindedness and sensitivity, his fund of information always at the disposal of his students, and his example of scholarly integrity.

Daniel Walker Howe

Davenport College
Yale University
June 1969

Contents

The Unitarian Conscience

Introduction

Henry Adams looked back with inimitable irony on the New England Unitarianism in which he had been reared. "Viewed from Mount Vernon Street, the problem of life was as simple as it was classic," he reminisced. "Politics offered no difficulties, for there the moral law was a sure guide. Social perfection was also sure, because human nature worked for Good." Reflecting upon the intellectual leaders of antebellum Boston, Adams found their optimism superficial and irritating. Yet, from his vantage point of final disillusionment, he mingled his sarcasm with nostalgia.

Nothing quieted doubt so completely as the mental calm of the Unitarian clergy. In uniform excellence of life and character, moral and intellectual, the score of Unitarian clergymen about Boston, who controlled society and Harvard College, were never excelled. They proclaimed as their merit that they insisted on no doctrine, but taught, or tried to teach, the means of leading a virtuous, useful, unselfish life, which they held to be sufficient for salvation. For them, difficulties might be ignored; doubts were waste of thought; nothing exacted solution. Boston had solved the universe.[1]

Unitarian Boston's answer to the problems of the universe will be the subject of this book.

MORAL PHILOSOPHY

What follows is neither an institutional history of Harvard University nor a denominational history of the Unitarian church. Instead, it represents an attempt to describe a certain frame of mind that prevailed at Harvard, and among many Unitarian clergymen trained there, for the first two thirds of the nineteenth century. For this purpose, "moral philosophy" as then defined provides a logical starting point. Today,

1

"moral philosophy" is a synonym for "ethics," and it is taught as a specialized branch of philosophy. But in those simpler times before the academic profession had become so fragmented, the term "moral philosophy" was used in a much looser sense, and the subject was treated in a broad and general fashion. At the typical American college of the early national period, moral philosophy occupied a large and important place in the curriculum.[2] It was a humanistic study; indeed (were it not for the great attention bestowed on the classics), one might almost call moral philosophy *the* humanistic discipline of the antebellum college, for it encompassed the whole study of human nature. All the twentieth-century social sciences—psychology, sociology, political science, economics—are daughters of the old moral philosophy.[3]

The moral philosopher of the nineteenth century mixed his social science with metaphysics and religion. He was equally at home describing or prescribing human activities. Since he did not separate epistemology and aesthetics from psychology or morals, he taught the theory of knowledge and the theory of art as well as the theory of human behavior. A moral philosopher at Harvard explained, "There is a general science of Human Nature, of which the special sciences of Ethics, Psychology, Aesthetics, Politics, and Political Economy are so many departments."[4] It did not then seem necessary to have these "departments" studied separately; one man could master them all. As if this were not enough, the scope of the moral philosopher was further enlarged by the almost invariable conjunction of moral philosophy with "natural theology," or the study of religious truths independent of Christian revelation.

At most of the old American liberal arts colleges, the course on moral philosophy was taught by the president. At Harvard, however, a special chair had been endowed through the generosity of a local merchant, John Alford. The first Alford Professor of Natural Religion, Moral Philosophy, and Civil Polity assumed his duties in 1817; some idea of how varied these duties were may be gained from the terms prescribed by the Alford bequest. The new professor (whose name was Levi Frisbie) was expected

to demonstrate the existence of a Deity or first cause, to prove and illustrate his essential attributes, both natural and moral; to evince and explain his providence and government, together with the doctrine of a future state of rewards and punishments; also to deduce and enforce the obligations which man is under to his Maker, . . . together with the most important duties of social life, resulting from the several relations which men mutually bear to each other; . . . interspersing the whole with remarks, shewing the coincidence between the doctrines of revelation and the dictates of reason in these important points; and lastly, notwithstanding this coincidence, to state the absolute necessity and vast utility of a divine revelation.

He shall also read a distinct course of lectures upon that branch of Moral Philosophy, which respects the application of the law of nature to nations, and their relative rights and duties; and also on the absolute necessity of civil government in some form, and the reciprocal rights and duties of magistrates and of the people resulting from the social impact; and also on the various forms of government, which have existed or may exist in the world, pointing out their respective advantages and disadvantages.[5]

Besides being the ancestor of the social sciences, moral philosophy was, in a sense, the successor of theology. The prominence of moral philosophy in antebellum American education apparently reflected a desire to supplement religious sanctions with natural bases for values.[6] In most of the old-time American liberal arts colleges, moral philosophy performed the integrative, synthesizing function theology had performed at medieval universities. This was especially so at Harvard, where the dominant Unitarians, while impatient of many theological intricacies that remained important elsewhere, were enthusiastic proponents of moral philosophy. In ranking the "comparative importance of the different branches of knowledge," Harvard professors gave first place to those treating "the mind, the means of moral and intellectual improvement, the social nature, duties, and destination of man"—that is, to moral philosophy.[7] If there was a Queen of the Sciences at Harvard in the first half of the nineteenth century, it was moral philosophy.

In the Harvard Yard, the moral philosopher trained the social, cultural, and religious leaders of eastern Massachusetts. What was said in the Cambridge classroom would be echoed for decades in Boston pulpits, lyceums, and public forums. When Dorothea Dix was thanking Andrews Norton for his support of her reforms, she wrote: "It is your happiness to be the Teacher of *Teachers*; the apostle to apostles: and yr. labors, though they may seem at a brief glance to be somewhat confined, are in fact *not to be measured.*"[8] There was more than flattery in her words. The Harvard moral philosopher was the official arbiter of values for his community—and nineteenth-century Boston took prescriptive values very seriously. Henry F. May has remarked that "a history of [American] moralism would come close to being a history of American thought."[9] The present work is offered in the belief that Harvard Unitarian moralism forms a significant chapter of that larger history.

HARVARD UNITARIANISM

On August 27, 1803, David Tappan, Hollis Professor of Divinity for eleven years, died, thereby bringing on a bitter power struggle for control of Harvard. Tappan had been a moderate Calvinist; his death upset the delicate balance between religious liberalism and orthodoxy on the College faculty. After two years of complicated fighting among the members of the Corporation and the Board of Overseers, Henry Ware, a known Unitarian, was elected to succeed Tappan. With the balance of power tipped in their favor, the Liberals pressed their advantage and replaced the orthodox acting president, Eliphalet Pearson, with a man of their own persuasion named Samuel Webber. Angry Calvinist Overseers vented their feelings in fruitless pamphlets; orthodox faculty members resigned in protest, creating more vacancies for Liberals to fill. The Unitarians had taken over the new nation's oldest institution of higher learning, and the defeated Calvinists could only retreat to Andover, Massachusetts, there, in 1808, to found a seminary of their own.[10]

The controversy over the Hollis Professorship had been a long time in the making. The emergence of Unitarianism in New England represented the climax of "a very gradual, almost an imperceptible, process."[11] For several generations Arminian opinions had been slowly gaining currency in the vicinity of Boston and its nearby college; but with the notable exception of Jonathan Mayhew (1720–1766), eighteenth-century Massachusetts Arminians had not been forward in placing their views before the public. The term "Liberal," which they applied to themselves, they used in the sense of "broad-minded" or "unsectarian." By this designation they expressed their unwillingness to accept adherence to a strictly defined Calvinist creed as a test for church membership. The most important characteristic distinguishing the Liberals from those who remained orthodox (whether Edwardsean or Old Light Calvinist) lay in their estimate of human nature. Beginning with such early Arminian statements as Lemuel Briant's *The Absurdity and Blasphemy of Depreciations of Moral Virtue* (1740), men from the eastern part of the Commonwealth had been entering protests against considering humanity depraved. Anti-Trinitarianism, which was the form New England Liberalism ultimately took, did not become manifest until after the Revolution.[12]

The changes in attitude, though gradual, culminated in a striking transformation. When nineteenth-century New England Unitarianism finally emerged out of the crypto-Arminianism of the eighteenth century, it stood revealed as a well organized philosophy of Christian humanism. Yet historians have seldom accorded this philosophy close examination. They have generally been content to regard the Unitarians as "transitional" figures, and grant them merely passing mention between discussions of their Puritan forbears and their Transcendentalist offspring. In fact, it has even been claimed that the Unitarians of Harvard "had no philosophy [at all] to give their views consistency."[13] Recently, however, informed scholars have called attention to the "distinctive, unique, and integrated theological synthesis" of nineteenth-century Harvard Unitarianism.[14] This "synthesis"—what one might call the classic Unitarian world view—represented a confluence of Protestantism with the Enlightenment.

The years covered by this study, 1805 to 1861, approximate the duration of the sway classical Unitarianism enjoyed at Harvard, beginning with Ware's celebrated election as Hollis Professor and ending with the Civil War. The war seemed to mark the alteration and decay of the old intellectual system, for during it the philosophical ideas of Sir William Hamilton substantially eroded Thomas Reid's common sense philosophy, which had formed the foundation for antebellum Harvard Unitarianism.[15] But, for the relatively long period between these dates, a firm consensus was maintained at Harvard on questions of fundamental importance, and this consensus is best studied as the moral philosophers organized it.

The Harvard Unitarians were, in a way, a peculiar breed. Scarcely existing outside the merchant class of northeastern Massachusetts, they occupied a tiny heterodox enclave in a Trinitarian Protestant nation. Even within the Unitarian denomination there were other competing schools of thought, such as the Transcendentalist Unitarians like Theodore Parker and the Socinian Unitarians in England and America who regarded Joseph Priestley as their leader.[16] Thus Harvard moral philosophy might well appear a subject of merely local interest.

Paradoxically, however, this highly distinctive group of intellectuals were more remarkable for their representativeness than for their distinctiveness. A close examination of Unitarian moral philosophy sheds considerable light upon the general outlook of Western man as he adjusted his inherited Christian views to the modes of thought of the Enlightenment. On some subjects, such as metaphysics, ethics, and natural theology, Harvard views were widely shared. In other respects, such as their belief in the perfectibility of the human personality, the Unitarians were unusual only in carrying widely held ideas to an explicit extreme. The Harvard moralists participated in a worldwide movement of religious thought; they kept in close touch with European intellectual developments and mingled their native attitudes with ideas acquired from abroad. The eighteenth-century New England Liberals, with their devotion to humanistic culture and their deprecation of theological subtleties, were the American counterparts (insofar as the difference of environment allowed) of the English Latitudinarians and the Scottish Moderate Presbyterians. The nineteenth-century Harvard Unitarians represented the culmination of what may be called "the Christian Enlightenment."[17] Thus, Harvard moral philosophy can serve as a convenient model for the study of a much larger historical development.

The Unitarian moralists certainly thought of themselves as heralds of a new and more liberal faith for mankind. "The religious reformation which is now going on, though very different in its character from that of the sixteenth century, is one of not less importance," asserted Andrews Norton in 1827.[18] Nor were the expectations of the Harvard moral philosophers unfounded: one of the features of later American culture foreshadowed in Harvard Unitarianism was modernist Protestantism. The rebellion against Calvinist theology which the Liberals of Massachusetts pioneered was gradually accepted and followed by mainstream American Protestants in general (albeit without a rejection of the doctrine of the Trinity). The Unitarian denomination itself always remained small, of course, but the Harvard moralists had resigned themselves to this very early. "Our object is not to convert men to our party, but to our principles," they declared. "Unitarians have done more . . . by promoting a real though gradual change for the better in the opinions of other sects, than by building up their own denomination."[19] By 1857 a Unitarian could estimate, with justification, that there were ten times as many covert Liberals in other denominations as there were professed Unitarians.[20] Orthodox professors at Yale and Princeton enjoyed the approval of a wider public in their day, but the long-range impact of the Harvard moralists on American religion was more significant.

More important than modifications of doctrine, however, was a change in men's very attitude toward theology. The emphasis on ethics rather than dogma, which the eighteenth-century Liberals pioneered, was one of the mainstays of nineteenth-century Unitarianism and eventually became characteristic of American Protestantism in general. When a Harvard moralist claimed that "a man is not a Christian in proportion to the amount of truth he puts into *creed*, but in proportion to the amount of truth he puts into his *life*," he was expressing an attitude that was becoming widespread.[21] As early as 1844, the influential Presbyterian divine Robert Baird confessed that theological problems no longer aroused much interest.[22] By the beginning of the twentieth century, most respectable American clergymen had little to say about the Trinity, atonement, or predestination.

THE BOSTON ESTABLISHMENT

Any student of Harvard Unitarianism quickly learns that it was—and was considered in its day—the religion of an elite. The moral philosopher in Cambridge was spokesman for a socially and culturally distinct class, centered in and around Boston. Indeed, a recent study calls the

Boston Unitarians "one of the few cohesive and exclusive patrician groups" known to nineteenth-century America.[23] Cohesive they certainly were, though their exclusiveness did not prevent many new men from gaining acceptance (particularly in the generation after the Revolution and the flight of the Tories) into their ranks through education, marriage, or acquired wealth. But whether their standing in the community was old or new, the prosperous merchants and their professional allies exercised leadership in Boston and in its Unitarian churches.[24]

In their political preferences, most Unitarians of eastern Massachusetts were staunchly Federalist down to the mid-1820's. Although Liberal religion did not imply Federalist politics everywhere in America, in the Boston area it usually did. The principal exception was a small group of Jeffersonian merchant-Unitarians in Salem who provided the Republican party of the state with some of its most talented leaders.[25] The Unitarians combined their potent political power with the domination of many local economic, educational, cultural, and philanthropic institutions. Outsiders were often irritated by what seemed to them such undue influence. Harriet Beecher Stowe recalled bitterly that when her orthodox preacher father arrived in Boston in 1825 "All the literary men of Massachusetts were Unitarian. All the trustees and professors of Harvard College were Unitarians. All the elite of wealth and fashion crowded Unitarian churches. The judges on the bench were Unitarian, giving decisions by which the peculiar features of church organization, so carefully ordained by the Pilgrim fathers, had been nullified [in favor of Unitarianism.]"[26]

The ecclesiastical arrangements that the Beechers found so objectionable gave control of church property and the hiring of ministers to the legally constituted "parishes" of the Standing Order in Massachusetts, rather than to the converted "saints" or communicants.[27] In most of the Commonwealth, all taxpayers were considered members of the Congregational parish of their township unless they served notice that they were members of a recognized dissenting congregation. But in Boston, Salem, and Newburyport, only those who bought or rented pews were accounted members of the parish. Thus, while the parish was a rather democratic body elsewhere, in these communities it was controlled by a wealthy minority. The pew-proprietor system gave a distinctly plutocratic tinge to the religious liberalism of maritime Massachusetts. Workingmen and their families, Unitarians themselves ruefully admitted, seldom attended the Liberal meetinghouses of Boston, where they had virtually no voice in church affairs.[28]

Like religion, higher education in eastern Massachusetts bore a strong stamp of mercantile Federalism. "Harvard in politics has always reflected the sentiments of the economic ruling class in Boston," confesses the official historian of the University. "With very few exceptions, none but a Federalist received an honorary degree from 1802 to the 'Era of Good Feelings.' " The only Republican on the faculty, the scientist Benjamin Waterhouse, was dismissed in 1812 amidst political controversy.[29] Such policies did not endear Harvard to everyone; the renowned Jeffersonian scholar William Bentley made a point of donating his library to the Massachusetts Historical Society and not to his alma mater. Resentment against Harvard by Republican yeomen farmers brought political, religious, and economic antagonisms all to a focus.[30] When Henry Ware, troubled by the evident estrangement between his college and many of its natural constituents, set out to account for its unpopularity, he pointed to three factors: (1) the fact that after the Revolution Harvard had "sided with the friends of order and government in opposition to the popular following which then broke out in insurrections"; (2) the religious controversy surrounding his own election as Hollis Professor; and (3) the relatively high cost of living in Cambridge, which discouraged many boys in other parts of the state from attending.[31] Whether they were swayed by political and religious feelings, or kept away by the tuition fees which the Liberal administration doubled in 1807, the evangelical Calvinist folk of western Massachusetts generally preferred to send their sons to Yale, Brown, or (after its charter in 1825) Amherst.[32]

But whatever political, religious, and educational isolation the Boston Unitarians endured was more than matched by their remarkable cultural influence. Between the War of 1812 and the Civil War, there can be little doubt that Boston was the most important literary center in the United States, or that eastern Massachusetts was the most intellectually exciting part of the country.[33] The merchant princes of the New England Renaissance supported literary endeavor much as the merchants of the Italian Renaissance supported painting and sculpture. Besides Harvard University, they maintained the Boston Athenaeum, the Lowell Institute, the Boston Public Library, innumerable learned societies, lyceums, publishing houses, and magazines, as well as the best public school system in the country. "The intercommunity of the learned in Boston and Cambridge" (as contemporaries called it) [34] provided a comfortable home for many of the leading scholars of antebellum America: Edward Everett in classics, Andrews Norton in biblical studies, George Ticknor in Romance languages, and Joseph Story in law, in addition to the German refugee scholars Carl Follen and Francis Lieber. Perhaps nineteenth-century Harvard scholarship left its biggest mark in historical writing; one thinks of Francis Parkman, W. H. Prescott, George Bancroft, J. L. Motley, Jared Sparks, John Fiske, John Gorham Palfrey, and Henry Adams, all of whom came out of the cultural milieu of New England Unitarianism. [35]

In creative writing, the Unitarians also made a disproportionately large impact. While American theology gradually declined in vigor and importance, American secular literature rose, and the contribution of New England Liberals to this literature was substantial. As F. O. Matthiessen pointed out a generation ago, Unitarian religion unquestionably played a crucial role in preparing the way for the "American Renaissance" of the mid-nineteenth century. [36] Emerson, Thoreau, George Ripley, Bronson Alcott—such Transcendentalists as these could never have written their splendid paeans to individualism if the Unitarians had not paved the way for them by destroying Calvinist doctrines of original sin. Though some Transcendentalists like Emerson eventually found it necessary to repudiate organized religion altogether, they still owed a tremendous debt to their Unitarian upbringing and environment. Other famous Transcendentalists, of course, like Theodore Parker and Frederic Henry Hedge, remained within the Unitarian church all their lives. [37]

If Transcendentalism was descended from Harvard Unitarianism by way of revolt, what is called the "genteel tradition" of American literature was descended from Unitarianism more directly. The Brahmin poets and literary critics of the middle and later nineteenth century maintained Unitarian standards of moralism, social conservatism, and respect for classical learning. Out of the Boston of the Unitarian moral philosophers emerged "the Boston of Longfellow, Holmes, Lowell, and the later Emerson, the Boston of the *North American Review,* the Athenaeum, the Saturday Club, and the *Atlantic Monthly,* the Boston called the 'American Athens.' "[38] When the spread of the railroads in the 1850's consolidated the nation into a single publishing market, Boston established itself for a time as the commercial, as well as the intellectual, capital of American letters. The fact that Andrews Norton was the father of Charles Eliot Norton may be taken as a symbol of the relationship between Harvard Unitarianism and American genteel culture.[39]

The Boston cultural leaders of the early Victorian age are not popular today; they put us off by their stuffy, humorless manner. Even their contemporary and co-religionist Harriet Martineau found them provincial, pedantic, and vain.[40] Yet to give the Boston establishment its due, one must admit that it was not only literate, but also relatively compassionate. New England Unitarians contributed almost as much to American philanthropy and social reform as they did to American letters. "The area that included Beacon Street, Cambridge, and Concord was the historical center not only of morality and culture but even, to some extent, of progress."[41] Contemporary observers and later historians seem agreed that it was among the most enlightened areas of the nineteenth-century world in its laws and charitable institutions.[42] The list of Unitarian reformers rivals the list of Unitarian writers; a historian of the denomination proudly cites the following in his roster of humanitarians: Samuel J. May, Charles Sumner, John G. Palfrey, Thomas Wentworth Higginson, George William Curtis, Horace Mann, Dorothea Dix, and Samuel Gridley Howe.[43] It goes without saying that such heroes often annoyed their less benevolent fellow churchmen by crusading for improvements. But despite their conservatism, the New England Unitarians, as a group, were by no means blindly complacent. In fact, they offer an instructive example of a patrician class giving responsible leadership to its community. For all its pretentiousness (and what elite has not been pretentious?), the Boston establishment compares quite favorably with other bourgeois establishments. The Unitarian mercantile oligarchy provided northern society with its counterpart to the Virginian plantation aristocracy in the South—and, during the nineteenth century, the Bostonians certainly proved themselves a more productive elite than the Virginians.

The Unitarian moralists who are the subject of this book, it will become increasingly clear, were men of many paradoxes. Religious liberals and social conservatives, at once optimistic and apprehensive, nationalistic and cosmopolitan, they were elitists in a land dedicated to equality, proponents of freedom of conscience who supported a religious establishment, and reformers who feared change. Underlying a number of these paradoxes was the ambiguous position the moralists occupied within Boston-Cambridge society. Though the Harvard faculty and the Liberal clergy formed part of an interlocking business and professional patriciate, they nevertheless were able to regard their own establishment with a certain scholarly detachment. If they were at times conservative defenders of the status quo, they were also capable of social criticism.[44] Tension between the intellectual and economic components of the Boston elite was always potentially present and tended to become more open with the passage of time. The Harvard moral philosophers offer an instructive example of the peculiar difficulties American intellectuals have experienced in defining their social role.

THE UNITARIAN MORALISTS

The sources on which this book is based consist of the works of twelve leading Unitarian intellectuals of the "Harvard school." Four of these men were the occupants of the Alford chair of moral philosophy during the period treated: Levi Frisbie, Levi Hedge, James Walker, and Francis Bowen. Since the formal title of a man's chair then, as now, did not rigidly determine what courses he could offer, I selected four other Harvard professors whose teaching and writing overlapped into the broad areas then contained in moral philosophy: Henry Ware, Sr. (Hollis Professor of Divinity) , Henry Ware, Jr. (Professor of Pastoral Theology and Pulpit Eloquence), Andrews Norton (Dexter Professor of Sacred Literature) , and Edward Tyrell Channing (Boylston Professor of Rhetoric and Oratory) . To help show how the precepts of Harvard moral philosophy operated outside the classroom, I have included four other Unitarian ministers, all trained at Harvard, in whose careers the principles of Unitarian morality found expression. These are John Emery Abbot, Joseph Stevens Buckminster, Joseph Tuckerman, and William Ellery Channing. I sometimes refer to all twelve men collectively as "the Unitarian moralists."

Levi Frisbie (1784–1822) was the first Alford Professor of Natural Religion, Moral Philosophy, and Civil Polity, installed in 1817.* (Though the chair had been founded in 1782, Harvard, plagued by post-revolutionary poverty and inertia, had waited a generation for the endowment to increase before implementing the terms of Alford's bequest.) He held the professorship but five years. After Frisbie's premature death from tuberculosis, his friend Andrews Norton published such of his lecture notes as were coherent. In his lifetime Frisbie was respected for his piety, acumen, and taste, but posterity has forgotten him. Few copies of his *Miscellaneous Writings* survive; they offer a clear exposition, in technical language, of the official Harvard philosophy.[45]

The second Alford Professor, Levi Hedge (1766–1844), was the father of Frederic Henry Hedge, the Transcendentalist. Of the twelve Unitarian moralists treated here, Hedge is the most obscure personally. Nevertheless, he is historically important because of his textbook, *Elements of Logick,* which first appeared in 1816 and went through many editions thereafter. It was widely used as long as Scottish common sense thought remained current, and enjoyed the ultimate compliment to a nineteenth-century scholarly work of being translated into German. After suffering a stroke in 1830, Hedge retired, and the Alford chair fell vacant again.[46]

James Walker (1794–1874), who rose to become president of Harvard, is a better known figure. Even before he was appointed to the Alford professorship he had been a recognized leader of the Unitarian party for some years. Among the most outspoken of the Liberals, Walker fiercely criticized orthodoxy, especially orthodox revival techniques. Unlike Andrews Norton, however, he was quite tolerant

*Further information on Frisbie and each of the other Unitarian moralists is given in the Biographical Appendix.

toward the young Transcendentalist heretics, and (though he did not share their views) permitted them to express themselves in the Unitarian *Christian Examiner,* which he edited from 1831 to 1839. In the latter year Walker was chosen third Alford Professor of Moral Philosophy, and by 1853 he seemed a natural choice for president of the University. It turned out, however, that he was no longer vigorous enough to be a successful administrator, and he retired in 1860.[47]

The ablest of the antebellum Harvard philosophers, Francis Bowen (1811–1890), served as Alford Professor for thirty-six years (1853–1889). Throughout that time he was a prolific scholar and a vigorous teacher. He was equally at home in metaphysics, economics, literary criticism, theology, and political science. The codifier of Harvard moral philosophy, Bowen often sounds more rigid than his predecessors. He was dogmatic and unpleasant in controversy, though by no means obtuse. Bowen has been called "one of the abler men of the nineteenth century in this country, who managed, because of his orthodox and conservative bias, to be wrong about almost every important intellectual tendency of the age."[48] Bowen did back some social reforms, however, and for all his tactless arrogance, he was at least willing to change his mind. His philosophical views went through three stages of evolution. Down to the Civil War he taught the straightforward Scottish common sense here described; in the 1860's he modified it along the lines of Sir William Hamilton; finally, in the 1870's he became a disciple of Hegel and German idealism.[49]

The event which gets Henry Ware, Sr. (1764–1845), passing mention in many American history books was his contested election, in 1805, as Hollis Professor of Divinity. He is also remembered for the theological dispute he carried on with the Calvinist Professor Leonard Woods of Andover, nicknamed the Wood'n Ware Debate. But Ware found his teaching and administrative duties more congenial than polemics, and his true lifework was the rebuilding of Harvard from its late-eighteenth-century nadir. In 1811 he began the University's first course of formal graduate instruction in divinity; from this grew the Harvard Divinity School.[50]

Henry Ware, Jr. (1794–1843), was minister of the Second Church in Boston, where Ralph Waldo Emerson served as his assistant pastor.

In 1830 Ware turned the parish over to Emerson and joined his father on the Harvard faculty, becoming Professor of Pastoral Theology and Pulpit Eloquence at the new Divinity School. Beginning in 1837 he taught a course in moral philosophy to the divinity students. Despite the handicap of chronically bad health, the younger Ware managed to be extraordinarily active. He was a zealous proponent of many religious and social causes, including Sunday schools, temperance, antislavery, and the ministry to the poor. A tireless poet (if not a gifted one), he wrote many sentimental verses to help promote his humanitarian enterprises.[51]

Edward Tyrell Channing (1790–1856), called "the most famous teacher of composition in the nineteenth century," was a younger brother of William Ellery Channing. In 1819 he became Boylston Professor of Rhetoric and Oratory at Harvard, being a successor of John Quincy Adams in that distinguished chair. For thirty-two years Channing held the Boylston professorship, from which he exerted vast influence. Together with his colleague Edward Everett he is said to have "created the classic New England diction."[52] Among Professor Channing's pupils were Emerson, Thoreau, Holmes, Sumner, Lowell, and Thomas Wentworth Higginson. In politics a Federalist, in theology "a Unitarian of the old school," and in philosophy a disciple of Reid, Channing "stood like a breakwater against the tides and currents of false and misleading fashions," wrote another of his students, Richard Henry Dana, Jr.[53]

An even more prominent defender of Harvard "orthodoxy" was Andrews Norton (1786–1853), dubbed "the Unitarian pope." In 1819 Harvard (despite qualms about his outspokenness) recognized Norton's intellectual abilities by appointing him Dexter Lecturer on Sacred Literature; the lectureship was subsequently converted into a regular chair. Norton participated in a learned controversy with the greatest of the American orthodox biblical scholars, Professor Moses Stuart of Andover, on the respective merits of their theologies. In the 1830's, however, he turned his attention from the Calvinists to the Unitarian Transcendentalists, and engaged in his most famous debate, the one with George Ripley on "the latest form of infidelity."[54] Norton's conduct of the internecine dispute caused great pain to many of his Unitarian contemporaries, but one suspects he never understood their embarrassment. He was a man to whom ideas and their implications were vitally important—too important to be smoothed over for the sake of other people's feelings.

Norton himself was not without feelings. In fact, he was extremely sentimental, especially where women and children were concerned, and he both read and wrote poetry fairly dripping with tender affection. On his trip to Europe in 1827 he sought out the company of romantic poets great and small: Wordsworth, Southey, Joanna Baillie, and Felicia Hemans. Forever hurting others, Norton was hypersensitive and easily hurt himself. Idiosyncratic, pugnacious, and prolific, he was a colorful figure who has yet to receive a sympathetic hearing among historians.[55]

Both "Ned" Channing's literary criticism and Norton's biblical studies were considerably indebted to their contemporary Joseph Stevens Buckminster (1784–1812), minister of the socially exclusive Brattle Street Church. Buckminster crowded activities into the eight years he occupied the pulpit in Brattle Square. More than any other man, he was responsible for the identification of New England Unitarianism with genteel literature. Buckminster took advantage of his family means and generous salary to travel extensively in Europe, acquiring an acquaintance with cultural institutions. Seeing the merchants of rising commercial cities like Liverpool turning their attention to the patronage of belles lettres, he labored to persuade his own prosperous countrymen to follow their example. Buckminster became the chief organizer of both the Boston *Monthly Anthology* and the Boston Athenaeum. A devoted defender of classical learning, he was an equally ardent proponent of the biblical criticism coming out of Germany. Buckminster was an epileptic, and his meteoric career was cut short when he died during a seizure at the age of twenty-eight, just after having been elected Dexter Lecturer at Harvard.[56]

What Buckminster was to Unitarian culture, John Emery Abbot (1793–1817) was to Unitarian piety. This strange youth, with his soft, effusive devotionalism, remains interesting chiefly as a spokesman for "the religion of the heart" and as an archetype of the genteel romantic character. A graduate of Bowdoin College, Abbot came to Cambridge to read divinity under the instruction of the Harvard faculty and William Ellery Channing. During a four-year pastorate at North Church, Salem, he showed how evangelical rhetoric and emotional appeals could be incorporated within "rational" religion. His early death from consumption helped make him, like Buckminster, a culture hero to nineteenth-century sentimentalists.[57]

Joseph Tuckerman (1778–1840), who carried the principles of Unitarian moral philosophy into the realm of philanthropy, came from an old New England family of mercantile wealth and public spirit. In 1801 he accepted the call of the church in Chelsea, a small seacoast village where the pastor's duties included serving as country physician to the inhabitants of the offshore islands. For a quarter century of contented, rather uneventful service he lived there. Then, in 1825, Tuckerman took leave of the people of Chelsea to return to Boston as minister-at-large, working to alleviate the plight of the urban poor. The next decade saw Tuckerman accomplish the pioneering work in social welfare for which historians of American philanthropy remember him. The minister from the small town was transformed into a dedicated crusader on behalf of the city slum-dwellers. The charitable institutions Tuckerman organized and the rehabilitation techniques he developed remained a model for urban reformers in Europe and America until the twentieth century.[58]

There remains, finally, the greatest of the Unitarian moralists, the close friend and co-worker of Tuckerman, Norton, and Henry Ware, Jr., William Ellery Channing (1780–1842). Dr. Channing does not appear in these pages at his full stature, for he is here treated primarily as an exponent of a point of view rather than as a man in his own right. My purpose lies in showing Channing as the representative of a school, the spokesman who best summed up Unitarian thought and displayed its religious, literary, and humanitarian implications, not in portraying the Federal Street pastor's many-sided character.[59] Considering that contemporaries regarded Channing as the leader of a theological party, it is ironic that one should have to apologize for classifying him with that party. Yet some historians have been misled by Channing's disclaimers of affiliation with Joseph Priestley's Socinian Unitarians into dissociating him from the Arian Unitarians of

New England and regarding him as an isolated figure.[60] Still others have preferred to call Channing a Hopkinsian or a Transcendentalist. As a result, the Unitarian angelic doctor has yet to be studied extensively as a Unitarian.[61]

The identification of Channing with Hopkinsianism seems to have been partly due to the mistaken assumption that no proper Harvard Liberal would ever have preached to the "affections" as Channing sometimes did. It is true, of course, that Channing heard the turgid, scholasticized "New Light" preaching of Samuel Hopkins while a young man in Newport, just as he heard the "Old Light" Ezra Stiles. Both these Calvinists made strong impressions on his youthful mind— impressions of revulsion he enjoyed retelling in later years. While Channing accepted neither man's theology, he admired their characters; but his typically generous tribute to the personal qualities of his antagonists must not be misconstrued into agreement with them.[62] In fact, orthodox theology never received harsher treatment than at the hands of Channing in "The Moral Argument Against Calvinism" (1820) and "Unitarian Christianity Most Favorable to Piety" (1826).

Probably an important reason why Channing has often been thought of as a Transcendentalist is that two of his memoirists—William Henry Channing and Elizabeth Palmer Peabody—were Transcendentalists themselves and hence primarily attracted by those aspects of the older man's thought which seemed proto-Transcendental.[63] A careful examination of Channing's philosophy as a whole, however, shows it markedly different from the intuitionist epistemology and monistic metaphysics of Transcendentalism, as well as from its ethical and aesthetic emphasis on spontaneity.[64] To be sure, Channing enjoyed the friendship of several of the young Transcendental Unitarians who revolted against the official Harvard philosophy in the 1830's. But even on a personal basis, his relations with this group were less than close. He refused to join the "Transcendental Club" which met sporadically. Channing long persisted in the hope that Levi's son Frederic Henry Hedge would moderate the Transcendental movement and keep it within the bounds of traditional Christianity. When this hope proved vain, however, he disowned the rebels.[65]

For their part, the Transcendentalists respected Channing as they did no other "Harvard" Unitarian. "In our wantonness we often flout Dr. Channing, and say he is getting old," Emerson is reported to have said once when Channing was thought near death; "but as soon as he is ill we remember he is our Bishop, and we have not done with him yet."[66] But Transcendental relations with the Federal Street pastor became strained after "he drew back in horror" from Theodore Parker's "Discourse of the Transcient and the Permanent in Christianity" of 1841.[67] When Channing died the following year Emerson was under no illusions that his "Bishop" had been a Transcendentalist. He noted in his journal that Channing had been the best of the Unitarian rationalists: "the nearest that mechanism could get to the flowering of genius."[68] Although the contributors to the *Dial* discussed the possibility of an article on Channing in the Transcendental organ, they never produced one. Their inability to decide what to say about the dead preacher is a revealing comment on the relationship between Channing and the Transcendental movement. That the New England Transcendentalists owed an enormous intellectual and spiritual debt to Channing (and to Harvard Unitarianism in general) one may wholeheartedly grant. To identify Channing's outlook with theirs, however, would be to confuse the parent with the child.[69]

Such qualified compliments as Emerson paid Channing pale beside the glory, laud, and honor Harvard Unitarians heaped on their favorite minister. While Andrews Norton was "the Moses in the Exodus from the orthodox realm, Dr. Channing [was] the Aaron," declared the Unitarian *Christian Examiner*. Boston's *North American Review* called Channing "the acknowledged leader of the Unitarian sect, as far as there can be leaders."[70] And if the kindly clergyman himself once told a Methodist correspondent, "I am little of a Unitarian," such ecumenical expressions were common among the Boston Liberals, whom Harvard's President Kirkland called "the unsectarian sect." The fact is that William Ellery Channing was "the man whom all in and out of the denomination thought of when they mentioned Unitarianism."[71] His Baltimore Sermon was the party's platform; his vestry on Berry Street held its ministerial conferences; his oratory graced the dedication of Harvard's Divinity Hall in 1826. Channing's fame as a representative New England Unitarian became widespread even in Europe.

"If he is not the founder, Channing is surely the *saint* of the Unitarians," affirmed the French historian Ernest Renan.[72]

In his reverence for moral philosophy, Channing was a typical Harvard Unitarian. The subject possessed "a usefulness so peculiar as to throw other departments of knowledge into obscurity," he insisted. He planned an enormous compendium of Unitarian moral philosophy which, in the words of his granddaughter and editor, "was designed to be the crowning labor of his life." It would, in fact, have been Channing's only full-length book. But the gentle pastor soon discovered that he was not temperamentally suited for a work requiring such perseverance and rigor. Like many another great churchman, Channing left behind him an uncompleted summa; only the introduction and a draft of the first eight chapters (i.e., less than a third of the book) were ever written. Even so, enough exists for the author to be unmistakably identified with the Harvard version of Scottish common sense philosophy.[73]

Clearly Channing was a very different sort of man from the indefatigable and meticulous Andrews Norton. The Unitarian moralists displayed many variations of talents and temperament, but they were all committed to the same philosophical and religious premises. Some, like Norton and Bowen, were irascible and contentious; others, like Dr. Channing and the elder Ware, were genial spirits who shrank from unpleasant encounters. Tuckerman and the younger Ware were compassionate social activists; Buckminster, a snobbish aesthete; Abbot, a placid quietist. Agreement on intellectual propositions, of course, is perfectly compatible with differences of personality.

THE PROBLEM OF PERSPECTIVE

I am not a Unitarian myself, and I have written about my subjects as an outsider. I did not, however, feel called upon to try to discredit them—or to "rehabilitate" them either.[74] Instead, I conceived my task as the imaginative reconstruction of a vanished world view. For the most part, I have confined my exposition of the Liberal New England mind to ideas that were expressed publicly. This did not restrict me to printed sources, however, since the spoken word could be almost as powerful and public as the written in antebellum America; manuscript notes of lectures and sermons proved useful along with articles in journals and longer published works.

There are two expressions that I have used in rather special senses, requiring some explanation. One of these is "Second Great Awakening." The term is sometimes restricted to the revivals of the year 1800, but Perry Miller, among others, employed it to cover the whole of evangelical Protestant activity in antebellum America (at least up to the "Third Great Awakening" of 1857–1858). In this broad sense, he wrote, "the steady burning of the Revival, sometimes smoldering, now blazing into flame, never quite extinguished (even in Boston) until the Civil War had been fought, was a central mode of this culture's search for national identity."[75] It is in this sense that I shall speak of the Second Great Awakening, and undertake to show how the precepts of Unitarian moral philosophy were applied in a society which—"even in Boston"—was undergoing an awakening of religion. The Unitarian moralists, it turns out, were quite preoccupied with America's quest for national cultural identity.

The second expression requiring clarification is the term "modern." I employ the word modern to designate a period of Western history extending, roughly, from Westphalia to Versailles. As I have already indicated, the Harvard moralists were very much men of their age. The frame of mind classic Unitarianism illustrates was that of the modern period; among its characteristic features were commitments to capitalism, theism, liberalism, and optimism. Perhaps because my interest in Unitarianism arises out of a concern with broader issues of intellectual history, I have felt it more important to describe those aspects of Unitarian thought that were relevant to the modern age as a whole than to stress what was purely local and peculiar. Moral philosophy, not dogmatic theology, was the "marrow" of Unitarian divinity; and through their moral philosophy Unitarian divines displayed a universality of mind that far transcended the idiosyncrasies of their Christology. My study of the Harvard moral philosophers has convinced me that they were not merely amiable, mildly eccentric provincials, but serious thinkers grappling with the central issues of their times. They were, in fact, archetypal modern intellectuals.

The place of Harvard Unitarianism in Western intellectual history is perhaps best summed up in the expression "Christian humanism." Humanism (that is, a philosophy centered on the development of human nature) was by no means peculiar to the modern era, though it was typical of it. Thus, Karl Barth has described the spirit of the Enlightenment as "a revival (a very peculiar one, admittedly) of the sixteenth-century Renaissance . . . The nature of this Renaissance is however explained by the idea of humanism, the latter to be understood in its widest sense."[76] The humanists of nineteenth-century Harvard drew heavily upon the ideas of earlier Christian humanists: Renaissance Erasmians, Cambridge Neoplatonists, and eighteenth-century British Latitudinarians. They shared with these other humanists not only their emphasis upon the dignity of man, but also a devotion to ideals of harmony, compromise, classical learning, and the supremacy of reason. In the first part of this book, I take the moral philosophers who taught at Harvard between 1805 and the Civil War and the Unitarian clergymen they trained as a small-scale model, representative in many respects if unique in others, of modern Christian humanism as manifested in America.

The late Perry Miller, more than any other man, has called attention to "the *representative* quality" (his italics) of the New England mind. He discovered that the intellectual development of New England from its beginnings through the early part of the nineteenth century provides historians with a "laboratory" for the study of "the relation of thought or ideas to community experience."[77] In the second part of this book, therefore, I have attempted to treat the Unitarian Awakening as a case study in the application of ideas to community experience. While Harvard moral philosophy remained essentially unchanged from the early nineteenth century to the Civil War, the United States changed a great deal, and Boston was not impervious to these transformations. Political democratization, westward migration, industrialization, sectional controversy—all of these gave Harvard moralists food for thought. The rise of mass-consumption book publishing and the rapid growth of revivalistic religious denominations had important cultural consequences for Unitarian intellectuals to consider. Though in a certain sense the case study is a restricted one, focused on a single school of thought, its range of concerns—religious, literary, educational, and social—offers an opportunity to examine the implementation of modern ideas in some breadth as well as detail.

We ourselves apparently live in some post-modern era whose shape is not clear. Although we are separated from them by only a century, the Unitarian moralists often sound strangely remote to our ears: it is not easy to sympathize with their complacent, dogmatic tone. As Henry Adams wryly remarked, "The keen joy of truth aggressive and triumphant blended in their consciousness with a tranquil conviction that the limits of truth had been reached."[78] In many ways we post-modern men stand closer to the anguished men of the Reformation era than to these nineteenth-century optimists. Still, it is the duty of the historian to try to understand not only what the people of the past thought, but also how they felt. I suspect the Unitarians were often less sure of themselves than they sounded. And, if they still seem overbearing and shallow at times, it is well to remember that they lived in a young nation, in a day when less had happened to refute confident expectations. Theirs was an age, Alfred North Whitehead observed, when even "wise men hoped."[79]

Part One

Theory:

The Harvard Moral Consensus

I / Mind and Matter

THE METAPHYSICAL FOUNDATIONS of Harvard Unitarianism were prepared by the Scottish common sense philosophers. The confidence with which Thomas Reid, Dugald Stewart, and their pupils solved the most perplexing epistemological problems appealed to the intellectual leaders of eastern Massachusetts. Like the humanists of the Renaissance, Unitarian humanists were academically oriented, and sought the cultivation of human nature within the framework of an organized scholarly curriculum. Upon the foundation supplied by the Scots, Harvard professors were able to construct a durable consensus, containing room for both Enlightenment aspirations and Christian principles.

THE PROBLEM OF EPISTEMOLOGY

"Modern metaphysics," Edwin Arthur Burtt has written, "is in large part a series of unsuccessful protests" against the disintegration of the medieval world view. Between 1500 and 1700 Copernicus, Kepler, Galileo, and others developed quantified physical science, producing an intellectual revolution that displaced man from his central position in the universe and replaced anthropomorphic purposive explanations of events with mathematical models. The task that early modern philosophers set for themselves was to incorporate the findings of the new science into some ordered system that would "reinstate man with his high spiritual claims to a place of importance in the cosmic scheme."[1] One after another, the great metaphysicians of the Christian Enlightenment—Descartes, Locke, and Berkeley—tried their hands at finding a substitute for scholasticism, but their systems provided no final resting place.

Descartes distinguished the existence of three substances: matter, mind, and God. Matter and mind were opposites—"mind" was our own consciousness, containing certain innate ideas; "matter," whose fundamental property was extension, was everything else. God made matter known to mind through the operation of our senses. The British empiricists each attacked a segment of Descartes' philosophy: Locke rejected the possibility of the mind possessing ideas not based on experience; Berkeley rejected the independent existence of matter; Hume rejected the assumption that we can rely on God to validate our sense data.[2]

Locke's *Essay Concerning Human Understanding* was chiefly concerned with perception. In the terminology Locke developed there, an "idea" was a content of consciousness, usually a mental representation of a thing. "Knowledge" consisted in the grasp by the "understanding" of the relationships among ideas. Although he argued that all our ideas derive from sense experience, Locke never explained how we can be sure that these ideas, once arrived at, correspond to anything in the real world. Yet he distinguished between the "secondary" qualities of matter (like color) which he acknowledged were purely subjective, and "primary" qualities (like "figure"), which he considered objective properties of things in themselves. How could one know the "primary" qualities? Though he had tried to rescue the mind from Cartesian isolation, Locke had in fact not solved the problem of how men could know things as they are, apart from mere appearances.[3]

Berkeley offered the solution of theistic phenomenalism. He demonstrated that Locke's epistemology implied an idealistic ontology. If the ideas in our mind were the objects of knowledge, said Berkeley, then it was pointless to refer them to some unknowable material reality: ideas (that is, perceptions) were themselves reality. Ideas which we did not conjure up at will were impressed upon our minds through the senses by God ("Vision is the language of the author of nature").[4] Causality, for Berkeley, lay ultimately in the orderly working of God's Mind. The Divine Will gave sequence and structure to our sensory perceptions.

Hume demolished the hope for a rational metaphysics by showing that the assumptions of British empiricism led straight to skepticism. If all we know is a stream of sense impressions, then everything else—including an external world—is a "fiction." The traditional arguments for the existence of God fell before the corrosive logic of the Great Skeptic. Without God to guarantee the orderly progression of events, trust in causality was left a mere "custom." According to Hume, a man could not even know, in a rigorous sense, that he was the same person from one moment to the next. Twentieth-century logical positivists may find Hume a congenial predecessor, but to his contemporaries he posed a terrifying threat. Since patristic times, Western thinkers had engaged in metaphysical speculation. With Hume, the enterprise had led to bankruptcy. Men could know nothing about ultimate reality.[5]

This was the situation when Thomas Reid (1710–1796) determined to revive the conviction of ordinary men that the world really exists and that we can know about it. He realized that all the British empiricists, including Hume, had been following Descartes in assuming that the objects of knowledge were ideas in the mind. Why not challenge this assumption? The objects of knowledge, Reid boldly asserted, could be sensible things in themselves. The obvious alternative to discredited metaphysics was empiricism, that is, a study of sensory information which would ignore ultimate questions. But most eighteenth-century Europeans were unprepared for anything like logical positivism, so Reid could not afford to dismiss metaphysics altogether. Instead, he proffered a pseudo-metaphysics: the philosophy of common sense, which purported to underwrite empirical knowledge as ontologically "real." Reid was attempting to reassure modern man that despite the disappearance of his medieval authorities he could still rely on reason and common sense for objective knowledge. It was a brave front, and, for a time, it helped stave off intellectual chaos.[6]

Among the many philosophical disciples of Reid were George Campbell (1719–1796), James Beattie (1735–1803), Dugald Stewart (1753–1828), and the popularizer James Oswald (1715–1769). Their Scottish common sense philosophy, as it was called, enjoyed vast academic prestige in Britain and America between the mid-eighteenth and mid-nineteenth centuries. Later philosophers who worked along the same lines but introduced some new elements into the Scottish system included Thomas Brown (1778–1820), Sir William Hamilton (1788–1856), and James Ferrier (1808–1864).[7]

The common sense philosophers agreed upon three epistemological doctrines: (1) observation is the basis of knowledge; (2) consciousness is the medium of observation; and (3) consciousness contains principles which are independent of experience and impose order on the data of experience. These constitutents of consciousness composed what was known as "common sense." The principles of common sense were not innate ideas in the sense that men were born believing them, but rather ideas which, once they were presented, would seem self-evident.[8] Reid's principles of common sense were a miscellaneous assortment. Among the necessary truths were the axioms of logic and mathematics (e.g., no proposition can be both true and false at the same time). Other truths of common sense provided the rebuttal to Hume: they asserted that what we perceive with our senses really exists, and that the laws of nature will operate in the future as they have in the past.[9]

Reid and his disciples in the Scottish school were great admirers of Baconian natural science. The inductive principle, they believed, was an original constitutent of the human mind; common sense (or "intuitive reason") justified induction and empiricism. Reid granted Hume's contention that we do not understand causation save as regularity of temporal antecedence of one event to another. Yet Reid asserted that we were rationally justified in making predictions, whereas Hume had concluded only that we could not help venturing them.[10] The common sense philosophers believed that they had vindicated empirical science against disintegrating skepticism, though actually their efforts on behalf of science were superfluous. Natural science quantitatively describes objects as they can be known to the senses, but whether sensory data are ultimate "reality" is irrelevant to this activity.

If Hume had not actually undermined the foundations of future scientific effort, he posed a very real threat to religion. Christianity, even more than science, was a cause which the Scottish common sense philosophers were anxious to uphold against their great compatriot. Hume's thoroughgoing skepticism had identified in the minds of many philosophers the defense of Christianity with the defense of ontological realism. God, Reid and others reasoned, would not deceive men about their surroundings. Their insistence upon the reality of the world and the trustworthiness of our senses carried a great deal of emotional freight. If the visible world were not what it seemed, how could men believe in that world which was invisible? And without supernatural religion, most early modern men assumed, neither morality nor social order would be possible.

The common sense philosophers distrusted "abstract" rational discussions, and preferred observation or self-evidence to logical demonstration. Believing that they were constructing a new "Baconian" philosophy, they confined themselves as much as possible to their "data" —empirical and intuitive perceptions. Their philosophy was, in a way, a "no-philosophy" or an "antiphilosophy." This represented, of course, part of their revulsion against Hume; they were shrinking back from the abyss to which he had led mankind. Philosophy, they decided, was not really useful. The important philosophical truths were obvious; their demonstration was both unnecessary and impossible. "I despise Philosophy, and renounce its guidance," cried Reid; "let my soul dwell with Common Sense."[11]

On the western side of the Atlantic, Scottish common sense was eagerly snatched up by many diverse groups. Perhaps it answered the desires of an expanding, dynamic society especially well by accepting material things at face value and discouraging idle speculation; in any case, it doubtless helped further the decline of Calvinist theology.[12] By 1803, the diehard Princeton Calvinist Samuel Miller was already lamenting that "the word *metaphysics* is seldom pronounced but with contempt, as signifying something useless, unintelligible, or absurd."[13] But nowhere else in America was Scottish common sense philosophy accepted so enthusiastically or unqualifiedly as at Harvard.

HARVARD LOGIC

"The Scottish Enlightenment was probably the most potent single tradition in the American Enlightenment," Herbert W. Schneider has stated, and there is no reason to dispute his verdict.[14] Common sense philosophy was part of the substantial store of intellectual baggage that John Witherspoon brought with him from Scotland when he accepted a call to serve the struggling College of New Jersey in 1768. At Princeton, Witherspoon set about replacing the Calvinist idealism of Jonathan Edwards with his own variant of Calvinist common sense realism. In the hands of his successors (at Princeton and elsewhere), Witherspoon's system was shaped into a veritable "Protestant scholasticism."[15] Near the opposite end of the American theological spectrum, Thomas Jefferson was also an admirer of the Scottish philosophers.[16] But neither Jefferson nor the common sense Calvinists fully shared the outlook of the Scottish school of philosophers. Jefferson certainly did not participate in their concern for the preservation of organized Christianity. And American Calvinists could never swallow Reid whole so long as they retained a commitment to deductive logic and an insistence on human depravity alien to his Arminianism.[17] The true American counterparts and most faithful disciples of the Scottish philosophers were to be found in Cambridge.

The Ramean dialectic of the founders of Harvard College had given way to Cartesian philosophy before the end of the seventeenth century; in the following century, Descartes in turn made way for Locke. David Tappan introduced Scottish philosophy to Harvard in the latter part of the eighteenth century, and it rapidly became standard.[18] All of the occupants of the Alford Chair in the years before the Civil War— Frisbie, Hedge, Walker, and Bowen—were enthusiastic proponents of Reid's common sense. Scottish magazines, avidly consumed by the Boston establishment, strengthened the prestige of the Scottish textbooks used in Cambridge. Such journals as *The Edinburgh Review,* the *Quarterly Review, Blackwood's Edinburgh Magazine,* and Campbell's *New Monthly Magazine* (the latter a London periodical edited by a Scot) extended the influence of the Scottish Enlightenment on Yankee culture beyond the classroom.[19]

Harvard professors were gratified to feel that their support for Scottish philosophy put them in the mainstream of Western thought. When James Walker, toward the close of the antebellum period, brought out his carefully annotated abridgement of Reid's *Essay on the Intellectual Powers,* he observed with satisfaction that the moral philosophy "generally taught in England and in this country for the last fifty years has been that of the Scotch School of which Dr. Reid is the acknowledged head. The influence of the same doctrine is also apparent in the improved state of philosophy in the Continental nations and particularly in France . . . The name of Reid therefore historically considered is second to none among the British psychologists and metaphysicians, with perhaps the single exception of Locke."[20] New England Liberals admired the expository talents of Reid's disciple Dugald Stewart so much that in 1829, the year after his death, they issued a seven-volume memorial edition of his works.

The definitive presentation of the Scottish theory of knowledge as taught at Harvard is given in Levi Hedge's *Elements of Logick; or a Summary of the General Principles and Different Modes of Reasoning*. The first edition (1816) was among the earliest of a vast number of textbooks which antebellum American professors of common sense philosophy prepared for their college students.[21] The book completely overshadowed its author. As a man, Hedge will always remain an obscure figure, for his literary remains provide little that could give us insight into his personality. (Apparently he was very much the old-fashioned pedant, with dogmatic mannerisms students snickered at behind his back.) Yet the long-lasting popularity of his text may be illustrated by an anecdote. When Speaker of the House James G. Blaine was introduced to Levi's son Frederic Henry Hedge at the Concord Centennial celebration of 1875, Blaine, ever the charming politician, responded mistakenly, "One hardly needs to be introduced to the author of Hedge's *Logick*."[22]

Logic as it is known today formed but a portion of Levi Hedge's subject matter. To him, logic meant the whole study of human reasoning, and much of his book dealt with epistemology and cognitive psychology. Hedge addressed himself to what one of his successors called "the most profound problem of speculative philosophy": "How do we know that things are what they appear?"[23] "Judgment," Hedge began, "is an act of the mind, uniting or separating two objects of thought according as they are perceived to agree or disagree. Every act of judgment is grounded on some sort of evidence." In his classification of evidence, Hedge followed the scheme set out by George Campbell, an eighteenth-century Scottish philosopher. Three kinds of evidence were acknowledged: "intuitive," "demonstrative," and "moral."[24]

"Intuitive" evidence Hedge considered to be that which came from common sense. Judgments for which only intuitive evidence was available presented Hedge with his greatest epistemological problems. Intuition was the evidence he offered for such statements as "I know that I exist," "The things I see exist," "The events I remember really happened," "Everything that happens has a cause."[25] Such propositions were synthetic; that is, they asserted matters of fact and not mere definitions or explanations. How synthetic propositions could be known a priori was a problem Unitarian philosophers admitted to be vexatious. Scottish philosophy resolved it for them by teaching them to trust the structure of the human mind as created by God. Common sense gave the evidence for the synthetic a priori propositions; they could therefore be safely known as true, God Himself having vouched for them.[26]

"Demonstrative" evidence, by contrast, raised few problems; it was simply the evidence supplied by logical deduction from accepted premises. Judgments depending on demonstrative evidence were necessarily true, but abstract, timeless, and without connection to the real world.[27] Although twentieth-century philosophers would regard "demonstration" as the most secure mode of acquiring knowledge, Hedge and his Harvard colleagues had little interest in, or affection for, the topic. Hedge devoted much of his discussion of deductive logic to definitions and seldom rose above the level of grammatical analysis; his students apparently learned nothing of mathematical logic. (Hedge's neglect of implications and tautologies reminds one that mathematical logic as we know it does not antedate the time of Charles Sanders Peirce.) Harvard undergraduates, to judge by the workbook Hedge designed to accompany his text, spent their time learning rules rather than applying them to logical problems.[28] The aversion to deductive logic which the Unitarians shared with the Scottish school had its historical roots in Bacon's rejection of scholasticism, and had been reinforced at Harvard by contempt for Calvinism.

The third type of evidence Hedge recognized was "moral." Hedge's terminology may confuse a twentieth-century reader, for by "moral evidence" he meant empirical or sensory evidence.[29] This is the evidence upon which we rely for contingent judgments, that is, judgments about conditions in the real world. "Moral" reasoning, in contrast to the other two forms, allows different degrees of certitude. In the case of "moral" reasoning, Hedge explained, it may be necessary to weigh opposing evidence, and "give our assent to that, on which there appears to be the greatest weight"; this, of course, never happens in the case of intuitive or demonstrative evidence. But—and here Hedge took his stand with Scottish common sense—the highest degree of "moral evidence" was just as certain as demonstrative knowledge.[30]

Hedge described several types of "moral" reasoning: induction, analogy, and "reasoning on facts." "Reasoning on facts" was the expression he used for the art of the historian. "Facts" in this context were events believed to have occurred on the basis of testimony. Testimony consisted of reports of sensory perceptions, whether written or oral. Hedge offered rules for the interpretation of testimony, such as ideas for evaluating the credibility of witnesses (on the basis of their opportunities for observation, their disinterestedness, and the like).[31] In early nineteenth-century America, the Holy Scriptures were almost invariably interpreted entirely on a literal plane, as a historical record. Canons of historical evidence took on transcendent importance when applied to biblical narratives. In the various controversies that Harvard Unitarians engaged in with deists, Calvinists, and heretics of their own like Parker and Ripley, the authenticity of biblical passages became crucial.[32]

In putting his philosophy at the service of his religion, Hedge was only doing what any other good Harvard professor would have done. "Philosophy is not the master nor the author of religion," one of them wrote, "but its servant."[33] The whole purpose of Unitarian epistemology was to sustain the proofs of religion. The exaggerated insistence on the reliability of empirical evidence and testimony was but a device to exalt the Bible as providing historical proof of intervention in human affairs by a personal God. Religious faith, according to Unitarians, was grounded upon testimony, and differed from sensory knowledge only in not being first-hand. A form of vicarious sensation, religious faith was, in the first instance, nothing more than involuntary "rational assent to evidence." "Faith that is not founded on testimony, is no longer faith" but blind prejudice, Joseph S. Buckminster told his congregation. Our acceptance of the Gospel of Christ upon the testimony of the Evangelists is (at least initially) precisely analogous to our acceptance of the assertion that Saturn has rings around it, on the basis of testimony from astronomers who have seen them through a telescope.[34]

Unitarians, determined to maintain their integration of Christianity with the Enlightenment, identified religion with empiricism, and faith with evidence. Andrews Norton expressed the Unitarian conviction that the cause of true religion was the cause of all empirical knowledge. On the occasion of his inauguration as Dexter Professor, he proclaimed: "The temple in which we worship is placed within the citadel of human reason; and before it can be approached for the purpose of destruction, almost all our knowledge must have been surrendered. He who doubts the existence of God, has left himself no truth dependent on moral [i.e., empirical] evidence, which he can reasonably believe."[35] Supremely confident in human reason and the principles of common sense, the Unitarians felt they had secured their religion within the strongest citadel they could build.

COMMON SENSE ONTOLOGY

Professor Merle Curti has argued that the influence of Locke dominated the American mind until the middle of the nineteenth century.[36] While this is true, it represents a high level of generalization. To be sure, most antebellum Americans—and Harvard Unitarians in particular—subscribed to such Lockean principles as capitalism, representative government, and cosmic optimism. But a close examination of formal philosophy reveals qualifications within that broad outlook. Most American philosophical admirers of Locke accepted his thought as modified by Reid. Scottish realism was, in fact, the filter through which Lockean empiricism influenced America.

Reid blamed Hume's skepticism on the doctrine that we perceive only representations of things (i.e., what Locke called "ideas"). Locke had taken for granted an isomorphism between the objects of the real world and the ideas perceived in our minds, but had given no adequate justification for this assumption. Reid got around the difficulty by dispensing with Lockean "ideas" altogether. According to Reid, an idea was not a representation, but an activity. Things in themselves were the objects of the activity. One reason why Locke had believed the mind knew only ideas was that he could not conceive of "action at a distance" between the mind and an external object. But, complained Reid, to postulate a realm of ideas still did not explain the action at a distance between external objects and these internal ideas, so Locke's theory was actually no help. Nor did Reid find representative ideas useful in explaining memory and imagination. Let us say we are thinking of a centaur, he would suggest. The object of our imagination then is a centaur, and not an idea of a centaur, which would be something else. Thus, Reid invariably discarded the Lockean "idea" as a useless hypothesis.[37] Reid's modification of Locke was, in effect, the opposite of Berkeley's. Locke had attempted to maintain the existence of both ideas and objects. Finding this unsatisfactory, Berkeley had dispensed with the objects; Reid dispensed with the ideas.

Francis Bowen at Harvard sided firmly with Reid in the argument over ideas. "The hypothesis of mediate knowledge, of a perception of things only through the intervention of representative ideas, was the great mistake of the philosophy of the eighteenth century,—the capital error into which Locke fell," declared the Yankee philosopher. Locke, Bowen felt, had fallen into the trap of saying that knowledge came *from* sensation and reflection, whereas he could easily have avoided difficulty by saying that knowledge came *through* sensation and reflection.[38] As it was, however, Locke had left the door open for Hume. Reid's principles of common sense saved the day by informing men that their habits of cognition were God-given and justified accepting perceived objects as real.

Common sense philosophy was really a way of restoring faith in Lockean empiricism after Hume's devastating skepticism. This, at any rate, was how the Unitarians saw things: "The works of Reid are not a refutation, but a defence, of Locke." Hence, although common sense philosophy modified their acceptance of Locke, it did not keep Unitarians, or other Americans, from reading and admiring him.[39] When, in 1803, the first American edition of Locke's *Essay* was published, a Boston printer, David Carlisle, brought it out. Locke and the Scottish philosophers were studied concurrently much of the time in Harvard classrooms. An example of the diligence with which Harvard students perused Locke is the undergraduate notebook of George Moore, preserved in the Harvard University Archives. Moore spent fourteen weeks in the fall term of 1833 studying the *Essay Concerning Human Understanding*. Moore's notes consist of intelligent summaries of Locke's views together with a few comments of his own.[40]

It was not very difficult for the Unitarians and others to retain their reverence for Locke while also accepting Reid. Despite their different approaches to epistemology, Locke and Reid were not far apart in their ontology. Both were ontological realists. "Realism," in philosophy, may de defined as the attribution of objective independence to that which is known.[41] Medieval realists had ascribed such existence to abstractions. Locke and Scottish common sense realists ascribed it to the "primary qualities" of matter. Locke had tacitly relied upon what was nothing more than common sense in asserting the objective existence of these primary qualities; Reid simply made the assumption explicit when he proclaimed the principle of "common sense," that the things we perceive really exist. Reid's Unitarian disciples understood perfectly well that there was no *logical* way of demonstrating the validity of sensory impressions, but decided that since "every man, woman, and child believes in his or her own existence and in that of the outward universe," it must be "because we are so constituted as to make it a matter of intuition."[42] Common sense philosophers in Britain as well as America put their faith in direct perception (intuitive and empirical), neglecting and distrusting logical demonstration.

Ontological realism justified Lockean epistemology. Locke had placed firm reliance on the knowledge which God offered mankind through nature, knowledge which was independent of scriptural revelation. Yet without any assurance of the validity of his senses, did man dare trust this knowledge? Hume had left every man alone, lost in chaos and darkness. Common sense rescued man by transforming sensation into a reliable key to nature. God had implanted common sense in the human mind, the Scottish philosophers asserted, thereby enabling man to trust his perceptions and, through them, to apprehend God's ways. For a man like Channing, the universe became the "language" of God, revealing through "natural signs" metaphysical facts.[43] Common sense, which taught men to trust their senses, trust nature, and trust God, provided a convenient foundation for Christian natural theology. Confident in the validity of empirical knowledge, a Unitarian Thanksgiving Day preacher could rejoice in "the goodness of our maker" who had adapted "our organs of sense . . . to the perception of external objects."[44]

Common sense realism offered an ontological legitimacy to all forms of rational activity. Belief in our own identity, in our senses and memory, and in the general operation of laws of nature were (whether we realized it or not) prerequisites to any sort of scientific or philosophical investigation, according to the proponents of common sense. As Dugald Stewart put it, certain "fundamental laws of human belief" were "necessarily and unconsciously involved in the exercise" of the faculties.[45] But neither Stewart nor Reid nor any of their disciples achieved a precise enumeration of these "fundamental laws" or "principles of common sense." Reid never asserted that his own list was exhaustive, and it was certainly not very clearly organized. James Walker kept hoping that Reid's American followers could come up with such a list, but he waited in vain. Eventually Francis Bowen concluded that it would be a mistake even to try to draw one up: "the phenomena of intelligence being numberless, . . . the reduction of them to a few elements" would be "wholly arbitrary."[46]

A large and indefinite number of poorly defined principles, each of which is accepted as unanalyzable and self-evident, makes an awkward basis for a philosophical system. The trouble was aggravated because, with their aversion to deduction, the members of the Scottish school seemed actually to prefer to accept assertions as God-given without trying to deduce them from other assertions. Unitarians and other common sense philosophers showed little respect for the so-called principle of parsimony ("Occam's Razor") , to which mathematics, science, and philosophy have generally adhered, which holds that it is desirable to deduce or explain as much as possible from as few premises as possible.

Perhaps the fundamental defect in common sense ontology arose from its apologetical purpose. Scottish realism was basically a device to justify empiricism, to restore confidence in natural science and natural theology. It was, if you will, an ontological answer to an epistemological problem. The existence of material objects, which Scottish philosophy so loudly maintained, is something which few if any philosophers deny; the philosophical disagreements come when one tries to explain what "material objects" are, and what it means for them "to exist." No nontrivial metaphysical system can be falsified by empirical data; yet the fundamental claim of Scottish common sense philosophers (which was, in fact, their fundamental mistake) was that empirical data have one distinct metaphysical implication. Then they frequently compounded their offense by asserting that all other people really believed in this metaphysic, no matter how they might profess otherwise, because they did not attempt to walk through walls or plunge into fires.[47]

THE METAPHYSICS OF DUALISM

"The sensualist and the spiritualist may both lay down their arms and cease their useless warfare," wrote William Ellery Channing with characteristic pacifism.[48] The material and the spiritual were equally real to the Unitarian common sense dualist. Just as the irrefutable facts of consciousness vouched for the reality of a physical world without, they also testified to the existence of a mind (or spirit) within. Mind-matter metaphysical dualism had been common to both Locke and Reid. Though Locke is famous as the philosopher who denied "innate ideas," he actually granted the existence of one intuitive belief: our awareness of our own existence.[49] This was also one of Reid's fundamental "constituents of consciousness." The "I" or the "self" was a mind within which the powers of perception subsisted. The mind, Unitarian moral philosophers agreed, was a simple, indefinable entity, distinct from the body with which it was allied, indivisible, and preserving a continued identity through time.[50]

Unitarian and other common sense philosophers called the study of the mind "psychology," a term which Dugald Stewart had popularized.[51] Antebellum Harvard psychology bore little resemblance to either experimental or clinical psychology as these are known today; it was a descriptive "natural history" of the faculties. One of the favorite Scottish works on psychology at Harvard was Thomas Brown's *Philosophy of the Human Mind,* which Levi Hedge edited in a handsome two-volume edition (Cambridge, 1827). Hedge's own textbook also contained a section on psychology, as did several other Unitarian philosophical works, including Channing's unpublished study. All these books boasted elaborate classifications of the powers of the mind: "perception," "conception," "relation," "memory." The different enumerations contained variations that gave rise to such recurrent arguments as whether "consciousness" was really a separate mental faculty, or simply the sum of all of them.[52]

The faculty psychology of common sense philosophy was not the same as medieval faculty psychology. In medieval psychology the faculties had been conceived as distinct spiritual beings within the soul. Locke, any account of Western thought will relate, had swept this notion into the ashcan of history with his *Essay Concerning Human Understanding*. Actually, however, Locke and his successors were not done with the concept of faculty quite so easily. They retained the word but redefined it as a synonym for power. ("That I have one faculty of memory, and another of judgment, is a phrase which means nothing more, than that I am able both to remember and to judge," explained Francis Bowen.) [53]

Harvard psychology always remained closely bound up with metaphysical concerns. New England Unitarians were convinced that Christianity and the doctrine of immortality in particular were dependent on the existence of spirit. Consequently, they were anxious that nothing in their psychology should contradict their religious faith in men's souls. They were profoundly suspicious of materialistic psychological theories which attributed human behavior to nerve impulses.[54] How much more satisfying they found it to explain the operations of thought in terms of mental faculties—and then to equate the "mind" of Lockean philosophy with the "soul" of Christian tradition. Had not Locke himself assured them that only spirit acted, willed, and judged? The material body must be purely passive. Very likely it was the operation of mental faculties which produced physical activity, and not the other way around.[55]

Harvard Unitarians were fascinated with the theme of spirit triumphing over matter. God was spirit, the world was matter, and God ruled the world. Unitarians took over David Hume's argument that we cannot logically understand what causation means, and they did strange things with it. They concluded that the physical universe lacked all power to cause events, that nothing occurring in the realm of matter could be attributed to matter. Yet they insisted everything that happened had to have a cause. Therefore, a spirit universe must exist, consisting of God and the minds of men, to supply the power the material world lacked. Men's minds controlled their bodies and God's mind controlled the rest of nature. Mind and matter were equally real, but not equally powerful or equally important. Man had both a mind (that is, a spirit) and a body, but his destiny clearly lay in developing the power of the former.[56]

Unitarian theology manifested the preferred status accorded to spirit over matter in Unitarian metaphysics. "God is a Spirit," declares John 4:24, and the Liberals never let their orthodox adversaries forget it. William Ellery Channing rejected as "idolatry" the notion that Divinity might have clothed Himself in flesh. The doctrine of the incarnation was a product of weak and ignorant imaginations, lacking the "reflecting and purified mind" to worship God as "pure spirit, invisible and unapproachable." Trinitarianism represented "a relapse into the error of the rudest and earliest ages, into the worship of a corporeal God," he asserted in an unusual outburst of invective. "Its leading feature is the doctrine . . . of the Infinite Divinity dying on a cross; a doctrine which in earthiness reminds us of the mythology of the rudest pagans."[57] The crucifixion of the creator of the universe was altogether too preposterous, messy, and disgusting to be credible for one of Channing's enlightened temper. Nor could he bear to think that any act so purely physical as the torture of a man nailed to wooden beams could bring salvation to humanity: "I am astonished and appalled by the gross manner in which 'Christ's blood' is often spoken of, as if his outward wounds and bodily sufferings could contribute to our salvation; as if aught else than his spirit, his truth, could redeem us."[58] The worship of a human, suffering Christ was no more calculated to "spiritualize" mankind than the worship offered Mary by the benighted Papists.

Harvard metaphysical dualism revealed a definite streak of Neoplatonism. Like Plato's ideal philosopher, the Unitarian moralist mediated for men between the temporal and the eternal, between finite matter and infinite spirit. The man who elaborated this Platonic strain in Harvard Unitarianism the farthest was, of course, Dr. Channing. Channing was a devoted reader of Plato (most often in Cousin's French translation) and was anxious to Christianize the insights of the ancient pagan.[59] But he did not stand alone in his respect for Platonic philosophy. Besides Plato himself, many Neoplatonists had long been admired in New England; the Ramean dialectic of the founders of Harvard College had borne unmistakable traces of Renaissance Platonism.[60] After the Liberals gained control of the college they frequently turned for inspiration to the group of seventeenth-century English writers known as the Cambridge Platonists. The Cambridge Platonists, of whom the most often read in New England were Ralph Cudworth (1617–1688) and Henry More (1614–1687), proved attractive to the Unitarian moralists on many counts. They taught the freedom of the will and the power of human reason, advocated mutual forbearance among religious sects, promoted biblical scholarship, and subordinated theology to ethics. Under the gentle influence of these Cambridge men, the rigor of Plato's philosophy was suffused with a warm, quiet spirituality.[61]

Perhaps Unitarian philosophy is better termed "quasi-Platonic" than Platonic. The stern Athenian, after all, had regarded the material universe as a prison from which a wise man would seek to escape, or as a veil of delusive appearances that the true philosopher sought to penetrate.[62] The genial Harvard moralist tended to be less demanding; he granted the reality and legitimacy of material things, and desired not so much to *escape* from the physical as to *use* it, to subordinate it to his will. "We were placed in the material creation, not to be its slaves, but to master it," he proclaimed. His was not an ascetic creed, but a faith in spiritual triumph. "That the material and spiritual world are at war, I do not believe," affirmed Channing. "We can live in both worlds at once."[63]

Although the Platonic aspect of Unitarianism would be amplified by Emerson and the Transcendentalists, it is important not to exaggerate the proto-Transcendentalism of Channing and his fellow Harvard moralists. The idealistic monism of Jonathan Edwards and Emerson was condemned by Channing as "pantheism" and "mysticism." To the end, he remained a dualist.[64] Whatever idealistic philosophers he admired he fit into his own metaphysical scheme. "I am far from assénting to [their] speculations," the Federal Street preacher insisted, but "I still recur to them with pleasure, as indicating how readily the soul passes above matter, and as manifesting man's consciousness of the grandeur of his spiritual nature."[65] This imperative of subjugating matter and asserting man's spiritual grandeur leads directly from an examination of Unitarian metaphysics to the study of Unitarian ethics.

II / The Moral Nature of Man

ETHICAL THEORY lay at the very heart of the large body of subject matter which antebellum American academics called moral philosophy. Natural religion, political theory, economics, aesthetics—these and other subjects were all regarded as fundamentally moral. What was the nature of moral obligation, how men might know it, and whether they could act upon it were problems which Harvard moral philosophers, like others, pondered at length. Bowen, Frisbie, Walker, and the elder Ware treated these important questions in some detail and, though their discussions span half a century and more, with remarkable unanimity.

THE TWO TYPES OF ''MORAL SENSE''

Modern ethical theory, many historians of ideas agree, arose in reaction to the disturbing doctrines of Bernard Mandeville and Thomas Hobbes. These seventeenth-century cynics had argued (in somewhat different ways) that all human actions proceeded from self-regard, and that morality originated in the will of the strongest. Both propositions provoked a chorus of criticism; but the critics soon began to disagree among themselves. Those who concentrated on refuting Hobbesian egoism came to form one school, while those who emphasized more the objectivity of morality and its independence from any sovereign will founded another.[1]

The first of these schools has often been termed the "sentimentalist," for, in rejecting the assertion that men act entirely from selfish motives, it claimed that men are endowed with a "moral sense." This moral sense distinguished good from evil by an immediate emotional reaction, without any rational calculation of advantage. The moral

45

sense was a natural component of the human personality, though it might require some cultivation for proper development into maturity. Pioneers of this sentimentalist school were Thomas Burnet (1635–1715) and the Earl of Shaftesbury (1671–1713), the grandson of Locke's patron. Shaftesbury, who elaborated his ideas somewhat more fully than Burnet, related the moral sense to a natural human gregariousness, which prompted such "social affections" as benevolence.[2]

A more rigorous philosophical exposition of ethical sentimentalism was given by Francis Hutcheson (1694–1746), a clergyman of the Church of Scotland. Hutcheson regarded the moral sense as one of a number of inexplicable human impulses, including curiosity, imitation, and "sense of honor." Like Shaftesbury, Hutcheson recognized a distinction between active benevolence and the passive approbation of the moral sense. The moral sense gave emotional approval to benevolent emotion—that is, the moral sense was "an affection for an affection."[3] Why did the moral sense approve of benevolent impulses? Shaftesbury had said, 'Because the gratification of our natural benevolent urges is pleasurable.' Hutcheson, however, referred moral approbation to a feeling for what was beautiful and fitting: moral sensitivity was a form of aesthetic taste. An interesting aspect of Hutcheson's doctrine was that he postulated a moral sense in God, directing His will toward benevolence, although this defied the conventional belief that God does not have emotions.[4] Among other Enlightenment philosophers who espoused varieties of the sentimentalist approach to ethics were David Hume and Adam Smith.[5]

The reaction against Hobbes also fostered the development of another great school of modern ethics. The resolute reaffirmation of the independence and immutability of moral values imparted new vigor to an old ethical doctrine known as "rational intuitionism." The rational intuitionist approach to ethics, which goes back to Plato, typically treats "goodness" or "rightness" as simple, indefinable ideas, perceived intuitively by human reason. The difference between good and evil, or right and wrong, is regarded as part of "the nature of things" and self-evident.[6] The first great modern proponent of rational intuitionism was the Cambridge Platonist Ralph Cudworth, whose *Trea-*

tise Concerning Eternal and Immutable Morality was published post-humously in 1731. In that classic work, Cudworth took issue with Hobbes, claiming that morality has an objective existence, dependent upon no command or will. Not even God could create or change moral principles, according to Cudworth; instead, He recognized their validity and was guided by them. To put it another way, God's will was subordinate to His intellect.[7]

Probably the greatest philosopher of this ethical intuitionist school before the twentieth century was the Rev. Richard Price (1723–1791), British Unitarian theologian and sympathizer with the American Revolution. In his *Review of the Principal Questions in Morals* (1758), Price treated "right" and "wrong" as ideas inherent in the very process of reasoning, along with such other concepts as "substance," "existence," "duration," and "cause," which were similarly indefinable, indispensable, and intuitive. Ethical truths were not created by God, Price agreed with Cudworth, but were logical necessities. They were, in a way, "part of God," Price suggested; God's knowledge of morality was really self-knowledge.[8] The basic principles of morality, Price emphasized, were synthetic propositions asserting objective facts, not hypotheses, tautologies, or conventions. Invoking Locke's ontological concepts of "primary" and "secondary" qualities, Price applied the distinction to the subject of ethics. He complained that Hutcheson's ethical sentimentalism had relegated moral qualities to a "secondary," or subjective status, like sweetness or color, existing only in the mind of the perceiver. Moral qualities, claimed Price, should be regarded as "primary" qualities like extension or mass.[9]

Like Price, Thomas Reid was a graduate of Marischal College, Aberdeen, an early center of Scottish moral philosophy. Reid agreed with Price that moral values were both objective and self-evident. According to Reid, the assertion "such a man did well and worthily, his conduct is highly approvable," expressed a proposition with truth value (i.e., it might be meaningfully true or false); and it was *not* equivalent to the assertion, "the man's conduct gave me a very agreeable feeling."[10]

Although he was a rational intuitionist, Reid took over from the sentimentalists their term "moral sense," which he apparently liked because it suggested (to him) that moral truths were perceived with a directness and certainty similar to that with which our physical surroundings were known. He attached to this term, however, an entirely different meaning from that of the sentimentalists. The "moral sense" for Reid was no involuntary emotion but an active, rational power. Reid considered that the sentimentalists had, by reducing the moral faculty to an involuntary emotion, robbed ethics of ultimate validity and man of genuine moral responsibility.[11] He therefore redefined the "moral sense" to make it an aspect of human reason. Reid used the word "sense" to mean a rational faculty, as we do when we say, "He is a man of sense." Both "common sense" and the "moral sense" were, for Reid, powers of judging self-evident truths. As the down-to-earth Scot himself put it, "Good sense is good judgment."[12]

According to Reid, the moral sense "intuitively discerned" various "moral axioms" that provided the basis for conduct just as quantitative axioms provided the basis for mathematics. Unlike mathematics, however, ethics did not require elaborate deductions in order to reach useful conclusions. Nor, in Reid's opinion, was careful calculation of consequences usually necessary. Under normal circumstances, the moral sense could perceive the path of duty quite readily. "In the common occurrences of life, a man of integrity, who has exercised his moral faculty in judging what is right and what is wrong, sees his duty without reasoning, as he sees the high way. The cases that require reasoning are few."[13]

Professional philosophers, when writing about the history of ethics, have often used the term "moral sense theory" to refer specifically to the school of Hutcheson and Shaftesbury.[14] It is important, however, that the expression "moral sense" has been used by both sentimentalists and intuitionists. Reid's ethical intuitionism and his use of the term "moral sense" to designate a rational faculty were followed by Dugald Stewart and many others in the Scottish common sense school, including a number of Americans. (The most famous ethical proposition for which intuitive self-evidence has been claimed was that of Stewart's friend Thomas Jefferson: "all men are created equal.") In fact, the moral sense of Reid and Stewart was almost certainly a more influential concept in America than the moral sense of Shaftesbury and Hutcheson.[15]

THE MORAL SENSE AT HARVARD

If modern European moral philosophy was a sustained reply to Hobbes, Harvard moral philosophy was a sustained reply to Calvin as well. The terms of the dialogue remained much the same. Both the theologian from Picardy and the atheist from Malmsbury were psychological egoists, viewing men as selfish and bestial; both grounded moral values in the will of a supreme being—the Unknown God of Calvin, the Leviathan of Hobbes. Against Calvin, Harvard Unitarians maintained the same two assertions their European counterparts maintained against Hobbes: (1) men were capable of altruism; and (2) morals were not created by arbitrary fiat.[16]

In the early eighteenth century Massachusetts Arminians had not yet settled upon any specific ethical theory; Hutcheson's sentimentalism vied for their favor with various forms of intuitionism, including the elaborately deductive system of Samuel Clarke (1675–1729).[17] Perhaps what ultimately drove the Liberals into the intuitionist camp was Jonathan Edwards's brilliant adaptation of sentimentalism to the purposes of Calvinist orthodoxy. On the other hand, perhaps the Arminians were only reactivating the strain of ethical intuitionism that had been submerged in seventeenth-century Ramism.[18] Be that as it may, the influential Jonathan Mayhew took up rational intuitionism in his *Seven Sermons* of 1748, and by the nineteenth century this had become the official ethical theory of Harvard Unitarianism.

The intuitionist Richard Price, admired in Boston for his Arian theology, became a favorite ethical philosopher there as well. As a youth Price had studied under Isaac Chauncy, a Harvard graduate; later the British divine was elected a Fellow of Boston's leading learned society, the American Academy of Arts and Sciences. He managed to maintain a correspondence with the Rev. Joseph Willard, then President of Harvard, even during the Revolutionary War years.[19] After the war Price kept up his American contacts, and his influence remained strong among New England Liberals. In the philosophical debate Price carried on with Joseph Priestley, the sympathies of Harvard Unitarians lay solidly with the former.[20] During the early nineteenth century a Unitarian preacher could take it for granted that his congregation would be familiar with Price's works; in fact, Dr. Channing's oft-quoted remark that "Price saved me from Locke" and "moulded my philosophy into the form it has always retained" could have been made by any number of Yankee Liberals. When the Boston *Monthly Anthology,* the pioneer Liberal literary magazine, began publication, its first volume set forth the doctrines of Price on morality.[21]

Students at Harvard College in the early national period acquired a respect for most of the leading British intuitionists, including the Cambridge Platonists and the Scottish common sense philosophers as well as Price. The climate of opinion in Harvard Yard may be judged from Ralph Waldo Emerson's undergraduate Bowdoin Prize Essay for 1821, "The Present State of Ethical Philosophy." The young Emerson was straightforward in his evaluations of philosophers. "Dr. Cudworth attacked the system of Hobbes, in his 'Immutable Morality,' with ability and success, and modern opinion has concurred in his boldest positions," he avowed. Emerson concluded that if ethical philosophy were to achieve real progress in the future, it "must go on in the school in which Reid and Stewart have labored."[22]

Henry Ware's lectures show how the argument for an objective, intuitive ethical theory was presented at Harvard. The Hollis Professor of Divinity addressed himself to the question, 'Why should we promote the general good?' He offered three answers, each on a different intellectual plane. In the first place, he pointed out, one may reply, 'Because we know it is the will of God.' (This was where Calvin had laid his emphasis.)[23] Secondly, Ware observed, one may say, 'Because our emotional make-up is such that we like to promote the general good.' (This had been the answer of Hutcheson.) Yet neither of these answers offered a satisfactory resting-place for an intuitionist moral philosopher. So Ware moved on to his ultimate answer to the question, 'Why promote the general good?' He groped for words as he tried to explain that the only reason for doing so is that we know it is right. "Right" is a word we understand but cannot explain, an indefinable, "invariable and universal" conception, he told his students.[24] After the class was over, the professor continued to ponder the issues he had raised. "It seems to me that right and wrong are qualities existing in the nature of things," he reflected. "To perceive these fitnesses—to distinguish right from wrong—is an intellectual exercise, and we have faculties for performing this office." These "faculties" composed, for Ware, man's rational "moral sense."[25]

The other Harvard moral philosophers echoed Ware's doctrine. Levi Frisbie taught his classes that morally right actions have "an indefinable excellence in themselves"; Andrews Norton considered it essential that students grasp "the intrinsic nature of right and wrong."[26] James Walker, while President of the University, took advantage of the compulsory attendance of the students at chapel to instruct them further in the intuitionist theory of ethics. There are three axiomatic principles of conscience, the President informed his charges: (1) "right" is different from "wrong"; (2) "right" is a simple, i.e., indefinable, idea, and everyone understands its meaning; (3) the idea of "right" implies the idea of "obligation" (to do the "right"). These three principles were necessary, intuitive, "fixed and absolute."[27] William Ellery Channing carried intuitionist moral philosophy into his pulpit on Federal Street. "It belongs to reason to comprehend universal truths," he instructed his parishioners. The principles of morality were such universal truths: "It is conceivable that we might have been so framed as to prefer darkness to light, or to find nourishment in what is now poisonous. But a being so constituted as to see baseness in disinterested love and venerableness in malignity would be an inconceivable monster. In truth, we can no more imagine such a moral being, than we can imagine an intelligent being who could think of a part as being greater than the whole."[28] For the Unitarian moralists, ethical obligations were logical necessities that could not be otherwise than they were.

Harvard moral philosophers helped define their ethical views through the criticisms they directed at rival theories. Professor Frisbie set forth a plausible critique of egoistic hedonism. (1) As a description of human behavior, he argued, the Hobbesian principle that men act from a desire for happiness is false. Basic drives like hunger, curiosity, and gregariousness are not derived from a rational commitment to "happiness" in the abstract. In practice, "happiness" is not an end in itself, but a by-product of the gratification of these impulses. (2) As a description of the concept of "virtue," egoistic hedonism is likewise false. It leads to the conclusion that it is virtuous to be selfish, which runs counter to the way everyone uses the word "virtuous." "Should I say of a merchant, that he made a very virtuous voyage, I should be thought to talk nonsense."[29]

Unitarian opposition to the doctrine that moral values originated in the will of a sovereign power dated back to the mid-eighteenth century. Mayhew's great *Discourse Concerning Unlimited Submission and Non-resistance to the Higher Powers* (1750) had taken issue with Hobbes and Calvin to deliver a warning to London. Even God was limited, the Whig preacher had proclaimed, by the "eternal *laws* of truth, wisdom, and equity, and the everlasting *tables* of right reason— tables that cannot be *repealed,* or *thrown down* and *broken* like those of *Moses.*"[30] Long after the crisis over parliamentary power had passed, later generations of Liberal moralists continued to proclaim that God was a constitutional monarch. God obeyed principles of morality which He had not created and could not change. "It is not within the power even of Omnipotence ... to alter the moral relations of thoughts and acts and our judgments of them," asserted one Unitarian. Consequently, moral principles did not depend for their force of obligation on the commandment of God, another pointed out; a foundation for moral distinctions would still exist without reference to religion.[31]

Still another target for the shafts of Harvard moral philosophers was the ethical theory of sentimentalism. Levi Frisbie's critical "Examination of Dr. Adam Smith's Theory of Moral Sentiments" appeared in the *North American Review* for March 1819. According to sentimentalists like Smith, moral judgment was only a description of feeling. In Smith's view, the emotion upon which ethics was based was that of "sympathy" (i.e., empathy) . If people are motivated by the same emotions we ourselves would feel in their situation, Smith held, we approve of their conduct. Frisbie objected to this theory: (1) "There are numerous cases of sympathy without approbation." We may sympathize with an art collector, and delight in his acquisitions, but we do not on that account consider his purchases virtuous. We may even sympathize with a skillfully portrayed villain like Macbeth while deploring his deeds. (2) According to Smith's theory, Frisbie declared, evil men should approve of their own vices when these are manifested in others. Obviously this is not the case. (3) We often approve most highly of men's conduct when we know full well that we ourselves would be incapable of imitating their virtue. (4) We judge men's motives right or wrong according to their "intrinsic character," without regard for whether we can "sympathize with" them. Emotional identification with virtuous men, like emotional abhorrence of evil men, is a result, not a cause, of the moral judgment that we pass. Smith's mistake lay in misapplying the term "moral approbation" to an emotion "which is properly only a consequence of it."[32] As Frisbie told his students in class, moral ideas are perceived by rational intuition, like mathematical axioms. Moral feelings are only the results of moral judgments; they can vary from person to person and from time to time in the same person without the judgment itself changing.[33]

The rational moral sense, in Unitarian doctrine, was the greatest gift of God to mankind. By means of it, men had been granted the ability to perceive the eternal truths of morality as readily as God Himself did. Through this faculty, which they shared with God, men could participate in the divine homage to virtue. This was the burden of William Ellery Channing's prose hymn to conscience in his famous address "Likeness to God."

It is conscience within us which . . . interprets to us God's love of virtue and hatred of sin; and without conscience, these glorious conceptions would never have opened on the mind . . . Men, as by a natural inspiration, have agreed to speak of conscience as the voice of God, as the Divinity within us. This principle, reverently obeyed, makes us more and more partakers of the moral perfection of the Supreme Being.[34]

THE UNITARIAN CONSCIENCE AS AN INTELLECTUAL POWER

Harvard moral philosophers distinguished two elements, or components, in the "conscience"; these were the cognitive element and the volitional. It was one thing to *know* the right; another thing to be motivated to *do* the right. This division was a commonplace of Scottish philosophy, both Reid and Stewart separating the "intellectual powers" from the "active powers" of man. Actually, as Reid admitted, these categories were little more than new names for the "understanding" and the "will," which had long been distinguished by Western thinkers. It was the intellectual faculty in the conscience which "intuitively discerned" the "axioms" of morality.[35]

"Men are moral beings because they have a moral nature, that is, a conscience, an innate inextinguishable sense of right," proclaimed President Walker from the pulpit in Harvard College Chapel. "This disinterested principle in human nature we call sometimes reason, sometimes conscience, sometimes the moral sense or faculty," answered Dr. Channing from across the river in Boston. "But, be its name what it may, it is a real principle in each of us."[36] Innate faculties—that is, innate capacities—are not the same thing as innate ideas,[37] and it was the moral "faculty" which Walker, Channing, and their colleagues regarded as universal. Men were born with a potential ability to make moral judgments; but Unitarians did not imagine that men were born actually knowing certain precepts. When a normal adult reflected on certain relationships, they claimed, the ethical implications would be self-evident to him. The Unitarians recognized, however, that all men did not avail themselves of their moral capabilities. The "moral sense" did not perceive truths unless a man consciously directed his attention to them, or trained himself to perceive them habitually. It was quite possible to ignore the principles of morality, Frisbie pointed out, just as "a man may, for years, add 2, 4, and 8, . . . without ever observing, what is intuitively true, that these numbers are in geometric ratio."[38]

Whether the conscience needed training was the subject of a spirited argument between William Ellery Channing and Theodore Parker. Like a good Transcendentalist, Parker defended the competence of man's spontaneous natural morality. Parker conceded that the intellect needed education to present facts properly to the conscience, but felt the conscience itself "infallible." Channing retorted that conscience was "like the *eye,* which might be dim, or might see wrong." According to Parker's record of the conversation, Channing "thought a man late in his life (in a case I put), who had not hitherto consulted his conscience, would, coming to that adviser, make great mistakes, and therefore be punished for his past sin of neglect."[39]

Since the power to understand ethical obligation and distinguish right from wrong did not require knowledge of the revelation of God through Scripture, the moral sense was possessed even by heathens.[40] This doctrine made it necessary for the Unitarians to reckon with the fact that mankind has displayed an amazing diversity of moral codes in different times and places. How could one maintain the existence of a universal moral sense in the face of such apparent ethical variation? Harvard thinkers adopted several modes of dealing with this problem. First, they could claim a consensus on meta-ethical matters: all societies recognized the concepts of "obligation" and "right," however they might disagree over their proper application. Second, Unitarians could argue that differences among the moral values of societies were more apparent than real. In some societies, for example, men killed their maimed children and senile parents; yet if they did so from merciful motives, their customs were not actually so startling. Third, Unitarians could point out that it is a mistake to judge the state of morality in a society from a few notorious examples; the conduct of Nero, claimed Professor Frisbie, illustrated the emperor's personal immorality rather then the prevailing code of ancient Rome.[41]

The various arguments employed by Unitarians on behalf of the universal moral sense reveal a certain vagueness on their part about the function of this faculty. The Unitarians were probably on their firmest ground when they maintained that, by simple analysis (or "intuition"), men could accept certain meta-ethical principles, e.g., that "right" implies "obligation," or that normative judgments are different from descriptive ones. But the Harvard moral philosophers were very seldom content to leave their claim on that remote theoretical plane. They usually maintained that the moral sense also intuited certain positive "obligations." (An "obligation" is a general principle of ethics, such as that promises should be kept.) When it came to specific "duties," however, i.e., what a person should do in a given situation, Unitarian theory acknowledged considerable difficulties: "Absolute certainty belongs to [a moral] proposition only when couched in general terms. It can be applied to particular cases only by approximation." Actually, the moral sense did not discover duties; it stopped with knowledge of obligations. Duties were calculated by prudential reason, on the basis of factual knowledge and experience.[42]

The Unitarian moral sense was obviously based on the same kind of assumptions about reality as Unitarian common sense. Just as common sense intuited descriptive, ontological truths, the moral sense intuited prescriptive, ethical truths. In fact, common sense and moral sense were little more than names denoting two different activities of the intellect. Their special function, as far as Unitarian and other philosophers of the Scottish school were concerned, was to endow sensory knowledge on the one hand, and ethical values on the other, with an assurance of authenticity. As Reid had put it, "The testimony of our moral faculty, like that of the external senses, is the testimony of nature, and we have the same reason to rely upon it."[43] The ethical principles which were known through the moral sense were regarded, by Price, Reid, and the Harvard philosophers, as objective truths— "primary qualities," in their terminology. It was for this reason that intuitions of moral values were entitled to be termed genuine "perceptions," not mere subjective "sensations." Unitarian ethics, like Unitarian metaphysics, may be characterized as a search for objective justification. As common sense had provided the answer to Hume's skepticism, the moral sense provided the answer to Hobbes's cynicism.

Ethical intuitionism offered Harvard Unitarians—and many other respectable men of the Enlightenment—means of escaping from the theocentric ethics of the Reformation without surrendering belief in the validity of moral standards. The doctrine that neither the will of God nor the will of man could change the moral order was attractive in an era of many "immutable" principles, "fixed" constitutions, and "eternal" verities. If sixteenth-century Calvinists had felt the ultimate truth about the universe to be the existence of arbitrary Power, enlightened Unitarians believed the ultimate truth about the universe was the existence of moral values. The older attitude had fostered piety; the new one fostered rectitude.

THE UNITARIAN CONSCIENCE AS AN ACTIVE POWER

In considering the conscience as an intellectual power, the Unitarians had exalted moral principles into objective and immutable truths, but left unanswered the question of how men could live up to these ideals.

Yet the latter was, in their eyes, the more important concern; "abstract rules assented to as true and right" mattered much less than the "real *springs of action* existing in the individual himself."[44] In their treatment of the conscience as an active power, Harvard Unitarians addressed themselves to the problem of motivating men to be good. Hobbes and Calvin had denied this was possible without recourse to compulsion or supernatural intervention. The Unitarians themselves admitted it was extremely difficult; much of the easy confidence with which they claimed knowledge of the right was lost when they turned to the task of its implementation.

Seventeenth-century Puritans, Perry Miller has explained, believed in a hierarchical ranking of powers within man, "vegetative," "animal," and "rational." Puritans viewed the human being as a "Microcosmos," possessing "a springing life as Plants . . . a sensitive life as Beasts, and . . . a rational life as Angels." The disposition to interpret human nature in this way was by no means peculiar to the Puritans, although they were the ones who carried it to Massachusetts. Long before, Plato had distinguished various components within the soul, ranking them in an order of rightful precedence.[45] Through the Middle Ages and the Renaissance, elaborate conventions developed that recognized successive stages of being, beginning with mere existence, and rising through animation and sensation to understanding. Man, possessing all of these attributes, represented a tiny world within himself. The "great chain of being" could be a model for man's own nature, as well as for the universe around him.[46]

During the Enlightenment, the conception of human nature as a replica of a hierarchical cosmos continued to flourish. Among its advocates were Richard Price and Joseph Butler, the Anglican philosopher-bishop of Durham.[47] The two thinkers who most influenced Harvard Unitarians with their views on this subject were, however, Thomas Reid and Dugald Stewart. Reid classified the "active powers of man"—i.e., the impulses prompting him to action—as "mechanical," "animal," and "rational." The mechanical powers were the automatic reflex actions over which there was no conscious control, like eye-blinking. The animal powers included "appetites," "desires," and "affections," all of which were characterized by being involuntary in origin and yet subject to the conscious will in some degree. The rational powers were two: prudence (self-regard) and conscience or the moral sense (regard to duty).[48]

When Levi Frisbie undertook to explain "the moral constitution of man" to his classes, he avowedly followed Reid's system almost exactly, although his discussion of "mechanical powers" was confusing. The "appetites" were the three periodic physical urges, hunger, thirst, and sex, the first two being necessary for the preservation of the individual and the last for the preservation of the race. The appetites required regulation by higher powers, but were not in themselves evil. Indeed, Frisbie told his students, "Instead of considering man as degraded by his appetites, let us consider them, as they really are, striking instances of the goodness of our Creator . . . It is not the legitimate use, but the abuse of the appetites, by which man is degraded."[49] The "desires," in Scottish and Harvard terminology, were instinctive propensities such as curiosity and gregariousness. They differed from appetites in that their object was emotional, rather than physical, gratification.[50]

The third, and most important, type of animal power comprised the "affections." The affections were emotional attitudes toward other persons. Frisbie followed Reid in subdividing them into "malevolent" and "benevolent." Malevolent affections included envy, resentment, contempt, and the like. Examples of benevolent affections would be gratitude, pity, friendship, and parental and filial love. The benevolent affections were natural and unreflective, seeking the good of others without conscious selfishness. Since they reflected a mere "instinctive sympathy" they did not partake of virtue until blessed by the rational moral sense.[51] Yet the benevolent affections were beneficial, even essential, to the individual, since they provided the basis for society, without which man could not exist. Apparently it came to seem unfitting that such noble motives should bear the somewhat derogatory label of an "animal" power, because the Unitarians often preferred Dugald Stewart's expression, "instinctive or implanted propensities," as a euphemism. The benevolent affections (or, as they were also called, the social affections) played a crucial role in Harvard thought. The Unitarians trusted them to provide a basis for human community even in a strange New World, hoping that, through them,

Americans could escape the frightening Hobbesian alternatives of tyranny or anarchy.[52]

Although the Unitarians did not accept Francis Hutcheson's sentimentalist theory of ethics, they greatly admired his description of the benevolent affections. If Hutcheson had not persuaded them as an ethical philosopher, he had certainly convinced them in his capacity as a psychologist that man possessed altruistic impulses. William Ellery Channing was so powerfully impressed by Hutcheson's defense of man's capability for "disinterested affection" that he recalled his first reading of it as a kind of religious experience. What "suddenly burst" upon the young man's mind, however, was not a vision of God's glory but a "view of the dignity of human nature."[53]

Possession of the two rational powers, prudence and conscience, distinguished men from all other created beings. They represented the spiritual aspect of man's complex nature, as the mechanical and animal powers represented his bodily aspect. In this way, the Unitarians carried their dualistic metaphysics into their study of human behavior. The function of prudence was "to provide for our good on the whole, by the regulation, balancing, and use of the primary appetites, desires, and affections." Prudence (or "self-love," as it was also called) aimed at "happiness"—i.e., "the sum of the several enjoyments" of the lower powers—but it did not control them completely, as the egoistic hedonists had mistakenly imagined. Self-love was not sinful per se, in the opinion of Harvard Unitarians; like every other human active power, it had a legitimate function and was good as long as it was kept in its proper place. Only when perverted did self-love degenerate into selfishness.[54]

The source of morality was, of course, to be found neither in prudence nor in any lower faculty, but in conscience. Conscience, or the moral sense, was rightfully the supreme faculty, judging all the others and determining to what extent they might properly be indulged. The authority of conscience was—or rather, ought to be—"supreme and final over every other *kind* of human motive and inducement," intoned President Walker. "Should a conflict arise, our sense of what is right ought to prevail, in all cases, over our sense of what is expedient or agreeable.[55]

The Harvard moral philosophers thought of the conscience primarily as a judge of motives supplied by other powers. Whether the conscience alone could motivate action was doubtful. Reid had taught that the conscience did have some motive force, but another Scottish thinker admired by the Unitarians, Lord Kames, denied this. Francis Bowen at one time asserted that the conscience possessed power to motivate, but he later changed his mind.[56] Even those who granted conscience the ability to motivate preferred it to act in concert with other powers. Frisbie taught that the moral sense regulated the appetites and controlled the emotions, but could think of only one case in which the sense of duty should act alone to prompt action: when inflicting pain (e.g., in punishment). In all other cases, Frisbie held, the conscience should invoke the assistance of some other power—probably prudence or a benevolent affection—to supply motivation.[57] Like any wise monarch, the moral sense should enlist the aid of its subjects, not try to tyrannize over them. Consequently, the effective functioning of the conscience as an active power implied the effective functioning of the entire personality.

If there were a single conception that dominated Harvard Unitarian thought, psychological, social, and religious, it was the conception of harmony. The Unitarian conscience was not a repressive, but an expressive faculty: not to crush, but to harmonize, regulate, and balance, was the task of the ruling power. In twentieth-century psychological terminology, the Unitarians regarded a firm sense of values as essential to an integrated personality. Only when a man was following the guidance of prudence and the moral sense was he free, Reid had written, and Unitarian preachers agreed; the man who was not the master of himself was the servant of sin. They frequently led their congregations in the contemplation of the balanced character of a virtuous man. To be overcome with passion was, in Unitarian opinion, to be enslaved by a usurping tyrant.[58]

When they rejected the doctrine of innate depravity, Unitarians were led to espouse the view that sin consisted of a breakdown in the internal harmony, an abdication by the higher faculties of their dominion over the lower. No longer was sinfulness considered inherent in the human condition; instead, it was an abnormal state of disorder, "the abuse of a noble nature." Sin represented a failure to regulate impulses that were not in themselves evil. Virtue, conversely, could be identified with *"universal moderation."* "Moral strength," the younger Ware preached, "stands opposed to violence and to self-indulgence, both of which are characteristics of feebleness. Conscious strength is calm."[59] The Unitarian ideal of a "balanced" character contrasts sharply with the romantic ideal of uninhibited self-expression. William Ellery Channing condemned the notion that "genius" lay in "a kind of fever, madness [or] intoxication." True greatness, the New England Unitarians always insisted, lay in "self-mastery."[60]

The major difficulty Unitarians sensed in maintaining the harmonious personality as they conceived it was that the relative strength of the impulses in man seemed to vary inversely with the rank assigned them. The two rational faculties simply did not possess the driving power that the emotions did. There was a trace of pathos in the words of Bishop Butler, so often quoted by Unitarians, that if conscience had might, as it has right, it would govern the world.

The Harvard Unitarians have generally been denominated "rationalists," and the label certainly is justified by their doctrine of the conscience as an intellectual power. In their theory of the conscience as an active power, however, the term "rationalist" must be qualified. The Unitarians, to be sure, believed that men *ought* to be governed by reason (including the moral sense) but this is very different from believing that men always *were* so governed. James Walker was capable of warning the Cambridge community not to "overrate" the power of reason compared with that of the affections. Francis Bowen criticized not only Hobbes, but also Locke, for treating men as though they were rationally motivated.[61] Scholars have repeatedly reminded us that children of the Enlightenment were by no means necessarily naively optimistic about the power of reason to govern men. "The ruling passion conquers reason still," the poet Pope declared, while such political writers as "Publius" warned that man's passions required a close watch. The Harvard Unitarians, like a number of other Enlightenment thinkers, found cause for concern in the strength of the emotions.[62]

Unfortunately, any of the desires or affections might "take a direction fatal to the virtue and the peace of its possessor" and challenge the legitimate supremacy of conscience. When this happened, the rebelling faculty was designated a "passion."[63] As a rightful sovereign over the kingdom of the soul, the moral sense had to guard against the emergence of such demagogic passions. If the moral sense did not consistently maintain its sovereignty over the other powers in the soul, a passion might sweep into control of the will, carrying everything before it. Once such a passion had come to power, the perceptions of the moral sense would be obscured, and the disordered "enthusiast" lose even the ability to realize that he was doing wrong. Eternal vigilance was the price of preventing such internal revolutions.[64]

How could the conscience maintain its authority? Or, to put the question another way, how could the mind retain its freedom? The moral sense was, as we have seen, more a judicial than an executive faculty, and like all judiciaries, stood in need of some power to implement its decisions. It could acquire this additional power, Unitarians believed, by borrowing strength from other faculties. These other faculties were evil only when they defied conscience; working in harmony with conscience they could supply plentiful power for good. Prudence, the other rational faculty, rendered great service to conscience. Man also had a number of useful emotions, which the moral sense could rely upon to enforce its judgments. "To find out what is true, we should use our reason; but having found it out, if we would give effect to it, we must call in the aid of the feelings."[65]

Perhaps the most valuable emotions for aiding the conscience were the ones called "sentiments." A sentiment was an emotional regard for a rational principle. "Sentiment is not mere feeling," Dr. Channing explained; "it is feeling penetrated with thought."[66] Patriotism, for example, being an emotional commitment to an abstraction, was a sentiment. Sentiments occupied an exalted place in Harvard moral philosophy. They offered Unitarians great hope for the implementation of man's nobler ideals. To achieve their aspirations, the Unitarians invoked those "affections in man, which not only suppose reason, but are founded on it; such as the love of truth, the love of beauty, the love of virtue, and the love of God." By cultivating such sentiments as these, a man could maintain contact with the spiritual world, and elevate himself above the mundane. For this reason, James Walker called the sentiments "the highest distinction and glory of man."[67]

"The love of virtue" was the sentiment most directly related to conscience. Unitarians (and others) called this sentiment by the name "moral taste." Moral taste was the aesthetic, emotional delight in virtue that followed upon the rational moral judgment. "A sense of duty is a conviction that we are bound to conform to the laws of rectitude; moral taste delights in this conformity."[68] Moral taste was gratified by the contemplation of virtue, whether our own or others, in literary fiction as well as in actual experience. The Unitarian doctrine of moral taste had been anticipated by Price and Reid, both of whom had acknowledged that a perception of objective moral truths was followed by the experience of subjective emotion.[69]

Moral taste helped to reinforce and strengthen moral perception. The man who had cultivated this sentiment possessed (in the younger Ware's words) "not the cold judgment of the intellect alone, in favor of what is right, but a warm, glowing feeling of preference and desire." A refined moral taste provided an important incentive to virtue, Edward Tyrell Channing pointed out: "self-imposed duty soon becomes a pleasure."[70] By making virtue a source of pleasure, moral taste enabled Unitarians to regard virtue as its own reward. "The satisfactions of a heart overflowing with kind affections," Frisbie wrote, "harmonized to a love of order, delighting in whatever is pure and excellent, constantly seeking and acquiring new degrees of goodness, in short, being and doing good; these are the true, the essential reward of virtue."[71] Nineteenth-century Unitarians no longer thought of the good life primarily in terms of obedience to God; for them the good life meant achieving a delight in virtue.

Combining the moral sense with moral taste enabled Harvard Unitarians to have the best of both worlds. By this ingenious intellectual twist, they were able to find a place for sentimentalism within an ethical theory that was formally rationalistic. The moral sense assured them that morality had an objective validity; the moral taste, however, made these stern absolutes seem warm, human, and delightful. If the moral sense was universal, the moral taste was not; the former held all men morally accountable, but the latter conferred a special authority on the man of refined sentiment.

THE PRUDENTIAL INCENTIVE TO VIRTUE

The faculty of "prudence" was also sometimes called "reason" or "self-love" and the three names are suggestive of the three functions it performed. In the first place, prudence regulated the desires, affections, and appetites on the basis of their contribution to the happiness of the individual, just as the moral sense regulated them on the basis of obligation. But second, prudence was also the deliberative, reasoning faculty, so its cooperation was necessary in arriving at any specific moral judgment: the moral sense intuited the obligation, but only prudential reason could evaluate the facts of the situation so as to arrive at a duty. Third, prudence itself supplied a motive to action: self-love.[72]

Self-love had a legitimate place in the personality. It was entirely possible for the same action to be prompted both by self-love and by conscience, although if the selfish motivation became excessive, conscience would withdraw its approval.[73] Indeed, Unitarians expected that conscience and self-love would normally reach the same conclusions. Conscience might, of course, demand that one forsake personal happiness and welfare in response to its dictates, but Unitarians were convinced that, in practice, the good would generally prosper. On this basis, Francis Bowen could even rehabilitate the doubtful morality of Poor Richard: "So far, therefore, as Poor Richard shows the intimate connection between virtue and well-being, so far as he proves that to be honest and true is the best mode of becoming wealthy and happy, he is a sound moralist. Nor will any great objection be made to his doctrine, if he holds up this fact as *one* of the inducements to virtuous conduct." Of course, Bowen hastened to add, we must not let the prudential incentive to virtue confuse us: "to say that all virtuous actions are also useful . . . is quite a different thing from saying that actions are right *because* they are useful."[74]

An author whom the Harvard moral philosophers found helpful in their efforts to inculcate a prudential motive to virtue was William Paley (1743–1805), archdeacon of Carlisle. Paley was a spokesman for the extreme Latitudinarian wing of the Church of England, as well as a writer on moral philosophy and natural and revealed religion. His *Principles of Moral and Political Philosophy* (1785) espoused a doctrine that has become known as theological utilitarianism. This theory may be summed up, in Paley's own words, as follows: "Virtue consists in doing good to mankind, in obedience to the will of God, and for the sake of everlasting happiness."[75] Paley's views are of some historical interest, as foreshadowing those of Bentham, but as ethical philosophy, they are extremely naive. He grounded the "right" in the will of God, with all the difficulties that entails; then, by saying that actions were only virtuous if performed for the sake of a heavenly reward, reduced all virtue to calculated self-interest.[76]

Despite its glaring inadequacies as ethical theory, Paley's *Principles of Moral Philosophy* was an assigned textbook at Harvard (and many other American colleges) during much of the antebellum period. Harvard professors, without accepting Paley's *definition* of virtue as that which was rewarded in heaven, were quite willing to impress upon their students that the *consequence* of virtue would be happiness hereafter. In the supernatural sanctions emphasized by Paley, Harvard moral philosophers found their most powerful prudential incentive to virtue. Unitarians were somewhat apologetic about employing this tactic; fear of future retribution had its limitations, as Henry Ware, Jr., pointed out. "It stops far short of the true end. It may begin but it cannot finish. It can do nothing more than restrain from evil; it cannot lift to excellence."[77] But even a beginning on the road of righteousness was something, so Paley, like Poor Richard, was accorded his due.

The theory of religion, no less than of pure ethics, sanctions an appeal to man's instinctive desire of future happiness, as a motive and an incitement to an upright and holy life. This is but a preparatory step, it is true; for that virtue is imperfect, is even mean and grovelling, which is not practised for its own sake.[78]

There was little danger that Harvard students would swallow too much of Paley's theoretical hedonism. Harvard professors felt free to subject ethical thinkers to critical examination in class and relegated Paley to his proper place during their lectures.[79] Furthermore, the other readings that were required in courses on moral philosophy often denounced Paley in no uncertain terms. Dugald Stewart's *Philosophy of the Human Mind,* normally assigned along with Paley, undertook a lengthy attack upon several forms of utilitarianism, including Paley's. Thomas Brown's *Philosophy of the Human Mind,* which Levi Hedge edited, called Paley's doctrine "the most degrading of all the forms which the selfish system [of ethics] can assume."[80] It should not, therefore, be surprising that the undergraduate Francis Bowen could win a Bowdoin Prize with an essay dismissing Paley's theological utilitarianism as "undoubtedly erroneous" at a time when Paley was still on Harvard reading lists. One Harvard alumnus from this period recalled that Paley's book was actually nicknamed "immoral philosophy" by the students.[81]

Harvard philosophers often took issue with Paley's ethical theory in their writings. In 1819 Levi Frisbie declared that the "popular doctrine of Paley, which at first seems to furnish so easy an explication of the difficulties which embarrass the theory of morals, will be found, we are persuaded, the more it is examined, more and more inconsistent with sound philosophy and safe practice."[82] Dr. Channing, while praising some of Paley's work in other fields, complained that he had carried moral philosophy "backward." Henry Ware, Sr., regarded all forms of utilitarianism as essentially prudential and not truly "ethical" in the only sense that he, an intuitionist, could accept. James Walker's views on Paley were best explained in an article he wrote for the *Christian Examiner.* He believed there was a place for Paley's book, "regarded merely as a practical work for the use of [Christian] believers," but the Unitarian would "hardly go to the extent of clearing it from all reasonable objections as a scientific treatise."[83]

The prudential incentive to virtue, though it had its uses, always possessed an unfortunate "moral tendency." Utilitarianism did not foster such a high standard of rectitude as intuitionism did, it seemed to Harvard men; and the hazard implicit in theological utilitarianism appeared even plainer in the secular, Benthamite version. The hedonistic calculus of Bentham did not elevate and refine the character, as Unitarians expected the study of moral philosophy to do. Harvard moralists conceived of virtue as involving a balanced personality, and insisted that the faculty of rational prudence should not be allowed to overshadow all the other active powers. Furthermore, Francis Bowen accused the Benthamites of equating "happiness" with mere physical pleasure.[84]

Bowen spoke for all the Harvard moralists when he insisted that the proposition of the utilitarian, "Whatever is useful, is right," ought to be inverted to read, "Whatever is right, is useful." To be sure, society benefited from the moral law; without morality we should live in a Hobbesian state of nature, our lives "solitary, poor, nasty, brutish, and short." But the immemorial moral law did not exist for the sake of society, and virtuous actions should not be performed merely because they were socially useful. For in the last analysis, "though the pride of the state should be humiliated, and its power be diminished, and its prosperity should receive a real or seeming check, the law of right must be obeyed."[85] That such sacrifices were seldom if ever demanded was due to the merciful Providence of God. In His beneficence, the divine Being had so ordered all things that mankind would benefit, both individually and collectively, from obedience to the moral law. God had provided for the recompense of virtue; the righteous would prosper here on earth and receive a heavenly reward as well. The hard teachings of Unitarian ethical theory were made to seem easier and more attractive by Unitarian religion.

A NOTE ON FREE WILL

One of the distinguishing theological characteristics of the Boston Unitarians was their Arminianism, that is, their belief in the freedom of man to work out his own salvation. Under the circumstances one might expect that they would have produced an apologetical literature defending free will against Calvinist determinism. But the student who seeks for a comprehensive Harvard Unitarian refutation of Edwards's *Careful and Strict Enquiry into the Modern Prevailing Notions of the Freedom of the Will* (1754) is disappointed.[86] In fact, the antebellum Harvard moralists devoted remarkably little energy to the issue of free will, either as a logical or a psychological problem. Edward's argument seemed to them unassailable and yet unconvincing. So they were content to accept the freedom of the will as a datum of consciousness, that is, as a principle of common sense, and declare that it required no proof. "The moral freedom of man is not a question of speculation, to be settled by abstract reasoning," asserted Levi Hedge. "It is a question of fact to be decided by feeling . . . We believe we are free, because we feel that we are so."[87] Not even Doctor Johnson could be more dogmatic: "Sir," said he to Boswell, "we *know* our will is free, and *there's* an end on't."[88]

III / Reason and Revelation

Natural Theology, for centuries a recognized scholarly discipline in the Western world, was the study of the existence and attributes of the divine Creator as these could be inferred from the evidence of His works. Treatises on moral philosophy in the Scottish tradition normally included a section on natural theology. There was little that was distinctive about Harvard natural theology; other Protestant common sense philosophers treated the subject in much the same way.[1] Sons of the Christian Enlightenment, the Harvard Unitarians were confident that nature spoke to man of God, revealing a divine order at once intellectually satisfying and morally uplifting.

NATURAL AND REVEALED RELIGION

"Nature" and "revelation" were the two accepted fountains of knowledge in the Middle Ages. The truths of nature, as used in this sense, included all knowledge obtained by man's unaided reason, that is, all knowledge not derived from the Word of God. The truths of revelation, on the other hand, had been supernaturally communicated to man and recorded in the Old and New Testaments. The fundamental assumption of medieval scholarship was the complete harmony between natural and revealed knowledge.[2] Well into modern times, Western man continued to accord equal authority to these two types of knowledge, partially overlapping and perfectly compatible. Thus, John Locke put his great epistemological innovations at the service of a traditional expression of the relationship between reason and revelation.

Reason is natural revelation, whereby the eternal Father of light, the Foundation of all knowledge, communicates to mankind that portion of

69

truth which he has laid within the reach of their natural faculties. Revelation is natural reason enlarged by a new set of discoveries communicated by God immediately, which reason vouches the truth of, by the testimony and proofs it gives that they come from God.[3]

The God of Newton, Boyle, and Ray also remained the God revealed in Scripture. And the authority of the Scottish common sense philosophers helped maintain the harmony between natural and revealed religion down to the middle of the nineteenth century. Not until the impact of Darwin on the one hand, and biblical higher criticism on the other, was this durable synthesis finally shattered for English-speaking Protestant intellectuals.

The Unitarian moralists kept up this traditional view of the dual sources of knowledge, or as they called it, "the Christian conjunction" of faith with reason. A sympathetic interpreter has described Harvard Unitarianism as "a half-way house to the rationalistic and scientific point of view, yet a house built so reverently that the academic wayfarer could seldom forget that he had sojourned in a House of God."[4] Neither reason nor revelation, the two pillars of divine wisdom, could be abandoned, lest the integrated structure of Liberal Christianity come crashing down. Every third year from 1755 on, the Dudleian Lectures at Harvard rehearsed the standard formulas of "Natural and Revealed Religion." Paul Dudley's endowment gave Massachusetts its provincial counterpart to the Boyle Lectures in London (started in 1692), where Anglican divines expounded identical themes.[5] Interest in the reconciliation of human and divine knowledge reached a peak in Boston under the auspices of the Lowell Institute, founded in 1839. When James Walker delivered the first series of Lowell Lectures on natural theology, two thousand people filled the Odeon Theater on Federal Street to capacity twice a week to hear him.[6]

Together, reason and revelation provided Unitarians with an epistemological dualism analogous to the ontological dualism of mind and matter. The Harvard philosopher candidly confessed that he possessed in advance (from revelation) many of the conclusions he sought to confirm by natural reason. "To investigate the principle of an admitted rule is much easier, and followed by conclusions far more satisfactory, than when the principle and the rule are both to be discovered," acknowledged Levi Frisbie. "Our inquiries are guided by truths already known."[7] Unitarian philosophy existed to ratify and elucidate Christian religion.

THE BOOK OF NATURE

Henry Ware's two-volume *Inquiry into the Foundation, Evidence and Truths of Religion* typified Unitarian interest in nature. Compiled near the end of his life, the *Inquiry* was based upon Ware's Harvard lectures on "natural and revealed religion." These he had delivered, almost without change, to generations of students from 1805 until his retirement in 1838. The debates surrounding his appointment as Hollis Professor must have seemed far away to the old man, and he evinced no desire to relive them. Increasingly, Ware and his fellow Unitarians shied away from controversial speculations on the Atonement and Grace, finding an alternative mode of religious expression in natural theology. The "book of nature" (as they called it) would reveal more beauty and more truth about the universe than the tomes of Calvinist pedagogues had ever contained.

Natural theology expressed what might be called the "rationalistic" strain in Unitarianism, that is, the disposition to regard religion as an inquiry into divine knowledge. Rejecting the ancient paradox attributed to Tertullian *(credo quia absurdum est)*, Unitarians believed that only what was rationally plausible could be accepted in religious faith. Religious assertions should be evaluated on exactly the same basis as other assertions about the world, such as those of history or science. Searching by the light of nature, Ware's *Inquiry* discerned a great "chain of being" in the universe, ascending from inert matter up through men to the divinity. Before he was through, Ware had found rational evidence for God's existence, unity, omniscience, and omnipotence.[8]

Men like Ware had a view of nature that was a remarkable amalgam of the old and the new, of modern science and medieval Christianity. A historian of science has summed up their outlook as an attempt "to weld into a single philosophy . . . two not entirely compatible conceptions: one, the idea of nature as a law-bound system of matter and motion, and two, the idea of nature as a habitation created for the use and edification of intelligent beings by an omnipotent, omniscient, and benevolent God."[9] In the early nineteenth century the state of scientific knowledge had not yet discredited this attempt. By and large, it was a time of little conflict between science and religion; the threat to natural theology still came from only a few skeptical philosophers.

The typical British or American scientist of that age was a Christian, more or less pious as his individual temperament might incline. The dominant school of early nineteenth century geologists, for example, "accorded complete philosophic validity to whatever results Baconian induction might bring them; [but] they also required these results to display the structure and development of the material world as the history of an intending Providence with a moral purpose."[10] Science of this kind was the welcome ally of religion. Boston Unitarians (like their American orthodox contemporaries) gloried in the scientific achievements of the Enlightenment. "When I consult nature with the lights modern science affords," William Ellery Channing exulted, "I see continually multiplying traces of the doctrine of One God."[11]

When the accumulation of scientific knowledge, particularly in geology, raised disturbing questions, Boston Liberals were reluctant to admit that the early modern synthesis of science and religion might be on the verge of collapse. "There is nothing . . . in the scientific study of nature to hinder men from . . . becoming religious," a Harvard moral philosopher bravely asserted, while his colleague condemned "ill-judging divines [who] discredit and defame the most eminent geologists of the day." "Geology declares without hesitation, and with as much distinctness as Holy Writ, that time was when the earth was without form and void, and before the dry land appeared." As late as 1855, Francis Bowen remained optimistic. "I have no fears of any conflict between the truths of real science and those of either Natural or Revealed Religion." Darwin's *Origin of Species,* coming in 1859, was received with dismay and disbelief by its Unitarian reviewer.[12]

Natural science in the early nineteenth century was generally divided into two great branches: natural history, which included geology, biology, and anthropology; and natural philosophy, consisting of astronomy, chemistry, and physics. As an influence upon the Unitarian world view, natural history was considerably the more important of the two. Natural philosophy dealt entirely with inanimate matter, and such divine order as it revealed often appeared remote from human needs. The methods of natural history—then chiefly description and classification—seemed more relevant to religious concerns, lending themselves to doctrines like the great chain of being and providential benevolence.[13] It is hard to escape the conclusion that Unitarian ethical theory, particularly in the classification of the hierarchy of the faculties, revealed the influence of contemporary natural history. Likewise, Harvard epistemology sang the praises of a common-sense empiricism more relevant to natural history than to the controlled experiments and quantified data of natural philosophy.[14]

Unitarians drew on a rich literature of early modern natural theology. When Ware taught natural and revealed religion at Harvard, he was able to assign a long list of writers famous throughout Protestantism.[15] One of the most interesting of these, Abraham Tucker (1705–1774), was an eccentric English squire whose multivolume life-work, *The Light of Nature Pursued,* is a rambling and amusing relic of a bygone age. James Walker gave the first American edition of this work (published in Cambridge by Hilliard and Metcalf in 1831) a favorable review in the *Christian Examiner.*[16] Perhaps the grandest enterprise of natural theology was the "Bridgewater Treatises," a series of eight studies by eminent British scientists written under the terms of a bequest from the pious Earl of Bridgewater. The fame of the Bridgewater Treatises reached across the Atlantic to New England and the Unitarians. Henry Ware, Jr., had the fictional paragon of his didactic stories, David Ellington, keep his family on bread and water all one summer in order to save enough out of his carpenter's wages to buy a set of these elevating volumes.[17]

But the most well-known and widely used of all works on natural theology was Archdeacon Paley's handbook of that name first published in 1802. Paley was an expounder of the theories of more academic religious writers. He popularized the ideas of John Ray (1627–1705), William Derham (1657–1735), and others in much the same fashion that Bishop John Robinson has diffused the theology of Bultmann, Tillich, and Bonhoeffer in our own day.[18] Paley treated natural facts as the conscious contrivances of a benign Providence; his favorite analogy was that between the intricacies of human or animal physiology and the workings of a watch or some other machine. The systematic ranking of biological species into genera and classes also indicated to him the rationality of the deity.[19] Paley summarized, in language everyone could understand, the favorite clichés of an era that loved to see the hand of God in nature. Something of his vast prestige may be judged from the fact that the famous British Whig politician, Lord Brougham, and Sir Charles Bell, an eminent surgeon of the day, collaborated on a five-volume annotation of Paley's little book.[20]

Notwithstanding their serious misgivings about Paley's *Moral Philosophy,* Harvard Unitarians unreservedly accepted his *Natural Theology.* Ware used it in class, probably from 1812 on, certainly by the 1830's, and his lectures echoed its interpretations.[21] Its fundamental assumptions were congenial to Enlightenment Christians, and its simplified presentations proved an asset to the religious educator. In the opinion of Unitarian philosophers, the most important quality of any book was its "moral tendency." Though Paley's presentation was not very profound, it was wholesome and morally elevating. Antebellum Harvard professors retained enough of their Puritan heritage to believe that the education they offered should include ethical and religious values. Paley's pious work was an eminently practical example of knowledge applied to the service of Christian morality.

Early nineteenth-century Harvard Unitarianism does not appear to have been especially favorable to science when compared with other branches of Anglo-American Protestantism (certainly not if compared with Priestleyan Unitarianism). Even sympathetic contemporary observers agreed that the Liberal moralists tended to superficiality in their attitudes toward natural science. Thus, a fond classmate recalled that Joseph S. Buckminster could "illustrate the topics of literature on which he descanted by appropriate allusions to the success of scientific principles. But here his intercourse with the sciences, especially the abstract sciences, ended. The principles themselves he never investigated."[22]

When it came to either quantitative or deductive thinking the New England Unitarians betrayed a tendency to "glorify reason rather than use it."[23] They sang with Pope, "Nature and nature's laws lay hid in night;/God said, 'Let Newton be,' and all was light." But the Harvard moralists really had little interest in the higher mathematics of the *Principia*. Buckminster, typically, preferred to write a poem in praise of mathematics rather than do mathematics itself.[24] During the first decades of the nineteenth century Harvard lagged slightly behind the Princeton of Joseph Henry and the Yale of Benjamin Silliman, Sr., in the field of science. The 1840's saw the founding of the Lawrence Scientific School and the arrival at Harvard of two outstanding scientists, Asa Gray and Louis Agassiz—though it is worth noting that both were brought in from outside New England Unitarianism, the former being an orthodox Presbyterian from New York and the latter a Swiss disciple of Schelling's *Naturphilosophie*.[25]

As one scholar has observed, for all the admiration that New England Unitarians expressed for natural science, in practice they "tended to subordinate it to a complex religious and humanistic heritage."[26] The reasons for this subordination are rooted in Harvard metaphysics and its subordination of matter to spirit. "Outward, material Nature derives its chief power of contributing to our happiness, by being a manifestation of mental or spiritual excellence," taught a Unitarian philosopher. "No one truly enjoys the creation, but he who sees it everywhere as radiant with *mind,* and as for ever showing forth the perfection of its author."[27]

Unitarian sermons and prayers frequently praised God for the beauties of nature and expressed awe at its marvelous contrivance. Like medieval schoolmen, the Harvard moralists listened reverently to "the music of the spheres." Buckminster's sermon, "The Providence of God as Displayed in Nature," is perhaps the best example of how the doctrines of Liberal natural theology could be put to devotional purposes. It would be unthinkable, Buckminster insisted, for God to create a universe without taking a constant interest in it thereafter. Did He not co-ordinate the paths of stars so they did not collide? Even "more striking," asked the moralist, turning from natural philosophy to the field of natural history closer to his hearers' experience, did God not provide animals with instincts that were direct manifestations of divine intelligence? The ant storing food for the winter was responding to the prudential promptings of Providence.[28]

Some thirty years after Buckminster preached that sermon, Henry Ware set down its conception of nature in his volumes. And the old man's son, who enjoyed composing a little verse, expressed it another way:

> All nature's works His praise declare,
> To whom they all belong;
> There is a voice in every star,
> In every breeze a song.[29]

So hymned the Unitarian poet; the transition from rationalistic to rhapsodic natural theology came easily. Whatever its influence may have been on other men, among New England Liberal Christians natural theology stimulated literature more than science.

THE TELEOLOGICAL ARGUMENT

In the summer of 1838, the attention of the Cambridge community was diverted from the country's worsening economic crisis by a shocking address which an apostate Unitarian minister named Ralph Waldo Emerson had delivered at Dean Palfrey's Divinity School on the fifteenth of July. The hazards implicit in the innovations of the "New School" of Unitarian heretics had been evident to reflective Harvard men for some time, Orestes Brownson having raised the standard of working-class radicalism more than a year before. Andrews Norton had already felt forced to chastise the dangerous views on revelation which George Ripley was advocating in the *Christian Examiner*.[30] But Emerson's Divinity School address was particularly galling. The speech was given in the hallowed halls of Harvard; Emerson made use of a forum provided by the Unitarian seminary to subject Unitarianism to some most unflattering criticism. This was not only subversive; it was (in Harvard eyes) poor taste. The churches had lost the spirit of poetic intuition that was the essence of true religion, Emerson charged; they accepted a feeble second-hand faith instead of provoking men to seek direct inspiration through mystical union with nature. Professor Norton's hot-tempered retort was not slow in coming, but it only embarrassed many Unitarians the more. Men like the stolid James Walker had no relish for such contention.[31]

Henry Ware, Jr., his father's colleague at the Divinity School, attempted to counteract Emerson's address with a sermon he preached in the Harvard Chapel soon after classes resumed in September. Ware entitled his own address "The Personality of the Deity" and focused his attention upon the doctrine of God. He contrasted Unitarian orthodoxy (if the term be not contradictory) with certain other opinions he let remain nameless. The Unitarian God stood above and beyond the natural order, as Ware defined Him, and should not be confused with nature itself. Furthermore, to use the word "God" to refer to abstract concepts like "beauty" or "virtue" was "to violate the established use of language." God was a conscious personality, and to apply His name to either the universe itself or to inanimate abstractions was a pitiful disguise for atheism. While the younger Ware politely refrained from identifying any local crypto-atheists, his target was obvious. Even so, his statement elicited no rebuttal from Emerson. Ware himself did not press the issue further, very likely because he and Emerson had long been personal friends.[32]

Yet Emerson's talk had seemed to implicate official Unitarianism in the Transcendental novelties, and it would take a more forthright and thoroughgoing defense than Ware's to erase the stigma. What was needed was a point-by-point elucidation of the Unitarian position, to manifest before respectable men throughout the English-speaking world that Harvard was no hotbed of "enthusiasm." Frances Bowen, twenty-six-year-old Harvard instructor, rose to the occasion. His review of Emerson's *Nature* had already marked him as an enemy of the "new views" when Bowen commenced a series of articles in the *Christian Examiner* and the *North American Review* aimed at discrediting the idealistic philosophies seducing some Yankees.[33] Though definitely *pièces de circonstance*, these essays also provided a definitive exposition of Unitarian doctrine, particularly in the field of natural theology. Since (as Bowen finally realized many years later) the American Transcendentalists were not really much interested in formal philosophical systems, one may conclude that his papers are more significant as statements of classical Unitarianism than as criticisms of its Transcendentalist offshoot. In 1842 the articles were collected and republished under the title *Critical Essays on a Few Subjects Con-*

nected with the History and Present Condition of Speculative Philosophy.[34]

Like Ware, Bowen regarded the conception of the Deity as the heart of the matter. His essays deal at length with the arguments for the existence of God. These arguments, having been thoroughly threshed out by philosophers over the centuries, may be reduced to certain standard forms, each with its designation.[35] The argument which Bowen, in common with the Wares and other Unitarians, considered the most convincing was the teleological, or the "proof from design." The teleological argument, the one Paley popularized, infers the existence of God from the harmony of the universe, both inorganic and organic. Innumerable examples of apparent design in nature are marshaled as evidence of conscious contrivance. Just as the workings of a watch testify to the existence of a watchmaker, so, the argument runs, the orderly universe indicates the existence of a Purposeful Designer. All the philosophers of the common sense school, beginning with Reid, reposed great confidence in this teleological argument.[36]

There were also several a priori arguments purporting to prove the existence of God by logical demonstration. A Unitarian philosopher had to reckon in particular with two of these arguments, widely known in early modern times: the cosmological argument employed by Samuel Clarke (1675–1729) and the ontological argument of Descartes. The cosmological argument derives the existence of God from the existence of the universe. Most often, it takes the form of an argument for a First Cause. Locke had devised a form of the cosmological argument, a rather weak and uninfluential form, in fact. The Harvard Unitarians did not accept it, but they charitably refrained from criticising the philosopher to whom they owed so much. Instead, they directed their shafts at Samuel Clarke. Clarke had attempted to demonstrate the necessity of a God from the postulated existence of infinite time and infinite space. Bowen objected that Clarke's "argument, at the utmost, proves only that something exists," though Clarke had assumed that this "something" must be God.[37]

Descartes' ontological argument detained Bowen somewhat longer. It had recently received endorsement from Victor Cousin, and Bowen evidently feared this would encourage the American Transcendentalists, for he devoted considerable attention to refuting it. Bowen summed up the ontological argument well: "In the idea of God are combined all the attributes of a perfect being; but necessary existence is one of these attributes; therefore, he necessarily exists." His specific objection to the argument was that it wrongly assumed existence to be an "attribute." Even more important, Bowen felt that all such deductive "proofs" of the existence of God were instrinsically incapable of bearing the weight their advocates placed upon them. Against the a priori arguments, Bowen invoked the epistemological rule he had learned from Levi Hedge: the conclusions of demonstrative reasoning, even if valid, could never reveal anything about the real world. They could never show that God was an active and conscious personality, as the Unitarians conceived of Him. A "God" whose existence was a logical "necessity" would be only an abstraction, Bowen snorted, "a fantastic thing of man's device, a mere word, [with] neither substance nor reality."[38]

The teleological argument, on the other hand, was compatible with the Unitarian conception of a personal God. The argument was constructed as an a posteriori induction from empirical ("moral") evidence. As such, it led to the claim that the existence of God was a scientifically respectable "fact" and not a mere definition or abstraction. Besides the real existence of God, the teleological argument was also capable of inferring one of His attributes: His unity (from the alleged unity of design in the universe).[39]

Common sense philosophy, which taught that God had endowed men with organs of sense that they might perceive and admire His works, dovetailed perfectly with the teleological argument. But the philosophy of Kant, which New England Transcendentalists were then praising, posed a threat to Unitarian natural theology. Kant called into question the ultimate authenticity of empirical knowledge. The order which men found in the universe might not "really" be out there, the German idealist warned; men imposed upon their perceptions certain categories which were characteristic of the operation of the human mind rather than of external reality. Bowen thought he had heard this argument before: "Kant simply established Hume's doctrine on a different basis."[40] In fact, Kant, like Hume, did reject the teleological argument for the existence of God. God, Kant asserted, was a postulate of the "Practical Reason" along with immortality and free will. This was too much for a Harvard Unitarian to swallow; God could not be a mere hypothesis.

Bowen's attempted refutation of Kantianism fell considerably short of adequacy; for the most part he simply criticized its "moral tendency." The political consequences of the Critical Philosophy were downright dangerous, the New Englander complained. From his American perspective, Bowen endowed Kant's speculations with social implications which the staid Prussian professor would scarcely have recognized: "[Kantianism] has brought a reproach on the very name of philosophy, and, through the mournful perversion of terms which it has occasioned, has given too good cause for regarding a system of philosophical radicalism as a mere cover for an attack on all the principles of government and social order."[41] By discrediting Kant, Bowen thought he was helping to save America from Transcendental fanatics.

How are we to account for the preference which the Harvard Unitarians showed for common sense philosophy and natural theology over the more sophisticated doctrines of Hume and Kant? Their fear that new philosophies would foster political radicalism is only part of the story. Perhaps a fuller answer is that common sense and the teleological argument spoke directly to their experience. Nineteenth-century Unitarianism was a religion for respectable people in a commercial, industrializing society. Francis Bowen, ambitious young Harvard instructor, was the academic spokesman for a class of modern men who prided themselves on being practical and sensible. To the minds of men like Bowen, the philosophies of Hume and Kant seemed far-fetched. Such men wanted religious assurances that were at once tangible and conventional. Basing Christianity upon empirical evidence satisfied this desire; it endowed traditional belief with the prestige of the new science and (probably even more important) the prestige of the new technology. "If we were shown for the first time a complex piece of machinery, a power-loom or a steam engine, we should not hesitate a moment in ascribing it to human contrivance."[42] Inferring God from the contrivance of nature appealed to men enchanted by the mechanical inventions of their age.

The teleological argument would also have seemed plausible to men who were relatively well off. The universe they inhabited was indeed, from their point of view, well designed. Unitarian writers, like generations of Christians before them, wrestled with the problem of evil in a creation their religion taught was fundamentally good. But one often gets the impression that for Bowen and his colleagues it was a remote and academic problem. When they dismissed pain and suffering as incidental to some higher good, they did so a little too easily to carry conviction.[43] Francis Bowen inferred the benevolence of God from the overwhelming happiness of the human race, and this overwhelming happiness he inferred from the contented situation of his own social class. He apparently could not believe that any sufferings bourgeois Bostonians did not experience were a very important part of human existence. "How many of those who read this page," he asked, rhetorically, "have been plagued by famines, innundations, earthquakes, the assassination of friends, robbery, ravenous beasts, tyranny, the necessity of slaying a fellow creature for sustenance, or the like? And if, which is very improbable, there be an individual who has experienced one of these calamities, how small a portion of his whole existence has been immediately saddened by the event?"[44] The lives of Bowen's readers probably did tend to corroborate the view that a benevolent power controlled the universe. If Harvard Unitarianism was remarkably optimistic, it may have been so because it was the religion of a fortunate group of people.

Still, one cannot help wondering if the Boston Liberals were always perfectly sincere in their avowals of philosophical complacency. The ideas of Hume and Kant threatened to undermine the whole Platonic heritage of cosmic order, on which Unitarians had staked so much. Their own assault upon Calvinist orthodoxy illustrated the vulnerability of all intellectual traditions. Did the Harvard moralists ever have to conceal fears that, after all, they themselves might prove to be wrong? "In our best moods, everything in natural religion is clear; in our worst moods, everything is dark," James Walker once confessed.[45] How much of Unitarian rhetoric represented whistling in the dark we can never know.

REVELATION

Professor Andrews Norton resigned his chair at Harvard in 1830, thereby gaining relief from the demanding teaching and administrative duties it imposed. Independently wealthy since his marriage to the daughter of a Boston merchant, he could afford to give up the salary. From then until his death in 1853, Norton labored singlemindedly on a multivolume work entitled *Evidences of the Genuineness of the Gospels.* The task to which Norton dedicated his life was to prove, by the most sophisticated scholarly tools available to him, the trustworthiness of the Gospel narratives. Within the Harvard Unitarian system of values, no more important or practical project could have been undertaken. Though it does not possess the romance or the general interest that the narrative histories of Prescott or Motley have retained, Norton's work on the New Testament deserves to be remembered along with them as a major product of antebellum Unitarian scholarship. His impressive labor of love appropriately indicates the respect in which Harvard Unitarians held the Scriptures.[46]

Divine revelation, as Norton and his fellow Unitarians understood it, supplemented reason in two general ways. In the first place, it clarified the great truths of natural religion, assisting man to employ his reason properly in noticing indications of providential planning.[47] Second, revelation gave man a knowledge of obligations and doctrines he could never have discovered by the light of nature alone. Through revelation God had supplemented the dictates of conscience with additional positive commandments. Usually, the latter were elaborations of, and subsidiary to, the former; thus, that we should worship our benevolent creator was considered a self-evident obligation, but that the Sabbath Day should be set aside for this purpose was a revealed law. God's commandments could, indeed, only bind morally to the extent they they were compatible with the immutable principles of right— but God, who conformed perfectly to the moral law Himself, would never command anything contrary to it.[48] (Of course, many moral truths, e.g., "Thou shalt not kill," were known through both reason and revelation.)

But the most important function of revealed knowledge was not the additional obligations it enjoined, but the additional *motives* for virtue that it supplied. Although the principles of morality were independent of religion or God's will, God loved and enforced them. Hence, when acting from a sense of duty, men should be aware that they were fulfilling a "religious obligation" as well as an ethical one. The knowledge that his conduct was pleasing to God filled a good man with joy, thus making religious pleasure a motive to virtue. In this way, revelation enlisted the religious affections in support of the moral sense. Revelation also helped bring prudence into line behind conscience by supplying knowledge of a future state of retribution.[49]

"Faith," Locke had written, "cannot be afforded to anything but upon good reason." Revelation was accepted by Harvard Unitarians, as by their master, Locke, only on the basis of evidence to its authenticity. The truth of revelation was "decided at the bar of reason."[50] Religious faith, for the Harvard Unitarians, consisted in accepting the Bible (at least for the most part) as a true historical record of events. Justifying this acceptance was the testimony of the authors of Scripture to that which they had seen. The true believer, Buckminster told his congregation, "is indeed, like Thomas, on recognition of the Savior, ready to exclaim, 'My Lord and my God!' "[51] Like Thomas! The faith of the doubter who would not believe until he had seen and felt the evidence was the faith this Lockean religion extolled.

The canons of empirical epistemology, as Levi Hedge had laid them down, governed Harvard attitudes toward the Scriptures. Hedge's doctrines about "reasoning on facts" came straight out of the *Essay Concerning Human Understanding*. "Facts," in this sense, were events recorded in the Bible or any other historical work and accepted on "the testimony of others, vouching their observation and experience."[52] In accepting such facts, one was substituting the sensory perception of another person for one's own. As natural religion was based on empirical evidence, revealed religion was based on vicarious empirical evidence. So, as Buckminster explained to his parishioners, faith was not "opposed to reason," even though its objects were "beyond the reach of personal experience." "Christianity," William Ellery Channing could boast, "is a rational religion."[53]

There were, of course, those who denied the rationality of revealed religion. Most of these were deists, men who, while accepting natural religion, were unconvinced by the pretensions of revelation.[54] Some of the deists, like John Toland (1670–1722), were disciples of Locke who felt their master had erred in supposing that the Scriptures were substantiated by adequate evidence. Others, however, like Lord Herbert of Cherbury (1583–1648), had arrived at deist views quite independently of Locke.[55] Deism had passed its peak in England by the middle of the eighteenth century, but its influence (like that of many other European cultural developments) was felt more slowly in America. Thomas Paine, who occupied an anomalous position as an English, French, and American deist, typified the connection between religious and political radicalism that disturbed Federalist Unitarians. His *Age of Reason* (1794) was the deist tract most hated and feared by Boston Liberal Christians. Arminians and Calvinists stood shoulder to shoulder against him in New England; while Timothy Dwight of Yale warned against "the nature and danger of infidel philosophy," John Thornton Kirkland of Harvard was lecturing on the "poison of the skeptical and disorganizing philosophy." In 1796 every student at Harvard was given a copy of the Anglican Bishop Richard Watson's *Apology for the Bible* in an all-out effort to combat Paine's terrifying popularity.[56]

Unitarian attacks on deism were slow to subside. Continually confronted with the taunt that their religion was a way station on the road to infidelity, Unitarians self-consciously proclaimed their devotion to the Scriptures. "I know of no sentiment in which Unitarians are more entirely agreed," claimed the elder Ware in 1821, "than in the absolute authority of Divine Revelation." James Walker was still fighting the old battle in 1837.[57]

In their defense of revelation against deism (which was an indirect defense of their own Christianity against the aspersions of the Trinitarians), Harvard Unitarians relied heavily upon the arguments developed by Church of England controversialists in the eighteenth century. Many of these writers were naive by twentieth-century standards, but Joseph Butler (1692–1752), Bishop of Durham, was not. Butler endeavored to answer the deist charge that Scripture, with its riddles, contradictions, and ambiguities, its obscure passages and problems of translation, was intrinsically a poor vehicle for divine revelation. How much better sense it would make, Paine and his coadjutors had argued, to suppose that God had revealed Himself fully and equally to all men through nature, rather than to one obscure tribe through peculiar means. The deists had set up a sharp distinction between natural religion, which was readily intelligible, and revealed religion, which was inherently implausible. In the words of Paine, natural and revealed religion were "true and fabulous theology," respectively.[58]

Butler replied that the contrast between natural and revealed religion that the deists had made simply did not exist. The problems and perplexities of natural religion were fully equal to those presented by Scripture, he pointed out. Nature too was full of mystery. This, Butler claimed, would not surprise the Christian, who maintains that both nature and Scripture have the same Author, but it should embarrass the deist. Our experience of life is complex and puzzling, granted Butler, but the Christian revelation fits it about as well as one could reasonably ask. As a rejection of deist claims for the superiority of the religion of nature, Butler's *Analogy of Religion* (1736) was brilliant. His argument is the *tu quoque,* which has served Christian apologetics longer and better than any other: the argument that commitment to Christianity is no more irrational than an alternative commitment.[59]

Butler was a High Churchman in ecclesiastical politics, yet he had much in common with the "Latitudinarians" at Harvard. He agreed that revelation had to be subjected to the test of reason; he also had a firm commitment to the facts of everyday experience congenial to common sense philosophy. Butler's *Analogy* was treasured by New England Unitarians as an arsenal for weapons against deism; indeed, Boston Liberals boasted that Butler had no more loyal admirers than they. President Walker told Harvard students that the *Analogy of Religion* was "the most original and profound work extant in any language on the philosophy of religion."[60] But the English bishop's importance for Massachusetts Unitarians went beyond the confines of formal philosophy, and influenced their deepest feelings about nature and the world.

Butler's sense of mystery and awe toward nature did much to counterbalance the superficial rationalism fostered by Paley. Henry Ware, Jr., manifested this more sensitive, pietistic attitude. The Christian "walks as a child . . . amid the wonders of the universe," he wrote. "While every leaf and flower and insect presents its crowd of marvels to his admiring thought, he is drawn to God, rather than repelled, by the inexplicable . . . He is drawn to Christ, not repelled, by the mingled atmosphere of light and darkness in which he robed his spiritual teachings."[61] William Ellery Channing was another New England Unitarian influenced by Butler (one of the "master-spirits of the human race," he called him). "There is an impenetrable mystery in every action and force of the universe, that envelops our daily presence with wonder and makes sublime the familiar processes of the commonest arts," agreed Channing.[62] The natural religion of Bishop Butler fed a stream of preromanticism in Boston Unitarianism.

Butler had rebutted the charge that revelation was too irrational to be true, but the deists had another accusation against the Bible that Unitarians had to acknowledge: the Bible was too immoral to be true. Especially in the Old Testament, God is often depicted as vengeful and outrageously partial. His Chosen People perpetrate atrocities with His blessing. Could this book be an accurate revelation of the divine perfection? Paine said no.[63]

The Harvard Unitarians accepted the criterion of morality in judging revelation. They could not afford to admit that the Bible, of all books, might have a bad "moral tendency." A true revelation must contain nothing absurd or immoral. Reason and the moral sense are, so far as they go, trustworthy guides, divinely implanted, and God must be presumed not to contradict Himself. "A religion, for example, commanding us to hate and injure society, reason must instantly discard." We can make no a priori assertions about what a revelation will contain (if we could we would not need the revelation), but we can confidently assert that it will *not* contain anything contrary to morality.[64]

Having granted Paine's premise that an alleged revelation must be moral to be authentic, Unitarians were at great pains to show that Biblical religion was moral. Henry Ware attempted to explain away a number of apparent injustices related in the Old Testament, such as Noah's curse on Ham's descendents for Ham's offense. Our conception of the morality taught in the Bible must be derived from "the general tenor" of the Scriptures, and not from selected short passages, argued Buckminster.[65] And Francis Bowen avowed that the moral faculty was worthy to sit in judgment on Scripture, deciding which passages could be accepted literally and which could not. "In the perusal of Scripture," he wrote, "the only reason for construing a passage in a metaphorical sense is, often, that by a literal interpretation, it would convey a doctrine utterly repugnant to all our moral feelings. The law written on the heart expounds the law graven on tables of stone."[66] The Unitarian conscience was a tool of biblical criticism.

So far, the Unitarian defense of revelation had been merely negative. The Bible was not too irrational or too immoral to be true. But did it bear any positive authentication of its message? The system of arguments by which the Unitarians claimed to validate the Christian revelation has become known as "supernatural rationalism."[67] This consisted of the presentation of empirical evidence that the teachings recorded in the Bible came from God. The favorite evidence was that of miracles—particularly the miracles wrought by Christ. These were taken as proof that Christ was a divine messenger, empowered to perform marvels to demonstrate His commission. Supernatural rationalism was by no means peculiar to Boston Liberals. The attitude is at least as old as Nicodemus the Pharisee: "Rabbi, we know that thou art a teacher come from God: for no man can do these miracles that thou doest, except God be with him" (John 3:2). In the eighteenth century, the argument for Christianity from the biblical miracles was almost universally accepted. By the nineteenth century, the argument, although still popular, was losing its power to convince many intellectuals (as the Transcendentalist controversy made clear). Mainstream Harvard Unitarians, however, following in the footsteps of Jonathan Mayhew, steadfastly defended supernatural rationalism.[68]

The greatest exponent of supernatural rationalism had been John Locke, and Unitarian commitment to it was bound up with their dedication to his empiricist epistemology. In both the *Essay Concerning Human Understanding* and *The Reasonableness of Christianity,* Locke took the position that the miracle stories authenticated revelation. However, the Harvard Unitarian version of the authentication of revelation by miracles contained a subtle but significant distinction from the doctrine of Locke. As Locke elaborated his views in *A Discourse of Miracles* and *A Third Letter Concerning Toleration,* he took the position that the sole function of a miracle was its impact upon the beholder, creating awe and inciting trust in the miracle-worker. He therefore defined a miracle as an event "above the comprehension of the spectator, and in his opinion contrary to the established course of nature." By this definition, a miracle need not contravene any law of nature *in fact*; it need only create the impression of doing so. But Harvard philosophers found Locke's definition distasteful. They insisted that a miracle must be "a sensible deviation from the known laws of nature" and "contrary to the established constitution and course of things." The loophole which Locke had left open for subjective interpretations of miracles was closed by Unitarian moralists.[69]

The firm commitment of Harvard Unitarians to the supernatural was summed up by William Ellery Channing's famous statement in his Dudleian Lecture of 1821: "Christianity is not only confirmed by miracles, but is in itself, in its very essence, a miraculous religion." Others might find miracles incredible, but not the great New England Liberal. "The miracles of Christianity, so far from shocking me, approve themselves at once to my intellect and my heart," declared Channing.[70] The rest of the Harvard moralists concurred; Henry Ware, Sr., expressed amazement that "some of the German divines do not believe in miracles, and yet pretend to believe in Christianity." The younger Ware likewise cautioned his students against attempting to "explain away" the miracle stories in naturalistic terms.[71]

Besides miracles, other types of evidence were cited by the supernatural rationalists on behalf of Scripture. The confirmation of Old Testament prophecies in the New was, of course, invoked; so was the fairly rapid success of Christianity in the face of many handicaps (which was taken to indicate divine favor). All such supernatural authentication was considered crucially important.

> Had [Christ] wrought no miracles, had no prophecies received their accomplishment in his person . . . and had he delivered no prophecies that were afterward fulfilled,—however his doctrines might have claimed our assent as valuable truths, and his precepts deserved to be received as rules of life, they would have had no peculiar authority.[72]

Marshaling "evidence" for the Gospel seems to have been accompanied by a certain loss of focus upon the Good News itself. Even Dr. Channing was convinced that, should supernatural wonders prove incredible, it would be "fatal to Christianity."[73]

The Liberals managed to call supernatural rationalism into play during their theological disputes with orthodoxy. When Calvinists pointed to the creeds of the Reformation Era as authoritative statements of Protestant belief, Channing retorted, "On what ground, I ask, do the creed-makers demand assent to their articles? . . . What has conferred on them infallibility?" "Show me your proofs," he taunted them. "Work some miracle. Utter some prophecy." When no Calvinist marvels were forthcoming, the Unitarian concluded triumphantly, "You are unaided men like myself."[74]

Obviously miracles were open to objection as evidence for revelation. Far from confirming the truth of the Bible, Tom Paine complained, the miracle stories only added to its incredibility. Long before, Hume had argued that miracles are inherently unbelievable, since by definition they contradict all previous human experience.[75] In their own time and place, the Unitarians faced such formidable antagonists of supernatural rationalism as the erudite Theodore Parker and the caustic, secular-minded Richard Hildreth.[76] To defend their reliance upon miracles in the face of such critics, Harvard philosophers argued that every event in the history of the universe represented a separate and immediate volition of the Creator. If nature appeared generally uniform, this was only because God normally chose to act in certain patterns. The Unitarians found nothing improbable in His acting differently whenever His purposes might be served by doing so. Hume's argument was generally rejected as begging the question. "It asserts that miracles are contrary to universal experience; when the very question is, whether or not they have been met with in human experience." If one accepted the possibility of a God, and the possibility that He might wish to authenticate a revelation to man with signs and wonders, then, the Harvard philosophers maintained, one would have to admit that a miracle was possible. The natural history of the time seemed to confirm the possibility of miracles: early nineteenth-century geology provided scientific evidence (as it was then interpreted) of sudden catastrophic convulsions in the earth's primordial history. Such findings were taken as indications that God did, on occasion, intervene spectacularly in the processes of nature.[77]

It might seem contradictory to infer the truth of natural religion from the stable order of nature, and the truth of revealed religion from the breakdown of that order, but Harvard Unitarians were convinced that the two modes of argument were compatible. God was free to display His power through either regular or irregular modes of action. Andrews Norton told the Cambridge community that a good theologian must "perceive the harmony between the two revelations which God has given us;—that, which is taught us by the laws which govern the world, . . . and that, whose divine origin was attested by the presence of a power controlling and suspending those laws."[78] When the Transcendentalists called into question the centrality of miracles to revelation, and of revelation to religion, they were undermining the whole structure of classical Unitarian orthodoxy. Many Unitarians, who had fought for years to dissociate themselves from deism, could not bear to have their subversive younger generation discredit them. It is not surprising that Norton, the greatest of the Unitarian biblical scholars, should have leapt to denounce this "latest form of infidelity."[79]

If the message of the Bible were plausible, and the evidence that it came from God were likewise plausible, then there remained but one important stumbling block to the acceptance of Christian revelation. The record itself might be historically unreliable. Corruptions, fabrications, mistranslations and the like might have crept into the Scriptures since the time when the events they describe purportedly took place. Nor had the enemies of revelation failed to bring this accusation to bear. Paine had argued that the testimony of the biblical writers was worthless, on the grounds that most of the books of the Bible had not been written by their traditional authors and were therefore forgeries.

Harvard Unitarian scholars were far from denying the existence of many obscurities and corruptions in the text of the Bible as it was usually received. They were good classicists, most of them, and perfectly familiar with the problems presented by ancient texts. Nor did they shrink from applying the accepted modes of critical scholarship to Scripture; "the Bible is a book written for men in the language of men," they affirmed, "and its meaning is to be sought in the same manner as that of other books."[80] Furthermore, their doctrinal views, particularly their rejection of the doctrine of the Trinity, provided encouragement to seek in biblical scholarship substantiation for their case. Henry Ware, Jr., explained why Unitarians looked to biblical criticism for Arian apologetics: "The most important corruptions which have crept into the records of our faith have been of a character to favor an opposing system [i.e., Trinitarianism], and . . . the more the Scriptures are restored to the precise words of their writers, the greater is the support which they give to the rational system [i.e., Unitarianism]."[81] Biblical scholarship had indeed turned up evidence embarrassing to orthodox Christians accustomed to justifying Trinitarianism by the Bible, and Unitarians seized upon it. The Old Testament in particular had passages which Unitarian scholars were happy to give up, passages which seemed to substantiate Calvinist conceptions of a God of wrath.[82]

But when full allowance had been made for all of them, the spurious passages in the Bible remained only peripheral, according to Harvard scholars. The "essential" teachings of biblical religion emerged unimpaired. Andrews Norton could agree with deist critics that St. Paul had not written the Epistle to Hebrews, nor Moses the Pentateuch, but he rejected their conclusion that the whole of Christian revelation was thereby discredited.[83] To rebut the more extreme charges against the historical accuracy of the Bible, Norton undertook his magnum opus. At the outset, he stated his case: "I mean to be understood as affirming, that [the Gospels] remain essentially the same as they were originally written; and that they have been ascribed to their true authors." The qualification, "essentially," was necessary; Norton was willing, for example, to reject entirely the first two chapters of Matthew as forming no part of the original manuscript.[84] The fruit of Norton's labors would be, he and his admirers trusted, the definitive defense of Scripture.

The six volumes which Norton produced before death cut short his project are a monument to industry, devotion, and critical acumen. They display a knowledge of biblical texts remarkable for their time and even more remarkable for their place.[85] For the sake of these writings, Harvard Unitarians forgave Norton his erratic and irascible temper. When Francis Bowen reviewed two of the volumes upon their publication in 1844, he voiced the pride of the Cambridge community:

The multitude will not read and cannot appreciate it; [but Norton's *Genuineness of the Gospels*] will take its stand upon the shelves of libraries as one of the great works in theological science of the present century. It will probably be better known and more highly valued a hundred years hence, than at the present day.[86]

The hundred years having passed, one reads with a sense of pathos this touching expression of faith in Liberal religion and genteel scholarship. Today one is tempted to dismiss Norton as a pompous buffoon; yet to do so is to miss the true significance of his failure. His career was essentially tragic, not comic. An intelligent and conscientious man, Norton was justly esteemed an expert on an important subject. The bankruptcy of his efforts renders a sobering judgment on human achievement.

IV / The Moral Basis of Religion

Natural Religion encompassed much more than the inference of a Providence from the harmony of external nature. In Christian tradition, "natural" knowledge was all knowledge not derived from revelation. The "realm of nature" was defined in epistemological terms, but not in terms of subject matter.[1] Natural religion included whatever nonsupernatural knowledge—of the physical universe, of politics, philosophy, or human experience—might be helpful to religious feeling and insight. The knowledge of man's moral and emotional makeup, and of its development, were valuable components of New England Liberal religious life.

THE ARGUMENT FROM CONSCIENCE

"Intra te quaere Deum" ("Seek God within thyself"), ran an ancient Christian saying. The Harvard moral philosophers did not forget this precept when presenting their teleological argument for the existence of God. The beautiful design of the human mind, with its interrelated functions and hierarchy of faculties, could be used as evidence for providential contrivance as well as the order of material nature. "It is the same thing," they declared, "whether we reason from the anatomy of the body or that of the mind, when the peculiar structure of each is the only ground for affirming, that it is the work of an intelligent Creator."[2] Levi Frisbie, in fact, considered that the primary purpose of his lectures on "the moral constitution of man" was to lead his students "to observe in the constitution of our active powers, indications of wise and benevolent design, no less admirable than in the mechanical contrivance of our bodies."[3] Some of the British writers on natural religion with whom Harvard professors were familiar, such

93

as William Derham and Lord Brougham, likewise laid considerable stress on the mental or "internal" aspects of the teleological argument.

Certain faculties were normally singled out for special praise as indispensable to human activity. Few were extolled more than the benevolent affections, those emotional impulses of fellow-feelings that Unitarians considered the basis for society. The presence of benevolent affections within man was a clear mark of providential solicitude, since without them social life would have been impossible. Not only the refinements of civilization, but human existence itself, were dependent upon God's gift of the social affections.[4] But the faculty most often discussed in the "internal" teleological argument for the existence of God was the moral sense.

Harvard Unitarian views on the role of the moral faculty in natural religion were heavily indebted to the great Bishop Butler. "Butler, like Plato, ascribed to human nature a certain hierarchical structure; some phases of it are higher than others and have a natural right to rule, the sovereign faculty [being] conscience."[5] The similarity between Butler and the Scottish moral philosophers has caused the Anglican bishop to be called "the Reid of England."[6] Butler emphasized, as the Scots did, the harmony which would characterize the optimal functioning of the faculties, especially the harmony between conscience and self-love. The experience of life, he argued, suggested that human beings were under a system of "moral government," in which virtue was, on the whole, more conducive to happiness than vice. Conscience, of course, was the faculty by which we distinguished virtue from vice; Butler believed the presence of this power was an indication of the existence of the Creator who gave it to us for our guide. If God had made men love righteousness, and rewarded them for it, very likely He loved righteousness too. Conscience thus acted not only as an assurance of God's existence, but also of His attributes; conscience taught that God drew moral distinctions and intended that men should also.[7] The trend of Butler's argument had been anticipated by the Cambridge Platonists (who called man's rational moral sense "the candle of the Lord" within him) ; Richard Price also invoked it. All these writers influenced the Liberal Christians of New England, and they were frequently cited in the elder Ware's classes, as well as in the triennial Dudleian Lectures on "Natural and Revealed Religion."[8]

Butler had been extremely moderate in his assertions; he did not argue that either conscience or any other fact of experience "proves" the claims of religion, but only that the world as we know it is "analogous" to the model of the universe set up by Christian theism. Butler's caution was, however, not imitated by the Harvard moral philosophers. From the fact that man possessed a conscience, a sense of obligation, they inferred that his Creator was a moral being and that the voice of conscience was also "the voice of God."[9] The moral values that man treasured, God must treasure also; for the very fact that man could perceive these truths showed that God wished him to do so. "The law of rectitude which [God] has written . . . upon the heart of every living man" ranked, with New England Liberals, alongside Scripture and the book of external nature as a third source of divine knowledge.[10]

In many respects, this mental or "internal" natural religion satisfied Unitarian moralists more than material or "external" evidence did. To them, the argument for the existence of God from the design of the human mind seemed "even more direct, logical, and convincing" than the argument from the design of the material universe. After all, mind was the active and superior substance, matter the passive and subordinate substance. Francis Bowen brought out this preference when he drew a terminological distinction between "natural theology," which dealt with the external universe, and "natural religion," which originated in the soul. "Natural *Theology*," he said, "makes us acquainted with the being and the natural attributes of the Deity, such as his infinite duration, power, and wisdom, *merely as facts of science, or truths for contemplation*. Natural *Religion*, proceeding from conscience, makes known to us his moral nature, his purposes and will." Between natural theology and natural religion, so defined, there was a relationship somewhat analogous to that between moral sense and moral taste: natural theology, like the moral sense, gave insight into objective, "external" truths; while natural religion, like moral taste, sprang from the inclinations of human nature. The latter two most preoccupied the practical Unitarian moralists, for they terminated, *"not in knowledge, but in action."*[11] As William Ellery Channing told Unitarian worshippers, "I would have you see God in the awful mountain and in the tranquil valley; but more, much more, in the clear judgment, the moral energy, the disinterested purpose, . . . of a good man."[12]

CHRISTIANITY AND HUMAN NATURE

"Thou shalt love the Lord thy God with all thy heart, and with all thy soul, and with all thy mind, and with all thy strength; this is the first commandment" (Mark 12:30). "The command thus given," Dr. Channing explained to his congregation, "is in harmony with our whole nature. We are made for God; all our affections, sensibilities, faculties, and energies are designed to be directed towards God."[13] The foregoing section has examined the Harvard Unitarian doctrine that man's psychic constitution gave evidence for the existence and attributes of a Designer. But Harvard Unitarians also held that human nature revealed the Designer's intention that man should be religious. "No people so barbarous, none so degraded, has yet been discovered, that the idea and worship of a supreme power has not been found with them," the younger Ware was pleased to affirm. Religion is as natural to man as gregariousness, James Walker agreed; "man, unlike the inferior animals, [is] a religious being."[14]

"Here, then," Walker granted, "is a view of religion quite distinct from the truth or falsity of any particular and definite form of it."[15] But this anthropological interpretation of religion did nothing to undermine Unitarian faith, as the elder Ware's *Inquiry* testified. Man was "disposed by the constitution of his nature to resort to some religion." Religion was uniquely, as well as universally, human; lower animals did not possess it. Despite this fact, there was no "religious sense" comparable to the "moral sense," to give all men a clear perception of reality. If religion had been a matter of intuition, all men would know the one true faith; but since religious propositions were not self-evident, as moral propositions were, men exhibited a much greater variety in religion than they did in morality.[16]

Then what were the factors in human nature that made man a religious creature? Of course, man's intellect was capable of inferring a designer from the contrivance manifest in the universe. But Ware also recognized deep-seated emotional factors fostering the rise of religion. Man—especially primitive man—sometimes feels ignorant and dependent on unseen powers. When in suffering and danger he longs for surcease. He fears death, and "this [fear] must inspire some wish, and that wish alone will be parent to some faint hope at least, that the life which seems to be extinguished by death may not be extinguished forever." In this way, the human condition, while not imparting the substance of religious knowledge, nevertheless "predisposes" men toward it. Ware concluded, quite frankly, that people would probably never have accepted the evidence for religion if they had not first desired to believe in it. The conclusion did not disturb him in the slightest. He blandly decided that this confluence of intellectual and emotional prompting toward religion must demonstrate God's providential design.[17] Just as the emotional moral taste reinforced the rational moral sense, the religious emotions harmonized with the religious convictions of the intellect.

Religious faith, according to the Harvard moralists, was a "sentiment," that is, an emotional affection for a rational principle. Levi Frisbie explained that the "sentiment" of piety implied "certain feelings, as well as perceptions of the understanding," and that the meaning of religion could not adequately be described without considering both these components. Francis Bowen elaborated the idea. "Religious sentiment" was analogous to moral taste: both emotions were dependent on rational judgments. "Blind and instinctive," the religious sentiment needed rational guidance. "Its object is not given along with it, but is left to be traced out by the active intellect, questioning and interpreting the operations of nature." God, in His mercy, had made it possible for that guidance to be offered through Christianity.[18]

Unitarians believed that everything in the world around them was part of an integrated system and served a purpose within that system. Applying the same principle to human psychology, they considered that man's faculties would function harmoniously if properly developed and exercised. If men had religious emotions (affections), these must have a proper function to perform. "The supreme good of an intelligent and moral being is the perfection of its nature," asserted William Ellery Channing.[19] Religion, it seemed, was an aspect of human nature which, by the aid of God-given knowledge, could be cultivated and developed to take its rightful place in the life of man. This "propensity" toward religion was a fundamental need, not merely an idle curiosity about the origins of the universe. "Man was made to submit and adore, as well as to understand."[20]

Christianity had been given to satisfy this need. Dr. Channing went through a long list of the faculties, showing how each of them found fulfillment in the religion of Christ: reason, moral sense, moral taste, aesthetic taste, and various social affections. Indeed, it was only in this sense that Channing was willing to call Christ "Saviour." Like other good Unitarians, he rejected the doctrine of the Atonement. Yet he believed that Christ had come to set man free—if not from the wrath of an angry God, then from the chains that had bound his faculties. "Jesus Christ is the great emancipator," Channing declared. "He came to give liberty to human nature."[21]

Probably the greatest statement of Unitarian doctrine on the subject of Christianity and human nature was James Walker's sermon, "The Philosophy of Man's Spiritual Nature in Regard to the Foundations of Faith." Walker, like a good Scottish common sense philosopher, appealed to the *"revelations of consciousness"* to witness the existence of "spiritual faculties" within man. Among these spiritual faculties were the conscience, the conception of perfection, and the sentiment of veneration. Religion being required to develop these faculties, it followed that piety *"enters essentially into our idea of the perfect man."* So far there was little unusual about Walker's address, but then he proceeded to invoke the principle of common sense to argue that since these spiritual faculties were a fact, an objective spiritual world corresponding to them must also be a fact. Walker had applied to religious experience the same ontological principle Scottish philosophy applied to sensory experience: "Our conviction of the existence and reality of the spiritual world is resolvable into the same *fundamental law of belief* as that on which our conviction of the existence and reality of the sensible world depends."[22] To Unitarian and other philosophers of the Scottish school, human activities had ontological implications.

Men were conscious, therefore mind existed; they had sensations, therefore matter existed. More than this, human desires implied a fulfillment in reality. As hunger presupposed food, scientific curiosity presupposed a rational cosmos, and conscience presupposed a moral law. On these grounds, why should not the religious sentiments also be self-authenticating? Walker's address has sometimes been considered a proto-Transcendentalist utterance, but it is basically an inspired elaboration of Reid.[23] Insofar as it does offer hints of later intellectual developments, the sermon foreshadows William James's argument for the existence of God from religious experience.

Of course, no Harvard Unitarian would have said he was accepting a religion just because it seemed attractive or useful. Boston Liberals were not irrationalists avowedly embracing a pleasing delusion; they were (or at least believed they were) good Lockean empiricists. William Ellery Channing was one of the Unitarian moralists who proclaimed the "deep wants" within the human breast which incline men toward religion. But at the same time he firmly insisted that the facts warranted faith in Christian revelation, quite apart from its spiritual gratifications.[24] In practice, the Unitarians were seldom content to rest with Walker's subjectivist foundation for faith. The miraculous "evidences" for the divine origin of the Scriptures provided objective justification for their will to believe. The Harvard moral philosophers were satisfied that Christianity was true, as well as psychologically helpful.

The doctrine that Christianity was revealed to help develop human nature fitted in nicely with Harvard Unitarian principles of biblical criticism. Any revelation, even a true one, they believed, would have to be conditioned by the cultural level of the people to whom it was addressed. "We must presume that the [revelation] will be accommodated to the actual capacities and wants of the people and the age," wrote President Walker. "Accordingly, we have a succession of revelations—the patriarchal, the Mosaic, and the Christian."[25] This justified the Liberal view that divine revelation had been "progessive," with the earlier portions of the Old Testament adapted to the simple understandings of a primitive people. "The dispensation of Moses," Channing explained in his famous Baltimore sermon, "we consider as adapted to the childhood of the human race, a preparation for a nobler system."[26] Passages depicting God as vengeful or passionate could properly be explained away on these grounds. Of course, assuming the purpose of revelation was to further the growth of man's faculties, it was obvious that nothing in the Bible could be interpreted so as to contradict the intuitions of the moral sense.

If Christianity were conceived in these terms, it followed quite naturally that dogmatic theology was of merely incidental importance. Doctrine was significant only insofar as it contributed to the development of human potential. This was the rationale which underlay the repeated Unitarian assertions that dogma was subordinate to ethics. Joseph Stevens Buckminster tried to explain the Liberal view to his father (who remained a Calvinist). "I have always considered it to be the object of the Christian dispensation to lead men to virtue and holiness," he wrote. "To this end the doctrines of the Gospel are auxiliary as means or motives, without any intrinsic value in themselves, or in the acknowledgment of them, except so far as they lead to this great end, the promotion of Christian excellence."[27] The older man was not persuaded. New England Unitarians, however, continued unashamedly to regard their religion as a means for moral and spiritual uplift.

THE MORAL TENDENCIES OF THEOLOGY

In April 1819 a group of Boston Unitarians journeyed to Baltimore for the ordination of young Jared Sparks (1789–1866) as minister of the newly formed Unitarian church in that city. Sparks was to go on to a career of distinction, becoming chaplain to the United States House of Representatives and an historian of note. But nothing else in Sparks's life would leave quite so large a mark in the annals of American religion as the day of his ordination. For at that ceremony, William Ellery Channing rose to present the most famous exposition and defense of New England Unitarianism ever made. Before it was even delivered, the address had been prepared for publication under the simple yet ambitious title, "Unitarian Christianity." Circulated more widely than any other pamphlet in America prior to the Webster-Hayne Debates, Channing's Baltimore sermon won its author a doctorate of divinity from Harvard and firmly established him as the foremost Unitarian spokesman of his generation.[28]

"I have thought it my duty to lay before you, as clearly as I can, some of the distinguishing opinions of that class of Christians in our country who are known to sympathize with this religious society," the visiting speaker began. Unitarian Christianity was based on natural and revealed religion, and Channing devoted considerable time to explaining the principles by which these were interpreted, e.g., God "never contradicts in revelation what He teaches in his works." Unitarians found no justification in either reason or revelation for the doctrine of the Trinity, nor for the belief that Christ had two natures, divine as well as human. After he had disputed these orthodox dogmas at some length, Channing moved toward the climax of his address: "I now proceed to another point on which we lay still greater stress. We believe in the *moral perfection of God* . . . We believe that God is infinitely good, kind, benevolent, in the proper sense of these words." In contrast to the benign God of Unitarianism, Channing painted a fearsome picture of the vengeful, capricious God of Calvinism, arbitrarily choosing a few men for salvation and then condemning the rest to torture for inadequacies they were helpless to remedy. Such a theology, Channing believed, had most unfortunate consequences for the characters of those who professed it.

It tends to discourage the timid, to give excuses to the bad, to feed the vanity of the fanatical, and to offer shelter to the bad feelings of the malignant. By shocking, as it does, the fundamental principles of morality, and by exhibiting a severe and partial Deity, it tends strongly to pervert the moral faculty, to form a gloomy, forbidding, and servile religion, and to lead men to substitute censoriousness, bitterness, and persecution, for a tender and impartial charity.

The Liberal preacher had hit upon a telling line of argument. The confrontation between Unitarian and Calvinist, avoided for a generation, had now finally begun.[29]

Inasmuch as the Harvard Unitarians regarded theology as a means to the formation of a virtuous character, it followed quite readily that they should evaluate competing theological doctrines on the basis of

their contribution to personality development. The charge that Calvinism had a bad "moral tendency"—i.e., that it was not conducive to
the cultivation of the proper sentiments—figured prominently in the
theological debates that Channing's Baltimore sermon provoked.
Moses Stuart and Leonard Woods of Andover promptly rebutted
Channing, while Andrews Norton and Henry Ware, Sr., rallied to his
support. The Liberals' charge that the Calvinists' God was unworthy
of worship became a central issue in what is known to American intellectual history as "the Unitarian controversy."[30] Just as they were to
find Transcendentalism inadequate on the grounds of its faulty conception of God, the Unitarians asserted that Calvinism perverted the
true idea of a perfect Being.

"The purity of a particular system is to be measured by the conception which it inspires of God," Dr. Channing declared. "Does it raise
our thoughts to a perfect Being? Does it exalt us far above our own
nature?"[31] The Calvinist doctrine of God did not satisfy the Liberals'
Neoplatonic criteria. The Calvinists were willing to qualify their
belief in God's goodness in order to maintain absolute insistence on
His omnipotence; whereas the Unitarians would circumscribe God's
power if by doing so they could keep His benevolence perfect. The disagreement was expressed in debates over whether such words as
"good" and "benevolent" had the same meaning when applied to God
as when applied to people. Unitarians maintained that these words
must be taken in their usual sense when being used as divine attributes; Calvinists held they could be used only in a "figurative" and
"limited" sense. Harvard philosophers argued that, if our ideas about
God's attributes had no reference to human experience, they were
devoid of content. "If God's justice and goodness are consistent with
those operations and modes of government which Calvinism ascribes
to him, of what use is our belief?" Channing asked. "All the divine
perfections are lost to us as grounds of encouragement and consolation."[32] The reverent agnosticism of Calvinism was too close to atheism for Unitarian comfort.

Unitarians were anxious that men should be brought to love God.
Their favorite classical thinker, Plato, was one of the few ancient phi-

losophers to emphasize that God should be loved. Yet love could be felt only for a benevolent God, they were convinced; God's other attributes—omniscience, eternity, and omnipotence—did not by themselves entitle Him to worship. An all-powerful but evil spirit would not deserve homage, "for power, when joined with selfishness and crime, ought to be withstood."[33] In order that statements about God's moral attributes might be meaningful, Unitarians resisted the assertions of Calvinist moral philosophers that ethical values were derived from the will of God.[34] For the Unitarians, a just view of the moral attributes of God was essential to the cultivation of a Christian character. If men were to take the divine perfections as the model for their own efforts, they must be able to predicate intelligible goodness of God. The inner peace and harmony which New England Liberals idealized were not fostered by dwelling upon a God of wrath.

Obviously the Calvinist doctrine of man was as repugnant to Liberals as the Calvinist doctrine of God. In the pamphlet debates between the Harvard philosophers and their counterparts at Andover, Yale, and Princeton, the issue of original sin loomed large. When confronted with the Unitarians' plausible and cheering statements of man's "likeness to God," orthodox scholars responded with the grim words of Scripture: "We are all as an unclean thing, and all our righteousnesses are as filthy rags, and we all do fade as a leaf" (Isaiah 64:6) .

Yet the actual differences between the contestants were often less than the shouting might suggest, especially when the Harvard Liberals were debating other New Englanders. By the third decade of the nineteenth century, Massachusetts Calvinists and Unitarians were not in substantial disagreement over what was the chief end of man, nor even over the number of men who actually attained that end in life. Both held that the union of all the faculties in joyful communion with God was the highest good; blessed is the man "with whom the glory of God is nothing but another name for his own greatest happiness," preached Buckminster, and a Hopkinsian would not have disagreed.[35] Likewise, both parties would have sorrowfully admitted that few men in nineteenth-century America achieved this beatific vision. Both, in fact, hoped for a national spiritual awakening. At bottom, the real issue between them came down to this: had those persons who attained true virtue done so by natural or supernatural means, through their own efforts or through the grace of God?[36]

The argument from "moral tendency," as employed in this controversy, generally took the form of showing that an opponent's views were not favorable to the revival of piety that both sides agreed America needed.[37] From the Unitarian point of view, the doctrine of original sin had a bad "moral tendency" partly because it was so repugnant to human feelings that no man of refined sensibility could be expected to adopt it, and partly because it would degrade the character of any man who had been brought up to believe it, leading him toward fatalism and despair. Unitarians sometimes added a class appeal, claiming that their version of Christianity was more helpful in keeping the educated and prosperous within the church. Calvinism, like Catholicism, tended to drive these important elements into skepticism.[38]

The Unitarian argument against the "moral tendencies" of Calvinism was difficult to substantiate on a personal basis. Even the Liberal controversialists themselves were hard put to find evidence that their orthodox counterparts were actually "gloomy, forbidding, or servile." Calvinism "does not produce all the effects on character which might be anticipated," William Ellery Channing admitted; indeed, he was quite willing to pay tribute to the personal kindness and intellectual integrity of many individual Calvinists. As a rule, of course, Harvard professors' condemnations of American Calvinism were directed less against their colleagues at other universities than against popular Calvinist preachers. The Unitarian moral philosophers professed to find the disregard some of these evangelists showed for moral values extremely dangerous. The elder Ware warned Professor Woods of Andover that desperate men might find the doctrine of innate depravity attractive: it could provide them with "a complete and satisfactory excuse for . . . every crime, . . . however great."[39]

James Walker took up this line of attack and pressed it even harder. Revivalistic Calvinism "administers an opiate to the consciences" of men, he charged in an outburst of youthful zeal. Lazy men like to be told that grace is "free" and bestowed without regard for "the character of the recipient." The doctrine of election appeals to ignorant men, giving them a feeling of importance and of belonging to "the initiated few." In such ways, Walker charged, Calvinist preachers pandered to the desire of men to gain unearned salvation. In the hope of cheap grace, men have always been willing to do all sorts of things: assent to fearsome and recondite creeds, permit their "passions to be acted on and wrought up to any pitch," and even to "fast and confess." "In short," Walker concluded, "they are willing to submit to anything that shall come to them as a *substitute* for plain practical religion—to anything that shall relieve them from the difficult and endless task of establishing and preserving an upright character."[40]

American Calvinists were quite capable of fighting fire with fire and countering Harvard criticisms with a "moral argument" against Unitarianism. Traditional doctrines like the Atonement could be defended for their evangelical utility. "How faint must be your hope of success, how weak your expectations [in] striving to reconcile sinners to God, and yet presenting them with no other righteousness . . . but their own," the orthodox Dr. Buckminster told his Liberal son. "A worldly church may be built, men may be formed to external decency and order, but the corrupt fountain of the heart will never be cleansed . . . where the doctrine of Christ's atonement is disowned."[41] Despite the possession of such arguments as these in their armory, antebellum American Calvinists were evidently unable to maintain the purity of their doctrine. On balance, the argument from "moral tendency" seems to have gone in favor of the Liberals—if one judges by the trend American theology was taking in the nineteenth century.

Although the difference in religious outlook between the Harvard Unitarians and their Puritan ancestors was pronounced, the difference between them and their American Calvinist contemporaries was much less great. Some of the historical factors which had brought about the intellectual transformation in Boston and Cambridge had obviously been operating elsewhere as well, and undermining Calvinism. The first two thirds of the nineteenth century was an era of expanding activity for Trinitarian Christianity in America, but all of its bustling energy could not be contained within the creedal limits defined at Westminster and Dort. Evangelical Arminian principles were increasingly avowed in pulpits throughout the land. Even the professed Calvinists were weakening—except, perhaps, at Princeton. American Calvinism had indeed become a "cultural anachronism."[42]

The seeming success of Consistent Calvinism in the founding of Andover Seminary in 1808 proved in the long run but a hollow victory for the principles of Jonathan Edwards. The Andover theologians moved steadily in the direction of crypto-Arminianism. Liberal controversialists sensed that they had history on their side. "Calvinism," Channing rejoiced, "is giving place to better views . . . Society is going forward in intelligence and charity, and of course is leaving the theology of the sixteenth century behind it."[43] The New England Unitarians did in fact confront halfhearted antagonists, as the course of the debates revealed. The truth is that their orthodox contemporaries were often troubled by the same aspects of traditional New England theology as were the Harvard Unitarians. Pressing their advantage, Unitarians taunted their opponents with quotations from seventeenth-century Calvinist creeds.[44] Men like Leonard Woods of Andover and Nathaniel William Taylor of Yale "realized the force of the Unitarian 'moral argument' against Calvinism and sought to restate *their* Calvinism to meet it."[45] But, somehow, Calvinism did not survive their restatements. By the close of the antebellum period, the Harvard moral philosophers could claim at least partial vindication. Calvinist orthodoxy had disintegrated into a number of different schools, most of them greatly modifying those tenets the Liberals had found objectionable. Avant-garde Trinitarian theologians, though under suspicion from their co-religionists, were by then moving along trails the Unitarians had blazed. Indeed, a Unitarian reviewer of the great religious controversy, writing in 1857, had little but praise for the views of Edwards Park and Horace Bushnell.[46]

THE CULTIVATION OF A CHRISTIAN CHARACTER

Henry Ware, Jr., was outwardly gratified but secretly troubled. He had just published his tract *On the Formation of the Christian Character,* the fruit of four years earnest thought. The work represented the classic exposition of Unitarian religion conceived as a method of personality development. "Religion," Ware wrote, "is founded on man's relationship and accountableness to his Maker; and it consists in cherishing the sentiments and performing the duties which thence result."[47] Although he thus admitted that religion was "founded on" man's relation to his Creator, Ware had not, significantly, treated religion as "consisting in" the establishment of rapport with this Heavenly Father, or with His other children. Instead, Ware conceived the essence of religion to lie in "cherishing sentiments" and "performing duties." These two interrelated activities went together to form the Christian character. Religion, thus defined, was a means of self-culture.

What gave Ware his mixed emotions was the response to his handbook. It apparently answered a felt need of the times. "I am surprised to see how seasonable my little book has been, how widely it has been circulated, and how strongly people feel about it," he confided to his wife.[48] (The book went through fifteen editions of a thousand copies each in the United States, and also sold well in Britain; there were even those who called it a Unitarian *Imitatio Christi*.) [49] Men "speak to me of it with tears in their eyes," Ware continued. "It seems just to have met the wants of the crisis." All this naturally filled an author with "sincere and hearty pleasure." But it also reminded him of his own shortcomings. Inwardly, Ware knew that he had not achieved for himself the awakening of sensibility in which he instructed others. He cursed his hidden "inconsistency," and wondered that he did not feel even more guilty. "I hope I am not hardened forever. But, however it may fare with myself, I do rejoice and feel thankful, that I am able to do something to save others from the fate to which I am hurrying myself. Is not this strange?"[50]

Christians had, of course, employed devotional manuals for centuries; the Calvinists had them, and Ware's little volume may rightly be seen as an heir of this long tradition. On the other hand it can also be viewed as belonging to a different genre. This Unitarian tract represents an early example of the "how-to-do-it" manual, or, perhaps a better term, the "do-it-yourself" handbook, which eventually became so common a feature of American life. Ware was anxious to assure his readers that, however slow and difficult the process might be, the formation of a Christian character was within the reach of energy and devotion. "Be on your guard," he exhorted them, "against setting your mark too low . . . The higher you aim, the higher you will reach."

Ware put up a bold front to his public, and kept whatever misgivings he had to himself.[51]

The "formation of the Christian character," to which Ware encouraged his contemporaries, was achieved through the balanced development and harmonious integration of the faculties. Every faculty, Unitarians believed, could be developed through education, and the conscience was no exception. The moral sense could be relied upon to perceive certain basic "obligations" with certainty, but it required practice and special skill to apply these generalizations to concrete situations and know, specifically, what should be done. Harvard Unitarians, like their ancestors, shunned Antinomianism and "enthusiasm." In many cases the revealed will of God had to be studied to supplement the teachings of nature. The ethical wisdom relied upon by the Harvard moralists was much more than the primitive intuition of an untutored moral sense; it represented the accumulated moral understanding built up "by the studies and experience of all ages."[52]

But, if the conscience was susceptible of improvement as an intellectual power, how much more so was it as an active power. The ability of the conscience to regulate the personality as a whole was dependent upon long training. Conscience required that all of man's faculties should be bent to the service of morality. This could be attained only gradually. "Moral goodness admits of an indefinite variety of modifications and degrees," wrote Andrews Norton. "As we advance in improvement . . . our judgment is more correct, our moral sensibility becomes more delicate, . . . and our hopes, affections, tastes, and motives are changed."[53] Of all the aspects of personality that changed as a man grew in Christian virtue, the ones whose development seemed most striking were the sentiments. If the Harvard moral philosophers had a tendency to think of religion in terms of personality development, they also had a tendency to think of personality development in terms of the cultivation of the sentiments.

The attention that New England Liberals lavished upon their moral and religious sentiments was predicated upon the assurance they reposed in their ultimate judgments. That is, the Harvard Unitarians were confident they knew the truth, but they perceived a problem in achieving a proper relationship to that truth. Harvard moral philosophers did not need to ponder, "What is justice?" They found reason and revelation reliable guides; what troubled them instead was the problem, "How can we make men just?"

"Moral taste" was a case in point. The Unitarian philosophers held that evil should provoke an emotional repugnance as soon as it was rationally recognized. The difficulty was that although all men could presumably see what was self-evident, all did not have the same reaction. According to Harvard moral theory, the statement "stealing is wrong" was necessary and universal. Yet the statement "the contemplation of stealing produces an emotion of disapproval in most men" was only contingent—and, in nineteenth-century America, maybe not even true. The mere abstract knowledge of the moral sense would not be enough to control men's actions unless it could be reinforced by an emotional relish for the right. And the emotions with which men regarded moral issues varied enormously. So the Unitarian moralists set out to sensitize men, and to refine their moral taste.[54]

Religious sentiments were cultivated by the Liberal Christians on much the same grounds as moral sentiments. A Unitarian preacher took it for granted that the arguments for the existence of God were iron-clad, and that the cosmic significance of Christ's mission, attested by His miracles, was beyond question. The difficulty he admitted was in creating an emotional response to these truths. Recognizing few of the problems that vex twentieth-century Christian theologians, the Unitarian moralists were philosophically content. Yet they were also aware that all their students and parishioners did not take naturally or easily to religion.[55]

It was not to be wondered at, if Boston Yankees found piety difficult to achieve. Henry Ware's *Inquiry* had explained the origin of that sentiment largely in terms of man's helplessness, dependence, and fear. These qualities were not characteristic of New England merchants and Harvard men in the early nineteenth century. Yet their traditions taught New Englanders that the achievement of religious feeling was a matter of supreme importance. If secure, prosperous, and optimistic men were to remain religious, they would have to recreate artificially their ancestors' emotions. By strenuous effort, it might still be possible for Boston Unitarians to remain loyal to their inherited Christian values. Harvard moralists like James Walker joined Ware in exhorting them to "the assiduous and systematic cultivation of the religious affections."[56] When Calvinists and Transcendentalists called the Liberals "corpse-cold" rationalists, the insult must have hurt Unitarian moralists deeply.

Very likely a number of the Harvard moral philosophers shared Ware's difficulties in attaining the moral and religious sensitivity they prized. The Unitarian moralists were continually exhorting them selves, as well as others, to fill every moment not spent in work with careful self-improvement. Several of them left among their papers evidence of the highly self-conscious efforts they made to cultivate a Christian character. Elaborate schedules of projects, conscientious resolutions, and records of how many pages of worthy books they read each day testify to the diligence with which they pursued the development of their personality. Notwithstanding the confident rhetoric they habitually employed in public, few of them apparently found the yoke of the Lord easy. One confessed, "Christian virtue is something arduous and sublime; its attainment demands time, self-denial, circumspection, perseverance; . . . it is hardly won, and easily lost."[57]

Self-cultivation was the essence of Massachusetts Arminianism. When (after what was presumed to be careful conditioning) a man did achieve refined sentiments, Unitarian moralists regarded him with an admiration that seems a little exaggerated nowadays. The elder Ware held King David of Israel up as an example of "tenderness of heart" whom moderns would do well to emulate. David sinned, of course, but when he did, his exquisite moral taste rendered his remorse acute. Andrews Norton, eulogizing Levi Frisbie, held the "delicacy and purity of his moral principles and feelings" to have been the late professor's most valuable qualification for the Alford chair.[58] Though New England Unitarians regarded moral reason as the common property of all men, they prized moral emotions as the distinguishing characteristic of a cultivated elite.

Along with "cultivating sentiments," Ware had taught that "performing duties" contributed to character development. James Walker agreed. "The first step toward the formation of a truly Christian character [is] to watch over the influence which our daily conduct is having on our habits."[59] The goal was to make the performance of duty so routine, through the cultivation of good habits, that virtue would become automatic. Whereas the Calvinists often spoke of man's actions being determined by his "nature," Liberal Christians considered that most of men's deeds were the result of "habit." Not innate but acquired characteristics seemed to them to control human motivation. Harvard moral philosophers often spoke of the importance of early conditioning in forming the character. Human nature was improvable, but once habits—good or bad—had been formed, they were "almost irresistible." Bad habits enslaved the sinner to his vices. Good habits protected the Christian against temptations. "What our habits are, we are. If they are Christian, we are Christian; if they are pagan, we are pagan—no matter what may be our professions."[60]

Like his Puritan ancestor, the Harvard moral philosopher judged men on the basis of their disposition rather than their deeds, their character rather than their individual acts. Character was hard to develop and not easy to change. Yet Andrews Norton asserted that, before repentance was acceptable in the eyes of the Lord, the sinner must alter his whole character from bad to good. "We cannot . . . hope for the divine favour while in the habitual practice of any sin." "Do not imagine that any faith or love toward Jesus can avail you but that which quickens you to conform yourselves to his spotless purity and unconquerable rectitude," Channing warned his congregation.[61] It was ironic—since Liberal theology stressed the benevolence of the deity—but such remarks betrayed a conception of a God who was not really merciful: He bestowed His favor only on those who deserved it.

Having such an exalted conception of what repentance entailed, the Unitarian moralists expected few people to achieve it. Once a sinner had started down the path of bad habits, it was nearly impossible for him to return to the path of rectitude. Notwithstanding its rejection of predestination, Harvard moral philosophy retained an implicit tendency to classify people as "good" or "bad." Normally, the Unitarian moralists addressed their exhortations to people who were already respectable, though lacking in emotional sensitivity. Passages in the New Testament where Christ offers loving forgiveness even to chronic reprobates were not among the favorite texts of Harvard Unitarian preachers. However, James Walker's sermon on Luke 15:7 is a remarkable tribute to his ability to fit even an awkward text into his preconceptions. The verse reads: "I say unto you, that likewise joy shall be in heaven over one sinner that repenteth, more than over ninety and nine just persons, which need no repentance." Walker asserted that Christ could not possibly have meant that "a reclaimed sinner is an object of greater favour in the sight of God merely because he has been a sinner." Instead, Christ must have been saying that the reformation of a person who got off on the wrong foot and acquired bad habits in youth is so strange and unusual that God regards it with startled wonder.[62]

Although Unitarian religion was moralistic, it was not legalistic. The Harvard Unitarians did not conceive of religious morality as a body of laws or a code of rules. Religious morality was "a principle," which formed a part of a man's character and regulated all his motives, dispositions, and actions. Without this supreme organizing principle, men fell into "a copious source of practical error," warned Henry Ware, Jr. "They adopt and endeavor to follow religion, not as one thing—not as a perfect whole springing from one root, . . . but they address themselves to its distinct and separate parts; they attend to a certain set of doctrines, or a certain list of rules." The religious principle of Unitarianism, on the other hand, would regulate and unify the faculties under the leadership of the moral sense. Then the sovereign Unitarian conscience "would guide, control, [and] regulate everything."[63]

How did the Unitarians justify their constant striving for self-improvement? In the first place, Harvard moralists taught that "the cultivation and control of proper affections" constituted "obedience to the Deity." God could have implanted in man fixed instincts, like those of the social insects, to govern his life; that He had not done so indicated His wish for man to develop his active powers through conscious effort. In the second place, self-culture was a useful means to a moral end—a person should fit himself to do his duty. But chiefly, New England Liberals regarded self-culture simply as an end itself— an obligation a person owed to himself. Like all fundamental truths, the obligation to self-improvement was really self-evident, a matter of common sense, though natural theology taught the same lesson. The perpetual motion of the mechanism of the universe offered man a moral example of the virtue of "steady employment."[64] Unitarian character development was a peculiar mixture of moral conditioning, emotional stimulation, and learning to keep busy.

CHRISTIAN HUMANISM

New England Unitarianism had its "rationalistic" strain: a disposition to regard religion as an inquiry into divine knowledge. But there was also a "romantic," or perhaps more accurately, a "preromantic" strain in New England Unitarianism: a disposition to regard religion as the cultivation of human personality, and especially of the proper "sentiments." Both these strains reflect the Liberal concern to adapt Christianity to the Enlightenment. The Harvard Unitarians seem to belong in that tradition of aspiration and ceaseless striving which is known as Christian perfectionism.[65] The Liberal *Christian Examiner* expressed the Unitarian outlook very well when it proclaimed, "Living is an *art,* a difficult, elaborate, and most momentous art." [66]

The art of living, as Unitarians understood it, demanded the discernment of proper objects of gratification. Every motive arising from the human faculties was considered to seek some "object." The appetites, desires, and affections had rather well-defined objects. Thus, the object of hunger was food, the object of gregariousness was companionship, the object of benevolence was the happiness of others. The sum total of the proper gratification of all motives was called "happiness," and this broad concept was the object sought by the faculty of self-love.[67]

If man's self-love were truly rational, he would come to realize that only by the development of a Christian character could real happiness be achieved. Evil objects afforded but transitory gratification; licentiousness and greed soon cloyed the appetites they fed upon. The confirmed evil doer became benumbed, insensitive, incapable of pleasure. Before long, a sinner was pursuing his wickedness more from unbreakable habit than from any satisfaction derived from his profligacy. "Whosoever committeth sin, is the servant of sin," quoted the Unitarian moralist.[68] Ultimately, man could reach happiness only by the same method he reached virtue: by fulfilling his being in conformity with the law of his nature.

Inasmuch as man's various faculties had constantly recurring needs to gratify, the human personality was by its very nature active, striving, and incomplete. The New England Unitarian was "future-oriented," as we would say, and looked ahead for the fulfillment of his desires. In Harvard theory, the quality of life and the structure of the personality itself took on aspects of the objects toward which one aimed. The virtuous man was constantly growing and developing, discovering new delights as his faculties matured. The vicious man was stunted, his personality degraded.[69]

Some of the objects man desired seemed to lift him above the mundane sphere into a higher realm of aspiration. Man's religious, moral, and aesthetic sentiments longed for a spiritual fulfillment. Providence had not designed man to be a creature of this world only. Human nature could be finally fulfilled only in self-transcendence. "Why does the savage pause in his midnight journey to gaze into the fathomless depths of the clear and tranquil heavens?" asked James Walker. "It is the instinctive sentiment of the infinite, struggling after an object with which to be satisfied and filled. That object is found in God alone." Here, as elsewhere, the New England Unitarians revealed their pervasive Neoplatonism; William Ellery Channing felt "the desire of an excellence never actually reached by humanity, the aspiration toward that Ideal which we express by the word *perfection*."[70]

One must emphasize that Unitarian yearnings for the spiritual did not entail a rejection of the temporal. The religious impulses of which New England Unitarians were conscious did not end in self-abnegation. Aspiration, rather than repentance or humility, characterized Liberal religion. Unitarian preachers did not exhort their followers to renunciation, but to the enjoyment of a fuller, richer life. "Men must be made awake to the purpose for which they exist," cried the Unitarian moralist. "They must learn that rational and immortal man can rationally pursue only an immortal object; and that, as nothing is immortal but truth, virtue, and God, the object of life must be to possess himself of them."[71] In this remarkable way the Christian religious life, the duty of self-improvement, and the pursuit of happiness were all identified with each other.

The Harvard Unitarian moralists held out to man the happy prospect that "duty and pleasure [were] the same," and that "religious happiness [could] be looked for just in proportion to religious attainment."[72] The cultivation of a Christian character was the means to happiness, not merely in the life to come, but here and now. "Christians enjoy the world more than other men [and] find more satisfaction in it," President Walker rejoiced. The secret of their happiness was found in their sense of values. Because they understood true moral values, Christians understood how to find true fulfillment.

All men have their pleasures, but all pleasures do not satisfy . . . Wealth has its pleasures; and so has power; and so has appetite: but who ever heard of a man who was satisfied with these alone . . . or felt in having them he had enough? Hence those persons who pursue these objects as *ends* are never happy, in any proper sense of that word . . . Men who would be happy must pursue them as *means* only . . . The Christian gives them their proper place as means, and turns them to their proper use . . . Made to contribute to the great moral purposes of [man's] being, they satisfy him in the sense of making part of a whole life.[73]

"A whole life." Therein lay virtue, piety, and happiness, all integrated into a single concept of human destiny.

The Unitarian moralist tried to make energetic, optimistic Bostonians of the early nineteenth century feel that religion was essential to their self-development. How he did this may be illustrated with one of Walker's unpublished sermons. The text was, appropriately, Mark 9:23, "All things are possible to him that believeth." The preacher explained that the mysterious omnipotence of which Christ spoke was actually nothing more than the exercise of one's own "latent powers." Of course, before a man can accomplish anything, he must have faith in his undertaking. So, Walker encouraged his congregation, to make all things possible—to develop your powers to the fullest—believe in spiritual as well as material values. "As it is by faith in worldly things, that the worldly elements of the character are called out and realized, so it is by faith in the heavenly things, that the heavenly elements in the character are called out and realized."[74] Religious faith was a means to the emergence of man's full humanity.

Christian humanism, as the Harvard Unitarians defined it, was "the doctrine that human life is a season designed for the growth and perfecting of the human being." And Christian humanism summed up the Unitarian sense of values: "The aim of man's being . . . can be nothing less than to arrive at the full perfection of the nature with which God has endowed him. To stop short of this, is to leave the divine work incomplete."[75] By the development of his own personality, the New England Unitarian was actually participating in the divine creation. Thus the Harvard moralists reconciled self-love and love of God, self-fulfillment with obedience to God. The more one achieved for himself, the more one had achieved for God.

UNITARIAN CONVERSION

The "formation of a Christian character" was the Boston Unitarian version of the "conversion experience" of New England religious tradition. The Harvard Unitarians did not believe that man was innately good; they believed man was born morally neutral, neither good nor bad. Virtue was within his grasp, but it was still something which man had to *achieve*. "We are not born with a character, good or bad, but only with a capacity to form one," the Harvard moralist pointed out, and since man's destiny was not predetermined the character needed conscious cultivation.[76]

The doctrine that man's salvation lay in "a progressive purification of the personality," during which the faculties were gradually brought into their proper relations with each other, was not invented in the nineteenth century, nor original with Harvard Unitarians. Its origins go back at least as far as the seventeenth century. Prominent among the advocates of such a gradualist approach to religious experience had been Ralph Cudworth and the other Cambridge Platonists.[77] But antecedents of the Liberal doctrine of character cultivation can also be found closer to home, in the early New England Puritan doctrine of "preparation for grace." The emigrants from East Anglia in the 1630's had included a number of exponents of the belief that sinful man could prepare his heart for the reception of divine grace. Indeed, students of colonial history have discovered that differing attitudes toward "preparation" sparked the famous Antinomian Controversy.[78]

Thomas Hooker (1586–1647), the foremost first generation interpreter of the stages of preparation, declared it to be a "harsh and tedious" process, doubly so in that it was undertaken without certainty of success. Among those who developed and adapted Hooker's thesis was John Norton (1606–1663), collateral ancestor of Andrews Norton and, like him, a dedicated foe of "enthusiasm." To counter the pretentions of Quakers and Antinomians who claimed to require no law save the inspiration of the Spirit, Norton argued that a long and careful preparation was essential, if not for regeneration itself, at least for the assurance of regeneration. For John Norton, a painstaking, contrite preparation could not force God to extend His grace, but even so it was a moral duty and a prerequisite to church membership.[79]

The tension which was present from the start of the Massachusetts experiment between preparation and predestination, between proto-Arminian and quasi-Antinomian, increased as the generations passed. By the nineteenth century, evangelical revivalists, the heirs of colonial "enthusiasts," were concentrating their attention upon emotional conversions quickly whipped up; while for their part, Boston Unitarians had elaborated a conception of preparation going far beyond anything Hooker would have recognized. The mysterious, supernatural event that had climaxed the long preparation of the Puritan entirely vanished from Unitarian thought. In contrast to traditional "conversion," Unitarian character-development was a never ending process, and described in natural rather than supernatural terms.[80] What the Puritans had considered merely preliminary to an ineffable transformation became, for their more prosaic Liberal descendants, the regenerative process itself.[81]

One suspects that changes in the theology of regeneration reflected changes in the nature of religious experience. Even in the eighteenth century, Jonathan Edwards had been disappointed by the inability of many of his countrymen to sustain that rapture of pious mysticism which was his own chief delight. By William Ellery Channing's time, it seemed obvious that such an "elevation of thought and feeling is not designed to be the ordinary state of even the most improved human beings." Many men, Channing observed, "seem constitutionally incapacitated for such ardor."[82] As startling conversions became more and more inaccessible to middle-class urban Yankees, the alternative Liberal mode of regeneration was proposed.

We misunderstand the Unitarians if we imagine that their conception of character development was merely superficial. Their objective remained the same as their ancestors': "to receive a clear impression of God's all-embracing presence."[83] It was the means for attaining this goal, together with the theoretical framework within which the means were understood, that had changed. The Unitarian Yankee aspired to raise *himself* to God, not languish in hope and fear awaiting supernatural grace. Channing and his peers pursued the ends of Jonathan Edwards by methods more reminiscent of Benjamin Franklin.[84]

The New England Liberal doctrine of salvation through gradual growth was well explained in two sermons by Joseph Stevens Buckminster.[85] The preacher began by discussing conversion. Buckminster distinguished three senses of the word: (1) "conversion" from another religion to Christianity. This sense created no problems. (2) "Conversion" in the sense usually employed by Calvinists and revivalists, a definable moment of emotional experience which the recipient recognized as all-transforming and beyond his control. "Conversion" in this sense was not essential to achieve salvation, asserted Buckminster. (3) "Conversion" as the decision to commence conscious formation of a Christian character. This was the Unitarian sense of the word. But actually, Buckminster went on, Liberal Christians were not much interested in "conversion" per se; they were interested in "regeneration." "Regeneration" was the inward transformation of the personality which was the aim of Unitarian self-development. This "renovation of the heart and spirit" could be initiated in any of a number of ways: through childhood training, through intellectual conviction in adulthood—or even, perhaps, through a "conversion" of the traditional Puritan type. How it took place was dependent upon the temperament and environment of the individual involved. The insistence of classical Unitarians upon some form of "regeneration" for man was one of the issues dividing them from Transcendentalist Unitarians. "A religious character is an acquisition, and implies a change," Harvard Unitarians insisted; true religion was not spontaneous or innate. "The Christian is a new man."[86]

Other Harvard moralists joined in Buckminster's interpretation of regeneration. James Walker explained that character development was what St. Paul meant by putting away the "old man." Dr. Channing's sermons on what he called "the perfect life" offered elaborate guidance to parishioners seeking "awakened religious sensibility." Self-discipline and the thorough regulation of one's faculties were the prerequisites for communion with God.[87] Since character development was dependent upon individual effort, divine acceptance really waited upon human success.

What was the man like who achieved the ambitious program Harvard moral philosophers laid out for him? He resembled a well-ordered society, Henry Ware, Jr., explained at the conclusion of *The Formation of the Christian Character*. "Universal harmony reigns within him; no oppositions, no jarring contentions, mar his peace." Like a well-balanced society, the ideal man was self-sufficient. "The complete man is ... wise, watchful, self-governed, self-sustaining; every part of him is in its right place, and of its right proportion, and every faculty is obedient to his will." The good man was a man of conscious rectitude. Both violence and indifference being inimical to the proper functioning of the conscience, the model Christian had achieved a *via media* between enthusiasm on the one hand and insensitivity on the other. In Harvard moral philosophy, this golden mean of personal development was termed "moderation" or "calm."[88]

Although they did not think it could be easily fulfilled, the Harvard moral philosophers had an exalted conception of ultimate human potential. Through their continued pursuit of the divine, these heirs of the Puritans revived the Renaissance doctrine of the dignity of man: "Man, medially situated between spirit and matter, is able through his active intellect to attain almost deific excellence by subordinating the baser to the higher element in his complex nature."[89] The more man developed his potential, the closer he approached to God. This was what Jesus Christ had manifested. Christ was divine only in the sense that He was fully successful in developing qualities of excellence all men possessed. Thus the Unitarian doctrine of self-fufillment found theological expression in Arian Christology.[90] As Buckminster told his congregation: "If you love what you know of [Christ,] and imitate what you love, and study to know more and more of his character, you will see that he was in the Father, and the Father in him; for the more like God, the perfection of all excellence, you become, the more will you feel all that is godlike in his Son."[91]

The formation of a Christian character could be expressed as the formation of a Christ-like character, and, at last, of a God-like character. In daring to avow such an aim, the Unitarian moralists were manifesting the glorious optimism, the unlimited perfectionism, of early nineteenth-century America. "God becomes a real being to us in proportion as his own nature is unfolded within us," announced William Ellery Channing in one of his most famous sermons. "To a man who is growing in the likeness to God, faith begins even here to change into vision."[92] In the New England Unitarian aspiration toward "likeness to God," Christian humanism reached what was probably the highest development it ever achieved anywhere.

V / Moral Man and Moral Society

CIVIL POLITY in the early nineteenth century encompassed both sociology and political science, though it differed from those twentieth-century disciplines in its paucity of techniques and strongly theological orientation. Principles of providential harmony and moral purpose pervaded the subject as it was viewed by New England Unitarians. Like natural religion, civil polity was considered a branch of moral philosophy at Harvard: "Professor of Natural Religion, Moral Philosophy, and Civil Polity," read the title of the Alford Chair. But despite their theoretical integration, Unitarian religious and social thought lay uneasily alongside each other in the Harvard consensus, the progressive aspirations of the former contrasting with the conservative Puritanism of the latter. The combination of an exalted view of man's potential with a determination to preserve traditional social values was, perhaps, typical of Christian humanism.[1]

THE END OF THE COVENANT

Even the oldest of the Unitarian moral philosophers (Levi Hedge and Henry Ware) had been but children when Washington mustered his troops on Cambridge Common and quartered them in the Yard. The generation that dominated Harvard after 1805 was too young to have experienced the times that tried men's souls. The men of this new generation brought to their work preoccupations very different in emphasis from those of their Revolutionary fathers. Whatever objectives the fathers had in rebelling, the sons were determined to restrict the achievements of the Revolution to as narrow a compass as possible. By the eighteen hundreds, Harvard men wanted the American political experiment conducted with caution. Where the fathers had been concerned for liberty, the sons were concerned for order.

121

A remarkable aspect of this postrevolutionary change in mood was the sudden eclipse of John Locke and his social compact from Liberal Christian political thought. During the struggles against parliamentary supremacy, the Massachusetts clergy had been among the most influential advocates of the compact theory. Jonathan Mayhew, like other Americans, had proudly acknowledged Locke to be one of his political masters.[2] But Harvard moral philosophers had ceased to invoke the Lockean compact by the early nineteenth century. In 1782 the executors of the Alford estate had assumed the existence of a "social impact" [sic] and presumed the Alford Professor would teach about it.[3] Yet when Francis Bowen spoke out on the subject, half a century later, it was to denounce the compact.

The hypothesis of birth in a state of nature, original enjoyment of entire freedom, and subsequent formation of society, and voluntary submission to legal restraint, is fallacious and irrelevant . . . Man is eminently a social being . . . The true state of nature, far from being one of unlicensed action and self-government, is a condition of responsibility, submission, and trust.[4]

Locke had actually described two successive compacts in his *Second Treatise*, the first instituting society and the second, government. Though Bowen denied that the first type of compact had ever occurred, he could scarcely deny that the second type served as a model for American constitutional conventions. The Unitarians had placed themselves in an anomalous position by trying to reject Lockeanism in America.[5]

Their Puritan background helps explain the Unitarians' readiness to dispense with Locke. New England political thought since the seventeenth century had been characterized by tension between organic and contractual analogies, between an interpretation of institutions as natural (or divine) and an interpretation of them as artifical (or man-made).[6] The Unitarians chose to emphasize the conservative, organic component in this tradition. Just as they quietly laid aside the federal theology, the Liberals quietly repudiated the concept of a social covenant or compact.

William Ellery Channing's Election Sermon of 1830 manifested the Unitarian rejection of the Lockean philosophy of the American Revolution. "We are sometimes taught that society is the creature of compact and selfish calculation," he warned the governor and legislators of the Commonwealth. "But no. Society is of earlier and higher origin. It is God's ordinance, and answers to that which is most godlike in our nature," he assured them. "The chief ties that hold men together in communities are not self-interest, or compacts, or positive institutions, or force. They are invisible, refined, spiritual ties, bonds of the mind and the heart."[7] For Channing, human society was a product of the "instinctive" cravings of human nature; it was best preserved through the cultivation of the proper sentiments. His civil polity was truly a corollary of his moral philosophy.

Harvard instructors found an attractive alternative to Lockeanism in the social theory of Adam Ferguson (1723–1816). Professor of moral philosophy at Edinburgh, Ferguson rejected the contract theory in favor of an anthropological approach to civil polity. It is pointless to contrast a "state of nature" with civil society, he claimed, for civilization and barbarism are equally "natural." Man, like many other creatures, is by nature a social animal. Gregariousness and the need for the security of numbers cause people to associate in larger and larger groups. Political institutions arise from a desire to regulate human relationships within these groups. Compacts, charters, and such formal agreements are a late development in the process of social evolution.[8]

But the favorite political commentator of the Unitarian moralists was Edmund Burke. Tuckerman was his devoted admirer; Norton frequently cited him.[9] Harvard seniors were taught that Burke "went to the foundation of government, yes of society itself, in England and everywhere. He showed what sorts of innovation were to be dreaded, and what sort of deference to old feelings and old observances was useful and honorable." Burke's *Reflections on the French Revolution*, continued Edward Tyrell Channing, struck exactly the proper balance, falling neither into "a disgusting adulation of kings," nor into "a deceptive panegyric of freedom."[10] Surely this was a remarkable judgment to come from a New World republican.

When Francis Bowen was rebuking the Dorrite rebels of Rhode Island, he quoted Burke's famous passage: "The state ought not to be considered as nothing better than a partnership agreement in a trade of pepper and coffee . . . It is . . . a partnership not only between those who are living, but between those who are living, those who are dead, and those who are to be born."[11] Burke's feeling of community with those who had gone before was often evident among Unitarians. The elder Ware preached again and again on "reverence for the principles of our ancestors." Maintenance of the institutions and laws of the past was the proper function of the statesman, Professor Channing told his classes.[12] Norton expressed it this way:

The relations between man and man cease not with life. The dead leave behind them their memory, their example, and the effects of their actions . . . Our institutions have been founded by them . . . Our minds have been formed by their instructions. We are most intimately connected with them by a thousand dependencies . . . Their power over us remains.[13]

Bowen, defending a Burkean definition of the term "constitution," pointed out that "what is usually termed the Constitution in this country . . . is but a part, and a small part, of the fundamental law under which we live." Bowen considered the real "fundamental law" to include the whole Anglo-American political tradition; in this extended sense, he could assert, "Constitutions are not made, but they grow by an inherent law of progress and adaptation to changing circumstances. They are not contrivances of human wisdom, but are necessary products of men's habits and wants."[14]

If government were a legacy from the past, existing from time immemorial without the necessity for any voluntary agreement, did it depend for its legitimacy on the consent of the living? No, answered the most forthright of the Harvard conservatives; "We need . . . a more solid foundation for the authority of the state, than a mere bargain between it and its subjects." This alternative stronger foundation he found in human nature and "the general order of things," that is, in the immutable principles of morality. "Reverence for law" was therefore not only "spontaneous and natural," but also commanded by conscience.[15]

Burke himself believed the institutions of society had the sanction of an "eternal, immutable [moral] law." His opening remarks at the trial of Warren Hastings commanded the assent of Unitarian moralists. "We are all born in subjection, . . . high and low, governors and governed, [to a] pre-existent law . . . by which we are knit and connected into the eternal frame of the Universe . . . This great law does not arise from our conventions, or compacts; on the contrary, it gives to our conventions and compacts all the force and sanction they can have."[16] The moral principles underlying political obligation were seldom called into question, said Burke; politics as a rule was concerned with prudential calculations, with means rather than ends. Nevertheless, prudence, prejudice, and tradition derived their ultimate legitimacy from consecration to a moral purpose.[17]

Burke's approach to political morality answered the desires of the Harvard Unitarians beautifully. An apologist for the American Revolution but an enemy of the French one, he had just the right strain of conservatism for them. Like the Liberal Christians, he was a spiritual descendant of Richard Hooker.[18] His ethics (that is, the ethics he professed) coincided conveniently with common sense philosophy. His affinity with Butler has passed generally unremarked, but it is close.[19] The Whig politician and the saintly bishop had in common an organic, hierarchical conception of society and a conception of human life as a process of development. As sources of inspiration for Harvard professors, Burke and Butler complemented each other well.

The political conservatism of Boston Unitarians set them apart from their co-religionists across the Atlantic. Whereas British Unitarians were members of a persecuted sect (subject to penal laws until 1813 and excluded from political life until 1828), Massachusetts Liberals enjoyed the privileges of a religious establishment and political power. No American nobility overshadowed the bourgeois patriciate of Boston. The difference between the Harvard Unitarians and the British Unitarians is nowhere more apparent than in their respective reactions to Burke. Burke, the exponent of order and the masterly manipulator of conservative sentiments, attracted the Harvard Unitarians, while his moral traditionalism reassured them. But leading British Unitarians like Joseph Priestley, Richard Price, and Harriet Martineau became outspoken critics of Burke in his own land.[20]

THE ORGANIC SOCIETY

"None of us liveth to himself, and no man dieth to himself." The text was Romans 14:7, and the preacher was Joseph S. Buckminster. The occasion was the death in office, December 10, 1808, of James Sullivan, Governor of Massachusetts. Buckminster took advantage of the solemn moment to impress the mourners with the intimate, infinite interconnections among all members of society. The governor's death caused bereavement throughout the Commonwealth. Yet, since every man occupied a place in the social system, in a very real sense the death of any individual would have been felt by the whole community.[21]

The theme of social interdependence was a favorite one with Unitarian moralists. Biological analogies in sociological discussions were common long before the time of Darwin and Spencer, and the Harvard Unitarians used them often. The ideal commonwealth was an organic unit, composed, like a living body, of interrelated parts, each contributing its essential function. Thus, William Ellery Channing called upon New England to provide the American body politic with its conscience and rationality, while he expected the South to furnish its bold affections and graceful sentiments.[22] The Unitarian preoccupation with an integrated and balanced personality found its natural complement in Unitarian concern for the harmonious integration of society.

Unitarian theology, which taught that men were not innately depraved, colored Unitarian social thought. The early Calvinists had been disposed toward the Augustinian view that the social order had been instituted by God as a remedy for the sinfulness of man. Unitarians, in contrast, followed Richard Hooker and Thomas Reid in holding that man was a political animal and society the natural outgrowth of human nature as God intended it to be. "Man is evidently made for living in society," Reid had written. "His social affections shew this as evidently as that the eye was made for seeing."[23] Whereas the traditional Calvinist view of society had been somewhat negative and repressive, the Unitarian view was essentially a positive one, a view of society as an aid to the expression of human purposes. Good men made a good society, Unitarians believed, and also, a good society made good men. In the ideal community, men would labor dutifully in their callings, each as members of the body, and "the whole economy of civil society prove a school of virtue."[24]

One of the most dreaded threats to the Unitarian ideal of social integration and consensus was ideological conflict. The Unitarian moralists stood with Burke and the Scottish philosophers in their deep distrust of deductive rationalism. The doctrine of the social compact seemed to them a form of abstract theorizing that was potentially dangerous. Their rejection of the compact theory was associated with their general shrinking from profound speculation. Part of the Liberal rejection of theology, this aversion stemmed from a fear of contention. Political theorizing was associated with a "love of novelty" and "Utopian schemes" too often to suit the Boston-Cambridge establishment.[25]

Harvard professors did not encourage the philosophical examination of first principles in politics. "Men of speculation have in vain endeavored to fix a model of government" that can endure the test of varied circumstances, asserted Ferguson's textbook. An undergraduate fledgling orator contrasted "visionary schemes" and the "abuse of theories" with the wisdom of "the old and experienced statesman . . . desirous of keeping in the beaten path."[26] In their epistemology, the Harvard philosophers exalted empirical knowledge to an undeservedly high level of reliability, ranking it on a par with logical demonstration. By an interesting parallel development, they exalted experience at the expense of logic in their political thought.

Belief in objective, immutable principles of morality does not necessarily imply a high opinion of the rights of individuals vis à vis society, as the classic example of Plato shows. Individual rights, in the opinion of Unitarian moralists, could be limited by society. "It is indeed a first principle of social morality [though not a law of the state of nature], that every human being has a right to life, to property, and to the pursuit of happiness," declared Joseph Tuckerman. "But not one of these rights is illimitable; and just conceptions of their limitations in every case are as important as just conceptions of their reality."[27] Although conservatives, the Unitarians tempered their respect for property rights with a sense of community responsibility. The rights of property, like other rights, were subject to the needs of society. On these grounds Francis Bowen criticized the first American textbook of civil polity, which had been written by Francis Wayland. In *The Elements of Political Economy* (1837) the well-known Baptist moral philosopher had espoused too rigid and absolutist a doctrine of property rights. "Property is a social institution," Bowen objected, "and must therefore be subject to those limitations and instructions which increase its tendency to . . . the general welfare." Far from explaining society as instituted for the protection of property, Unitarian moralists justified property as conducive to the social good. Herein lay the basis for their appeals to the merchants for philanthropy.[28]

Willingness to accept the limitation of one's rights was a virtue highly esteemed by Harvard moralists. Andrews Norton interpreted "Blessed are the poor in spirit," to mean "Blessed are those who will give up their own rights, rather than disturb the peace of society." Since "rights" expressed nothing more than human relationships, every "right" implied a reciprocal "duty." (That is, if A has a right to have X done by B, then B has a duty to do X to A.) Americans were more likely to forget their duties than their rights—at least so it seemed to Unitarian moralists. "Our religion gives us no statement of . . . rights. Its doctrine of rights is to be found only in the duties which it inculcates," Tuckerman reminded his readers. One of the most attractive statements of the Unitarian emphasis on duties rather than rights was given by the younger Ware, when he wrote, "The interpretation of the republican principle seems too often to be, 'I am as good as you;' . . . the true interpretation is, 'You are as good as I.' "[29]

Another consequence of the rejection of the compact theory was an intensified awareness of the function of the family in society. If society could not be understood as a voluntary association, perhaps it could better be viewed as an extended family. Gladys Bryson has indicated the importance of the family and clan in eighteenth-century Scottish political theory. The state, in the opinion of Scottish thinkers, reproduced many characteristics of the kinship group. Butler and Burke similarly held that the family, rather than the individual, was the fundamental unit of society.[30] The Harvard Unitarians were prone to see both the church and the state as large families. When the inhabitants of a parish gathered for worship on Sunday, Unitarians beheld "as it were, a larger family assembled . . . about a domestic altar." They called the state "the common parent of all," and likened treason to parricide.[31] The welfare of both church and state was dependent on the cultivation of the domestic virtues and the maintenance of the integrity of the family.

Families are the smaller communities which go to constitute the larger; and as the community of the river must partake of the quality of the little rivulets which flow into it, so of necessity the character of the nation will be affected and modified by that of the families which compose it. Strict discipline, habits of order, obedience, and sobriety in the family circle, lay the best foundation for good citizenship.[32]

The disintegrating effects of geographical and social mobility, of urbanization and industrialization, seemed to threaten this family ideal. In a time of feminism, polygamy, slavery, and other challenges to the conventional mode of family organization, New England Liberals felt called upon to defend the sanctity of marriage and domesticity. Antebellum Unitarian moralists shared with many other American social thinkers, before and since their day, a concern for the future of the American family.[33]

How to achieve the organic wholeness they idealized in society was perhaps the most important practical problem the Unitarian moral philosophers faced. If one could not appeal to the consent of men freely offered in covenant or compact, what appeal could one make on behalf of social unity? An appeal to conscience was in order, since the structure of society had the sanction of the moral law. Yet the moral sense alone was weak, as all men knew; it needed help from other faculties. Reid had pondered this problem and concluded that the most important power cementing society together was not the rational moral sense but the benevolent affections. Indeed, he went so far as to assert that the "security, the happiness, and the strength of human society spring solely from the reciprocal benevolent affections of its members."[34]

The Harvard Unitarians accepted Reid's verdict. They enlisted the emotions of the individual into the service of his moral sense; likewise, they relied on the public sentiments to sustain the state. A sentimental description of patriotism, by an unknown disciple of Henry Ware, Sr., is typical of Unitarian regard for the social affections: "Love of country . . . is one of the most comprehensive and complex of the affections. It embraces the past and future with the present, and it includes all the regards we pay to the beings and objects around us; to our families and friends, and fellow-citizens; . . . to the means of education and the institutions of religion. And it is with religion, particularly, . . . that patriotism seems to be most naturally and strongly associated."[35] The proper role of religion was to reinforce the social affections, and avoid the contentiousness of dogma. Such affections as pity, magnanimity, and family love, given religious reinforcement, would bind society together far more securely than could either selfish interest or the stern injunctions of the Pentateuch.

If social cohesion depended on emotional appeals, it was obviously necessary to envelop institutions in some kind of mystical aura. Traditional institutions had an important advantage over newly contrived ones; they commanded more emotional veneration. It was hard to make any appeals on behalf of recent institutions except those of rational morality and prudence. Unfortunately, American society was new. "Our constitution, our government, our whole political organization, are the work of our own hands, and the work of our own hands we will not worship," a Unitarian lamented. Somehow, Harvard moralists believed, an emotional reverence for American institutions had to be created if society were not to disintegrate in the vast new continent.[36]

The attempts of Francis Bowen to give a Burkean interpretation to American institutions illustrate Unitarian yearning for tradition. Bowen relied on the historical continuity between English and American experience to achieve his effect. "I am no great believer in the natural excellencies of Anglo-Saxon blood," he readily allowed, "but I have great faith in the acquired excellencies of Anglo-Saxon institutions . . . Most of what is valuable in our civil polity has come to us by inheritance from our English ancestors." Bowen could cite trial by jury, representative government, and the authority of local magistrates as examples of America's debt to medieval England. "In this country, we are even now reaping the fruits of Edward the First, and of the acumen and wisdom of judges who occupied the bench during the reign of the Tudors."[37] The so-called revolution in America, Bowen explained, had been fought to defend established customs and the traditional rights of Englishmen. "It was not a Quixotic crusade in favor of human rights in general, nor a war undertaken only to show that all men are free and equal, and have a right to govern themselves as they see fit." As for the written constitutions drawn up by the emergent states, "They were not made by philosophers and theorists, but by practical men, . . . and were *founded on existing institutions.*"[38]

Bowen's Burkean analysis of the Constitution of the United States bears some resemblance to that of John C. Calhoun. Like the Southern conservative, the Cambridge Unitarian maintained that sovereignty was an indivisible attribute of an organic society—and that the several states, not the national government, were the true organic sovereignties. The Constitution was the product of cooperation among these legally constituted entities, not the creature of the people considered as an undifferentiated mass. Bowen once had occasion to express his opinion of Calhoun's *Disquisition* in a review article. Calhoun, it will be remembered, had distinguished "government" (an inevitable consequence of human nature) from "constitution" (a rational contrivance to prevent rulers from abusing their powers). Of course Bowen agreed that society and government were natural to man; the aspects of Calhoun's theory he criticized all had to do with "constitution." In other words, it was the Lockean element in Calhoun to which the Yankee conservative objected. Bowen did not even trouble to question Calhoun's postulate of human depravity. Instead, he concentrated his fire on the constitutional theory of "concurrent majority," calling it a typical example of abstract "speculation" leading straight to "anarchy."[39]

THE MORAL ELITE

It was an important day in Cambridge when Levi Frisbie inaugurated the long-awaited Alford professorship of moral philosophy on November 5, 1817. The academic ceremony subjected the new incumbent to a cruel ordeal, for he had suffered much from illness and was nearly blind. But Frisbie had been reared a Calvinist, and though he had by now repudiated his ancestral theology, he never shook off the grim impression it had made on him. He was a stern disciplinarian with an intense conviction of the obligations of duty. And so Frisbie rose to the occasion to deliver a long inaugural address, in which he undertook to instruct his audience in the function of moral philosophy. The terms in which the speaker analyzed this function were more social than philosophical. Frisbie's address, promptly published, became recognized as an authoritative exposition of American cultural conservatism.[40]

Moral philosophers, Frisbie explained, were practical men. They defended the welfare of society and disdained "metaphysical subtleties and abstract reasonings" with no application to the world. The service moral philosophers performed for society was twofold. In the first place, they were trained to investigate the more recondite ethical problems and prescribe such duties as might not be easily deduced from the simple intuitions of the natural moral sense. In this respect, they were the moral leaders of society, pointing out the directions progress ought to take. But the second function Frisbie assigned to moral philosophers was conservative. They were to counteract the "speculations of false philosophy." Since "there will always be a Hobbes, a Rousseau, or a Godwin" to subvert sound morals, "let us then have also our Cudworths, our Butlers, and our Stewarts" to defend them. Bad philosophies, if they become "embodied in popular fiction," will "find their way into the hearts of men," and have dangerous social implications. "The safety of society then requires, that such systems be subjected to the jealous scrutiny of a sound philosophy, and that there be men, whose habits and studies will lead them to a rigid superintendence of whatever is proposed."[41] The moral philosopher was a guardian of moral orthodoxy and a dedicated agent of conservatism.

Since he was a child of seven at the time, Francis Bowen probably did not attend Professor Frisbie's lecture. But twenty-five years later he echoed Frisbie's concern over the social function of philosophy. Writing, in 1842, a preface to his anti-Transcendental essays, Bowen recurred to the oft-cited example of the French Revolution to illustrate the dangers of philosophy run rampant. Bowen believed that New England's religious tradition was her best bulwark against the disintegrating power of ideologies. It followed that the wise policy for a Yankee philosopher was to serve New England religion. Unitarianism was the preferable form of that religion because Calvinism fostered too much controversial speculation. "An eminently metaphysical creed, [Calvinism] has entailed upon us a multitude of religious controversies ... The disputes that arise are conducted mainly by abstract reasoning ... The arena of theological contests is thus opened to the layman, the logician, and the specularist, and the weapons of attack and defence are borrowed from the popular philosophy of the day."[42] Calvinism encouraged philosophical thinking among common men and "impractical" intellectuals, with all the threat to social harmony that implied. The safer combination of Unitarianism and common sense conserved traditional values while eschewing speculation.

The Harvard moral philosopher, it has been said, conceived of himself as the "conserver of the Christian, scholarly, and gentlemanly virtues."[43] Indeed, the Unitarian moralist did think of himself as the custodian of the moral values of society, with a grave responsibility to posterity. He discharged his responsibility by acting as an intellectual arbiter, evaluating ideas on the basis of their social consequences. He applied to philosophical systems the same criterion he applied to theologies—that of "moral tendency." Systems like those of Jeremy Bentham and Richard Hildreth, which exposed traditional institutions to critical investigation, had a bad moral tendency.[44] James Walker was confident that David Hume, a sound political conservative, "would have been among the first to consign his [own] papers to the flames" if he had "so much as suspected" their evil implications for society.[45] On the other hand, Dugald Stewart's philosophy satisfied Unitarian criteria beautifully.

The doctrines which [Stewart] inculcates are those of vigorous common sense and sound morality, never deformed by love of paradox, and never compromising the interests of truth by straining after novelty, or by unseasonable attempts to appear ingenious or profound. The principles of social order and good government, and the great interests of virtue and religion, were never more impressively taught, or eloquently defended, than by this professor of Scotch metaphysics.[46]

Ideas which fostered class harmony and good manners, even if not "ingenious or profound," met with approval from the Unitarian moral elite.

Moral elitism was a New England tradition. The Puritan Commonwealth had been dedicated to a moral purpose, and the clergy had been the acknowledged exponents of that moral purpose. Through their pious erudition they discovered God's Will, and by their preaching passed on the Word to the rest of the community. The clergy continued to exercise great influence well into the nineteenth century, even though the era of their greatest prominence had passed. "There is no place on the face of the globe where so much attention is paid to ministers" as Boston, Buckminster boasted. The man in the pulpit enjoyed "something of the ancient reverence which belonged to the prophetic character among the Jews," another Unitarian remarked. As late as the 1820's a Bostonian layman found clerical prestige awesome: "On the topmost round of the social ladder stood the clergy; for although the lines of theological separation among themselves were deeply cut, the void between them and the laity was even more impassible."[47]

Notwithstanding a long tradition of Protestant laicism, Unitarian moralists espoused an exalted conception of the cleric. "I consider my profession as almost infinitely raised above all others," Dr. Channing wrote to a friend. The minister "is the proclaimer and expounder of the divine will," observed the younger Ware; "the majesty and awfulness of the message passes to him who is commissioned to utter it." James Walker did not even shrink from citing the Society of Jesus as a model moral elite, highly gifted in the techniques of practical persuasion.[48] If anything, the Unitarians probably stressed the importance of the clerical function a little more than their American orthodox contemporaries. New England Liberals tended to be somewhat "sacerdotal," putting emphasis on the clergyman as an educated leader of society, while the Calvinists tended to enhance the powers of the "church," i.e., the small group of converted laymen in each parish.

The influence exerted by the minister in early nineteenth-century New England was not confined to the two sermons he preached each Sunday. He remained a leader in community activities, especially in literary and charitable institutions. Lecture notes taken by a young man training for the ministry at Harvard Divinity School in the late 1830's indicate the type of leadership he was expected to display after ordination. Most Massachusetts townships put the minister on the school board, the Professor of Pastoral Theology told the class. But the minister should also keep a keen eye on the local library, for librarians have a tendency to stock books which will give young people "only a taste for novel readings" and the minister must see to it that religious works are circulated too. The minister should also advise his parishioners on their magazine subscriptions, lend them good books, and suggest where they should send their children for an education.[49] Such was the instruction the academic moral philosopher gave to the prospective minister. Through the power of the pastoral clergy, the moral philosopher brought his own power to bear on society.

A classic statement of Unitarian moral elitism was delivered by the elder Henry Ware when he preached the ordination sermon for Joseph Allen on October 30, 1816. Ware took for his text Jeremiah 15:19, "Let them return unto thee, but return not thou unto them." He called on young Allen to be a worthy successor to the prophets as a teacher and leader of the people. The Christian minister must form public opinion. "He is not to follow servilely in the track of others, but to lead and guide them, [and] never for a moment to remit his effort, or yield to the popular current." The new clergyman should be on guard against dangers that might compromise his position. Beware of indolence and false humility, which sap the strength of will, the preacher warned his new colleague. Above all, resist the temptations of time-serving, "the criminal spirit of compliance."[50]

The Unitarians often repeated Bishop Butler's famous dictum on the rightful supremacy of conscience, "If it had might, as it has right, it would rule the world." The moral elite was the conscience of society, and as such entitled to direct its purposes. As conscience should never give way before any lower faculty, the Unitarian moralists were determined never to allow themselves to be displaced as the final arbiters of social morality.

What qualified the Unitarian moralists in their own eyes for the role they assumed? After all, the moral sense was a universal faculty, possessed by all normal men. Did this not make the value judgments of one man as good as those of any other? Though some Americans reached that democratic conclusion (and some Transcendentalist-Unitarian heretics were among them), Harvard Liberals rejected it. Education and refined taste still counted in their theory, and these made the moral judgments of some men worth more than those of others. Dr. Channing was irritated when ignorant revivalists quoted Scripture: "God hath chosen the foolish things of the world to confound the wise" (I Corinthians 1:27). Obviously, education was required for the competent interpretation of Scripture, still an important basis of Unitarian morality. Furthermore, education enabled a man to discern relationships of ethical significance that might pass unnoticed to the untrained observer. Complex situations required complex ethical analyses, even if the basic premises were simple.[51] As for "moral taste," its emotional responses were an inestimable asset to the moral sense, yet they were not automatic. The heightened moral sensibility of the man of taste was the product of a long and careful training.

Unitarian moral elitism had distinctly Platonic overtones that bring to mind the Platonic influences on Unitarian natural religion and ethical theory. The faith Unitarian moralists placed in persuasion as a means of social control may have a source in Plato, but the most striking affinity between their social thought and his lies in their dream of an integrated and moral society.[52] Every man has a function in the good society, but every man is not qualified to prescribe the good for society. Men should be persuaded to desire that which is just, Plato and the Unitarians agreed, but justice does not depend on human compact or consent.

An integrated society under the moral leadership of an educated clerical elite was still a living ideal in Federalist New England. But forces that would eventually destroy the ideal had been at work for a long time. Beginning in the eighteenth century, revivalism registered popular protest against an educated clergy and a hierarchical social order. Liberal clergymen opposed revivalism just as they opposed French infidelity. Both the First Great Awakening and the French Revolution had threatened clerical privileges, and both had been condemned from Boston pulpits as forms of "enthusiasm." A century after the invasion of George Whitefield, the Harvard clerical elite was still fighting a holding action to maintain its status. But by Jacksonian times the Unitarian moralists could read the handwriting on the wall. "There is a tendency in the state of society to destroy the distinction between clergy and people," one of them admitted in 1835.[53] The Old World ideal no longer mirrored social fact in mid-nineteenth-century America.

What effect the ending of clerical leadership would have on society remained to be seen. The elder Ware expressed forebodings when ordaining young Allen: "Public opinion will be perverted," he warned, should clerical efforts fail. "The taste in morals, manners, and religion will sink down to a low standard."[54] Notwithstanding the attempts of Harvard civil polity to furnish America with a Burkean tradition, there were in fact few historical institutions in the United States to assist in the conservation of traditional values. Harvard moralists dreaded that, in this absence of conservative influence, Americans might lose sight of moral and spiritual ideals. If the academic moral philosophers and their disciples, the pastoral clergy, were to keep public opinion in safe channels, they would have to do it through persuasion. As a substitute for Old World institutional restraints, the moral elite hoped to inculcate "good principles and good habits, which are the conservative power of our free institutions," into the conscience of the public.[55] More was at stake here than customary church attendance or the status of the clerical profession. Could good manners, respect for education, and a sense of community responsibility survive in a democratic environment? The Unitarian moral philosophers, who associated such values with a hierarchical social order, had their doubts.

PURITANISM WITHOUT CALVINISM

According to Harvard moral philosophy, a good man was a microcosmic society in which a sovereign moral sense ruled, with aid from prudence and benevolent affections, over the baser passions and appetites. According to Harvard civil polity, a good society had an analogous structure. It possessed a moral elite: men who were the moral sense of the social organism. But like the moral sense of the individual, these men needed help from other powers to perform their function properly. How the moral philosophers and clergy were to maintain their rightful independence (that is, their rightful supremacy) and at the same time attract the support they knew they needed presented a touchy problem for elitists in a democracy. In practice, the Harvard moral elite looked to the wealthy for an alliance in the interests of social order.

Of course Unitarian moralists did not invent the idea that religion should underwrite the social order, nor were they the first to propose cooperation between the economic and ecclesiastical power structures. These attitudes have been commonplace throughout Christendom, and the Unitarians had simply inherited them from the Puritan colonists. The Unitarians greatly admired their Puritan forbears, despite a strong distaste for their theology. ("Far distant be the day," prayed one Unitarian, "when . . . Americans shall cease to venerate the character of the Puritans.") What the Unitarians liked about the Puritans was their social morality: their "deep tone of seriousness," their "disinterestedness," their "extreme cautiousness regarding outward conduct."[56] All these, together with their firm commitment to traditional patterns of social deference, endeared the Puritans to conservative Unitarians. Even while discarding Calvinist theology, Liberal clergy of the Standing Order cooperated with Boston merchants to keep Puritan social ideals alive. What nineteenth-century America really needed, Harvard Unitarians implied, was Puritanism without Calvinism.

Many precepts of the Unitarian moralists revealed old Puritan attitudes. When Henry Ware bade farewell to his parish in Hingham to accept the Hollis Professorship in 1805, his parting admonitions displayed an interpretation of social justice that had changed little since Stuart times. Ware enjoined his flock:

1. that the rich be not high minded, nor oppressive, nor trust in uncertain riches; but that they do good with their wealth;
2. that the poor be patient, honest, and resigned to the divine allotments;
3. that rulers keep in view the end of their appointment, and make a just use of the power committed to them;
4. that subjects submit quietly to rightful authority, and lead peaceable lives.

These homilies reflected Ware's view that the good life was to be found in "a conduct correspondent to the respective stations and conditions of men." Men should live together in loving community, but they should also respect status distinctions. Christian acknowledgment of the equality of every man in the sight of God was perfectly compatible with the recognition of "varieties of condition and talents and acquisitions and character."[57] Indeed, the variation in human condition was a positive advantage to Christian morality. "If every condition in life were comfortable, there would be no call for contentment in one, no exercise of compassion in another. If the ranks in society were equal there would be no need of humility and no place for condescension."[58] Unitarian moralists had no sympathy with social leveling. To be sure, Christ had commanded the privileged to invite the humble to dinner; but this no longer bound Christians, said a Harvard professor, now that there exist organized charities through which the rich can help the poor without mingling with them socially.[59]

Although "inequalities of property" seemed to the Unitarians "indispensable to the maintenance of civil society," their ideal social hierarchy was not so much an economic ranking as one of prestige derived from education and good character.[60] "Talents, united with correct morals and good manners," distinguished the true aristocrat from the man of mere wealth, according to Andrews Norton.[61] In the early days of the Bay Colony, there had been substantial factual basis for this ideal, since leadership had been exercised by gentlemen of piety and learning. Of course, wealth had commanded a certain amount of political influence in Massachusetts, but not so much as in some other colonies. A good education and the blessing of the clergy had been important assets for a politician in the Puritan Commonwealth.[62]

Unitarian moralists seem to have expected that political power would become more closely identified with money as time went by. In their opinion, the absence of a hereditary nobility of the Old World type only made the emergence of a purely economic aristocracy in American more likely.[63] Nor did the social democratization of the Jacksonian Era affect this judgment about economic consolidation. "We reveal no secret when we say that without the name, we have much of the spirit of office and rank, of the aristocracy of wealth and of power," claimed Joseph Tuckerman in 1838. As the Boston merchant princes grew in wealth, they were bound to grow in power, Francis Bowen predicted. "They will not need to have this [additional political] power expressly given to them by laws and constitutions; it will naturally and inevitably fall into their possession—so much of it, at least, as they shall deem necessary for their own security and happiness."[64] The self-appointed task of the Unitarian moral philosophers was to work with and through the consolidating commercial plutocracy, transforming it into a cultivated, socially responsible, stable aristocracy.

Eighteenth-century humanist attitudes mingled with those of seventeenth-century Puritanism in forming Unitarian aristocratic aspirations. The moral elite wanted the Boston merchants to display good taste as well as paternalism. Buckminster warned his wealthy congregation to help maintain the cultural standards of society, as well as to set a good moral example. "God grant that you may never feel the remorse of having deliberately contributed to the . . . corruption of an old or established principle . . . or assisted in the gradual encroachments of selfishness, vanity, pomp, and slavish imitation." In a similar vein, Henry Ware, Jr., admonished the graduating seniors of Harvard College that they should act "like so much leaven, to affect the whole community, pervade it with higher tastes, and give it a better tone."[65] Should the Unitarian moralists make good their claims to authority, they would train the emergent merchant class in respect for Old World values. Then, the newly rich of Mayhew's generation might become true aristocrats by Norton's definition.

Boston's wealthy classes might prove a convenient breeding-ground for "talents, . . . correct morals, and good manners." These criteria of Norton's invite comparison with those of Thomas Jefferson's "natural aristocracy." Not only talent and virtue, but also good manners, characterize the Harvard aristocrat. Now, while talent and virtue might be found anywhere, manners are a cultural advantage likely to accrue to the children of good families. The Unitarian natural aristocrat, then, was not only a person with a potential for leadership, he was also a person whose upbringing and education had realized that potential. The training of an aristocrat could be pursued in conjunction with the development of a Christian character. The businessmen of Boston, if they were willing to accept the tutelage of Harvard moral philosophers, could develop the habits necessary for enlightened leadership.

The implicit bargain that the Harvard moral philosophers were trying to drive with the merchants came down to this: the moralists would provide a rationale for capitalism and the protection of property, if the merchants would grant them the positions of cultural and moral leadership. Frank Gatell has preserved for us an apt illustration of how the bargain could work. John Gorham Palfrey, eminent Unitarian man of letters and moral reformer, sometime Dean of Harvard Divinity School, is writing to Amos Lawrence on September 1, 1835. He is asking the mill owner for a loan to enable him to buy the *North American Review*.

I believe you will agree with me that it is a matter of some general interest, what principles the work in question should maintain, and I venture to flatter myself that you give me some credit for attachment to sound principles in morals, politics, and literature . . . It is important to have it go into hands, such as . . . will prevent it from becoming the instrument of any hurtful influence.[66]

Lawrence sent the money. One is reminded of Emerson's sardonic observation, "Boston or Brattle Street Christianity is a compound of force, or the best Diagonal line that can be drawn between Jesus Christ and Abbott Lawrence."[67]

Of course, the Unitarians were by no means the only academics or clerics in American history to seek to safeguard their own position by an alliance with capitalists. Orthodox Trinitarians often did so too, the proslavery stance of southern clergymen being a well-documented example. Episcopalianism was long closely identified with political and economic reaction; it was no accident that Alexander Hamilton and Fisher Ames became Episcopalians. Nor did Boston Liberals ever descend to the crassness of a Russell Conwell or a Bruce Barton. Granting all this, the conservatism of the Harvard Unitarians still has a special interest. Nowhere outside eastern Massachusetts did the clergy have so clear a conception of the cultural and moral standards they were trying to achieve by their conservative posture, for nowhere else was the combination of transatlantic influence and clerical tradition so strong. And seldom, indeed, did religious disputes in the United States take on so many ominous aspects of class conflict, as did the great schism in Massachusetts.

Debate between Unitarians and Calvinists often included social slurs and recriminations. The Unitarian moralists shuddered at such controversy, which posed a direct threat to their ideal of a stable and hierarchical society. Calvinist condemnations of Liberal religion encouraged the common people to be critical of their betters, and this provoked anxiety at Harvard. The Calvinists had the impudence to accuse "those who guide public opinion, . . . [the] most distinguished magistrates, . . . ministers of religion, . . . scholars and literary men" of being "destitute of all real moral goodness, . . . hypocrites and reprobates," complained Norton petulantly. The mild spirit of William Ellery Channing was shocked that "men in those walks of life which leave them without leisure or opportunities for improvement" should "decide on the most intricate points" of disputed theology and "pass sentence on men whose lives have been devoted to the study of Scripture!" To Channing it seemed that religious controversy threatened the whole social order, ranging youth against age and female against male.[68]

To counteract such divisive accusations, Unitarian moralists sought to prove that Christianity should actually offer no basis for class bitterness. The Gospel of Christ, according to Buckminster, promoted social stability.

Our Saviour's instructions are not like those of Rousseau, adapted to men in an inconceivable state of Nature, to which this visionary enthusiast would recall them. They do not require men, like some of the ancient Stoics, to throw their wealth into the sea or to inflict upon themselves unnatural austerities. But everything about Jesus, in precept and practice, is mild, cheering, great; everything is suited to the precise wants of men in society.[69]

The Scriptures, of course, contain many denunciations of the rich. But Harvard moral philosophers (like others before and since) contrived to take the sting out of these by presenting them not as criticisms of the wealthy, but as expressions of pity for them. The poor, whose cause the Bible often espouses, were by this logic to be envied. Christ's condemnations of the wealthy were interpreted as applying only to the rich Jews of His own time, and not to the wealthy in general. The senior Ware, preaching on I Corinthians 10:24 ("Let no man seek his own, but every man another's wealth"), struggled to explain away its socialist implications. Various socialist ideologies were current in antebellum New England, but Harvard philosophers envisioned a moral society without an alteration in the economic structure of capitalism.[70]

Ethical theory came to the aid of religion in the Unitarian defense of the status quo. Harvard professors were familiar with the distinction between "absolute" and "conditional" obligations, the former being binding upon all men and the latter dependent upon the specific relations subsisting between the people involved. It was easy to employ the concept of "conditional" obligation to call upon servants to obey their masters and subjects their rulers. Ethical philosophy also provided John Emery Abbot with his interpretation of the Golden Rule. Abbot told his parishioners the precept meant we should do unto others as we might "in sound reason and good conscience, desire them to do to us, were their condition ours." By this interpretation, he subtly introduced a number of qualifications into the hard teaching, which he went on to make explicit. We are not obligated "to gratify all the wild wishes of others," but only such of their desires as *our* reason and conscience approve. Furthermore, since men have many various conditions, the distinctions of social rank and the claims of consanguinity are not to be overlooked in applying the Golden Rule. The Rule does not require us to treat all men alike, only to treat them as we might hope in conscience and reason to be treated by them were the relationship reversed. What Abbot had done was to impose upon the Golden Rule one of the "self-evident" ethical axioms from the system constructed by the Anglican philosopher Samuel Clarke. The axiom was called "the law of equity" and implied a distinctive set of obligations accompanying each social station.[71]

The Unitarian moralists never let the Boston merchants forget that responsibilities as well as privileges went with wealth and status. "Men cannot be equal in all respects; but the high should feel their elevation to be a motive and obligation to labor for inferiors."[72] The Christian doctrine of stewardship sounded forth from the pulpit as it had in Puritan times. All things are God's; the rich man is one whom He has made custodian of much; he will have to answer to Him for the use he has made of this bounty. Providence, Bishop Butler had written, held the rich responsible for the tutelage and protection of the poor. These were time-honored truths which young Buckminster cautioned the merchants to remember. "Forget not that you are instruments in the hands of Providence, by which he diffuses his blessings, and promotes his grand purposes."[73] If the wealthy man was regarded as fortunate, it was not because he could lead a life of luxury, but because of the power for good at his disposal. Harvard civil polity took it for granted that the wealthy man would possess great influence and prestige in the community, and taught that he ought to possess political privileges as well. But wealth bestowed still another form of power on its owner: it enabled him to undertake philanthropy. If all these powers were to be exercised responsibly, the merchant class would have to follow the guidance of the moral elite.[74]

Merchants were famous for their prudence, so the Unitarian moralists did not neglect prudential considerations when exhorting the merchants to do their duty. A degree of social responsibility was dictated by an enlightened conservatism. In 1827 Walker warned his congregation: "Much is said about the disorganizing doctrines and theories of the day; but, bad as these are, they are not likely to do so much to exasperate the poor against the rich, and break down the bulwarks of law and order, as the conduct of some among the rich themselves. The time was when the few could trample with indifference on the interests and feelings of the many, and make sport of their complaints with impunity; but that time has passed away."[75] The philanthropist would actually be safeguarding his economic and social position, the moralists pointed out. Tuckerman assured the merchants that, in the good society, where those in high station did not "neglect the claims of suffering humanity, . . . the inferior would render twofold respect for that which he received from his superior." The ultimate prudential incentive was, of course, the supernatural sanction. If rich men acted properly, as *"stewards"* of their wealth, Tuckerman felt they could be as hopeful as any of a heavenly reward. By balancing honest industry with philanthropy, "the rich man may daily be accumulating riches, and at the same time laying up for himself a treasure in heaven."[76]

THE SEQUENCE OF RIGHTFUL PRECEDENCE

The belief that the accumulation of temporal wealth might be evidence of virtue had long been characteristic of Yankees. It was an attitude that had gradually become intertwined with the doctrine of election during the eighteenth century. The temporal punishment of sin was part of traditional Christian belief; Butler and others whom the Unitarians admired had relied upon it to show that men lived under a system of moral government. Thus the idea that poverty was among the ways in which sin might be punished came naturally to Unitarians.[77] Henry Ware, Sr., believed in a "perceptible connection" between a man's character and condition in life, a connection which was "part of an established scheme" of Providence. Francis Bowen quoted Poor Richard's aphorisms with approval.[78] No doubt the merchants who owned Unitarian pews and made bequests to Harvard were not averse to hearing that prosperity was the recompense of virtue.

God has appointed that indolence shall lead to poverty and want, and thoughtlessness and folly issue in dishonor and ruin. But let the indolent and thoughtless turn to industry and prudence, and how soon his condition and prospects change with his character.[79]

Prosperity could not (in consistency) be held out like this as a reward for virtue unless the Unitarian moralists could bring themselves to accept the legitimacy of social mobility. But Harvard Unitarians, like some of their Trinitarian contemporaries, harbored suspicions of social mobility. The situation of the poor was enviable, they protested, and the poor should be contented with it. "The ploughman munches his mouldy crusts with as good a relish as the rich man eats his dainties with, for he has that best of sauces, hunger, to season his victuals . . . Nor is the lowest herdsman incapable of that sincerest of pleasures, the consciousness of acting right."[80] Orestes Brownson "exaggerates" the hardships of the "laboring classes," William Ellery Channing complained; "in truth, it may be doubted whether they have not the easiest lot," at least in America. "How often have I known professional and mercantile men toiling anxiously through the night, sacrificing health, while the laborer has been wrapt in oblivion of all his cares!"[81]

Instead of holding out hopes of rising in the world, Unitarian moralists usually felt it safer to offer a heavenly reward for honest toil. James Walker told his congregation that "our best preparation for death is to be found in a quiet, assiduous, and persevering discharge of [the] appropriate duties of our respective stations in life." Sobriety and industriousness were indispensable to the formation of the Christian character. They were, therefore, part of the duty one owed to himself, apart from any advantages that might accrue thereby. If people would only think of hard work simply as a development of their faculties, and stop hoping for worldly rewards, they would complain less about the injustices of this life, observed young Frances Bowen. Poverty, then, could be justified as a means to virtue. The hero of Henry Ware, Jr.'s didactic stories, David Ellington, rises early to labor diligently in his calling (that of a journeyman carpenter), but is praised for his lack of ambition to improve his station. Even the compassionate Channing, addressing a working-class audience on the subject of their "elevation," was careful to insist "that, by the elevation of the laboring mass, I do not mean that they are to be released from labor. I add, in the next place, that this elevation is not to be gained by efforts to force themselves into what are called the upper ranks of society." The change he had in mind was an "inward" one, an elevation of soul only.[82]

The trouble with Liberal exhortations to contentment was that they undercut the justification for social stratification in terms of moral desert. Should a man try to improve his condition or not? Unitarian moralists, caught between New World facts and their Old World ideals, did not easily find an answer. Frequently, they were guilty of grave inconsistency. They congratulated those who had risen into the ranks of Boston's plutocracy, but simultaneously tried to dissuade others from following their example.

The mixed feelings of the Boston cultural establishment toward social mobility manifest a classic American dilemma. Just as the Harvard intellectual system that challenged Calvinism was almost immediately thrown on the defensive by a still more radical Transcendentalism, the Boston social system which was transformed in the Revolution was soon thrown on the defensive by the continual efforts of still "newer" men to rise. In the intellectually and socially fluid society of America, nothing—and nobody—was secure. Every hard-won eminence, no matter how recently attained, must be entrenched at once if it would be saved from the next wave of attackers. Much of the Liberal infatuation with Burkean traditionalism can be attributed to the conservatism of the parvenu.[83]

In their search for some kind of order in a new country, Unitarian intellectuals constructed a social model derived from the teachings of moral philosophy. Harvard ethical theory ranked the faculties in a sequence of rightful precedence: (1) moral sense, (2) prudence, (3) appetites and emotions. Unitarian moralists believed the good society would preserve this hierarchy, and bestow influence first upon moral men, then upon prudent men, and last upon passionate men. When the moral philosophers translated these abstractions into terms of the society around them, they came out as follows: (1) the moral elite—clerical and academic men; (2) men of affairs—including not only the wealthy but also those middle-income professionals and salaried managers who shared a businessman's outlook; and (3) the lower classes, whom the Unitarians were in danger of ignoring and whom they were tempted to dismiss as the irresponsible poor.

The scheme was clearly inadequate for enabling the Unitarians to deal effectively with Massachusetts society. There were too many groups in between class 2 and class 3 who were left unaccounted for— yeomen farmers, respectable artisans, and the like. In their failure to communicate effectively with these people—the average citizens of Massachusetts, in fact—the Unitarian moralists made their biggest mistake. The moral philosophers seem to have enjoyed a considerable measure of success in persuading the Boston merchants to promote charitable and cultural enterprises. But the mind of the common people, in contrast, was a closed book to Harvard moralists. Henry Ware, Jr.'s fictional carpenter, David Ellington, is a sentimentalized and unconvincing character. The author, the grandson of a simple yeoman farmer himself, is evidently nostalgic and yet remarkably alien to the working-class world he tries to depict.

The moral sense needed support from the other faculties, and the moral philosophers needed support from other people. But Unitarian moralists did not achieve in their social practice the proper balance they idealized in their ethical theory. They leaned too heavily on one social group. The moralists generally concentrated on maintaining their good relations with the wealthy classes and seem to have assumed that they could count on the masses to follow respectfully at a distance. Andrews Norton's father had been able to preach to the servants in his congregation that they should be faithful to the station in life to which God had called them. After the first quarter of the nineteenth century, however, such preaching seemed incongruous and strangely remote from American reality. Norton the son recognized by the 1830's that social status could not be sharply defined in America and that social mobility was common. He hoped, however, that this might merely have the effect of minimizing class conflict.[84]

On the whole, Unitarians remained out of sympathy with the egalitarianism of the Age of Jackson. James Walker confided to the Harvard Chapter of Phi Beta Kappa that

there is nothing by which the people of this country are so likely to be deluded and betrayed as by the commonplaces which are continually rung in their ears, flattering to the national vanity and especially to their notions of liberty and equality. I hope I am a good republican, but I certainly cannot sympathize with those who would interpret and apply the glorious declaration in the charter of freedom, "all men are *born* equal," as to make all men *die* equal.[85]

As a Christian and an American, Walker could not deny that, in some sense, all men were created equal. But his inherited Puritan reverence for status, and his high expectations for a Boston aristocracy, made him an uncomfortable, elitist egalitarian. Walker was spokesman for a generation of Boston leaders who feared lest the American Revolution be carried too far.

Part Two

Implementation:

The Unitarian Awakening

VI / The Religion of the Heart

THE SECOND GREAT AWAKENING in America manifested a search for emotional community through religion, a search which was widespread in Western civilization during the first part of the nineteenth century. The New England Unitarians shared the view of many of their contemporaries, at home and abroad, that only Christianity could counteract the evils of nineteenth-century commercial society. Though the Harvard moral philosophers were proud of America's material achievements and felt generally optimistic about the course of history, they were troubled by the insensitivity, anarchy, and greed they often saw around them. "I am no foe to civilization. I rejoice in its progress," declared William Ellery Channing. "[But] without a pure religion to modify its tendencies, to inspire and refine it, we shall be corrupted, not ennobled, by it."[1] Like their Calvinist counterparts, the Unitarian moralists felt that what America needed was a spiritual reawakening.

UNITARIAN PIETISM

In 1810, while New England Unitarianism was still in its first bloom, a young man named John Emery Abbot came to Harvard to read divinity. After five years of study, he was ordained at North Church in Salem, where he served until his death in 1819 at the age of twenty-six. His bereaved parish erected a monument to his memory stating, "His life, though short, exhibited a pattern of the Christian virtues, and a model of the pastoral character." One can agree with those who knew him that the Reverend John Emery Abbot personified a Unitarian ideal.

The aspect of New England Unitarianism that Abbot illustrates

151

seems best termed Liberal "pietism." Pietism, in the words of one historian of religion, typically "stresses the emotional, devotional, and ascetic qualities of religion in preference to the intellectual, the ritualistic, and the ethical."[2] Within the Unitarian consensus, however, emotionalism, devotionalism, and otherworldliness managed to coexist with their opposites. In seventeenth-century Puritanism, "piety" and "reason" had been held together in uneasy tension. During the eighteenth century, "reason" had come to predominate among those sons of the Puritans called Arminians; yet the warmth of the affections was not wholly chilled.

The religious leaders from whom New England Liberals drew inspiration and encouragement included men who appealed to the heart as well as the head. As we have seen, the same Harvard moralists who revered Reid, Tillotson, and the Latitudinarians also idolized Joseph Butler and the Cambridge Platonists, with their rich emotional sensitivity. The Enlightenment, after all, was an era not only of Lockean rationalism but also of eighteenth-century sentimentalism, and both left their mark upon Liberal religion. Two English Dissenters who exemplified the strain of gentle, refined emotionalism that sometimes accompanied a "catholic" spirit and a more "reasonable" theology were Isaac Watts (1674–1748) and Philip Doddridge (1702–1751). These men tried to foster what they considered legitimate evangelicalism even while deploring "enthusiasm"; the hymns of Watts remain a lasting monument to his devotion. Watts, who in his last years entertained doubts on the doctrine of the Trinity, was especially influential in New England; he was an associate of Isaac Chauncy, the son of Harvard's president, and corresponded actively with most of the leading Bay Colony divines of his day.[3] Drawing upon the dual tradition of reason and sentiment illustrated by Watts, the Liberal Christians of Massachusetts contrived to find a place for pietism without rejecting the rationalistic aspects of religion.

The better known, rationalistic side of New England Arminianism found an early spokesman in Isaac Chauncy's grandson, Charles Chauncy (1705–1787). But the other facet of Liberalism, the tradition of sentimentalism, also possessed its eighteenth-century exponent in Boston. Benjamin Colman (1673–1747), the first minister of the proto-

Arminian Brattle Street Church, has been called "a rationalist who luxuriated in emotion": "He partook, although from afar, in that maneuver at the very center of English culture which, immediately upon the triumph of scientific reason, instinctively sought a counter-balance in the exploitation of the passions, especially, out of an over-whelming urgency, the 'benevolent' passions."[4] Though Chauncy was the great opponent of the First Great Awakening, Colman endorsed it until he was disillusioned by Davenport's excesses. In fact, the sympathetic correspondent to whom Jonathan Edwards addressed his famous *Narrative of Surprising Conversions* was the Liberal Benjamin Colman.[5]

Harvard moral philosophy, while insisting that ends must be determined by the intellect, acknowledged that emotions played an important part as means to religion and virtue. When chastising the revivalists of the 1740's, Chauncy had written, "An *enlightened* Mind, and not *raised Affections,* ought always to be the Guide of those who call themselves men; and this, in the Affairs of Religion, as well as other things."[6] But Chauncy's prestige did not prevent Unitarian pietists from qualifying his claim for the supremacy of the intellect. William Ellery Channing justified the invocation of the affections by citing the need for balance in a Christian character. "Some preachers, from observing the pernicious effects of violent and exclusive appeals to the passions, have fallen into an opposite error," he complained. "They have addressed men as mere creatures of the intellect; they have forgotten that affection is as essential to our nature as thought, [and] that the union of reason and sensibility is the health of the soul." Channing's pupil Abbot asserted that Christianity "calls us not to annihilate our feelings, but only to regulate them."[7] The man of well-regulated feeling was a man greatly admired by nineteenth-century Unitarian moralists.

The "sensibility" which Channing sought to unite with reason was a very special type of emotional sensitivity, a combination of religious affection and moral taste.[8] It appears that young Abbot actually possessed this quality other Harvard Liberals worked so earnestly to attain. "His natural dispositions and temper were undoubtedly good," Henry Ware, Jr., wrote of him. "He neither exemplified nor believed the doctrine of man's original depravity. His mind was finely strung, and its powers nicely balanced; and God seems to have given him no strength of passion, except sensibility. His sensibility was acute and delicate."[9] Abbot's sermons offer some of the purest examples of the "religion of the heart" among early nineteenth-century Unitarians. Otherworldly and quietist, they continually invoke the "religious affections." Abbot seems to have been completely impervious to the commercial spirit of America. True happiness, he preached, comes from the cultivation of a passive, affectionate, cheerful piety. A ministerial colleague described the effect of this preaching thus: "The mind of the hearer is tranquillized, and so totally dissolved in the gentle feelings he excites, that everything exterior is forgotten."[10]

Applying the pyschology taught at Harvard, Abbot taught that "susceptibility to religious impressions, and to devotional feelings, is given to us by nature; but, like all other intellectual and moral powers, it must be protected and nourished and strengthened by our exertions." Fortunately, God had provided means for this nourishment; He had designed the Gospel to serve as an aid in "purifying, elevating, and consoling" the heart of man.[11] The development of the affections was the essence of Abbot's message. When offering the traditional "right hand of fellowship" at a Unitarian ordination service, Abbot admonished his new colleague: "Christianity is peculiarly a religion of the affections. Other religions have been presented to their disciples in the form of rigid laws and stern exactions; but Christianity aims to sanctify the character and rule the life by breathing into the heart a fervent and influential charity."[12]

The charity of which Abbot spoke subsumed both benevolence and the religious affection—both love of man and love of God. He explained it in the customary terminology of Harvard moral philosophy.

God has warmed and ennobled our hearts with certain affections . . . Whenever an object corresponding to these affections, and suited, by its nature, to excite them, is presented with distinctness and force to the mind, these feelings are awakened . . . When they are directed towards human beings, they are benevolent affections, and constitute love of man, and when they are directed to the Creator and Father of all, they then constitute . . . love of God . . . The love of God perfectly corresponds, in its nature, with the love of man. It is composed of the same affections . . . and will be characterised by corresponding effects. The difference between the two dispositions arises only from the infinite disparity between their objects.[13]

In this interesting fashion, the Unitarian sentimentalist reconciled his pietism with his moralism, and attributed both to the same "affection." Jonathan Edwards had drawn a sharp distinction between the love of God and the merely natural moral affections. True divine love, or "benevolence to being in general," could come only through divine grace. Unitarians, however, made no such distinction; the benevolent and religious feelings Abbot described were entirely natural to man. What was required was not a supernatural gift, but simply practice in directing the charitable affections toward an unseen object. By cultivating the proper "sentiments," a man could achieve that "sensibility" required for the model Christian character. Through the development of his own emotional nature, the Liberal pietist hoped to ascend the ladder of love to God.

As an Arminian, Abbot taught that spiritual advancement was dependent upon men's own efforts. As a pietist, he devoted his efforts to cultivation of the affections. The "religious life" was one of constant emotional refinement. "It is impossible to remain stationary in respect to religious character," he told his congregation; unless one were careful to stimulate the virtuous affections, one would be in danger of falling prey to bad habits and spiritual deadness. Of couse, the evil affections did not give real happiness, though men could become addicted to them. The avaricious man, for example, was bound by the chains of his sin; despite all his "anxieties and cravings," in fact no "heaps of treasure or extent of possessions" ever satisfied him. To avoid such pitfalls, the Christian was wise to develop an elevated taste, an emotional attraction toward spiritual things. For one who achieved refined moral taste, sin would have no further appeal: "the charm of the world has vanished, and many of its temptations lost their power."[14]

Abbot was not the only Unitarian of his generation with pietistic inclinations. Buckminster and the younger Ware frequently joined in his celebration of the affections.[15] James Walker admonished the readers of the Unitarian journal that "the essential truths of Christianity are . . . addressed to the affections and to the conscience, as well as to the understanding. They must, therefore, be *felt* as well as perceived." "If enthusiasm be wild and furious, we are not to proscribe all ardour and zeal in the cause of religion," the elder Ware reminded Liberals. "Without denying any of the wildness of enthusiasm, we may cherish its anointing warmth."[16] Harvard Unitarian moralists found little difficulty in distinguishing dangerous "wildness" from safe emotional "warmth." Andrews Norton, for example, though hostile to Transcendentalist romanticism, reveled in the rich imagery of Anglican mystical poets.[17]

Many Liberal Christians found pietism a convenient escape from the legalism and futility into which some forms of American Calvinism seemed (to them) to be settling. Unitarian moralists had no desire to debate those whom they called "the scholastic theologues, hairsplitting metaphysicians, and long-breathed controversialists" of backcountry New England.[18] Rather than criticize Calvinism—or defend their own Arianism—from the pulpit, Liberal clergymen generally preferred to call for a simple piety. People "are not religious in proportion to the strength, the clearness, or the soundness of their faith," the moralists taught, "but in proportion to the hold which this faith . . . has gained over their feelings."[19] The Unitarian laity, for their part, were no longer interested in orthodox theology, and cared little to hear it refuted. Instead of John Foxe or Michael Wigglesworth, these sentimental descendants of the Puritans enjoyed reading Archbishop Fénelon, the French quietist. Traditional theological distinctions could not matter much to Yankees who praised a Roman prelate.[20]

Boston ministers made no attempt to revive their parishioners' flagging interest in the historic issues of Christian dogma, but dismissed theology out of hand. According to Buckminster, a "sincere" believer "does not perplex himself with fruitless inquiries into the precise nature of that relation which subsisted between Jesus on earth and the Supreme Deity; . . . it is to him of much more importance to ascertain the relation in which Jesus stands to himself—what Jesus is to him and he to Jesus."[21] It is surprising to find professional academics disparaging the value of intellectual discussion to the extent that Harvard professors sometimes did. "If religion and man have suffered from super-stition and fanaticism on the one side, they have equally suffered from logic, philosophy, and metaphysics on the other," declared the younger Ware.[22] The fact of the matter is that Boston Unitarians found "logi-cal subtlety" as distasteful as "enthusiasm"; it was just as suspect to think too much as to feel too deeply. In thought, as in feeling, *modera-tion* was their goal. Such an attitude heralded the coming of Victorian antiintellectualism. "Be good, sweet maid, and let who can be clever," was an injunction not far removed from the spirit of Liberal pietism during the Second Great Awakening.[23]

Besides emotionalism, Unitarians also manifested a second charac-teristic of pietism, devotionalism. "O thou who art a Spirit, inspire us with the spirit of prayer!" cried the Liberal minister from the com-munion table.[24] A life of prayer was an essential component of the cul-tivation of the Christian character. Since "temptation is abundant, and the Christian standard is strict and high," Unitarian moralists encour-aged men to turn to God in prayer for aid in fulfilling their spiritual aspirations. "It may be that our prayers are not answered as our short-sighted wishes could dictate, and return not to us in goods of this world," Abbot admitted. "But our prayers will not be in vain. They will be rewarded with what infinitely outweighs all earthly blessings—with the improvement of our own religious characters, and with God's eternal favor."[25] Invariably, the inward and subjective benefits of prayer were stressed rather than tangible rewards. During his short career in the pastoral ministry, Andrews Norton cautioned his congre-gation to pray, not for mundane things, but for spiritual things, for a purer heart. In later years, he told the readers of the *Christian Disciple* that prayer conferred only "real" blessings. By these he meant the pleasures of moral taste and religious sentiment, the pleasures that could never cloy.[26] Unitarian prayer was, in fact, an applied technique of Harvard moral philosophy.

Harvard philosophers subscribed to what we would call a "psycho-logical" theory of the value of prayer. Although they were staunch defenders of the historicity of biblical miracles, Harvard Unitarians were unwilling to ask God for miracles in their own time. The help they expected to derive from prayer came through entirely natural means. The effects of prayer were governed by "general laws," and were even predictable. It was the man who had been virtuous and formed a "holy character" who would find his prayers for spiritual strength answered. Of course, such an interpretation of prayer might appear to undermine the activity itself. If the benefits of prayer were purely natural and subjective, what sense did it make to ask God for them? To this, the Unitarian could only reply (as many other pietists have done), "The heart alone can understand itself . . . To be able to answer the question, What profit is there in prayer? we must enter into its spirit; and, as soon as we do enter into its spirit, we shall cease to take much interest in the question."[27]

Not all pietisms are alike; Unitarian pietism was very different from, say, that of Jonathan Edwards. Some sense of what their form of pietism was like may be gained by looking through such prayers of the Harvard moralists as have survived. In general, themes of thanksgiving and adoration predominate over supplication and repentance. Their piety was gentle, not harsh; warm, but not all-consuming. They prayed for the things they valued: "stability, uniformity, and constancy."[28] An air of contentment often suffuses even their prayers for assistance:

> Oh, may each day my heart improve,
> Increase my faith, my hope, my love;
> And thus its shades around me close
> More wise and holy than I rose.[29]

The third characteristic of pietism in the definition we have accepted is asceticism. Asceticism existed among Harvard Unitarians in only an attenuated and muted form; one can, however, detect traces of it in Abbot's otherworldly passivity and in some Unitarian literary sentimentality. Abbot espoused the "self-denying virtues" and renounced the "bold, turbulent, and daring" characteristics that made for success in nineteenth-century America. The young man was dismayed by the bustling materialism around him.

> Untouched by all the glories of country, [power men] seem hardly conscious of any relation to a spiritual world and an eternal existence. One can scarcely look without an emotion of . . . Must [the Christian] not feel how different are his views, his interests, his anticipation, from those of others?[30]

This life being but a "transient place of trial," the Christian should renounce earthly ambitions and fix his affections where true joys were to be found—in the next world. Notwithstanding his sense of religious alienation, Abbot was not estranged from his society politically. He produced no searching criticisms of its institutions, but preached contentment, family responsibility, and diligent labor in one's calling. Since everyone who knew him loved him, apparently no one felt threatened by the judgments he passed on his countrymen.

The ascetic search for redemption through suffering was alien to the dominant spirit of New England Unitarianism. Nineteenth-century Yankees generally pursued happiness, not pain. Harvard theodicy did, however, teach that suffering could be a useful device for character development. In consequence, there is a subordinate theme in praise of suffering which runs underneath the Unitarian chorus of joyful aspiration. Levi Frisbie's pupils pondered this question and answer:

Q. "How is it then that sickness and sorrow have a tendency to improve the character?"
A. "They soften the heart, by rendering us more dependent on the good offices of others; they make us feel the necessity of effort; and they serve to introduce religious thoughts and sentiments."[31]

Elements of ascetic teachings can be found in Harvard social theory. Hard work, even more than actual suffering, was useful in the formation of the Christian character. New England Liberals inherited something of the typical Protestant attitude that Max Weber has called "intramundane asceticism." The preaching of industriousness, contentment, and the renunciation of ambition to the poor had such a flavor about it. There was little ascetic about the lives of the Unitarian moralists themselves, however. They relished whatever luxuries their incomes and their provincial society afforded. Buckminster was a connoisseur of foods and wines as well as of books; Norton rode between the Yard and his mansion at Shady Hill in a splendid crested coach. Probably, like European bishops, the Unitarian scholar-moralists would have pleaded in extenuation of their self-indulgence that they were only maintaining the dignity of their station.

The poor, after all, could not avoid suffering. But it would have been asking a lot of prosperous Americans to mortify the flesh deliberately. The Unitarian humanists did not call upon them to do so. Instead, they recommended only that the fortunate *contemplate* suffering. Thus, while John Emery Abbot was convalescing from tuberculosis in Cuba, "he visited the prison, the slave market, and burial place of Americans, where he attended the funeral of a young man, a fellow passenger, and other similar places of suffering. When the fatigue attendant on such exertions was named to him, he replied that it was the duty of a clergyman to make himself familiar with such scenes, as they fitted him for the better discharge of his duty."[32] By acquainting himself with suffering, Abbot was practicing a precept of Harvard moral philosophy: fitting himself for the service of duty. What was a species of vocational training in a minister became a form of character refinement for other middle-class people. Through sentimental literature, many nineteenth-century Yankees tried to reap the moral benefits of vicarious suffering.

For some reason, several of the men who set the tone for the Unitarian awakening had weak, even delicate, constitutions and died young. Besides Abbot, there also come to mind Tuckerman, Buckminster, Frisbie, and Henry Ware, Jr.; the description is also applicable to others like William Emerson (Waldo's father) and Samuel Cooper Thacher, a close friend and co-worker of Buckminster. William Ellery Channing and Francis Bowen lived to be 62 and 79 respectively, but they were both small of stature and spent many years as semi-invalids. Possibly this helped infuse Unitarian preaching with a quality of poetic sadness. Certainly it contributed to the sentimental veneration in which the moralists were held after their deaths. The facts of their lives provided ready material for the nineteenth-century cult of frailty and mortality.[33]

EVANGELICAL UNITARIANISM

Seldom have men been able to indulge such hopes as in newly independent America. The material achievements of the new nation seemed to offer a foundation for unparalleled spiritual achievements. Despite the theological peculiarities that set them apart from their colleagues elsewhere, Harvard professors in the early nineteenth century were not immune to the contagious evangelical mood of their times.

The Harvard moral philosophers, like other evangelists, looked forward to infusing a warm Christian piety throughout the land. Though few people actually enjoyed the mystical peace Abbot did, the Unitarian moralists did not despair. Here on this continent men had more opportunity for self-fulfillment than they had ever known before. Everything would hinge on the ability of the moral elite to awaken Americans to a realization of their true destiny.

One of the most puissant instruments this moral elite possessed was, in their own opinion, the spoken word. In those times before the rise of mass communication, oratory remained a powerful tool for social manipulation; speeches, sermons, eulogies, and debates were all avidly devoured in antebellum America. The Harvard Unitarians attached great value to verbal eloquence and were anxious to take advantage of its persuasive powers. Through the eloquence of the pulpit, Unitarian moralists hoped to arouse Americans to a proper sensitivity toward Christianity and traditional moral values. But oratory not only inspired feeling; it also moved men to action. Through the preachers whom they trained, the Harvard moral philosophers aspired to bend the will of the people toward the religious and social objectives they held dear.

New England Liberal Christians were more than participants in the Second Great Awakening; they were among its pioneers. They were, for example, clearly among the first to challenge the Calvinist doctrine of moral inability that nineteenth-century American evangelists so largely abandoned. They were also among the first to put into their preaching that "new emphasis upon God's love and holiness" which became "the characteristic note of nineteenth-century evangelical Protestantism."[34] Such evangelical concerns as ecumenical catholicity and the primacy of ethics over dogma were manifested early among the Arminians of Massachusetts. Long before Miss Plummer of Salem endowed her evangelical "professorship of the heart" in 1856, Harvard had had its proponents of "experimental preaching."[35]

Both Edward Tyrell Channing (the Boylston Professor of Rhetoric and Oratory) in the College and Henry Ware, Jr. (the Professor of Pastoral Theology and Pulpit Eloquence), at the Divinity School lectured on the techniques of public speaking and on the opportunities for social leadership the orator enjoyed. The two teachers agreed that the written word could not rival the spoken in power over the affections of men. From their knowledge of classical antiquity, they derived lessons in the influence wielded, for good or ill, by effective public speakers. "The object of eloquence is always the same," Professor Channing told his classes: "to bring men, by whatever modes of address, to our way of thinking, and thus make them act according to our wishes." Exercised by a responsible moral leadership, oratory might work wonders of social transformation. "Preaching is the great instrument for reforming the world," exclaimed Professor Ware.[36]

Preaching was but one of four types of oratory that the Harvard Unitarians recognized (the others were occasional, legislative, and judicial speaking), and the aim of all was to "influence action." "Devotional sentiment and sincere purposes," however necessary, did not suffice to make a preacher effective, Channing taught; they had to be coupled with a knowledge of human nature. The preacher needed as deft a command of the techniques of persuasion "as any other orator." Ever since the seventeenth century, when Massachusetts preachers cultivated the Puritan "plain style," the clergy of the Standing Order had self-consciously contrived their sermons according to psychological and aesthetic theories. Jonathan Edwards in the eighteenth century had applied Lockean psychology to pulpit rhetoric; the Unitarians applied the doctrines of Scottish moral philosophy. As the Boylston Professor put it, "An effect is to be produced by presenting motives to the excitable, impressionable nature of man." Achieving this effect, he warned his students, required a sound philosophical foundation, for rhetoric was as much a "science" as an "art."

Edward Channing's counterpart at the Divinity School defined "experimental" preaching as that which had been scientifically designed to induce certain emotions and desires. Experimental preaching, Henry Ware, Jr., explained, "treats of religion not as a system of truth, but as a spiritual influence." Though the Harvard moralist wished his audience to undertake an elevating "Christian culture," he approached his own task with the down-to-earth attitude of a behavioral psychologist. His sermons were not so much expositions of doctrine as calculated stimulants. "He knew that speculative truth is good for nothing, except so far as it acts on the character, not by sim[ply] being explained, but by being made also interesting to the a[ffections] and urgent to the conscience."[37] The Unitarian philosopher [did not] wait upon supernatural grace to create either piety or virtue; he wa[s an] empiricist trying to produce a religious experience.[38]

Unitarian evangelists found fault with orthodox revivalists, how-ever, because they often failed to observe the proper balances in thei[r] appeals. A responsible orator would only rouse passion when there was "a warrant or justification for passion." The legitimate function of rhetoric was to enlist the emotions in the service of reason and the moral sense. A speaker who went beyond this was a demogague, a revo-lutionary who would overturn the established order of things. During the First Great Awakening, we have been told, Liberal "criticisms of the revival rested at bottom on an objection to the evangelical [Calvinist] evaluation of the place of the emotions in man's psychol-ogy."[39] During the Second Great Awakening, Unitarians again feared that all too many revivalists misconceived the proper role of the reli-gious affections. They preached "as if emotion [per se] were the great end of all eloquence" instead of merely a means to virtue.[40]

The camp meeting provided Unitarians with an object lesson in the evils of "enthusiasm," a word which they defined as "a dispropor-tionate strength of feeling and emotion, such as interferes more or less with the judgment."[41] What Boston Liberals (and many other good men of the Enlightenment) feared about "enthusiasm" was not its rap-tures but its irresponsibility, not depth of feeling but the abdication of the higher faculties. The hysteria which sometimes accompanied reviv-alism disgusted Unitarians; it seemed to rob men of all their individu-ality and reason. Liberal observers deplored the groaning and writh-ing that accompanied the excessive stimulations of some itinerants. The mood of the camp meeting resembled the excitement of "an elec-tion or a lawsuit" rather than that of true religion, one Harvard moral-ist complained.[42]

Among other revivalists, the great Charles G. Finney fell under Uni-tarian condemnation. William Ellery Channing and Henry Ware, Jr., visited the "burned-over district" of upstate New York while Finney's revivals were in progress and came away dismayed. James Walker denounced Finney as a hypocrite and a demagogue.

The inflammatory, or we should rather say, ferocious style of preaching, for which Mr. Finney appears to be distinguished, might easily be practised by a man possessing his peculiar turn of powers, though everything were feigned . . . The coarse passions, and those especially which are expressed in strong and boisterous tones and gestures, are easily affected; and there is something in the violent action of the speaker in such cases, that has the effect to excite him, and make him appear as if he were in earnest.

Walker was especially horrified that Finney should call upon children and servants to report whether their parents and masters were lacking in religious fervor.[43] In the course of their criticisms of nineteenth-century revivalism, New England Liberals recalled the First Great Awakening, and renewed Chauncy's quarrel with Edwards, Whitefield, and Davenport.[44]

Yet Unitarians by no means eschewed emotionalism in their own preaching. The good minister not only appealed to the "cool approbation" of men, Henry Ware the elder admonished a colleague; he imparted to his precepts "a glow of feeling." After all, Ware pointed out, religion was not "merely the act of assenting to the truth"; it represented the satisfaction of a powerful emotional need.[45] But in an age of self-confidence, it might be necessary for the preacher to create the need that religion would supply. The evangelist in Protestant America needed to awaken people rather than to instruct them. John Emery Abbot sensed the situation. The "design" of the Yankee parson, he noted "is less to communicate new truth, than to give impressiveness and efficacy to what is known." President Walker warned Liberals not to "underrate the influence of the *heart,* compared with that of the head."[46] For this reason Harvard instructors assigned Hugh Blair's *Lectures on Rhetoric and Belles Lettres,* which advised would-be preachers to avoid dry speculation and employ emotional appeals.[47] If their own exhortations were somewhat less "impressive" than those of the revivalists, Unitarian evangelists hoped they would be even more "efficacious."

Under the spell of the Second Awakening, Liberal clergy could rise to strong exhortations to their congregations for emotional commitment. At the Brattle Street Church, young Buckminster reminded his parishioners that "if God is to be loved, he is to be loved supremely." No source of infidelity was "half so much to be dreaded and to be lamented as that profound supineness and indifference to religion, which sometimes assume the name and honors of liberality." An evangelist demanded heartfelt conviction. Even "superstition" and "fanaticism" (that is, Catholicism and Calvinism) were preferable to the covert deism of those whose hearts were dead.[48] After Buckminster's efforts were cut short by epilepsy, Liberal leadership passed to the Federal Street Church, where William Ellery Channing continued the work of evocation. "The saddest spectacle in this or any world," Dr. Channing warned, is a man "smitten with spiritual death, alive only to what is material and earthly, living without God and without hope."[49] One of the most remarkable religious awakenings among the Unitarian churches of Boston was achieved at the Second Church under the leadership of Henry Ware, Jr. The smallest and least well-endowed parish in the city when he took it over in 1816, this historic institution (it had been the church of the Mathers) enjoyed a genuine renascence under Ware. "A man of rare religious genius," as one of the Transcendentalist ministers called him, Ware carried his evangelical ardor to Cambridge when he inaugurated the professorship of pulpit oratory at the Divinity School in 1830.[50]

Even appeals to the rational powers could be undertaken in an evangelical manner by Unitarian preachers. At the North Church in Salem, John Emery Abbot remembered to invoke the aid of prudence when exhorting his flock. The Gospel of Christ "draws its most powerful motives from its revelations of a future world," he warned. "We are thus continually called to consider consequences, and to look beyond this world to that of final retribution." The Day of Judgment loomed ominously ahead:

In that last convulsion of nature, the sun shall be turned to blackness, and the moon into blood, and the heavens being on fire shall be dissolved, and the world pass away with a great noise. Then shall the Son of Man come in his glory with all the holy angels and with a mighty shout. And the trumpet shall sound, and the dead shall arise, and all that ever breathed upon the earth shall stand before him in judgment . . . My friends, if these things are so, what should now be our conduct?[51]

Abbot's eschatological vision, while no doubt an extreme example, shows what Liberal religion was like at its most pietistic and evangelical.

The Unitarian evangelists did not forget to pay homage to the highest of human faculties. Conscience was so important a part of religion to them that in practice they made little distinction between awakening piety and invigorating men's moral powers. Professor Ware specified just how the appeal to the conscience should be carried out. Some people habitually paid so little attention to the light of conscience that they needed to be reminded of the very existence of a moral sense. Still others took note of only the most glaring obligations while remaining insensitive to nuances; they had to have their conscience "quickened" by moral taste. Most men needed guidance in applying the obligations of morality to the situations of everyday life.[52]

The awakening of conscience was indispensable to true religion, concluded Ware. Among the faculties, only the moral sense could be absolutely trusted. Here none of the qualifications that hedged about the other faculties applied. Though "moderation" might be the watchword for both the intellect and the emotions, no such limitation governed conscience. By definition, conscience could not be indulged excessively. All the historic evils of mankind—wars, persecutions, obscurantism—stemmed from "errors of the understanding or perversions of the feelings," that is, from the weakness of reason and the affections. These evils could have been avoided by an aroused conscience, equipped to enforce its rule over the other faculties.[53] The religion of the future, the Liberal Christianity that would take shape in America, would be a religion of the conscience. It would be a religion led by moral men, a religion for a moral society.

THE TECHNIQUES OF FOSTERING PIETY

Within a few years after joining the Harvard faculty, Henry Ware, Jr., began to feel that the promise of American Liberal religion was not being fulfilled. After a period of expanding activity around 1805 and another around 1820, Unitarian Christianity seemed to stagnate. In 1835, no longer able to contain his bitterness, Ware delivered himself of some *Sober Thoughts on the State of the Times, Addressed to the Unitarian Community*. It had long been the custom in Massachusetts parishes to hold two services each Sunday (a midweek lecture by the minister was also common) , but Ware observed that attendance by the upper classes at the afternoon service had started to decline. Unitarianism, the professor complained, was "encumbered" with more than its share of lukewarm adherents and "nominal Christians." Taking his approach from the traditional New England jeremiad, Ware warned his co-religionists that they were not living up to the ideals of their faith.[54]

Two years later, James Walker repeated the admonition. Though the evangelists had largely eliminated the threat of deism (if any), the threat of apathy remained. "There is less to fear," Walker counseled his listeners, "from the influence of an *avowed* and *active* scepticism than from the influence of a scepticism which is *unacknowledged and merely passive*." The preacher was appalled to note "the absence of that sensibility of soul by which men are made capable of feeling and appreciating spiritual things." Many Yankees still lay in a "spiritual death," from which they badly needed resurrection.[55]

The reaction of Unitarian moralists to religious apathy revealed their ambivalent objectives. Although they were motivated in part by a desire for the uplift of mankind, they also felt a powerful longing to recapture the spirit of their ancestors. Even while embracing a liberating new theology, Harvard Unitarians could not reconcile themselves to the loss of Puritan piety. The spiritual aspirations of the evangelical Unitarians were both "progressive" and, in a sense, "reactionary." When they were feeling optimistic, the Unitarian moralists could welcome men to expanded horizons and preach the fulfillment of human destiny. But at other times they were more concerned to recover the sentiments (if not the faith) of their fathers. In their dream of a successful awakening, and in their apprehensions of its failure, evangelical Unitarians manifested the mixture of humanism and Puritanism in Harvard moral philosophy.

According to the tradition that New England Unitarians still accepted, the ordinances of institutional Christianity—public worship, preaching, the sacraments—were "means of grace" through which men might find the new life promised in the Gospels. Other means of grace included private devotion and Bible study. All were aids God had given man for the course of progressive regeneration. The most hallowed of them, by long Christian usage, was the Supper of the Lord. The Holy Communion was not only a memorial of Christ's last meal, but also recognized as an "important means of spiritual improvement." Perhaps a wider participation in the sacrament would stimulate Liberal religion.[56] Solomon Stoddard, one of the first great New England evangelists, had shown how to use the communion as a "converting ordinance." Might not Liberal Christians follow his example? In the 1840's, many Unitarian churches in New England threw open access to the Lord's table to all who would come. But the practice garnered only a slender harvest for Liberal evangelists. "Open communion" provided no answer to the nagging problem of spiritual insensitivity. (Contemporaries often remarked that members of the male sex seemed particularly insensible to the appeal of the communion table.) [57]

The failure of open communion to revitalize Liberalism was probably related to the uneasiness Unitarian clergy themselves felt about the sacrament. The younger Ware confessed that the ordinance had been "founded on oriental customs of symbolic instructions and . . . does not coincide with our own institutions." The fact is that to many nineteenth-century Yankees, the central action of traditional Christian worship had become alien and almost meaningless.[58] When Unitarian moralists discussed the historic rite, they tended to apologize for it rather than to expound its significance. It will be recalled that Ralph Waldo Emerson left the Unitarian ministry rather than continue to administer the sacrament. His misgivings were actually widely shared, though few carried them out with such conscientious rigor. In short, Unitarian evangelists found the Lord's Supper more an embarrassment than an asset.[59]

Harvard moralists described the benefits one might hope to receive from communion as they described the benefits of prayer—in strictly naturalistic terms. The Lord's Supper, one of them cautioned, "has no mystical charm, no secret and magic power to bless you against your will. Everything depends on your own sincerity and devotion."[60] In effect, then, only those who already were on the road to regeneration could profit by the sacrament. Before a man could benefit from communion, "he must cherish the right disposition."[61] Everything came back to the need for a reawakening, and the responsibility for the reawakening remained with the minister. Unless he could persuade men to "make the experiment" and come to the Lord's table prepared to find grace, even the divine ordinance could have no effectiveness.

American Protestants in the early nineteenth century, wrestling with many of the same problems, came to many similar conclusions. One of these was that religious experience could be psychologically induced. The Unitarian indifference to the role of supernatural grace in the process of regeneration was followed in practice—and, to varying degrees, in theory—by most Trinitarian evangelists. Though his activities in the burned-over district were condemned in Cambridge, Charles G. Finney had a philosophy of evangelism that bore much resemblance to the one taught at Harvard. A revival, he declared, "is not a miracle, or dependent on a miracle in any sense. It is a purely philosophical result of the right use of the constituted means."[62] Antebellum Christian intellectuals were willing to resort to the secular to promote the spiritual, to rely on craft to induce sincerity.

In their efforts to remedy the emotional lacks of their society, Unitarian evangelists employed various techniques. It had long been the custom in Congregational pulpits for the minister to write out most of his sermons in advance and read them to his people. The Liberal preachers of Buckminster's day, influenced by European models, elaborated the traditional New England sermon form into polished essays, rich in refined sentiments. After a few years, however, Unitarian evangelists changed their tack, and took up extemporaneous preaching. Uneducated revivalists had long harangued the ignorant without benefit of a manuscript, but for the clergy of the literate to preach thus was a new departure. The new mode made it harder to discuss technical ideas, but it was defended on the ground that it offered greater scope for an appeal to the emotions. "The peculiar earnestness of spontaneous speech is, above all others, suited to arrest the attention and engage the feelings of an audience."[63] By the second quarter of the nineteenth century the practice of preaching with few, if any notes had gathered momentum. Unitarian ministers of this era looked back upon the sermon style of their predecessors as having been too formal. While continuing to revere the memory of Buckminster, they did not always follow his example in preaching, but often preferred to emulate other professional men, such as lawyers and legislators, who spoke extemporaneously.[64] "Religion ought to be dispensed in accommodation to [the] spirit and character of our age," the foremost Unitarian clergyman decided. He advised a colleague to preach alternately extemporaneously and from a manuscript, in order to strike the proper balance between heart and head.[65]

Unitarian evangelists were anxious to adopt methods which worked for respectable Trinitarian preachers. William Ellery Channing delivered many sermons on "affecting" subjects, with spiritual references that might have been made by any mainstream Protestant. Buckminster led his people in prayers that employed conventional Anglican rhetoric more for hortatory than theological reasons. John Emery Abbot even resorted to an imitation of time-worn Calvinist techniques.

Consider what prayer is—a direct address to the Lord God Almighty, to Him whose word brought all beings into existence; on whose will all, every instant, are dependent, and at whose word all would vanish and be annihilated: to Him in whose sight the heavens are unclean, and the myriads of glorified spirits that bow before him are impure. An address, too, offered by beings such as we are, frail, ignorant, erring, guilty creatures of the dust, whose strength is but weakness, whose best services are polluted, and who are continually offending that God whose awful presence we would enter.[66]

Through such old-fashioned rhetoric, the Unitarian evangelists tried to regain something of the old piety.

In the early years of the century, New England Liberals had been disposed to disguise their theological opinions in cryptic phrases to avoid weakening the Standing Order. But even after schism and disestablishment, Unitarian preachers continued to rely on traditional

Christian symbols. The new wine of Liberal theology was kept in old bottles bearing their accustomed labels. Prospective ministers were instructed to preach down to their congregations, even if this meant not being completely honest with them: " Never allow yourselves to be carried away by the whim that frankness and honesty require you to proclaim your modern flights into the clouds—to tell of your visions, or to declare every opinion of your own. The physician does not tell the patient all he knows about his disease, for it might be the death of him."[67] Ware's injunction reveals both paternalism and timidity. Of course, antebellum Unitarians were by no means the only clergymen who have employed this tactic of reticence. The price paid for its widespread use was an eventual decline in the intellectual standards of the American Protestant pulpit.

One of the most characteristic techniques for fostering piety employed in the Liberal awakening was the use of sacred music. Congregational hymn-singing had gradually replaced the "lining-out" of psalms in New England during the course of the eighteenth century. While the use of hymns transcended religious party lines, evangelical-minded Liberals were especially enthusiastic about their introduction. Most of the hymn lyrics were imported from England, and the favorite hymnographers were theologically liberal Dissenters like Philip Doddridge, Anna Letitia Barbauld (1743–1826), and, of course, the great Isaac Watts.[68] Along with hymns came the admission of musical instruments into New England meeting-houses. King's Chapel retained an organ from its Anglican past; the Brattle Street Church installed one in 1790; and within a generation most other Unitarian churches had followed suit. In the early nineteenth century Boston Liberals took another important step: they introduced professional choirs to replace singing by the congregation. The justifications offered by the Harvard moralists for this controversial action reveal that singing had ceased to be primarily an offering to the glory of God, and had become instead a device to "excite" the affections of the people. Professional choirs produced a more pleasing "religious effect," explained the *Christian Examiner*. At the Harvard bicentennial celebration in 1836, the new ode "Fair Harvard" was sung by a professional choir at the First

Church in Cambridge (Unitarian) .[69] The founders, whose Bay Psalm Book had proclaimed that "God's altar needs not our polishing," would have grieved.

The Unitarian preoccupation with improving the quality of church music was part of a more general tendency in the nineteenth century for Protestants in many areas of the world to return to religious ritual and aesthetic appeals. After hundreds of years of self-conscious plainness, a reaction toward the long-deplored "romish" ways finally set in.[70] One might even say that, in its own way, the religious awakening of Boston was a muted counterpart of the Oxford Movement in the Church of England. Unitarians began to decorate their church buildings with chandeliers and stained glass; after Appleton Chapel was erected in 1858 the Plummer Professor of Christian Morals who conducted Harvard's services there made use of elaborate ritual as well as music.[71] Some of the ideas for ceremonial changes came from King's Chapel, where a predominantly Anglican order of service continued in use even after the conversion of the congregation to Unitarianism. But of course, by its very nature, Unitarianism could never satisfy the yearnings for a devotional aesthetic as well as Episcopalianism itself. Like the Oxford Movement, the Unitarian awakening sometimes only whetted men's appetite for organic traditionalism and emotional satisfaction. By the mid-nineteenth century, many prominent Bostonians had converted from Liberalism to Episcopalianism. The climax of this development came on January 19, 1860, when Frederic Dan Huntington resigned as preacher to Harvard University to take Episcopal Orders.[72]

Despite all its devices, evangelical Unitarianism was ultimately a disappointment to its proponents. The gains registered for the Liberal faith in the first quarter of the nineteenth century were not followed up effectively in the remainder of the pre-Civil War period. Unitarian evangelists were slow to move outside their own geographical area and social class, and, as a result, missed many opportunities. At first missionary efforts did not even seem desirable to them. When Dr. Channing declared that "there is not on earth a body of men who possess less of the spirit of proselytism than the ministers of this town and vicinity," he was not apologizing; he was boasting. Henry Ware, Jr., not only declined an offer of a pulpit in New York City, but also discouraged those of his colleagues who were tempted to leave the neighborhood of Boston for posts elsewhere.[73] One of the most promising projects for diffusing Unitarian principles was a plan, mooted in 1827, for a seminary in New York State to be operated jointly by the Harvard Unitarians and the "Christian Connection" (not the Disciples of Christ but a sect of Unitarian Baptists prominent in the burned-over district). Notwithstanding the close theological affinity between the two groups, their cooperation foundered on the rock of class distinctions.[74] The foundation of a seminary at Meadville, Pennsylvania, in 1844, proved to be too little and too late. Even within their home grounds, the Unitarian moralists did not bring many people back to the communion table. In the years after about 1825, Unitarianism fell behind in the rush of evangelical Protestant activity in America, and it declined in relative importance as a denomination.[75]

The shortcomings of Unitarian evangelism were, one suspects, felt keenly by the Harvard moralists. Harvard rhetorical theory taught that only a person who had experienced an emotion himself could hope to arouse it in others. Although this was a universal rule of oratory, it was particularly applicable to the creation of refined sentiments like piety. "The great essential requisite to effective preaching," according to the younger Ware, was "a devoted heart." "Coldly and feebly will he inculcate that truth, which has made no impression on his own heart," his father warned a young ordinand. "The life and sensibility which we would spread must be strong in our own breasts," acknowledged William Ellery Channing. By implication, then, the deficiencies of Unitarian evangelists may have seemed an indictment of their "sincerity" as well as of their "art."[76]

As an ecclesiastical enterprise, the Unitarian awakening was a failure. Liberal moralists sought consolation in their optimistic view of human nature. "Religious sensibility is an essential element in man, and, however smothered for a time, it will break forth again with power," predicted Channing.[77] It was left to the Transcendentalist "church reformers" (as they have been called) to revive the fervent emotions Jonathan Edwards had aroused a century before.[78]

VII / Genteel Letters

LITERATURE was, for the Unitarian moral philosophers, an important means of social control as well as an invaluable aid to personality development. It helped form the taste, refine the sentiments, and determine the manners of a people. As theology ceased to dominate the New England mind, literature attracted more attention than ever before. Though converts might not crowd Unitarian churches, Harvard moralists did not despair. To supply the moral and spiritual needs of their society—needs for which the mechanisms of institutional religion appeared no longer adequate—Unitarian moralists turned to elevating literature. Liberal Christians were among the leaders in that campaign to develop an American literary culture which followed the formation of the new nation. It is safe to say that no other religious denomination in the country devoted so large a proportion of its energies to literary activity, or reposed so much confidence in belles lettres. Indeed, Harvard Unitarianism probably had its greatest impact on American society through its influence on American letters.[1]

THE MAN OF LETTERS

As the youngest of the twelve Unitarian moralists, Francis Bowen never knew Joseph Stevens Buckminster, but, like all literate Bostonians of his day, Bowen knew Buckminster's achievements well. After the political turmoil of the Revolution and Confederation—an era conservatives shuddered to think about—Buckminster had helped restore order through "the cultivation of literary taste and the quiet pursuits of the scholar." Furthermore, Bowen acknowledged, Buckminster had shaken off the dour old Puritan "plain style" in literature, and introduced Yankees to "the more animated and impressive manner, the unction" of European literary models.[2]

174

Unitarian writers marveled at Buckminster's contributions to Boston literary culture. To his awed contemporaries, the energetic and sophisticated young minister seemed "one of the most eminent men whom our country has produced." His friend Samuel Cooper Thacher credited Buckminster with fusing English neoclassic and French preromantic standards of taste. George Ticknor remembered him as the man who brought German learning to New England. Andrews Norton likened Buckminster's sermons to "the ethereal and dazzling eloquence of Edmund Burke."[3] Unitarian hagiographers seemingly vied with each other in praising "the singular grace of his oratory, his wonderful social charm, his eager and diligent enthusiasm as a scholar." Forty years after Buckminster's death, they said, "there were Boston merchants who could not speak of him without tears." Looking back from the vantage point of the 1880's, Joseph Allen concluded that Buckminster's literary enterprises had been more significant in the history of Unitarianism than Henry Ware's election as Hollis Professor.[4]

Buckminster also played an important role in the forming of Unitarian social attitudes. As a Massachusetts clergyman of the postrevolutionary generation, he was keenly aware that his profession no longer exercised the power in Commonwealth affairs it had wielded in the days of the Mathers. Born to a family of piety, learning, and political conservatism, he resented the rise of popular political leaders during the Revolutionary period.[5] Such men, Buckminster sensed, posed a challenge to the status of Harvard-educated clergy as social arbiters. While Americans ignored their scholars, he complained, "every blustering demagogue who strutted his hour upon the stage of our revolution has come down in triumph to posterity."[6] Buckminster's answer to the problem of providing society with safe leadership was to broaden the base of the moral elite.

Buckminster came to grips with an obvious fact of New England society at the end of the eighteenth century. No longer did the clerical profession comprise the entire intelligentsia; other professions—especially the law—had risen to prominence. No longer could the clergy hope to perform their traditional functions alone. Significantly, whereas in the seventeenth century over half of the Harvard College graduates had entered the parish ministry, by Buckminster's time the

proportion was down to about one fifth.[7] If the moralists were to preserve their influence, they would have to expand their appeal. Buckminster envisioned a class of educated gentlemen, who, substituting
polite letters for theology as a medium of expression, might continue
to perform the function of New England intellectuals. These gentlemen-scholars would set the moral tone for society and regulate the
public taste. As the nucleus of such an expanded moral elite, Boston's
clergymen could retain their position of leadership.

In 1803 Buckminster founded Boston's first literary gentleman's
club, the Anthology Society. Of its original fourteen members, six
were clergymen, three were lawyers, three were merchants, and two,
physicians. All were Unitarians save one: the Episcopal rector of Trinity Church, J. S. J. Gardiner. Later, the nonclerical membership was
substantially increased.[8] Buckminster and his fellow Anthologists
established a "reading-room" that developed into the Library of the
Boston Athenaeum. During his visits to Europe, Buckminster gathered valuable books for both the Athenaeum and his own personal
library (the largest in New England).[9] The Society also put out a critical journal, the *Monthly Anthology and Boston Review,* "containing,"
its title-page proclaimed, "sketches and reports of philosophy, religion,
history, arts, and manners."[10] Suffice it to say that the *Monthly Anthology* was simultaneously a Liberal religious organ, a Federalist political
manifesto, and the precursor of the genteel tradition in American literature. The first volume also made clear the *Anthology's* advocacy of
Unitarian moral philosophy: it reprinted Richard Price's essay "On
the Principle of Action in a Virtuous Agent."[11]

Buckminster's literary efforts enjoyed a considerable measure of success. The Athenaeum grew, and set the example for other libraries.
The *Monthly Anthology* struggled against the commercial distress of
embargo and European war, finally going bankrupt, but it paved the
way for a greater successor. When peace and prosperity returned to
Boston, another society of ambitious young literati was organized, with
Edward Tyrell Channing taking the lead this time. Richard Henry
Dana, Josiah Quincy, and President Kirkland of Harvard were among
its members. Starting in May 1815, these men joined forces with William Tudor, their merchant-patron, to publish the *North American*

Review.[12] Cooperating in these cultural enterprises with businessmen and politically conservative professionals, the Unitarian clergy continued to enjoy high prestige for another generation. Thus it came about that Boston's version of the Second Great Awakening witnessed a revival of letters as well as a revival of piety—and the former was the more portentous. Buckminster's small-scale counterreformation laid the groundwork for New England's literary Renaissance.

Despite his remarkable accomplishments, Buckminster never seems to have outgrown a certain personal immaturity. His private journals (which may still be found in the Boston Athenaeum) reveal a self-centered, rather snobbish, young gentleman-of-the-world, quite different from his public image as a devoted scholar and affecting preacher. But it was the public man who entranced educated Boston, and for whom the city mourned magnificently in a great funeral after his sudden death (from epilepsy) in the summer of 1812. Thirty years later his remains were moved, with appropriate ceremonies, to rest beneath an imposing monument in the new Mount Auburn Cemetery. The Buckminster legend had become a part of literary Boston's self-identification.

THE DANGERS AND DUTIES
OF THE MAN OF LETTERS

The central document of Buckminster's campaign for the creation of an American literary elite is the address he delivered before the Harvard Society of Phi Beta Kappa on August 31, 1809, entitled "The Dangers and Duties of Men of Letters."[13] In that speech, the ambitious young preacher set forth his hopes and fears for America's cultural destiny. Among those in the audience was Edward Everett, the future Whig politician, who in later years remembered the "indescribable charm" of the speaker and the "sterling sense" of his words.[14]

It were better to have lived in Athens than in Assyria, began Buckminster, better to dwell in a republic of letters than in a mighty empire. Yet, looking ahead, the speaker felt more confidence in America's future physical growth than in her intellectual progress: "In the usual course of national aggrandizement, it is almost certain that those of you who shall attain to old age will find yourselves the citizens of an empire unparalleled in extent; but is it probable that you will have the honour of belonging to a nation of men of letters?"[15] With this question, Buckminster raised the apprehensions of his academic audience. Then, employing the convention of the jeremiad, he compared the sorry state of the New England intellect of his own day with the high standards of colonial times. They were giants in those days, sons of the Puritans acknowledged; they were "more accomplished scholars" and "conversed more familiarly than their children with the mighty dead."

Buckminster laid the blame for this intellectual declension on the American and French Revolutions (his maternal grandparents, the Stevenses, had been Tories). No doubt it was true that New England educational institutions had suffered seriously during the turmoil of war and inflation, yet Buckminster focused his complaints not on these factors but on the democratic ideals the revolutions had fostered. Of course, he was harshest in his condemnation of the French Revolution, which had left a "foul spirit of innovation and sophistry . . . not yet completely exorcised" in its wake. Buckminster took it for granted that the "pernicious notion of equality" was inimical to literary achievement, for he assumed that literature was based on the classical education of a leisure class. The American educational system, this elitist feared, showed the defects of egalitarian ideology. "A little observation of the state of knowledge in this country brings to mind the remark of Johnson on the learning of Scotland: 'that it is like bread in a besieged town, where every one gets a little, but no man a full meal.' So it is among us. There is a diffusion of information widely and thinly spread, which serves to content us, rather than to make us ambitious of more."[16] With neither the social nor the intellectual climate favorable, America had not developed a class of gentlemen-literati.

The two revolutions had not only distracted men from the cultivation of humane learning, observed Buckminster sadly; they had brought classical education itself into disrepute. The educational traditionalist had good reason to be disturbed. New England in early national times was the scene of a renewed "battle of the books," in which the old-fashioned classical curriculum came under attack from proponents of a more utilitarian system of education. The "ancients," as the defenders of the classics were called, were roundly condemned by the "moderns," who felt vocational training would be more useful in building the new nation.[17] Buckminster turned the logic of the "moderns" against themselves, by arguing that a classically educated elite could serve a socially useful purpose. They would "direct our taste, mould our genius, and inspire our emulation"; in fact, they would be "the depositories of our national greatness."

If America were to achieve a national literary culture, the intellectual must carve out some kind of a niche for himself in American society. Buckminster proceeded to describe what he conceived to be the responsibilities and the temptations of educated men—"the dangers and duties of men of letters." In the first place, they must avoid political "factions" and not seek to ingratiate themselves in popular favor. On the other hand, they should not flee into scholarship as a shelter from public responsibility. "In the actual state of the politics of our country, this opposite temptation has been already felt by many studious minds," Buckminster acknowledged. Some intellectuals, he was sorry to say, retreated to their libraries "to enjoy a certain mild delirium of the mind, regardless of the claims of society."[18]

Neither demagogy nor withdrawal, but responsible moral leadership was the duty of the man of letters. The scholar should never forget the debt he owed society, his family, and the church, who had given him his education and advantages, and whom he should repay with the very practical service of moral guidance. "Learning is not a superfluity," Buckminster warned, "and utility must, after all, be the object of your studies." As model moral leaders, he held up the examples of the natural theologian Paley ("who makes truth intelligible to the humblest"), the preacher Fénelon ("who imparts the divine warmth of his own soul to the souls of his readers"), Dr. Johnson, and Lord Chief Justice Mansfield. When he became specific about the social responsibilities of the intellectual, Buckminster's own political bias was quickly revealed. Though he claimed intellectuals should be above "factions," in practice Buckminster equated support of conservative factions with responsible leadership. He considered the conservative political activities of Cicero and Burke perfectly legitimate but deplored the "temporary degradation" of Milton's genius to the service of a revolutionary movement.

Buckminster's conservative social views provide the key to understanding his hopes for the future. The Unitarian moralists expected American society to become more stratified, with economic power more consolidated. From Buckminster's standpoint, this augured well for the development of literature. Like most Harvard Unitarians, he anticipated an alliance between the power of wealth and the power of intellect. "Go to the rich," he advised New England scholars, "and tell them of the substantial glory of literary patronage!" Buckminster did not doubt that the merchants could be persuaded to sustain a literary elite. What was good for Boston businessmen would be good for American literature.[19]

Though he had begun his speech on a note of fileopietistic self-criticism, Buckminster quickly shifted to a tone of optimism. In a little while, America might be less troubled by the "want of leisure" and the "necessity of turning our knowledge to immediate account" that had crippled the cultural achievements of the present generation. "If we are not mistaken in the signs of the times, the genius of our literature begins to show symptoms of vigour, and to meditate a bolder flight; and the generation which is to succeed us will be formed on better models, and leave a brighter track."[20] Twenty-eight years later to the day, Ralph Waldo Emerson delivered his "American Scholar" address to the Harvard Society of Phi Beta Kappa. Buckminster's prophecy that his own generation would be followed by a greater one was fulfilled. The young Brahmin conservative would have been unpleasantly surprised, however, to learn that the mood of New England's greatest literary flowering would be one of radical antitraditionalism.

THE LITERARY MORAL ELITE

If the Transcendentalist Unitarians broke away from the pattern that Buckminster had prepared for the American scholar, many Harvard Liberal Christians did not. A genteel tradition in Cambridge and Boston maintained conservative literary ideals until well after the Civil War. New England Unitarians conceived of culture (including literature and art) as something consciously contrived and morally prescriptive. Within this framework, Brahmin intellectuals struggled to balance social conservatism with social reform, cultural nationalism with cultural cosmopolitanism, and their elitist ideals with increasingly democratic facts.

The Harvard Chapter of Phi Beta Kappa provided an ideal forum for Unitarian moralists to voice their cultural aspirations, and there, in 1827, James Walker rose to repeat Buckminster's call for an American literary moral elite. Walker deplored the egalitarian notions with which Americans were deceiving themselves, and declared that what the country really needed was a literary establishment of gentlemen-scholars, to form "the taste and intelligence of [the] people on all subjects."[21] A good many years later, when Walker became president of Harvard University, his ideas on the topic had changed little. He still believed in an intellectual elite, distinct from the moneyed elite, yet allied with it to keep out "follies and extravagances."[22]

Another exponent of this conception of America's proper culture was Andrews Norton. Like Buckminster and Walker, Norton considered that a major stumbling block to the attainment of a true national culture was American democracy. "In this land, where the spirit of democracy is everywhere diffused, we are exposed, as it were, to a poisonous atmosphere, which blasts everything beautiful in nature and corrodes everything elegant in art." As early as 1805 Norton had been calling for someone to set the standards of taste in America (as, he suggested, Addison had done for Britain).[23] When Levi Frisbie was inaugurated Alford professor of moral philosophy, Norton looked to the new incumbent with high expectations for cultural leadership. "The literature which we want is effective, practical, useful literature, the literature of the intellect and the heart. The men whom we particularly need are those who may guide and form public opinion and sentiment in matters of taste, in morals, in politics, and in religion; men who will think and write like [Levi Frisbie.]"[24] Unfortunately Frisbie died before he had a chance to fulfill his friend's hopes. Alienated from the dominant trends of the Age of Jackson, the first sage of "Shady Hill" (the house in Cambridge where Andrews' son, Charles Eliot Norton, also lived) was left to cry through the years of America's need for "literary men."

Henry Ware, Jr., joined the other Unitarian moralists in espousing the view that the intelligentsia properly formed a special class, with special moral obligations. Whereas Norton, Walker, and Buckminster had complained mostly about American democracy, however, Ware perceived the enemy as materialism. In his conception, the literary moral elite had the responsibility of elevating society out of the strictly mundane to spiritual goals, much as the moral sense might be expected to do for the individual. "The development of the public resources, the rapid advancement in wealth, the spirit of enterprise, all tend to bind men's hearts to the world," Ware warned. "Who are to make opposition to this tendency? Who is to give strength to the principles of truth and higher interests?" The answer was clear: "There must be these men, who shall hold intellect and law and truth supreme; . . . whose profession it shall be to see to it that the love of gold, the passion for display, the thirst for power, the appetite for pleasure, do not get the ascendancy in the community."[25] Ware's condemnation of the mercenary ethos reminds us that the literary moral elite he envisioned were to prescribe the goals of society, and judge society when necessary. The Unitarian man of letters, like the colonial clergyman, was supposed to be a moral leader, and his function was not confined to rationalizing the status quo. With characteristic optimism, the Harvard Unitarian philosophers hoped that Yankee businessmen would follow and support a group of potential social critics.

Among Unitarian prophets of American cultural development, none stood higher than William Ellery Channing. His essays on Milton, Fénelon, and Napoleon had already won him international recognition when, in 1830, he addressed himself to the basic issues of American culture.[26] Channing's "Remarks on National Literature" expressed the fear that "however we surpass other nations in providing . . . elementary instruction, we fall behind in . . . forming great scholars." The good pastor was not one to disparage America's achievement of mass literacy, but he did observe that amidst much "superficial knowledge," there was little "devotion to high intellectual culture." As a result, he pointed out, Americans still "rely chiefly for intellectual excitement and enjoyment on foreign minds."[27] In calling for a national "literature," Channing, like the other Harvard moralists, had in mind not only creative writing, but liberal scholarship and humanistic pursuits in general. The American people must be taught the "usefulness" of history, poetry, pure science, and—"above all"—moral philosophy. Only when America had developed her own intellectual leaders would she have attained real independence; for "the true sovereigns of a country are those who determine its mind, . . . its taste, its principles, and we cannot consent to lodge this sovereignty in the hands of strangers."[28]

The tensions between moral leadership and conservative apologetics, and between elitism and democracy, were related to a third source of strain in New England Unitarian literary thought. This, as Channing's remarks illustrate, was the tension between nationalism and cosmopolitanism. Though the Harvard moralists aspired to create an American national culture, they defined their objective largely in Old World terms. Thus, while the Federal Street minister's brother, Professor Edward Tyrell Channing, feared the power of British reviews to stultify American literary efforts, the critical standards he wished native journals to apply were patterned on British models. Dr. Johnson, not Noah Webster, was the authority on English usage whom members of Buckminster's Boston Anthology Society accepted.[29] Even while responding to the currents of nineteenth-century nationalism, the Unitarian moralists carried over from the eighteenth century a sense of belonging to a trans-Atlantic civilization.

Boston Unitarians bore some resemblance to the British Whig aristocracy, and the comparison would have pleased the Harvard moral philosophers.[30] There can be little doubt that the Unitarian moralists would have liked to create a Yankee cultural "establishment" modeled on the clubs, the universities, and the literary reviews of Britain. Writers in the *Monthly Anthology* looked enviously upon the Anglican ecclesiastical sinecures that enabled their holders to devote time to literary and scholarly pursuits. When Francis Bowen contemplated English society, he found useful lessons for American political and cultural conservatives.

[Much] of the present aspect of English literature [and] the conservative tone of British politics . . . is to be ascribed to the influences at work within the walls of the two great universities of England . . . We do not refer merely to the number of authors, politicians, and public men, who were educated at Oxford and Cambridge. It is rather the great body of the English gentry, the wealthy, influential, and intelligent classes, who really hold the reins of power in the country, . . . who hear what authors, politicians, and reformers have to say, and then decide upon the character of what they have heard.[31]

At Harvard, the Unitarian moral philosophers were trying to educate responsible, sensitive American gentlemen, comparable to the graduates of Oxford and Cambridge. With the aid of literary institutions like the Boston Athenaeum, they hoped to endow New England with a genteel culture that would be "worthy of commendation even in Europe."[32]

The great respect which Boston intellectuals had for British opinion exposed them to frequent hurt by British snubs. "The educated and reflecting portion of our people, who are naturally cordial well-wishers to England," wrote a pained Francis Bowen in 1856, feel "surprise and indignation at the insolent and domineering tone habitually assumed about everything pertaining to America" in the British reviews.[33] Yet British contempt for America was rooted in aristocratic values whose legitimacy New England Unitarians often admitted. When, for example, the *Edinburgh Review* charged that American cultural attainments were destined to remain trivial as long as the new nation lacked a leisure class, Unitarian moralists were in no position to protest. Unfortunately, Harvard did not dominate American life to the extent that Oxford and Cambridge dominated English life, and the cultivated Unitarian merchant exerted only local influence. Bowen had to admit that "the want of an influential and highly educated class" on a national scale created a serious problem in America.[34]

The deference which the Unitarians of Boston and Cambridge paid to British literary models has been subjected to frequent criticism, both in their own day and since. Orestes Brownson, for one, bitterly condemned Unitarian imitative cultural standards and bared their antidemocratic implications. Henry Adams, in one of his most savage cuts, remarked, "The true Bostonian always knelt in self-abasement before the majesty of English standards; far from concealing it as a weakness, he was proud of it as his strength." The Unitarians did indeed come dangerously close to reversing their Puritan ancestors' ideal, by looking to England to redeem America.[35] However, it is also true that a disproportionately large number of American literary men have emerged out of the context of New England Liberalism. Perhaps, then, the tension between nationalism and cosmopolitanism was invigorating, rather than debilitating, for Yankee culture.[36]

In any case, there was more to the Unitarian concept of the man of letters than mere Anglophilia. The Harvard moralists had a far more exalted opinion of the function of the intellectual than any they could have obtained by observing British attitudes and habits. The Unitarian moralists were trying to maintain the American Puritan conception of the role of the intellectual in an era when literature and humanistic scholarship had largely replaced theology as media of expression. They made use of British models because these were convenient and seemed to help clarify their aspirations; they looked abroad for images of literary men. But though New England Arminians might read Addison or Pope to find examples of fashionable polish, they had acquired their fundamental values at home. Educated men, in the New England tradition to which the Liberals remained loyal, would "descend from their lofty position," if they were to "forsake this honorable vocation" of moral leadership.[37] What really drove the Harvard moral philosophers to their self-appointed task of cultural guardianship was the memory of New England's colonial past, and the sense that they must live up to the Puritan ideal of the "calling" of an intellectual.

THE EPISTEMOLOGY OF ART: COMMON SENSE AESTHETICS

The Harvard moral philosophers belonged to that antebellum American "upper class" (to use William Charvat's words) "which felt itself competent to legislate, culturally, for other classes." According to the aesthetic theory held by Harvard moralists, artistic judgments were statements of fact, and best left to informed experts. The expert most qualified to pass judgment on art was, not surprisingly, the moral philosopher. The Unitarian moralists' literary criticism tended to be "judicial," rather than "appreciative"; they were more concerned to

evaluate a work of art than to understand it.[38] The question they typically asked, upon opening a volume, was not "What is the author
trying to do?" but "How well has the author done what (we think) he
should be doing?"

The definitive exposition of Unitarian aesthetic theory was given by
Edward Tyrell Channing as Boylston Professor of Rhetoric and Oratory from 1819 to 1851. Channing's views on aesthetics were published
posthumously in *Lectures Delivered to Seniors in Harvard College*
(Boston, 1856). The Boylston professor considered that judgments of
aesthetic value were judgments of objective fact. As a good Scottish
Realist, he regarded all matters of fact as having an existence independent of our knowledge of them. Thus, aesthetic standards were
absolute and immutable, depending upon no changing views,
"whether held by an individual, by a school, or by the whole world."
There was no place in this theory for "custom, fashion, or unstable
opinion"; to judge the beauty of something was to judge by "fixed
characteristics."[39] The Boston Unitarian literary journals applied the
same standards of aesthetic absolutism in their reviews of books that
Channing taught in the classroom.[40]

In aesthetics, as well as ethics, the Harvard Unitarians were disciples
of Thomas Reid. The Scottish philosopher had held that aesthetic
taste was a God-given faculty of the mind, just as the moral sense was,
and that we must believe its perceptions refer to intrinsic characteristics. Reid discussed aesthetic taste primarily as an "intellectual power"
(a power of cognition), rather than as a capacity for emotional response.
Judgments of aesthetic value, according to him, were rational verdicts
on the qualities of an external object and not merely descriptions of
the subjective feelings these qualities evoked.[41] Two other philosophers in great favor with Harvard Unitarians who may have disposed
them toward aesthetic objectivism were Adam Ferguson and Richard
Price. The aesthetic theories of these men dovetailed nicely with their
ethical theories. Price, for example, insisted that beauty was a "primary quality" intrinsically present in some objects. Aesthetic judgments, like moral ones, were based upon a recognition of what was
"fitting" or "excellent."[42]

Aesthetics, like all other branches of human knowledge that Scottish common sense philosophy recognized, had its foundation not only in the nature of external things, but also in the structure of the human mind. Not only did beauty have objective existence, but men had a special power for perceiving it. E. T. Channing called this the faculty of aesthetic taste, "an original faculty or operation of the mind, [which] has its laws or principles as fixed as those of any power."[43] The study of aesthetics, then, was at once ontological and epistemological, the study of what beauty was, and of how men came to know it.

The faculty of aesthetic taste, "like any other power," Channing taught, required "a thorough cultivation for a full development." Reid had likewise held that the faculty of taste could be improved through training. The necessity to cultivate aesthetic perceptions was something on which the Harvard moral philosophers were insistent. Knowledge of aesthetic facts, they maintained, was not innate, but acquired. The expert would see more in a work of art than a novice, and the more complex the work, the more important the acquired expertise. The educated elite were, after all, the moral sense of the social organism. When the average man accepted the decisions of the critics on a work of art, he was not so much bowing to an authority as obeying his own instructed mind.

There was more to aesthetics than rational decisions about beauty and fitness; Harvard Unitarians realized that people were supposed to *enjoy* art. Just as the recognition of moral good or evil was followed by an emotion of approbation or revulsion, so the discernment of beauty or ugliness provoked pleasure or disgust. As Reid put it, "Our judgment of beauty is not, indeed, a dry and unaffecting judgment, like that of a mathematical or metaphysical truth. By the constitution of our nature, it is accompanied with an agreeable feeling or emotion, for which we have no other name but the sense of beauty."[46] "For which we have no other name"—Reid's confession was an important one. The Harvard moralists suffered because their nomenclature lacked a specific term for the emotional response to beauty. In their ethical theory, the Unitarian philosophers labeled the power of perception "moral sense" and the dependent emotional reaction "moral taste," but in their aesthetic theory no correspondingly convenient terminology developed. Frequently, they employed the term "taste" to mean both the power of recognizing beauty (a rational function) and the subsequent (emotional) enjoyment.[47] But, though it meant struggling against the poverty of their technical vocabulary, Harvard scholars managed to distinguish "the power of deriving pleasure from beauty" from "the faculty of distinguishing or discriminating between the objects of [aesthetic] pleasure or pain."[48]

Aesthetic taste in the emotional sense—the power of deriving pleasure from beauty—was a "sentiment." Like "moral taste," it was an affection for a rational principle. The two feelings had much in common, Francis Bowen pointed out, for they were respectively "a capacity of being deeply moved and affected by a view of right actions and beautiful scenes."[49] Harvard Unitarians tended to assume that the two capacities would go hand in hand. The man of refined sensibility whom they idealized would have an acute emotional sensitivity to both virtue and beauty.

Besides the ideas of Reid, the Harvard Unitarians drew upon a long tradition of Western aesthetic thought, going back to Plato's concept of beauty as an objective quality identified with orderliness. They invoked quite a number of eighteenth-century British writers: Hugh Blair, Edmund Burke, Lord Kames, Sir Joshua Reynolds, Dr. Johnson, Archibald Alison, and Dugald Stewart among them. These men were by no means fully agreed among themselves upon questions of aesthetics, but the Harvard philosophers seem to have selected from their writings those passages that spoke to their own wants, ignoring the rest.[50] Actually, the Harvard moralists were more concerned to defend the objectivity of literary judgments as a means of maintaining the moral influence of the cultivated class than they were with the specific characteristics of "the beautiful."

Unitarian aesthetic theory obviously manifested the same preoccupation with preserving certainty and order that Unitarian ethical theory did. The aesthetic emotions, like the ethical ones, were to be kept in subjugation to the intellect and cultivated according to "the wholesome discipline of rules."[51] Unitarian aesthetics was also tied to political conservatism. Just as the Unitarians were worried about religious revivalists and political demagogues, they were also concerned about the emergence of a mass literary culture that did not defer to established rules. Only by maintaining a conception of art as something prescriptive and imposed from above could the Unitarians justify their own role as cultural guardians.

But one need not try to explain the Unitarians' views on aesthetics simply in terms of self-interest. The callousness and heedlessness widespread in nineteenth-century America posed a real threat to the values of humane letters. The Harvard moralists shared what Samuel Holt Monk has called "the wholly admirable desire to preserve the humanistic enlightenment of the Renaissance" from the depredations of a philistine society.[52]

THE ETHICS OF ART: DIDACTICISM

The Harvard Unitarians maintained the traditional view, dominant in Western civilization since classical antiquity, that the artist ought to be a moral and religious teacher. The Unitarian moralists took it for granted that the genteel writer would be just as faithful a servant of God as the medieval sculptor had been. As the images of saints and martyrs had made the Gospel vivid for the lords and peasants of a bygone age, edifying prose and poetry were expected to reinforce the sanctions of morality and religion among a literate middle-class people. The artist, then, was conceived as an active influence upon his society. He should not rest content with being a recording observer; it was his obligation to be a "force for good."

Literature, as far as the Harvard moral philosophers were concerned, was important chiefly for its practical effect upon readers. "A large portion of the most effective precepts and exhortations that have been addressed to men," Andrews Norton observed, "have been conveyed to them in some form of fiction." [53] Nor did the moralists value literature only for its explicit exhortations to virtue. Even if it contained no overtly didactic message, a literary work might still fulfill their purposes if it fostered the personal development of the reader, "refining his sensibilities," perhaps, or "softening his heart."

The moral philosophy taught at Harvard made no provision for disinterested artistic creativity. There was something unseemly about reading or writing that served no moral purpose. Modern literature, like the classics, should be read for benefit, not for idle amusement.

"Art for art's sake" would have seemed a frivolous, if not unintelligible, principle to the Unitarian moralists; they expected art, like learning, to serve an ulterior end. The criterion of "moral tendency," which Unitarians employed in philosophy and theology, was invoked in their literary criticism as well. In this respect, the Harvard moral philosophers were strikingly different from some of their southern contemporaries, like George Tucker (professor of moral philosophy at the University of Virginia) or Edgar Allan Poe, who espoused a pure aestheticism.[54]

"Moral beauty," according to the Harvard moral philosophers, was the most suitable subject an artist could treat. Levi Frisbie believed the artist's highest vocation was to depict examples of virtuous behavior: "A rational agent, animated by high principles of virtue, exhibiting the most generous affections, and preferring on all occasions what is just to what is expedient, is the noblest picture which the hand of genius can present." The standards of beauty, after all, were set by the virtuous. Vicious people might enjoy "the gratification of depraved passions," but artists should not pander to their corrupt tastes. Good art was the art good people liked.[55]

An artist was, of course, obliged to speak the truth. Since moral values had the status of necessary truths, an artist who seemed to deny them was guilty of gross falsification. The notion that a well-turned phrase might compensate for moral inaccuracy was indignantly rejected. An artist qua artist must conform to the same absolute standards he must conform to as a man. Since the purpose of art was largely moral, and moral standards were objective, it was altogether fitting that aesthetic standards should be objective too, and, in fact, that aesthetics should be conceived as a branch of ethics. As Andrews Norton put it, "there is nothing false in that splendid revelation of ancient philosophy that perfect goodness and perfect beauty are the same."[56]

Norton's dictum indicates the Unitarians' consciousness of their debt to Plato and various Neoplatonic writers. The Harvard moralists not only subscribed to the Platonic doctrine that the perception of beauty is an intellectual recognition of harmonious interrelationships; they also put Plato's moralistic canons of artistic criticism into practice. Norton endorsed Plato's judgment that Homer and a number of other ancient poets were not morally elevating and hence not good literature.[57] Obviously, the Harvard philosophers accorded literature a more honorable place in their moral armory than Plato had; even so, they evinced some of the same misgivings the ancient Athenian felt about depicting vice in art.[58] The Unitarian moralists were unanimous in asserting that a wise literary artist shrank from portraying evil, lest young readers have their "moral health" polluted. Harvard Platonism was destined to remain an important component of the American genteel literary tradition.[59]

Many Unitarian evaluations of the literary merits of authors inevitably jar a twentieth-century reader. Neither depth nor originality in a writer counted much with them, unless coupled with conventional morality. The earthy eighteenth-century works of Fielding, Swift, and Smollet were roundly condemned, along with some of the unfortunate moral lapses in Shakespeare and Pope. Wordsworth and Sir Walter Scott received high marks, but the greatest favorites of the Harvard moralists were two didactic English ladies, now relatively obscure: Maria Edgeworth (1767–1849) and Felicia Hemans (1793–1835) .

Maria Edgeworth was a novelist who enjoyed considerable popularity with British and American readers in the early nineteenth century, while neoclassical standards were still strong. Andrews Norton made extravagant claims on her behalf: "By the uniform employment of her rare talent to afford gratification to some of our best feelings, and to recommend and strengthen some of our best habits of action, she has conferred obligations upon the world, which entitle her to a reputation as enviable, perhaps, as that of any writer in English literature." In 1834, after Miss Edgeworth's reputation had begun to wane, Norton remained convinced that her contribution to literature and morality would prove lasting. "Miss Edgeworth's works will go to increase the small number of those which form the library of mankind," he asserted. "There is nothing in them of a perishable nature." Perhaps the most remarkable testimony to the esteem in which the Harvard moralists held this woman was Levi Frisbie's praise of Tacitus as the Maria Edgeworth of historians.[60]

Felicia Hemans was the ideal poet of genteel Unitarians, just as Maria Edgeworth was the ideal novelist. If she is remembered today, it is probably for her sentimental poem, "Casabianca" ("The boy stood on the burning deck ...") , a favorite recitation "piece" for nineteenth-century schoolchildren. Mrs. Hemans' lyrics possessed the "holy and purifying power" Harvard moralists were looking for in literature. Andrews Norton brought out a lavish edition of her poetry in the United States, magnificently bound in two volumes. "It is believed that no handsomer or more correct reprint of any foreign author has appeared in our country," he announced proudly. Norton paid Mrs. Hemans royalties on her works, though the primitive international copyright laws of the time did not require it.[61]

Harvard moralists were worried about the flood of popular novels that catered to the enlarged reading public of the nineteenth century. There is an old saying that no young lady was ever ruined by a book. Unitarian moralists were not so sure. The "fair sex" seemed in special danger from corruption by books. Henry Ware, Jr., in a "Letter to a Young Lady," warned her against frivolous literary romances. A girl should be preoccupied with developing a good character and "it is madness to suffer . . . constitutional gaiety or youthful sportiveness to counteract [one's] persuasion of duty." Romantic reading, and the daydreams it encouraged, had no place in the formation of a Christian character.[62] Many of the popular books Unitarian moralists condemned as "trash" certainly deserved the name, though Alexander Dumas and George Sand no longer strike us as dangerously licentious.[63]

To help remedy the paucity of suitable literature for the growing crowd of impressionable readers, a number of the Unitarian moralists themselves wrote didactic fiction and poetry. Norton, Tuckerman, Frisbie, William Ellery Channing, and the younger Ware all tried their hands at creative writing.[64] In their stories and poems, frequently dashed off for occasions of one kind or another, they usually did their best to follow their own literary prescriptions. A favorite theme concerned a young person (with whom the reader would, they hoped, identify) behaving in ethically ideal patterns when confronted with familiar problems. The works of Henry Ware, Jr., offer some good examples. His *Recollections of Jotham Anderson* attempts to inculcate such favorite Unitarian virtues as studiousness and religious tolerance, as well as more obvious ones like piety and domestic affection. "Robert

Fowle," a short story, seems a precursor of the famous tales of Horatio
Alger. (Alger himself, a product of antebellum Harvard, was a Unitarian minister.) Ware's hero is a poor but honest boy falsely accused
of theft, whose Christian virtue pays off in the end.

The defects of Harvard Unitarian artistic judgment are obvious
enough. There remains, however, something to be said in defense, or
at least in palliation, of the Unitarian moralists as critics and writers.
In an era when literature was rapidly expanding its appeal and books
were no longer the luxury of the few, it was natural for scholars to be
concerned with the values disseminated by literature. Indeed, American intellectuals from those times to ours have never ceased to worry
about the moral consequences of popular culture.

In some respects the moralists applied their principles with com-
mendable restraint. Whatever their conventionality and paternalism,
they never went to the extremes of the Englishman Thomas
Bowdler.[65] They compiled no Protestant *Index*. They neither possessed nor desired any power to enforce their judgments upon the
public. Though the Harvard moral philosophers thought there were
sound social reasons why "immoral" books should not be published,
they repudiated government censorship. In literature, as in other
spheres, the Harvard moralists wanted reform to be voluntary and private, and they put their faith in moral suasion rather than coercion.
Good Christian Liberals and optimists, the Unitarian moralists
wanted the average man to think for himself and to form his own opinions. They merely wished to show him how to do this properly.[66]

One can even argue that the Unitarians' critical standards exercised
a liberating effect on American culture. Today, their didacticism
seems narrow-minded and trite; yet in a nation profoundly suspicious
of the arts, the doctrine that imaginative literature could serve a moral
purpose once helped give to creative writing a much-needed legitimacy.[67] The Unitarians were at least willing to grant art an ancillary
function, and the artist a subordinate place, in society.

They were too scrupulous interpreters of religious obligation, who for-
bade to Christians the arts of music and painting, and all ornamental
accomplishments. [The arts] are not, it is true, to be ranked with the
labors of instructors, pastors, magistrates, and philanthropists. But they

fill a necessary place. Society could not well do without them. They are like the inferior members of the body, less honorable than the head and the main limbs, but not therefore to be despised.[68]

Most antebellum literary critics in the North agreed that literature should be judged by moral standards, but the Unitarians had faith where some others feared. Harvard moralists were less restrictive in their literary taste than many of their Calvinist counterparts: Professor Samuel Miller of Princeton, for example, declared that "if it were possible, he would wholly prohibit the reading of novels." Henry Ware, Jr., debated against Miller's contention that the average minister of religion had no business reading fiction. Looking back after sixty years, Josiah Quincy gave Harvard's Levi Frisbie credit for being a pioneer in the view that novels need not be harmful.[69]

THE PSYCHOLOGY OF ART: SENTIMENTALISM

Though the Harvard moral philosophers were consistent "rationalists" in their respect for objective "truths"—ethical, religious, and aesthetic—they did not have a very high estimate of the power of human rationality as a motive to action. The Unitarians believed men ought to be controlled by reason and the moral sense, but they recognized that in practice much, if not most, human behavior stemmed from emotional impulses. Unitarian psychology taught that the will was more dependent on the appetites and affections than upon reason for its impulses.[70] In consequence, it was essential that the emotions be enlisted in the cause of reason and morality. If literature were to fulfill its didactic function, it must arouse the emotions of men. In aesthetics, as in ethics and religion, the Harvard moralists first established objective "truths" through the use of reason, and then devoted their efforts to awakening an adequate emotional response to these putative facts.

Just as conscience needed aid from the affections to control an individual personality, the moral philosophers sought aid from poets and novelists to stimulate the benevolent sentiments of society. The purpose of art was to supply motivation to virtue. It was not enough that a work of art be objectively beautiful or moral; it should also create an emotional impact on the beholder. Of course the writer must limit himself to ends approved by the moral philosopher.[71] Literary sentimentalism, in Unitarian philosophy, was a psychological device for fostering approved emotions. The extraordinary seriousness with which Harvard Liberals took sentimental moralism is illustrated by Andrews Norton's comments upon the speech of the shepherd-boy Sylvius in the closing scene of *As You Like It* ("To love is to be made all of sighs and tears") . What was to Shakespeare a bit of gentle spoofing becomes for the American Victorian a matter of deadly earnestness: "I should hold it little less than prophanity [sic] to attempt to express my admiration" for the lessons of these lines, he declared.[72]

What made sentimentalism seem so important to nineteenth-century Unitarians? In the first place, literary sentimentalism was an instrument of social control. Harvard moralists considered the creation of a national literature essential to the common values and community feeling they were convinced America sorely needed. This literature would address itself to those "benevolent affections" which constituted the bonds of society. They hoped that such affections as family love, patriotism, and philanthropy might be stimulated through literary appeals. Second, and perhaps even more important, literary sentimentalism served a religious function. By arousing a heightened emotional sensitivity, it might aid the progressive regeneration of the personality. Harvard Unitarians took their knowledge of religion and morality for granted; they felt deficient, however, in their emotional responses to this knowledge. Literature provided them with a way of cultivating feeling and developing a Christian character.

As far as the Harvard moralists were concerned, the artist shared the hortatory function of the evangelical preacher: both were dedicated to emotional appeals on behalf of religion and morality. In their middle-class society, fast becoming urban, it made sense to try using the writer as a stand-in for the preacher; "in this age of reading," Edward Tyrell Channing noted, "men do go very generally to books for light upon many religious subjects, and for increased animation to their Christian motives and hopes."[73] The Unitarian moralists hoped to disseminate Christian values through genteel literature. Reading could make a Christian, as well as a gentleman. "In its legitimate and highest efforts, [poetry] has much the same tendency and aim with Christianity"; wrote Professor Channing's clerical brother: "to spiritualize our nature."[74] Through their standards of literary criticism, the Harvard moral philosophers were seeking to prevent the divergence of literature from religion in nineteenth-century America.

The canons of taste laid down by the Scottish clergyman-aesthetician Hugh Blair (1718–1800) offered New England Unitarians an attractive way to make literature serve religion and morality. "Mild, moderate, amiable, well-born, and refined," Blair had promoted much the same kind of clerical literary awakening in his country as they were attempting in theirs. Blair's textbook, *Lectures on Rhetoric and Belles Lettres* (1783), was a favorite at Harvard for many years.[75] The *Lectures* breathed a genial, eclectic spirit; they synthesized preromantic elements with neoclassicism by invoking the gentler emotions inside a framework of superintending rationality. Blair taught that polite letters provided a means of refining the sensibilities and bringing feeling into perfect harmony with judgment. His doctrines answered to the wishes of men who conceived of literature in terms of moral suasion. The *Lectures on Rhetoric and Belles Lettres,* a Unitarian magazine exulted, "brought religion into the parlor."[76]

Edward Tyrell Channing's views on rhetorical technique show the strong influence of Blair and his eighteenth-century standards on nineteenth-century Unitarian sentimentalism. Rhetoric, as the Harvard instructor conceived it, was the science of persuasion, as much a branch of psychology as of aesthetics. Professor Channing was a firm believer in supplementing intellectual argument with the judicious stimulation of the emotions, whether one were a public speaker or a didactic writer. The literary artist should choose his words with careful attention to their emotional impact, he told his classes. "A single word may set the mind on fire, but the word itself must burn." Emotional "excitement" should "follow and mingle with conviction," but could never, of course, "take the place of it." Naturally, the sentimental writer, like the experimental preacher, was expected to share the feelings he aroused. "No poetry affected another, which had not produced a throb in the breast of the poet who wrote it."[77]

So far, nineteenth-century Harvard rhetoric might appear similar to the rhetoric taught at seventeenth-century Harvard, which had also analyzed the psychology of a balanced appeal to the faculties. Yet when one turns from rhetorical theory to practice, sharp contrasts are visible. The graceful sentimentality of Unitarian literary taste was far removed from the sparse utilitarianism of the Puritan "plain style." In fact, could the Puritans have heard a nineteenth-century Unitarian sermon, they would probably have found its style similar to the flowery "carnall eloquence" they detested in Anglican preachers.[78]

As long as the emotions awakened by literature were carefully contrived, Harvard Unitarians assumed they could "work safely" under rational control, without usurping supremacy and becoming "turbulent masters." Indeed, emotions of the proper kind—such as the more elevated "sentiments"—could reinforce the power of the rational faculties. Andrews Norton found Mrs. Hemans' poetry "so full of deep sentiment, so pure and elevating," that it "allies itself to everything belonging to the better part of our nature." William Ellery Channing declared that sentimental poetry could liberate the conscience when "the thralldom of an earthborn prudence" threatened to stifle it.[79] Unitarian sentimentalism always remained subordinate to a rational and moral end. In this respect, Harvard moralists retained their faith in an ordered and hierarchical cosmos.[80]

THE NATURAL THEOLOGY OF ART: LITERATURE AS A MEANS OF GRACE

Christian natural theology, with its teleological argument and its chain of being, led many a Liberal preacher into rhapsodies on the plenitude of creation. The beauty and order of nature that were praised in the pulpit provided obvious themes for lay treatment as well. Among those who rejoiced in the harmony of nature were the scientist and the literary artist.

Unlike some of their romantic contemporaries (such as Whitman and Fenimore Cooper), the Harvard Unitarians sensed no hostility between the scientific and the artistic approach to nature. They conceived of both art and science in terms of the perception of harmonious relationships. "Science and Poetry, recognizing, as they do, the order and the beauty of the universe, are alike handmaids of Devotion," Henry Ware, Jr., informed the eager citizens who crowded in to hear him at the Boston Lyceum.[81] "Natural beauty is an image or emblem of harmonious qualities of the mind," observed William Ellery Channing in accents reminiscent of Jonathan Edwards. "It is a type of spiritual beauty," he continued, employing the ancient Christian convention called "typology."[82] But where Edwards had been attracted by the scientific study of nature, the Unitarians, with generally less rigorous minds, turned to literary appreciations of natural harmony.

Poetic celebrations of God's wisdom in creation offered Unitarians a welcome alternative to theological disputations. "A little flower from the garden-bed" often provided them with "a more convincing argument" for the existence of God than all the logic of the schools.[83] Hence, while they found the formal discipline of theology sterile and unilluminating, theological premises continued to inform their literary efforts. Unitarian writers went beyond a merely didactic, rational use of nature to illustrate God's providence; they drew emotional inspiration from nature and natural descriptions. Natural theology had "spread life over the inanimate creation," giving it power to call up countless imaginative associations, the *Christian Examiner* pointed out. For example, in the continual rebirth of life in nature Unitarians could feel "a secret intimation of the most sublime of human hopes, immortality."[84] By the use of their senses, Unitarians quickened their sensibilities.

From an admiration of the benign contrivance of the universe, New England Liberals moved to a fascination with nature's vastness and infinity. Mountain-climbing in the Alps, Joseph Stevens Buckminster paused at a barren summit to let his surroundings take effect. "Here nature had thrown off the veil, and appeared in all her sublimity," he recalled. "We seemed to have reached the original elevations of the globe o'ertopping forever the tumults, the vices, and miseries of ordinary existence." To express the feelings aroused by the scene, the young tourist quoted:

> Dans ces sauvages lieux tout orgueil s'humanise.
> Dieu s'y montre plus grand; l'homme s'y pulverise![85]

Buckminster's reaction was typical. Harvard Unitarians believed that communion with the awesome powers of nature would nourish their spiritual health, and sought it out on that account. For supposedly "corpse-cold" rationalists, the Liberal moralists were strangely infatuated with the mysterious, the mighty, and the remote.

The Unitarians' delights in the awe-inspiring aspects of nature were summed up for them in the word "sublime." The writings of many eighteenth-century aestheticians, including Reid, Blair, Kames, and the Unitarian political idol, Edmund Burke, were drawn upon in order to explain the full import of this suggestive term; Burke's *Enquiry into the Origins of our Ideas of the Sublime and the Beautiful* (1756) was quoted especially often. Whereas moral philosophers defined "beauty" as an objective quality, "sublimity" was defined subjectively, in terms of the feelings of the beholder.[86] Like patriotism and moral taste, the emotion of sublimity was a sentiment, and one which a sensitive man would cultivate. Vagueness, mistiness, and obscurity were favorable to the experience of the sublime. There was just a touch of fear in the emotion, too; for whatever was sublime was also powerful. Obviously, God, the omnipotent and incomprehensible One, was the ultimate example of sublimity. Unitarian moralists related the sentiment of sublimity to the religious sentiment, for both were responses to infinity. We may assume that Yankee Liberals pursuing the experience of sublimity in nature were essentially seeking a substitute for the Edwardsian experience of God.[87]

The Unitarian relish of sublimity bore overtones of their quasi-Platonic metaphysic. When nature seemed "to lose its material aspect, its inertness, finiteness, and grossness," in mists and distance, then it reminded Unitarians of the world of spirit. When it spread out "into a vastness which is a shadow of the Infinite or when in more awful shapes and movements it [spoke] of the Omnipotent," nature helped lift them out of themselves and into the realm of Eternity.[88] Emotions of the sublime, by drawing out man's own spiritual nature, developed a Christian character. Unitarian moralists invoked the sublime as a counterpoise to the mercenary materialism they feared was hardening the hearts of their parishioners. "An excessive love of the gains of worldliness obscures all the faculties and sentiments," warned Buckminster. "A worldly man . . . has no place for what is sublime."[89]

For the Unitarians (if not for some of their more forceful contemporaries) relish of the sublime implied no spirit of rebellion. Whether nature were misty and evocative, or clear and rational, it always pointed to a benevolent deity. Sublimity, for Unitarians, was a religious sentiment, and no counterpart to the blasphemy of Ahab. Unitarians found the titillations of sublimity pleasurable precisely because they were confident that behind the mist there was an order. Sublimity, after all, was only a subjective feeling; but the beauty of harmony was really "out there."

In their literary criticism, Unitarian moralists always demanded a certain kind of order. They were quite willing to dispense with mere orderliness of form, so long as the fundamental moral order was retained. Thus, the preromantic pastoral poetry of Thomas Gray was a Liberal favorite, for Gray joined his somewhat allusive and sentimental style to a thoroughly "sound" morality.[90] On the other hand, a rigid neoclassical stylist like Dryden disturbed Unitarian critics by his lack of "pathos, tenderness, or delicacy." Dryden, Andrews Norton concluded sadly, "has no sublimity, least of all anything that approaches to moral sublimity."[91] Among romantic writers, there was a world of difference between the Christian moralizing of the elderly Wordsworth and the "satanic" satires of Byron.

The sublimity Harvard moral philosophers approved was a mild and wholesome stimulant. If romantic authors aroused stronger and stranger emotions, however, the old distrust of "passion" reasserted itself. Levi Frisbie objected to *Childe Harold* because its "desolate misanthropy" created "an impression unfavorable to a healthful state of thought and feeling." Faustian, rebellious romanticism shocked and angered the Unitarian moralists. To permit emotions to violate the moral order was to encourage a revolution by passion against reason. Andrews Norton complained that Goethe threatened civilization with "a revolution of taste, or moral sentiments, of philosophy, and of religious faith, as improbable as it would be disastrous."[92] Even the saintly Dr. Channing gloated over Byron's personal misfortunes, "a fit recompense of his guilt."[93]

Romantic writers, of course, were not always content to be constrained within the limitations acceptable to Unitarians. Byron's *Don Juan* provoked the following comments from the *Christian Disciple:*

Thoroughly immoral.

Written in . . . drunken defiance . . . of all that is decent.

Its wit consists in degrading the better and holier affections by association with something mean and vile.

It has been said that there are passages of fine poetry in this publication. It may be so. We are not intrepid enough to admire and relish fine poetry, when found in such a connexion.[94]

Norton's frank admission, "We are not intrepid enough," reveals the subjugation of Unitarian artistic appreciation to conventional moral standards. The delicate, escapist, and artificial emotions of Walter Scott and the female sentimentalists appealed to the Unitarians, but titanic, untamed romantics like Goethe and Byron frightened and repelled them. As literary critics, the Harvard philosophers remained prisoners of their morality.

THE CULTIVATION OF A GENTEEL CHARACTER: LITERARY HUMANISM

"We can often determine to which sect a man belongs by his looks, tone, and gait," observed the *Christian Examiner* in 1829; Liberals "incline to the amiable and pacific virtues," and Calvinists, "to the stern and self-denying virtues."[95] Literary pursuits provided one way in which Unitarians cultivated their amiable and pacific virtues. The "scholar," or man of letters, whom Buckminster praised before the Harvard Chapter of Phi Beta Kappa was not merely—or even primarily—a learned man, and still less a creative artist. He was a sensitive man, a man who had developed all his faculties, moral, rational, and aesthetic. It was less important that he be a man of genius than that he be a man of "taste"; his innate endowments need not be especially great, but he "must have cultured and burnished them." This man was not so much a producer of literature as an educated consumer, not so much an artist as a critic. Such a man was qualified for membership in an aristocracy of talent, virtue, and manners. This was the man who, Unitarians hoped, would become the American *gentleman*.[96]

Buckminster and his Monthly Anthologists belong in that group of late eighteenth- and early nineteenth-century literary men who were searching for "a broader and more intense awareness through the cultivation of feeling."[97] Refinement of feeling, along with refinement of perception, was assumed to be part of the qualification for membership in the Unitarian literary moral elite. Only a man who had fulfilled his ideal nature, who had achieved a balanced personality under the guidance of reason, could perceive the subtleties of true beauty. When a man had realized his full potential for sensitivity, he could legitimately act as the moral and artistic arbiter for society.

There was a close relationship between Unitarian humanism and that of the European Renaissance. Not only did the Unitarians share the Renaissance confidence in man's freedom and potential, they also accepted the Renaissance world view: a unified, hierarchical cosmos, presided over by a beneficent deity who revealed Himself through nature and Scripture alike.[98] The high value Unitarians placed upon such notions as "balance," "toleration," "reasonableness," and "liberality" marks them as heirs of Erasmian humanism. Sixteenth-century Erasmians had striven to escape scholastic logic-chopping, putting in its place a graceful Latin and a simple piety. Three hundred years later, New England Unitarians were combining the pietism of the Second Awakening with the classical flourishes of the *Monthly Anthology*. In biblical studies, Harvard scholars were also following trails blazed by Erasmus. The Unitarian moralists were quite aware of their indebtedness and proclaimed the genial philologist of Rotterdam their hero. Indeed, many Harvard Liberals flattered themselves that they stood in the same relation to orthodox American Protestantism that Erasmus had stood toward Rome.[99] If the pedagogues of Princeton were heirs of Augsburg, Dort, and the traditions of "Protestant scholasticism," then perhaps the Harvard moralists might be called "the Erasmians of the Protestant Counter-Reformation."

Like good Renaissance men, the Harvard Unitarians regarded the arts as a means for man's self-fulfillment. But they added to this a nationalistic aspiration—a hope that the New World might be the place where man would find his greatest fulfillment. The Unitarian moralists became evangelical humanists, trying to awaken Americans to a respect for traditional European cultural values. "Music might here be spread as freely as in Germany," William Ellery Channing pleaded. "What is now wasted among us in private show and luxury . . . would furnish [Boston] with the chief attractions of Paris, with another Louvre."[100] By means of polite culture, the Harvard moralists tried to refine the taste of the American public, and especially that of the wealthier classes in whom they reposed special trust. In this way, they hoped, an isolated provincial people might broaden its horizons and become acquainted with other forms of experience. The intention of the Unitarian literary moral elite was to make Americans not only more religious, but also more cosmopolitan, more sensitive, and more compassionate—in short, more fully human.

The Unitarian moralists' task was complicated, however, by a profound conflict of ideals between them and most of their fellow-countrymen. Typically, early nineteenth-century Americans admired qualities of natural power and untutored genius, rather than cultivation or refinement. The success of political figures like Andrew Jackson demonstrates the hold this attitude exerted upon the popular imagination. A good deal of the best American literature of the period also drew upon this national trait for its inspiration. Melville's Ahab was its most exalted manifestation, all the greater for the ambivalence with which the artist regarded his mythic creation. Even the aristocratic Fenimore Cooper had enough contact with the democratic ethos to extol Leatherstocking and Uncas. But the Harvard Unitarians did not participate in this national romance. Acquired characteristics, not native ones, mattered most to them. No doubt this lies at the heart of their persistent reputation for un-Americanism—a reputation which, in view of their preoccupation with American culture and destiny, is not wholly accurate.

The well-rounded Renaissance (or eighteenth-century) gentleman had other drawbacks as a Unitarian literary ideal. The miscellaneous variety of topics treated in the *Monthly Anthology* illustrates a dangerous dilettantism, while the emphasis on the amateur also had its bad effects.[101] Too often Unitarian intellectuals snubbed the professional artist or scholar in favor of the gentleman who did not "write for money." The founder of the Boston literary Renaissance did not conceal his contempt for those who tried to make intellectual talents yield a living; "every starvling pedant writes for bread" nowadays, he sneered incredulously.[102]

The Boston Unitarians had a tendency to look upon literature too much as a means to the cultivation of a well-rounded character, and not enough in terms of serious achievement. In the long run, this attitude enervated Boston letters. Even after the period we are concerned with, Bostonians continued to prize such writers as Longfellow, Dr. Holmes, and Emerson (when he became domesticated) more as dignified and congenial personalities than as creative artists. In those areas of activity where their humanism could draw the most strength from old Puritan traditions, Harvard Unitarians could still turn in solid accomplishments. Bowen in political economy, Tuckerman in philanthropy, Dr. Channing in preaching, Norton in Bible studies—these were men of energy who lived up to the ideals of Unitarian humanism. So were the great nineteenth-century Unitarian historians. But in the realm of creative literature the humanistic ideal was less well fulfilled. There it turned soft and degenerated into elegance and sentimentality.[103]

The Harvard Unitarians deserve credit for keeping alive an appreciation of the traditional arts in America, but they contributed little that was original in poetry or fiction.[104] The Unitarian literary moral elite did not provide America with artistic trailblazers, but only with custodians for a genteel establishment.[105] The greatness of the New England Transcendentalist writers lay to a large extent in their ability to invigorate their Unitarian literary heritage, reuniting its humanistic aspirations with an authentic Puritan ardor, and then synthesizing it with the American ideals of democracy and natural genius.

VIII / Unitarian Whiggery

MID-NINETEENTH-CENTURY AMERICA has been well characterized as "a capitalistic society in the state of rapid economic and geographical expansion," in which "the social class, the family, the church, and the state, for better or worse, were losing their hold over the individual, their ability to dictate opinions and conduct in the interest of an ideal of community."[1] Such changes in social experience naturally produced alterations in social thought. While the fundamental values cherished by the Unitarian moralists did not change, the methods by which they sought to protect them did. Through various and sometimes shifting tactics, the Liberal moralists fought to preserve good order in America. It does credit to their confidence that they never gave up hope of success, even in a fast-developing country where—as one of them observed—"no man has a fixed position, [and] the imagination is at work continually on the distant and vast."[2]

POLITICAL MORALITY

The Harvard moral philosophers assumed that those who governed should be morally and intellectually qualified for public trust. While they did not necessarily expect office holders to be clergymen or professors (though some were, like Edward Everett and John Gorham Palfrey), they did hope that statesmen would share the values of the moral elite and be willing to follow its guidance. But the faculty of prudence as well as conscience came into play in the complex task of making political decisions; even though the moral ends at which society should aim might be given, the delicate means by which these could be achieved were still discovered only by careful calculation. The special knowledge political leaders most needed was not abstract or logical,

205

but was the practical wisdom of experience. This knowledge would most likely be possessed by men of affairs, the class of "prudent" men whom the moral elite trusted. From the ranks of the wealthy merchants and the liberally educated professional men—that is, from the gentlemen—the political leaders of Massachusetts and the country would (if Harvard moralists had much to say about it) be drawn.

J. R. Pole has described a "Whiggish" outlook common in pre-Jacksonian America which approved patterns of social deference and the near-monopoly of political office by an educated, prosperous elite.[3] The Unitarian moral philosophers tended to carry the political attitudes of this eighteenth-century Whiggery through most of the antebellum period. Every man "entitled to the protection of the laws" is not necessarily "competent to make them," Edward Tyrell Channing cautioned Harvard seniors. Legislators should be sufficiently independent "to do what they hold to be their duty," and not merely defer to those who elected them.[4] By the time Professor Channing's lectures were published in 1856, his Burkean theory of representation had long since been replaced in American practice by the Jacksonian attitude that any honest man was competent to hold office and that legislators should reflect the views of their constituents. Yet, in the same year, the president of Harvard was cautioning the congregation in the College Chapel that public opinion was of little value as a guide to public policy. The masses might have sound basic instincts, but they could not be trusted with complex questions of statecraft. Though a wise statesman would never "needlessly defy" public opinion, James Walker remarked, "he will be more influenced by conclusions deliberately arrived at by a single individual of an honest and gifted mind, who has really examined the subject for himself under the best lights of an advancing science and civilization, than by the consent of many thousands, where this consent is obviously a matter of tradition, or policy, or sympathy, or drill, or mere echo."[5] The Unitarian philosophers held high the torch of Enlightenment rationalism and elitism even while being engulfed by the tides of mass democracy.

According to Unitarian moral philosophers, the good statesman was engaged in a disinterested pursuit of the general good. The legislative process was conceived as an inquiry after truth, and the legislator was properly a "deliberative" man. Unlike the advocate at the bar, the political spokesman was "supposed to have adopted no opinion which he will not abandon for a better." Unitarians, with their organic conception of society, presupposed the existence of a common interest on the part of all members of society. Hence the lawmaker should not "think so much of bringing a majority to his side, as of ascertaining which side is the true one for all." To this end, it was essential that political men exercise "mutual forbearance" and tolerate honest disagreements until these could be definitively reconciled.[6]

Among the Unitarians' most attractive traits was their professed commitment to free inquiry. "I call that mind free which jealously guards its intellectual rights and powers, which calls no man master, [and] which does not content itself with a passive or hereditary faith," declared William Ellery Channing.[7] Unitarian preachers could defend freedom of inquiry with sentiments worthy of Jefferson:

No article of faith is too sacred, nor any doctrine too true, to be the subject of enquiry, [insisted the elder Ware.] It is not truth, but error and imposture, that are endangered by being thoroughly investigated ... Truth will always appear the brighter for its collision with doubt or error; and it will stand the firmer for having had its foundations attempted to be shaken; like the oak, that gathers strength and stability by the buffeting of the tempest.[8]

Harvard professors taught that government action to control opinions or their expression was appropriate only on those rare occasions when they directly threatened the commonwealth (for example, a Protestant government might legitimately forbid Papists to teach that allegiance was not due Protestant rulers).[9] Channing belonged to that small group of Federalists, led by John Marshall, who joined Republicans in opposing the Alien and Sedition Acts.[10]

Enlightenment rationalism was, however, intermingled with Puritan moralism in Unitarian political views. A list enumerating the duties of rulers among the Papers of Henry Ware, Sr., illuminates this aspect of Harvard thought in the nineteenth century:

first, to form the subjects to good morals.

to take care of the support of religion . . .

to entrust public employments only to persons of probity, and capable of fulfilling them well.

to levy taxes and subsidies only in cases of pressing necessity.

to preserve ... the goods of the subjects, and also to procure the increase of them.

to prevent factions.[11]

Not only is there nothing here about doing the will of one's constituents, there is not even anything about protecting their life and liberty. The emphasis is primarily upon moral paternalism, and subordinately, upon economic conservatism.

Conservative Whiggism tinged with paternalism characterized the political ideas of Francis Bowen. During the Dorr crisis, Bowen defended the antiquated constitution of Rhode Island with arguments reminiscent of those used to defend the sovereignty of the unreformed British Parliament. "In the United States, and in every other country on earth, wherein the right of the people to manage their own affairs and govern themselves is asserted and exercised, 'the people' is understood to be a specific and peculiar phrase, not comprehending 'all persons,' but assuming by prescription to represent all."[12] Thus, persons whose consent was not required in the political process were still obliged to obey constituted authority. Bowen explained that, in order to be entitled to allegiance, a government must (1) promote the "well-being of the subject" and (2) consult, "in some degree," the subject's wishes. The second requirement did not imply the necessity of consent to the government's actions—it was enough if a government were willing to entertain petitions. Bowen boldly denied the favorite principle of nineteenth-century nationalism, the right of self-determination. Colonists or subject peoples unrepresented in their imperial government had no "right of revolution" unless actually oppressed.[13]

For all their conservatism, the Massachusetts Unitarians were certainly no apologists for repression or despotism. They believed a good polity, like a good personality, should be balanced; and the needs of the masses were one legitimate interest to be balanced with others. But the fact that the *needs* of the people should be consulted did not require that their *wishes* always be heeded. Moreover, "balance" in the sense Harvard moralists used it meant harmonious integration rather than opposing force. Ideally, an office holder was a representative of the community as a whole, not a special pleader for a geographical, economic, or other interest. Dr. Channing expressed "distrust" for the expedient of pitting "men's passions and interests against each other, to use one man's selfishness as a check against his neighbor's." Publius had tried to make ambition counteract ambition, but the New England moralist warned that "the vices can by no management or skilful poising be made to do the work of virtue."[14]

The Unitarians were not always consistent, however, in maintaining that disinterested inquiry was the only true basis for statecraft. At times they were willing to concede something to the weakness of human nature, and grant that a proper political balance might more likely be struck if the different interests to be protected were each given representation in the government. In fact, the Liberal clergy of the Congregational establishments in New England had been traditional opponents of both "levelism" and "tyranny," and defenders of mixed "Aristicrato-Democratical" government. And so the antebellum Unitarians generally supported such devices as bicameral legislatures in which one house represented people and the other, propertied interests.[15]

The Constitution of the United States seemed to the antebellum Unitarians an instrument admirably suited to the proper balance of social interests. In particular, it prevented the masses from exercising too much power.

From many of the dangers peculiar to [democracy] we have been secured by the wisdom and foresight of the founders of the Constitution. They devised restraints on the action of the people, and . . . the people submitted to those restraints, and voluntarily tied their own hands. The frame of government under which we live is a system of checks and balances nearly as complicated and artfully arranged as that which forms the British constitution.[16]

Such a system was devised not so much to enable the majority to rule, as to protect the just rights of both the majority and the minority, and enable them to coexist in harmony. Just as a wise man would prescribe for himself rules of life to avoid succumbing to temptations, a wise people would surround itself with checks and restraints. What the danger of "passion" was to an individual, the danger of "faction" was to society. The great value of the American Constitution lay in the defenses it erected against mob rule. Demagogues, appealing to the worst motives in men, always lurked in the fears of Unitarian moralists, ready to pounce upon the land and destroy its carefully nurtured equilibrium.[17]

Among the leading exponents of "mixed government" in America was, of course, Massachusetts's own John Adams. Former President Adams, himself a Liberal Congregationalist, contributed to Buckminster's Liberal *Monthly Anthology* an essay on the importance of developing a responsible class of political leaders in the country. At his death, full of years and honors, Adams was held up to Unitarian congregations as an example of the ripe development of human faculties.[18] Governor James Bowdoin of Massachusetts (1726–1790) was another local statesman who exemplified Harvard ideals. Bowdoin, a Boston merchant and philanthropist, was the Federalist governor of the Commonwealth who suppressed Shays's Rebellion. A patron of arts and letters, the governor dabbled in natural history and natural philosophy, serving as first president of the American Academy of Arts and Sciences. Bowdoin was also a Liberal Christian and a member of the socially exclusive Brattle Street church. Buckminster's eulogy of him, preached twenty-one years after his death, was still being reprinted by nostalgic conservatives in 1848.[19]

The concept of a political elite taking guidance from a moral elite was institutionalized for Harvard Unitarians in the Massachusetts "Election Sermon," delivered annually for two hundred and fifty years.[20] On this occasion, the governor, his council, and both houses of the General Court (traditional title of the Massachusetts state legislature) assembled to be instructed in their duties by a minister of the Standing Order. It was a moment of great solemnity, and the preacher, selected from among the most eminent in his profession, regarded the sermon as a high point in his career. Exodus 18:21 was a typical text: "Thou shalt provide out of all the people able men, such as fear God, men of truth, hating covetousness; and place such over them to be rulers."[21] The preacher might warn his audience against legislating on behalf of special interests or showing favoritism to their own localities at the expense of the community as a whole. He might even instruct the politicians that state pride should bend before the welfare of the Union, and patriotism give way before the Christian ideal of fellowship among all nations.[22]

One of the most striking aspects of Unitarian political thought as expressed in the Election Sermons is the extent to which the old Puritan sense of corporate moral responsibility remained. God's moral government extended over communities as well as individuals. "In the laws which govern the lot of nations and the retributions which they receive, the justice of heaven is sometimes signally manifested," Henry Ware, Sr., warned his countrymen. Christian ethics applied to "collective bodies of men," and the institutions of society, like the actions of its members, came under the judgment of God. "Indeed," Ware instructed the Massachusetts politicians, "there is nothing in the intercourse of men with each other, in any of the political, or civil, or social relations, which will not be affected" by the demands of Christian fraternity. If the American political experiment were to succeed, the nation would have to show itself worthy of divine favor.[23]

One of the greatest Election Sermons in the history of the institution was delivered on May 26, 1830, by William Ellery Channing. The preacher told the politicians in his audience that they had concerned themselves too much with the material and not enough with the intellectual and moral—too much with means, and not enough with ends. We pride ourselves on living in a free and wealthy country, he observed. But what do we do with our freedom and riches? Are we taking advantage of our blessings to consecrate ourselves to the pursuit of wisdom and the welfare of mankind? American intellectuals are still asking their politicians the same questions.[24]

THE IDEAL OF A CHRISTIAN COMMONWEALTH

The American Revolution apparently did little to shake the strong tradition of religious establishment in Massachusetts. The state constitution adopted in 1780 provided for government support of religion as follows:

The legislature shall, from time to time, authorize and require the several towns, parishes, precincts, and other bodies politic, or religious societies, to make suitable provision, at their own expense, for the insti-

tution of the public worship of GOD, and for the support and maintenance of public Protestant teachers of piety, religion, and morality, in
all cases where such provision shall not be made voluntarily.

And the people of this commonwealth have also a right to, and do,
invest their legislature with authority to enjoin upon all the subjects an
attendance upon the instructions of the public teachers aforesaid, at
stated times and seasons, if there be any on whose instructions they can
conscientiously and conveniently attend.[25]

In some respects these constitutional provisions were actually reactionary, and they were ratified over the strong protest of religious
dissenters.[26] The legislation implementing these articles did away with
the exemption Quakers and Baptists had been enjoying from religious
taxation, requiring them instead, like Episcopalians, to pay their
church rates to the town clerk. This official was then supposed to turn
the dissenters' money over to their own religious leaders, but many a
Congregationalist clerk was notoriously reluctant to do so. The Massachusetts bench, dominated by conservative Federalists, compounded
the difficulties of dissenters by repeatedly ruling against them in law-
suits involving church taxes, often on infuriating technicalities. In one
case, a Baptist group spent four years and a hundred dollars in litiga-
tion to recover four dollars from a recalcitrant clerk.[27]

With regard to theology, however, the Constitution of 1780 was per-
missive. While retaining the traditional principle of religious
establishment, it omitted any reference to the Westminster Confession
or other creedal statement. There was consequently no legal basis for
requiring the parish churches publicly maintained by each township
to subscribe to Calvinist doctrines, even as a formality. Given the
Massachusetts polity of congregational independency, the way was
clearly open for the emergence of a Unitarian wing within the Standing Order.

Harvard had been founded to provide an educated ministry for the
Standing Order in Massachusetts, and after the Liberals gained control
of it in 1805 the College remained as much a stronghold of the religious establishment as ever. Liberal Harvard professors justified the
establishment in terms of the social utility of religion. "In preventing
atrocious crimes by its hold on the consciences of men, in restraining
the turbulent, impure, and selfish passions, [and] in contributing to

domestic peace and social order, religion is the friend of every human being," declaimed the Dudleian Lecturer for 1811 in a typical passage.[28] Benevolent affections, patriotic sentiments, and feelings of family responsibility were all reinforced by the church; religious exercises also fostered an emotional sense of corporate unity that was especially valuable in the amorphous society of America. The "public worship" (as it was always called) offered in Unitarian churches was a social as well as a devotional activity, symbolizing the organic wholeness of society. Public worship seemed "a natural method of supplying a public want." From the important services the church rendered to the state, Harvard moralists deduced the "right and duty of government to provide for the support of religion by law."[29]

Of course, social utility was never the ultimate concern of the Unitarian conscience. Above and beyond utilitarian considerations there stood the moral issue. Government support for religion testified to the rightful supremacy of Christian teachings in the commonwealth. "Public questions are and ought to be subjected to the moral judgment of the community," William Ellery Channing pointed out, and for Unitarian moralists, this meant referring them to Christian principles.[30] A religious establishment provided the good society with a means of consecrating itself, as a body, to purposes transcending the mundane.

The first Alford Professor of Moral Philosophy indignantly rejected the suggestion that support of religion fell outside the proper scope of government action. In his argument, Frisbie manifested an old-fashioned Federalist conception of strong government. "Surely the province of government is not merely to provide directly for the security of the persons and property of the citizens; its proper sphere is whatever can promote the peace and happiness of society, in the widest view of the subject." Government-maintained churches fell into the same category as government-maintained schools. The individual who found either not to his liking was free to attend a sectarian meeting or send his children to a private academy.[31] Taxation for public worship should not be construed as a grievance, even by those who did not attend: "Religious institutions are indispensable to the Commonwealth," James Walker insisted, "and on this account undoubtedly every enlightened patriot, whether he believes in any religion or not, will cheerfully contribute his proportion to their support."[32]

In defense of established religion, New England Liberals were able to draw on both their major intellectual traditions, Puritanism and the Enlightenment. They were proud to invoke the wisdom of their seventeenth-century ancestors, who "thought, and not without reason, that religious institutions . . . were of the utmost importance, [and] that the parishes, as by law established, were the only effectual provision for this object." Those old Puritans may have subscribed to a now-outmoded Calvinism, said James Walker, but they were "experienced and sober-minded statesmen, [and] not willing to see [ecclesiastical] institutions broken up and destroyed."[33] Eighteenth-century Whigs like Paley and Burke were also well known for their arguments in favor of the establishment of religion; Harvard Unitarians must have found the ideas of Burke on the organic union of church and state in a "Christian Commonwealth" especially attractive.[34] Even in America, many eighteenth-century rationalists of conservative temper agreed with Massachusetts Unitarians that a state church could be a valuable instrument of social control. With some justice, Unitarian moralists could claim George Washington shared their views.[35]

Defenders of the Standing Order in nineteenth-century Massachusetts were able to make certain kinds of appeals that would be impossible in twentieth-century America. They could assume the dissenters were Protestant Christians who preferred the established church to atheism. (Catholic immigration became significant only after religion was already disestablished.) They could also take it for granted that most people desired to see certain types of official privileges accorded Protestant Christianity: laws against blasphemy, laws regulating activity on the Lord's Day, the incapacity of atheists to testify in court, and prayers in the public schools. Under the circumstances, many dissenters could easily be accused of inconsistency when they objected to tax-supported worship in the parish churches.[36]

Harvard moral philosophers did not think of themselves as at all narrow-minded in upholding an official establishment of religion. Like Richard Hooker, John Locke, and many other Christian rationalists, they believed the social advantages of a state church should be compatible with intellectual freedom. Within the established church, they claimed a wide latitude for individual belief. Provided a man would accept Jesus Christ as the Son of God, Unitarians would not, theoretically, question his right to membership in the church of the state.[37] In actual practice, Harvard Unitarians proved less tolerant than they imagined themselves to be; for not only did they often harass dissenters, they also came close to excommunicating those Unitarian clergymen who (like William Bentley, Theodore Parker, and John Pierpont) deviated from the Liberal party line on social or theological issues. Still, Harvard moralists saw no real reason why all Christians (or at least all Protestants) could not unite under the banner of an established Liberalism. Unitarian Christianity, which tried to reduce theology to the least common denominator of all the sects, seemed to them ideally suited to be the church supported by all.[38]

The "catholicity" of which the Harvard Unitarians boasted was chiefly manifested in a distaste for theological argument with the Calvinist wing of the establishment. "No duty is more binding upon Christians," Henry Ware, Sr., told his divinity students, than "a readiness to be silent upon points of difference, or, when there is occasion to speak of them, to do it with gentleness, decorum, and mutual respect."[39] Differences of opinion must not be allowed to produce factionalism within the Standing Order, Unitarians felt, for though heresy need not cause alarm, schism was deplorable. When their orthodox colleagues called them to debate, Liberal clergymen were slow to come forward. Among the Harvard moralists, only Norton (and, for a time, Walker) really had much stomach for controversy with the Calvinists; William Ellery Channing, though famous for the gauntlet he belatedly threw down at Baltimore in 1819, had persistently tried to smooth over differences and muzzle the outspoken Norton.

If, as Alan Heimert tells us, the Boston Liberals were reluctant revolutionaries, they made even more reluctant schismatics. All during the turmoil of Revolution and the partisan strife between Jeffersonians and Federalists that followed, the Unitarians managed to avoid an open breach with the Calvinists. As long as deism and Jacobinism threatened, the two wings of the established church made common cause in defense of true religion and good order. Not until after the

Battle of Waterloo did the great theological controversy finally get under way. Even then, the fight had to be forced on the Liberals by an aggressive Calvinist from Connecticut, Jedidiah Morse.[40] During the acrimonious debates that followed, Unitarians claimed to be protecting religious toleration and freedom of conscience against repressive, cantankerous bigots. However, the most capable Trinitarian Congregationalists, like Moses Stuart, pointed out that Unitarians were actually not so much defending free religious expression as trying to hush up an embarassing division in the establishment.[41] The hesitancy of Harvard Liberals to stand up and be counted might be charitably attributed to an ecumenical spirit. But it also manifested their deep-seated social conservatism: their fear lest the weakening of the Standing Order by internal strife pave the way for disestablishment.

Despite the warnings of the Unitarian moralists, zealous Calvinists pressed ahead with their "denunciation and exclusion" of Liberals.[42] To maintain what they thought was ideological purity, Jedidiah Morse and his cohorts sacrificed the temporal interests of their church. Events proved the Unitarians right; schism heralded disestablishment. Reflecting upon Morse's great assault on the Liberals, James Walker wrote the epitaph for the Standing Order in Massachusetts: "From that hour the ascendancy of Congregationalists, for some time the sole, and until then the predominant sect, was at an end in this State. The house was divided against itself, and it fell."[43]

THE DISESTABLISHMENT OF RELIGION

The Standing Order, as long as it existed, gave some kind of symbolic guarantee to the hierarchical social order the Harvard moralists idealized. "Contrast . . . the seriousness, the silence, the . . . respect for the speaker, who alone conducts the services [in church], with the turbulence and rancor which are often seen in other assemblies," Edward T. Channing noted.[44] Amidst a disintegrating society, Unitarians could still find in their parish church a speaking aristocracy and silent democracy. "The doctrine of 'instructions' in politics is of very doubtful expediency," observed Edward's brother in good Burkean fashion; "but that instructions should issue from the congregation to the minister we all with one voice pronounce wrong."[45] Yet what else could possibly be the result of making the minister dependent upon popular contributions for his livelihood? Would not the democracy inevitably dictate to the pulpit the style of preaching it would hear? The vision of Harvard graduates competing with illiterate revivalists for the favor of the crowd was disturbing.

Unitarian moralists made no secret of their concern for the future of the clerical profession if civil aid to the church were withdrawn. Without their legally secured stipend, ministers would become time-servers, "the servants of men rather than of God." Under such circumstances, Harvard moralists feared the ministry could no longer attract men of talent. Even with towns obliged to support religion, the clerical profession demanded considerable financial sacrifice from a capable man. If people were free to hire any minister or none, "preaching will be literally an article in the market, and men will chaffer for it at the cheapest rate."[46] Harvard moralists had good reason to fear for the status of the clergy. Recent scholarship seems to confirm their apprehensions that the security and prestige of the clerical profession were gradually declining in nineteenth-century New England.[47]

In nineteenth-century Massachusetts, it proved impossible to maintain the Puritan conception of a tax-supported Standing Order. In former times the society had been homogeneous enough to share common goals, and the church had expressed this corporate consecration. By the third decade of the nineteenth century, however, the situation was changing. Religious dissent had grown steadily, particularly among yeomen farmers and urban workers, and its increasing strength was reflected in the ominous enlargement of the Democratic Republican Party in Massachusetts.[48] A divided establishment no longer provided clear spiritual guidance, and there was doubt whether its political guidance could keep the Bible Commonwealth Federalist much longer. When a convention to revise the state constitution met in 1820–21, church-state relations became a source of bitter debate.

The constitutional convention was made necessary by the separation of Maine from Massachusetts, a secession Boston Federalists accepted because it detached a predominantly Republican bloc of voters from their commonwealth. Once assembled, however, the convention could not be allowed to get out of hand. The selection of John Adams and then, when the patriarch declined, of Chief Justice Isaac Parker as presiding officer demonstrated that conservative Unitarian Federalists still maintained control of the state political machinery. A number of Unitarian clergymen and intellectuals had been elected to the convention, proof that old habits of political deference had not entirely passed away from New England. Henry Ware, Jr. was in the delegation from Boston, as were Josiah Quincy (future president of Harvard), William Prescott (father of the historian), the Reverend James Freeman, and, of course, Daniel Webster. Joseph Tuckerman was the natural representative of Chelsea, for besides being its minister (thereby, ex officio, the intellectual and spiritual leader of the community) he was by far the richest man in the town. Such Unitarian Federalists as these displayed remarkable vigor in preserving their traditional political privileges and staving off democratic reforms. The apportionment of the State Senate according to taxable property, which gave Boston substantial over-representation, was preserved, as was the integrity of the Unitarian-dominated judiciary. Most remarkable of all, however, the Unitarian Federalists managed to save the religious establishment.[49]

The schism between Liberals and orthodox was approaching the height of its bitterness in 1820, and this did not seem to augur well for conservatism. A major fear of the Unitarian delegates was that the Calvinist Congregationalists, hitherto their allies in Federalism, might join with the dissenters to disestablish the church.[50] By subtle maneuvering the Unitarian Federalists managed to prevent this realignment from occurring at the convention. Harvard moralists roused the delegates' fears that, if state-supported religion were abandoned, state-supported education would be the next to go.[51] Then, led by the canny Webster, the Unitarians beat back a movement for complete disestablishment by substituting for it a complicated amendment that included some concessions to dissent. The amendment failed to satisfy the dissenters, who voted against it when it was submitted to the people for ratification, and the Standing Order emerged unscathed from its close call. "All the credit is due to Webster," Henry Ware, Jr., wrote delightedly to a Liberal friend upon the outcome. "He is a wonderful man."[52]

On the issue of a religious test oath for office holders, the Liberals were not so lucky. Tuckerman and Ware both took to the convention floor in a last effort to stop the repeal of this constitutional article. "If our religion be from God," Tuckerman demanded, "shall we open the door of office indiscriminately to those who believe, and to those who reject this revelation of God's will?" The rhetorical question seemed to admit of but one answer, yet the moralists' stand was in vain; Webster reluctantly concluded that the odds were against the perpetuation of the oath and conceded this much to secularism and dissent.[53]

All in all, the Federalist Unitarians did well at the Convention, and the elder Henry Ware voiced their satisfaction in his Election Sermon of 1821. The results of the Convention had been "the most gratifying, the most encouraging, and the most honorable, that could have been expected," he told Governor Brooks and the General Court.[54] Even as the reverend professor spoke, however, events were moving toward the final demise of both the Massachusetts Federalist Party and the Standing Order beloved of Harvard moralists.

By the famous Dedham Decision of 1820, handed down just before the Constitutional Convention met, the Massachusetts Supreme Judicial Court had ruled that title to all properties of the Standing Order was vested in the parishes and not in the churches themselves.[55] In New England tradition, the "church" was the body of "professed" and "visible" saints, who usually constituted but a small fraction of the "parish" (or "religious society") supporting the minister. There were many towns in eastern Massachusetts where a majority of the Congregationalist parishioners (not necessarily a majority of the total population) had become Liberals, but the "church" remained dominated by orthodox Calvinists. Church members were admitted by a process of co-optation, and often the requirements for admission included theological examinations Liberals had difficulty passing. After the Dedham Decision, however, it was clear that members of a Congregational parish could settle a minister of their choice, regardless of the wishes of the church.[56] If, as happened in Dedham, the parish proceeded to choose a Liberal, the disaffected Calvinist church members could secede only at the cost of abandoning all ecclesiastical temporalities—meeting-house, parsonage, endowments, records—to the Liberals.[57] This is precisely what occurred in scores of Massachusetts townships, where open schism between Unitarian and Trinitarian left the newer faith in possession of the old buildings and lands. That so many Calvinists were willing to sacrifice this property, and rebuild their religious institutions from scratch, is a tribute to their Christian integrity. But the loss of centuries of pious benefactions to heretics left its legacy of bitterness. To the orthodox Congregationalists, the judgment of the Unitarian-dominated court seemed legalized plunder.[58]

The impact of the Dedham Decision (and the Brookfield Decision that reaffirmed it) was felt when more than a hundred Massachusetts parishes became Unitarian, while over eighty "exiled" Calvinist churches began an uphill struggle for existence as dissenters from the official religion of their towns. No longer did there seem much reason for the orthodox to support a religious establishment that was effectually expropriating them. The campaign of Jedidiah Morse and his followers had backfired catastrophically. Those who had tried to denounce and exclude Liberals from the Standing Order ended up being excluded themselves. Thus, at last, the orthodox Congregationalists came to espouse the cause of disestablishment.[59]

Then the fears of the Unitarians materialized: Calvinist Congregationalists made common cause with dissenters. The old Federalist coalition stopped working when the Unitarian-commercial wing of the party forced the nomination of Harrison Gray Otis for governor in 1823. Otis was wealthy, a Unitarian, a member of the Harvard Corporation, a former leader of the Hartford Convention, and utterly unacceptable to the orthodox-agrarians. As a result the Republicans carried the state, and Massachusetts Federalism went into its final decline. The election sealed the doom of the old ideal of a Christian Commonwealth. Only the continued strength of Federalist Unitarians in the state senate postponed the *coup de grâce*. In 1833 the Republicans (now called Democrats), with overwhelming Calvinist support, finally amended the constitution of Massachusetts to disestablish religion.[60]

It was only with reluctance that the Harvard moralists reconciled themselves to the transformation of Unitarianism from a theoretically comprehensive, public body into one little church among many.[61]

Although Liberal ministers had begun meeting in annual "Berry Street Conferences" in 1820, no effort at organizing their party within the Standing Order was made until 1825, when the American Unitarian Association was formed. Few Unitarians joined the association; Andrews Norton and William Ellery Channing, among others, declined to play active roles in it because they felt a Unitarian "sect" would hinder the spread of Liberal ideas within the older Christian groups. Only after the Civil War, in 1865, did Unitarians finally confess the defeat of their dream of catholicity and set up a regular denomination.[62] By coincidence, the orthodox Congregationalists gave up their struggle to define Christianity as Calvinism in the same year; 1865 saw the National Council of Congregationalism in Boston strike out all reference to Calvinism from the declaration of faith.[63] The great ecclesiastical schism in Massachusetts turned out to be a conflict both sides lost.

THE AMERICAN EXPERIMENT

After the Democratic Republican electoral victory in Massachusetts of 1823, the Unitarian moralists became increasingly aware that social change was out of their control. It matters little to what extent the event had only symbolic significance; a close reading of Unitarian sources shows that from the mid-1820's on, the moralists tried hard to reorient their thinking and take account of the disintegration of society. If they were slow to adapt their ecclesiastical institutions to religious pluralism, they were not blind to the many transformations occurring around them. They attempted to come to terms intellectually not only with their own declining political and religious influence, but also with such broad trends as industrialization, the swings of the business cycle, urbanization, the aspirations of the common man for education, and (eventually) the sectional crisis.

As usual, it was Dr. Channing who gave the Unitarian attitude its most eloquent utterance. In one of his last major addresses, May 11, 1841, he talked to the Mercantile Library Association of Philadelphia on "The Present Age." "The commanding characteristic" of the present age, he declared, was "the tendency in all its movements to expansion, to diffusion, to universality . . . Human action is now freer, more unconfined . . . The multitude is rising from the dust. Once we heard of the few, now we hear of the many." The speaker found this progress good, but fraught with dangers. Advancing scientific knowledge, for example, might tempt men to "question the infinite . . . and rush into an extravagance of doubt." The same ambiguity surrounded cultural developments. "Books are now placed within the reach of all." This was welcome, of course, yet it allowed works "deficient in taste" to circulate, catering to men's passions rather than to their higher powers. In political affairs, change was perhaps most manifest of all: "Once government was an inherited monopoly, guarded by the doctrine of divine right . . . Now office and dignity are thrown open as common things, and nations are convulsed by the multitude of competitors for the prize of public power." Channing acknowledged mixed feelings toward this transformation as well. Finally, the expansion of commerce entailed both good and bad effects. It promoted international peace and technological progress, and brought Christianity to distant peoples. On the other hand, however, it exposed the "uncivilized brethren" to exploitation and enslavement, while it fostered "a feverish, insatiable cupidity, under which fraud, bankruptcy, distrust, and distress are fearfully multiplied." What would come of all these changes in the end? America, the country where change was farthest advanced, had a special historical function as an experiment in liberty and progress.[64]

After the first quarter of the nineteenth century had passed, Harvard moral philosophers hardly ever called for government intervention in support of their claims to moral leadership. Once defeated on the issue of church-state union, they shunned the political arena. Making a virtue of necessity, Liberal moralists concluded that state action would not do them any good. They abandoned their Federalist hopes for a good society through government paternalism, and substituted an evangelical faith in moral suasion. The disestablishment of religion left the Unitarian moralists with an antipolitical bias. In the many philanthropic and reform efforts they initiated during the second quarter of the nineteenth century, they were usually quick to disavow any intention of political activity. "Even great enterprises can better be accomplished by the voluntary association of individuals than by the state," insisted Channing.[65]

Considering their organic view of society, it may seem strange that the Unitarians should have become exponents of little government. Their shift can be understood best by remembering that the Harvard moralists had always viewed government as only one of a number of means of preserving unity and order in society. The state differed from other means of social control, such as preaching or poetry, in that it could employ temporal sanctions to coerce obedience. Thus, while the precepts of literature and the pulpit were often addressed to the sentiments and other affections, the injunctions of government commanded the attention of the faculty of prudence or self-love.[66] Acting in concert, these various mechanisms marshaled all the faculties of man into the service of social morality. After the rise of the Jacksonian Democrats, the Unitarian moralists decided it would be a sign of weakness in society if politics overshadowed other forms of activity, for government was essentially negative, offering "little positive benefit" to man. "Government does little more than place society in a condition which favors the action of higher powers than its own," they explained.[67] As Burke had written, "Manners are of more importance than laws . . . The law touches us but here and there, and now and then. Manners are what vex or soothe, corrupt or purify, exalt or debase, barbarise or refine us."[68]

The Harvard philosophers never became dogmatic in their commitment to little government or, for that matter, to republicanism. They maintained that no political forms were universally appropriate: centralized monarchies might work best in some countries and republican federalism in others. New England Liberals were not prepared to offer such generalizations as "that government governs best which governs least"; each people was best ruled under the system for which manners, tastes, and traditions had suited it. The American Constitution owed whatever success it had enjoyed to inherited Anglo-Saxon social values, especially the Puritan virtues. The preservation of political freedom was therefore dependent on the conservation of moral values. Particularly after popular political participation widened during the Jacksonian era, Unitarian moralists felt it a matter of crucial importance that the influence of education and morality be brought to bear on the public. This was the task of Harvard moral philosophy.[69]

America, because it was a country with a weak, decentralized government, must serve as an example to the world of the strength of religion, morality, and good taste. America had to become a tangible refutation of Thomas Hobbes, in reaction against whom most of modern moral philosophy had been written. The Hobbesian state of nature had a terrifying reality for the Boston Liberals, who could see on the frontier of their country men leading a "solitary, violent, brutal existence."[70] If Hobbes were right, the anarchic and selfish competition of man in nature could only be controlled by despotism. The Harvard moralists were resolved to promote internalized restraints on conduct that would render Leviathan unnecessary. Then liberty could be reconciled with order, for the more men were taught to control themselves, the less control they would need from the state. "The voice within which approves or disapproves," declared a Harvard moral philosophy textbook, "has in it a restraining force more powerful than a thousand gibbets."[71] Through teaching moral philosophy, preaching a purified Gospel, and fostering a national literature, the Unitarian moralists tried to provide a free society with alternatives to coercion.[72]

A distinguished visitor to New England who shared the Unitarian moralists' concern for the future of liberty, as well as their vision of America's place in history, was Alexis Clerel de Tocqueville. Tocqueville and his traveling companion, Gustave de Beaumont, spent a considerable portion of their brief visit to the United States (1831–32) in the company of Boston Unitarian Whigs. Though Daniel Webster disappointed them, they found a kindred spirit in Joseph Tuckerman and lauded his philanthropic achievements in their official report on American penology.[73] Like most tourists, the two young Frenchmen were also anxious to pay their respects to the world-famous Dr. Channing. In conversing with him they discovered that religious liberalism coexisted with social conservatism in his mind. "It seems to me that Catholicism had established the government of the skilful or aristocracy in Religion, and that you [Protestants] have introduced Democracy," Tocqueville teased his host. "Now, I confess to you, the possibility of governing religious society, like political society, by the means of

Démocratie does not seem to me yet proven by experience." The Frenchman noted down Channing's reply:

I think that you mustn't push the comparison between the two societies too far. For my part, I believe every man in a position to understand religious truths, and I do not believe every man able to understand political questions. When I see submitted to the judgment of the people the question of the tariff, for example, dividing as it does the greatest economists, it seems to me that they would do as well to take for judge my son over there (pointing to a child of ten). No. I cannot believe that civil society is made to be guided directly by the always comparatively ignorant masses; I think that we [Americans] go too far.[74]

Tocqueville's great work on American life and institutions may well bear traces of the large number of Harvard and Boston informants upon whom its author relied. Dr. Channing had repeatedly issued such warnings as these: "Civil liberty is not enough. There may be a tyranny of the multitude, of opinion, over the individual . . . Popularity enslaves." "In a country called free, a majority may become a faction, and a proscribed minority may be insulted, robbed, and oppressed."[75] Tocqueville was similarly anxious about the danger of a tyranny by the majority, and he looked around for ways of preserving individual integrity and group order in a mass society. Yet Tocqueville was not offensive to American sensibilities (as so many European travelers were), and his hopes for the new nation outweighed his fears. Appropriately enough, then, the first American translation of *De la démocratie en Amérique* was made by the Alford Professor of Moral Philosophy at Harvard, Francis Bowen.[76]

A noteworthy parallel between the views of Tocqueville and those of the Harvard moralists was the contempt they shared for the patronage-oriented politics of their day. "*Great* political parties," Tocqueville declared, "are not to be met with in the United States at the present time." By this he meant that "the parties by which the Union is menaced do not rest upon principles, but upon material interests." Not since the demise of the Federalists, Tocqueville believed, had a party system worthy of respect existed in America. Like Tocqueville, the New England Liberals stigmatized political parties as "factions" and regarded them as "a necessary evil" at best. Parties in the state entailed all the evils of sects within the church; they conflicted with the dispassionate inquiry and mutual tolerance that were the ideals of Unitarian statecraft. Indeed, the American parties seemed institutional embodiments of a base passion: the lust for power over other men.[77] Political parties and the irresponsible journalism that fed upon them caused public issues to be debated in an atmosphere of "vulgar and unfounded abuse." This not only made rational policy decisions difficult, it also "disgusted the virtuous and high minded with [public] service, and"—as Tocqueville had also complained—"induced them to withdraw altogether" from public life.[78]

Unitarian condemnations of political parties were evidently not incompatible with a considerable measure of party regularity. William Ellery Channing, for example, was an unusually ardent Federalist in youth, even by Harvard standards. A bitter opponent of "Mr. Madison's war" with England, he led Boston's ostentatious rejoicing at the downfall of Napoleon in June 1814. In the 1820's Channing supported the apologists for the Hartford Convention even after it had fallen into general disrepute. When Andrew Jackson came into office Channing found him "headstrong [and] arbitrary" and termed the new President's spoils system "a prostitution of executive patronage."[79] Others among the Harvard moralists, notably Francis Bowen and Edward Tyrell Channing, were even more strongly identified with Federalist-Whig political views; yet in politics, as in religion, the older Channing brother became something of a symbol of Boston Unitarian moralism. David Henshaw, the Democratic Party chieftain in Massachusetts, conceived a most intense personal hatred for him. Recalling the preacher's opposition to the War of 1812, Henshaw once proposed this sarcastic toast at a Jackson Day dinner: "To the patriotic Dr. Channing—who eloquently enforced in time of war, the injunction of the Prince of Peace: 'Love Your Enemies.' "[80] Henshaw, an unscrupulous Jacksonian man-on-the-make, personified most of the things Channing disliked about American society. His sneer leaves the Liberal moralist in a better light than the political hack intended.[81]

GOD AND MAMMON

"Political Economy . . . is properly considered as one of the Moral Sciences," wrote Francis Bowen, spokesman for the Harvard moral philosophers on the subject of economics.[82] Of course Harvard professors weighed ethical considerations heavily in their study of economics, but Bowen intended more than this by his assertion. He meant that economic activity was governed by human nature and, ultimately, by the laws of God. The term "political economy" as then used was somewhat broader than our usual conception of economics. In Bowen's expression the word "economy" possessed a double meaning: not only did it denote the careful management of costly resources, it also referred to the Creator's plan, His special dispensation. Theological and teleological overtones pervaded most academic discussions of economic problems in early nineteenth-century America, and Unitarian writings were no exception.[83]

The Unitarian moralists hoped to build spiritual achievements upon a foundation of material achievements, and so, as a rule, they welcomed material progress. National prosperity seemed essential to the sensitivity and culture they wished to introduce to America. After all, only a man of secure economic position could really lead the rewarding life of self-development and refinement idealized by the Unitarians. "There is a harmony between all our great interests, between inward and outward improvements; and by establishing among them a wise order, all will be secured."[84] The cultivated Unitarian gentleman might well admire the beneficent Providence that reconciled his material and spiritual well-being, giving him "all this, and heaven, too."

The only large-scale work on economic theory produced by the twelve Unitarian moralists treated here, Francis Bowen's *Political Economy,* did not appear until 1856. The text reflects the ability of Unitarian moral philosophers to adapt to the changing economic conditions of the nineteenth century: Bowen's work breathes the spirit of a new age. It is not quite the book that would have been written at Harvard in earlier years; it advocates, for example, a protective tariff and a mildly inflationary fiscal policy favorable to industrial expansion, rather than free trade and sound money, which eighteenth-century Boston businessmen would have preferred. "Political economy" was first taught at Harvard in 1817 or 1818; apparently the shift to protectionism by Boston-Cambridge opinion leaders occurred in the mid-1820's.[85]

The Liberal consensus that had served a mercantile-agrarian society

in colonial and early national times could be adjusted to the industrialization of mid-century. The political, cultural, and philanthropic
functions that Unitarian intellectuals had previously expected ship-
owners to fulfill, Bowen now entrusted to millowners and railroad
magnates. He dedicated his text to a textile manufacturer and Cotton
Whig who was a close friend of John C. Calhoun.

To *Nathan Appleton,* one of the most eminent living representatives of
a highly honored class, *the merchant princes of Boston,* who have earned
success by sagacity, enterprise, and uprightness in all their undertakings,
and have dignified it by the munificence of their charities, and by their
liberal support of letters, science, and the arts, this work is respectfully
inscribed.

The old partnership between State Street and Harvard Yard was still
an aspect of Unitarianism in the 1850's. When a new College Chapel
was needed for the use of the evangelical Professor of Christian Morals,
Frederic Dan Huntington, the money was donated by the Appletons.

Bowen's large volume on political economy was a sophisticated work
in many respects.[86] The author began his task with a healthy distrust of
economic theorizing. Probably this was largely carried over from the
typical Unitarian distrust of dogma and abstract logic, whether theological or philosophical. Furthermore, the Unitarian moralist viewed
society as an integrated whole, in which men's conduct was influenced
by tradition and prescription, by tastes and emotions, as much as by
rational calculation. He was consequently suspicious of the concept of
an "economic man" familiar to classical economic theory. Economics
should be studied in relation to a specific social and political context,
Bowen believed, and it was the purpose of his textbook to "apply" the
basic principles of the subject to "the condition, the resources, and the
institutions of the American people." The chief defect of British economists, Bowen thought, was their disposition to generalize economic
insights valid only for their own time and place; "if Adam Smith were
living in our own day, it may be doubted whether he would be the
uncompromising advocate that he was of the principles of Free
Trade."[87]

Bowen was a loyal supporter of the Whig Party, and one of the
objects of his book was to endorse a protective tariff. He professed to

believe that protectionism was more valuable to the wage-earners than to the industrialists of the young country. If American industry were forced into direct competition with British, the pressure would depress the wages American employers could afford to offer; yet a virtually inexhaustible supply of destitute Irish would continue to accept jobs. After a generation of free trade, Bowen claimed, American industry would have cut prices and wages to their British levels. Yankee capitalists would have retained their profit margin, but the American workingman would have suffered a severe loss of purchasing power.[88]

Bowen found local conditions and the cultural context important variables when analyzing the accumulation of investment capital by various societies. A disposition to save money was not innate, Bowen noted, but was an acquired trait. Among primitive peoples there was practically no accumulation of capital, the tendency being toward immediate consumption, even waste, of any surplus. After comparing several societies with respect to their economic development, Bowen concluded that the causes for different rates of growth were primarily "moral" (i.e., pertaining to moral philosophy; we should probably say "sociological"). Internal political stability would provide security for property. A large urban population would provide both a trained work force and a good local market. Nor was the Unitarian moral philosopher who lauded the virtues of thrift and diligent labor blind to the economic implications of his ethic. It was vital to the material development of a country, Bowen maintained, that even humble people be encouraged to add their savings to the capital investment fund. In America, custom frowned on forms of conspicuous consumption common in Europe, and savings banks mobilized the resources of the people for the use of the financier.[89]

But the best way to foster capital growth was to offer encouragement to capitalists. The capitalist must be assured "as high a rate of profit and as large a measure of physical comfort, social consideration, and political influence as possible," to compensate him for foregone consumption and the risk of investment. The author's own Commonwealth of Massachusetts was, of course, an example par excellence of a society favorable to capital: where power and prestige rewarded the successful entrepreneurs among its law-abiding, concentrated population skilled in diverse callings. To the antebellum Harvard economist, his own society was a model for mankind, and its crowning glory was the enlightened merchant prince.

Bowen's chief purpose in writing on economics, he stated, was to reconcile the public to the functioning of an economic order that rewarded capitalists so lavishly. For a citizen of a country relatively free of class conflict, Bowen evinced a surprising degree of class consciousness and fear of class revolution. He acted on the assumption that economic discontent was rife and had to be mollified. Ideas that pitted class against class constituted a "danger from which no civilized community is entirely free," warned this Harvard conservative. Bowen dreaded "lest the several classes . . . should cherish mutual jealousy and hate, which may finally break out into open hostilities, under the mistaken idea that their interests are opposite."[90] Bowen's concern had a considerable history among Harvard Liberals. Some twenty years before, William Ellery Channing had pleaded with the workingmen of Boston not to be "so insanely blind to their interests [or] so deaf to the claims of justice and religion, . . . as to be prepared to make a wreck of the social order, for the sake of dividing among themselves the spoils of the rich."[91]

The sanctity of private property was one of the few economic principles Bowen considered immutable and independent of the cultural context. "No nation has ever been discovered on the earth, so low and brutal in their inclination and habits, so destitute of any idea of right, that the institution of property, to a greater or less extent, does not exist among them."[92] Antebellum American economists quite commonly insisted that the "laws" of classical economics were God-given and, indeed, illustrated the same beneficent design the physical universe did. And Bowen, despite his reservations about Manchester free trade principles and the abstract "economic man," was sometimes willing to treat laissez faire as though it were a divine ordinance. We catch him in this mood in his pages devoted to the "natural theology" of economics. Borrowing heavily from the Anglican Archbishop Whately, Bowen maintained that the operations of a free market economy "manifest the contrivance, wisdom, and beneficence of the Deity, just as clearly as do the marvellous arrangements of the material universe." Ambition and avarice, though among "the lowest passions of mankind," were yet providentially turned to good "in their operation upon the interests of society." Thus the Unitarian economist fell back upon the time-hallowed device of invoking God to justify the ways of man.[93]

A popular myth of nineteenth-century America was the idea that all real wealth was produced by agriculture. Commerce, manufacturing, and finance were regarded by many (especially by Jeffersonians and Jacksonians) as essentially parasitic. To refute this myth and assert the interdependence and equal worth of different economic enterprises was another of Bowen's hopes. The Harvard professor was convinced that urbanization and economic diversification were keys to national prosperity. "Cities and towns are the great agents and tokens of the increase of national opulence and the progress of civilization," he declared. So long as the population was largely self-subsistent and agricultural, it could never acquire the purchasing power to become a good home market. Production and consumption were, Bowen recognized, interdependent. Economic diversification created a good internal market for all producers; but "a country, the population of which is chiefly or altogether devoted to agriculture, cannot become wealthy, whatever may be the fertility of its soil or the favorableness of its situation."[94]

Francis Bowen's *Political Economy* is a statement of faith in the potentialities of industrial America. There were, however, certain problems which the American economy posed for the Liberal moralists, particularly in its exploitative, speculative, and anarchic aspects.

INDUSTRY VERSUS SPECULATION

The subordination of the material to the spiritual, which Harvard moral philosophy required, provided a basis for Unitarian social criticism. Once a man, or a society, had achieved a competence of material things, he or it was expected to turn to spiritual development. Furthermore, the habits acquired in the process of material advancement—prudence, industriousness, sobriety, and the like—ought to serve as the foundation for this higher, moral development. "If our liberty deserves the praise which it receives," Dr. Channing pointed out, "it opens to us an indefinite intellectual progress."[95] The ultimate success of the American experiment would not be achieved until a wealthy and free people had also become sensitive, enlightened, and truly Christian. The propects for this spiritual "awakening" hinged upon the means men used to pursue material wealth. One could not expect to make a silk purse of a sow's ear, or a virtuous nation out of a reckless, gambling, selfish people.

The Unitarian distaste for speculation clearly represented a continuation of traditional Puritan disapproval of avarice, "luxury," and economic "oppression." It was also typical of the high Liberal value on moderation. The distinction between honest industriousness in one's private calling and grasping speculation was the difference between liberty and license. Speculation was the vice that developed when the profit motive became excessive and licentious. The speculator elevated money to the highest end and ignored the character-building qualities of hard work. Money gained through such speculative activities as trading in land scrip represented no reward for diligent labor, but only luck. Interestingly enough, the stigma of speculation came to be attached to gambling as well as to venturesome capital risks. The 1830's saw a novel wave of moral disapproval for gambling and lotteries sweep Massachusetts; the private sale of lottery tickets was banned in 1833. Only a few years before, Harvard had financed the building of Holworthy Hall with the proceeds of a lottery. But get-rich-quick schemes had come to seem too dangerous and widespread to be sanctioned any longer. As James Walker explained it, "God never meant that things should come easily; he always meant that they should come hard . . . Money got by gambling, lotteries, and speculation proves a curse as often as a blessing."[96]

More often than the money itself, it was the "passion" for easy money that Unitarian moralists declared a curse. Early in the century J. S. Buckminster had implored merchants to "beware of an engrossing love of profit, which invariably narrows the capacity, and debases the noblest tendencies of the human character." As time went by such warnings became increasingly frequent and insistent. "The freest institutions of the world may become the nurseries, the hot-beds . . . of the most eager cupidity of wealth, and of every narrow interest and lawless passion by which individual character may be degraded," Joseph Tuckerman cautioned churchmen. Francis Bowen shifted the role of the moral philosopher from evangelical preacher to embryonic social scientist in telling Americans that their national obsession for wealth could lead to "mental anxiety" and a high insanity rate.[97]

The national pursuit of wealth was related to the absence of fixed social stations in America, as Liberal moralists saw clearly. In countries "where the aristocracy of birth and of wealth has long been established" custom restricted cupidity and ambition, Tuckerman observed. But in America traditional limitations were absent, and an unrestrained determination "to rise in wealth and power" infected all classes. The ambivalence and discomfiture with which Harvard moralists regarded social mobility was intertwined with their disapproval of the speculative and mercenary temperament. Concerned as they were about working-class discontent, the Unitarian moralists were more worried about aggressive speculators. In his analysis of the celebrated Charles River Bridge Case, William Ellery Channing declared, "The great danger to property here is not from the laborer, but from those who are making haste to be rich."[98] The stable and responsible patrician class Liberal moralists tried to foster in America would have the leisure and the security to rise above the race for riches.

The rapid westward migration of the American population was at once a manifestation and an encouragement of the speculative mood Boston moralists disliked. Abundant cheap land provided a standing temptation to people "to leave behind them all the means and appliances of civilization, and to become squatters and backwoodsmen in the wilderness." The frontier was, to say the least, uncongenial to the moral values and cultural refinements New England Unitarians held dear; geographical, as well as social, mobility posed a threat to social cohesion. The threat that land hunger posed to spiritual development and community responsibility had long been evident to Puritans and Yankees.[99] Reflecting their misgivings about westward expansion, Liberal moralists opposed federal internal improvements, a homestead act, and agitation for war over Oregon.[100] William Ellery Channing's open letter to Henry Clay on the Texas question, arguing against annexation, is a moving and articulate dissent from Manifest Destiny. Channing denounced the Texans as irresponsible, greedy speculators who had entered Mexico at their own risk and who had encountered few difficulties not of their own making. To annex Texas would embroil the United States in war with Mexico and serve as prelude to aggression in the Caribbean. Worst of all, Texas would strengthen and encourage the perpetuation of slavery in this country. Acquisition of Texas, then, might transform America from a peaceful exemplar of well-ordered liberty into an aggressive, imperialistic power.[101]

When financial panic hit the United States in 1837, the Unitarian moralists saw it as evidence of the evils of speculation. The Democratic Administration, southwestern state legislatures, and a diffuse "spirit of commercial gambling" were all to blame.[102] In the tradition of the New England jeremiad, the moralists called upon America to repent of her collective sins under the prompting of God's judgment. "What a blessing would our present commercial agony be, would it only free us from the accursed thirst for unbounded gain," reflected Dr. Channing. "Infinitely better for us would it be," cried Dr. Tuckerman, "that our commercial embarrassments . . . should indefinitely be increased, than that returning prosperity should bring with it increasing luxury and extravagance, . . . recklessness and depravity."[103]

It would be wrong to conclude from such social criticism that the Unitarian moralists despaired, for they did not. On balance they accepted America, her political institutions, and her economic order. A certain amount of apprehension as to the outcome of the American experiment was, after all, not only justified but apparently widespread among citizens of the new nation.[104] The Unitarians expected America to profit from her mistakes and go forth with "an indomitable energy, which after rearing an empire in the wilderness, is fresh for new achievements." The frontier, for example, gave cause for encouragement as well as alarm. "All our accounts of the West make me desire to visit it," remarked Channing. (He never did.) "I learn that a man there feels himself to be a man, that he has a certain self-respect which is not always to be found in older communities." The Boston moralist hoped the West "may learn from us the love of order, the arts which adorn and cheer life, the institutions of education and religion."[105] When striving to preserve the humanistic values of the past, the Unitarian Whig did not lose pride in the present. "I see the danger of the present state of society, perhaps as clearly as any one. But still I rejoice to have been born in this age."[106]

IX / Problems of Moral Leadership

SOCIAL INSTITUTIONS provided the context within which the Unitarian moral elite functioned. To some extent, the cultivation of individual character could compensate for the relative weakness of a disestablished church and a laissez-faire state. Yet even a voluntaristic approach to the problems of social control required philanthropic and educational institutions to channel men's moral energies. Only through some organizational framework could the Boston-Cambridge intelligentsia stimulate and direct the conscience and sentiments of their community. Benevolent societies and educational institutions became scenes of struggle for positions of leadership in a splintering society.[1]

OBJECTIVES OF UNITARIAN PHILANTHROPY

The Harvard moral philosophers rejoiced to live in "an age singularly prolifick in schemes for doing good to men." The numerous reform movements of early nineteenth-century America have fascinated historians, and it is not surprising that they should have captured the imagination of contemporary intellectuals as well. "A spirit of benevolence has diffused itself abroad, alike wonderful for its extent and its activity," cried Henry Ware, Sr., in 1820. "Asylums, hospitals, and schools, . . . the Bible Society, . . . the Peace Society, [and] missionaries, [all] bear witness to a religious zeal never before paralleled."[2] It was natural for the Unitarian moralists to associate this awakening of compassion with an awakening of piety; it seemed to Henry Ware, Jr., as to many historians since, that "those who have drunk most deeply the spirit of Jesus, and entered most fully into the genius of his religion, have been distinguished for their labors in behalf of their fellow-men."[3]

The benevolent Boston moralists regarded their efforts in the context of a worldwide Christian enterprise. Attempts to improve the condition of the soldiers in the Crimea, the primitive savages of Oceana, or lunatics in American asylums all seemed to James Walker parts of a gigantic, integrated philanthropic movement. "Men are beginning to feel, as they never did before, that there is an important sense in which every one is his brother's keeper," the Harvard President observed with satisfaction.[4] The Unitarians drew especially heavily on British reformers for inspiration and example. Their favorite political theorist, Edmund Burke, was a well-known advocate of a number of reforms in Britain and the Empire. Enlightened English aristocrats like Anthony Ashley Cooper and Sir James Mackintosh seemed to New England's would-be aristocrats ideal reformers.[5] In truth, the objectives of upper- and upper-middle-class British humanitarians in the early nineteenth century did bear much similarity to the moralism and essential conservatism of the American Unitarians. Unitarian philanthropy, like Unitarian philosophy and literature, manifested a cosmopolitan, trans-Atlantic cultural orientation.[6]

Although Harvard Unitarian philanthropy shared a great deal in common with Protestant philanthropy throughout the Western world, it had its own special development. The rise of organized philanthropy among New England Unitarians was related to the decline of the sacramental functions of the "church" (as distinguished from the "parish") among them. Traditionally, only the converted members of the church had received the sacrament of the Lord's Supper. But as belief in predestination withered and Arminian ideas of self-cultivation gained acceptance in the vicinity of Boston, the old theological basis for distinguishing the "elect" from the "damned" was eroded. When (as we have already related) the Liberal meeting-houses began to open their communion tables to all, the church was left without its customary special function.

If the church were to retain its corporate identity, it would have to develop a new purpose. A project for reviving the church and providing it with a raison d'être in changed circumstances was undertaken by Nathan Parker, minister of the Liberal South Parish in Portsmouth, New Hampshire. Beginning in 1813, Parker devoted the meetings of his church to the consideration of charitable needs in the parish. At the Berry Street Conference of 1822, Parker urged his practice upon the other Unitarian parishes. The ultimate outcome of Cotton Mather's "Essays to Do Good" (1710), Parker's plan transformed the church from a sacramental fellowship into a benevolent association.[7]

The Harvard philosophers regarded philanthropy as a spiritual exercise, as well as a community responsibility. They valued philanthropic magnanimity quite as much for its benefit to the donors as for its benefit to the recipients. To be sure, society was helped by philanthropic contributions, but the philanthropist himself also developed his personal virtue. The opportunity for generous giving enabled the well-to-do to cultivate their moral powers in an especially effective manner. "By no [other] means could those in the propertied classes be so advanced in the best qualities of the christian character," insisted a Unitarian moralist.[8] Among New England Unitarians, the exercise of philanthropy and the reading of improving literature tended to replace traditional religious forms as means of spiritual nurture.

Since the typical Harvard student or Unitarian pew-owner was a potential donor, not a potential recipient, of charity, it is not surprising that moralists should have often adopted the donor's point of view when addressing them. "You know not what means of personal good and happiness you are disregarding while you neglect . . . Christian benevolence," Joseph Tuckerman told the prosperous. The memory of philanthropic beneficence "will bring more gladness to your heart in the prospect of death than a remembrance of all your worldly success," he reminded them.[9] The efficacy of philanthropy in building a well-balanced character was a favorite sermon theme of the elder Henry Ware. And for those whose sins were great, philanthropy offered a way to get right with God again. Buckminster informed self-made men they could "atone for [their] rapacity" by charitable contributions.[10]

The quality that the philanthropist was supposed to cultivate through his munificence was "rectitude," that is, love of virtue. Consequently, it was not so much his objective to make the recipients of his alms happy, as to make them virtuous.[11] Harvard moralists frequently cautioned against charity that reflected mere benevolent impulses. Giving, in order to be effective, had to be rationally disciplined, and designed to do the most good in the long run. "We may find it hard to refuse a profligate beggar," warned John Emery Abbot, "but by gratifying him we may injure others by tempting them to negligence, encouraging them to idleness and improvidence, and holding out indemnity to vice."[12] Invariably, the Unitarians' charity was intended to reform and uplift the poor, not merely to mitigate their sufferings. The recipient would probably get an exhortation along with his dole, for unless it could be proved otherwise, most nineteenth-century Yankees assumed that poverty was the result of shiftlessness and sin.

Unitarian moralists were continually cautioning themselves against overindulgence of the vices of the poor. "We had better not cultivate a charity for other men's faults on principles which will lead us to be equally charitable to our own," warned President Walker. "We should remember, too, that it is God, all merciful as he is, who has made the wages of the transgressor hard; and it is not for such as we to interfere with this discipline."[13] The Unitarians were no more extreme than many other middle-class Protestant philanthropists in holding these attitudes; antebellum American philanthropy was often a device through which the middle classes sought to impose their moral values on the lower classes.[14]

If such a calculating and scrupulously "moral" attitude toward philanthropy had its arrogant and callous aspects, it was still not without its merits. Precisely because it placed such a premium on rationality and prudence, this attitude fostered a proto-scientific approach to social problems. Harvard moralists prided themselves on their rational investigations of society's ills: Henry Ware the younger amassed statistics on the evils of intemperance; tough-minded Francis Bowen studied statistics on prisons and concluded that the "Philadelphia System" of solitary confinement had disastrous effects on convicts.[15] The Unitarian moralists repeatedly expressed contempt for the impulsive largess of medieval nobles. "Unguarded, indiscriminate, profuse charity is no charity at all," they said, "for its tendency is to encourage indolence and wastefulness."[16] Their own philanthropy was intended to be judicious and discriminating, designed to get to the root of problems. "The best resources for improving the condition of the poor are *within themselves*," maintained Tuckerman; "they often need enlightenment respecting these resources more than alms."[17] Obviously the antebellum Unitarian moralists suffered from what seems to us their primitive sociology and oversimplified economics. Yet, in their attempts to apply quantitative methods, in their desire to eliminate the need for philanthropy, and in their honest belief that it would be best if the poor could help themselves, one can perceive the germs of enlightened social welfare.

Actually, the Harvard Unitarians were much less hardboiled in their approach to charity than many of their contemporaries. Tuckerman rebelled against the impersonal tone of much of the writing on the subject of pauperism. The poor, he complained, "have generally been treated merely as topics of political economy," and not as human beings.[18] The teachings of Malthus and the more extreme Manchester School economists (who maintained that philanthropy only raised the birthrate among the poor, canceling any amelioration of their condition) were indignantly rejected at Harvard. "Away with the misnamed philosophy which would lead to a result like this!" cried a student orator. "We need not argue against such doctrines, for we find a refutation of them in our own hearts."[19] Malthusianism contradicted the plain perceptions of the moral sense. Francis Bowen's textbook argued elaborately against Malthus. Human reproductivity was not an insurmountable stumbling block to progress, insisted Bowen. Sexual profligacy was the result of ignorance, apathy, and tyranny; eliminate these and the poor would check their birthrate. If the lower classes could be educated to aspire to a higher standard of living, and could feel assured that opportunities were really available, the Unitarian economist was sure they would marry late and keep down the size of their families. "Whatever tends to keep men hopelessly poor is a direct encouragement . . . to an increase in population," wrote Bowen. "It is not the excess of population which causes the misery, but the misery which causes the excess of population."[20]

Though poverty might be a punishment for sin, it was also clear to Unitarian moralists that the conditions of poverty could lead to sin. "The great calamity of the poor is not their poverty, understanding this word in its usual sense, but the tendency of their privations, and of their social rank, to degradation of mind," explained Dr. Channing.[21] Unitarian philanthropy sought to put into practice the precepts of Harvard moral philosophy by removing the pitfalls surrounding the poor on the path of virtue. Christian revelation taught that all men were immortal moral agents; Unitarian natural religion taught that all were capable of indefinite personal improvement. "Every human being has a nature by which he is qualified [assuming proper instruction] for endless intellectual and moral progress."[22] Yet, all about him, the Unitarian moralist could see human "capacities to an immense extent wasted or perverted"—especially "in the laboring and dependent classes." Here was an apparent violation of the Christian principle that all men are equal in the sight of God. "Christianity would remove, or enable every individual to surmount, every obstacle in the way to the highest moral completeness within his attainment," insisted Tuckerman. "It would make the hewer of wood and the drawer of water, the mere drain digger and the scavenger, morally as complete a being as it would make the most exalted [minister of religion]. It would make the servant morally as perfect as his master." By working to achieve the "equal relative perfection" of all human personalities, the Unitarian philanthropist rendered his "filial obedience to God."[23]

Tuckerman, who had more experience with actual philanthropic activity than any of the other twelve moralists treated here, drew inspiration for his efforts from the doctrines of Harvard Unitarianism. "There is no human being, however depraved, who is yet totally depraved," he valiantly asserted; "no one for whom moral efforts are not to be made as long as God shall uphold him in being." The dignity and perfectibility of every personality "was a first principle of that theory of human nature with which I entered upon my ministry [to the poor]; and every step of my way . . . has convinced me of [its] truth." Tuckerman credited his faith in this principle with enabling him to rehabilitate derelicts from the slums, whom "otherwise I should hardly have been induced to make an effort" to save. To the

Unitarian humanist, the doctrine of perfectibility was the foundation for all efforts to aid the poor. Tuckerman thought that a Calvinist preacher who went into the slums teaching predestination and depravity did more harm than good.[24]

The obstacles that Unitarian moralists conceived to stand in the way of the moral progress of the poor were environmental, not hereditary. Harvard thinkers recognized, of course, that men were born with variations of temperament; they considered that in consequence different men were vulnerable to different types of temptation. But they rejected all theories of genetic determinism, including racism. Though prejudice against the Irish and the Negroes was strong and periodically violent in antebellum Boston, the Unitarian moralists did not give way to it. William Ellery Channing and James Walker were among those responsible local leaders who deplored the excesses of anti-Irish-Catholic nativism. Later, Walker warned Harvard undergraduates in chapel not to be carried away by the "extreme" notions concerning "distinctions of race and blood" popular with the masses.[25] On the subject of American Negroes, Tuckerman wrote: "In regard to these fellow beings, the colored, our prejudices (for such are our opinions and feelings) are altogether unworthy of us not only as Christians but as Republicans."[26] Among Dr. Channing's friends and regular callers was a black schoolteacher. Reflecting upon the situation of the Africans (as he termed them) in Boston, the Federal Street pastor burst out, "What powers, how much *mind,* how much *heart,* what treasures, are contained in them! Shall all be lost?" he asked in exasperation. Channing hoped for an educational program which would "awaken a sense of their true dignity and true excellence" within black children.[27]

Unitarian moralists often celebrated the heroic efforts of those who triumphed over degrading environments to achieve personal integration and virtue. "There are none who have reached a higher moral elevation, who deserve a more exalted and enduring fame" than these, according to the younger Ware. It was invigorating to know that there were people who, in spite of hardship and misfortune, had managed to "assert the dignity of their being."[28] In the didactic tales the moralists wrote, models of virtue were usually taken from the poor, rather than the rich, in an effort to encourage the former and make the latter more compassionate. Such stories were attempts to bridge the gulf between the classes, and persuade the prosperous that the poor shared a common humanity. Tuckerman even included Negroes among the heroes of his "real life" stories.[29] The Harvard Unitarians, whatever their political conservatism and frequent timidity, were at least theoretically loyal to the doctrine that "a *man,* be his nation, complexion, condition, or capacity what it may, is an image of God."[30]

THE PRACTICE OF UNITARIAN PHILANTHROPY

The twelve representatives of Unitarian moralism treated in this study expressed support, at one time or another, for most of the charitable and reform movements of their day. Among the causes for which one or more Unitarian moralists labored were the Bible Society, temperance, peace, orphanages, opposition to dueling, prison reform, legal reform, and reform of the treatment of juvenile offenders.[31] The Unitarian reaction to slavery, a problem of special gravity and complexity, will be discussed in the next chapter. In the present section, it seems best to concentrate attention upon the philanthropic activities of one man who devoted a great deal of thought and energy to this phase of Unitarian moralism, the Reverend Joseph Tuckerman.[32]

Like the clergy of the Social Gospel two thirds of a century later, Tuckerman worked to awaken middle-class Americans to the plight of their urban poor. He sought to describe the slums of Boston—which then stood within five minutes walk of the best houses in town—to people with little awareness of the misery existing so near them. The frequent indifference to suffering that Tuckerman found in the city outraged his moral consciousness.[33] His Unitarian social theory accepted inequality, of course, but only an inequality which included the exercise of Christian charity. The Unitarian philanthropist resembled the Unitarian literary artist: both were concerned to create a greater emotional sensitivity, accompanied by a greater sense of moral responsibility, among the members of the middle class.

The lot of the poor is always and everywhere hard, and even in the relatively open society of antebellum America slum life was sufficiently appalling. The population of Boston quadrupled in the first four decades of the nineteenth century, and as the city grew, the economic cleavages in society became sharper than they had been in colonial times.[34] An urban lower class, drawn largely from uprooted rural populations in both New England and Western Europe, was developing. The most unfortunate members of this class constituted what Yankee contemporaries called "the poor." Immigrants and free Negroes, widowed and unwed mothers, the sick and the cripples, with large numbers of alcoholics and prostitutes among them, Boston's poor were an identifiable element by the second quarter of the nineteenth century. During recurrent economic slumps, the ranks of the poor were swollen by hordes of unemployed laborers. As the city enlarged, "neighborhoods" developed, corresponding to the growing economic stratification. The brick tenements of the later nineteenth century had not yet been built; poor neighborhoods then consisted of wooden shacks or "shanties." Along the waterfront, two or three families sometimes lived in one-room cellars. Both shanties and cellars lacked sewage or sanitation of any kind, and were periodically plagued by destructive fires.[35] A Unitarian observer could only marvel that a "kind and merciful Father" should treat His children so unequally. "In the same nation, whole classes [live] in luxury and comfort; [while] other classes, by their side, hardly grope their way through wretchedness and toil to a scanty and precarious subsistence."[36]

Before Tuckerman turned to the problem, Boston's poverty had attracted little attention. A crude program of "outdoor" relief, administered by annually elected officials who kept few records, was the mainstay of municipal social action. Even this system was better than that prevailing in many other Massachusetts townships, where the relief of the poor was farmed out at auction to the lowest bidder.[37] The church did not make up for the lack of interest on the part of the state. Indeed, the ecclesiastical establishment seemed only too willing to ignore the growing masses of the slums. By the 1830's the population of Boston exceeded the seating capacity of the churches by 20,000. Since pews were normally rented or sold, when poor persons did attend church they were relegated to humiliating galleries designated "free."[38] Such treatment did not go down well in Jacksonian America; it is no wonder that only 58 percent of the families in Boston had "regular connexions" with organized Christianity.[39] Though an occasional Liberal minister had called attention to the sufferings of the poor (young Buckminster did what he could during the frightful unemployment of Jefferson's Embargo), the record of Boston churches in the first quarter of the nineteenth century had not been noteworthy. Henry Ware, Jr., confessed that the Standing Order had allowed the urban poor to become "debased [and] abandoned."[40]

The Unitarians of Boston (like other conservatives throughout American history) had been reluctant to admit that anyone moral, willing, and able could be poor in their favored land. The poor, as we have seen, they tended to identify with the "profligate," "passionate," and "vicious" element in society. In 1818 it still seemed to Andrews Norton that "honest industry" could secure to any American "all the necessaries and many of the conveniences" of life.[41] Furthermore, Unitarian natural theology sometimes belittled the extent of human misery. Yet there were other components in the Unitarian world view that made for a compassionate response to the demands of civic responsibility, once these became clear. The Liberal Christians prided themselves on their ability to face facts, to study problems rationally, and to translate religious concerns into ethical action. "The happy community is that in which its members care for one another, and in which there is, especially, an interest in the intellectual and moral improvement of all," taught Harvard civil polity.[42] And so, beginning in 1822, a small "association of [Unitarian] gentlemen" met once a week in Boston to consider ways of relieving the distress of the poor. William Ellery Channing and Henry Ware, Jr., were among those who took an active part in the meetings.

Like many good middle-class people, the Unitarian gentlemen looked upon the poor with mingled pity and disgust. Ware observed: "Amidst dark and comfortless cells, where hunger and cold are perpetual afflictions, ... where parents and children converse only in words of blasphemy and reviling; where the whole intercourse is that of ignorant brutality, ... it is difficult to say whether the wretchedness be more deplorable, or the depravity more hopeless."[43] What bothered these reflective Liberals most was the degrading and inhibiting influence the slum environment exerted upon its inhabitants. The conditions of slum life were inimical to the cultivation of a Christian character, to the self-development and self-fulfillment that Unitarians prized as the essence of religion and the chief end of man.

Despite its good intentions, the little association found it had neither the time nor the money to work with the poor on the scale that was needed. In 1826 the gentlemen persuaded the American Unitarian Association to establish a full-time ministry to the poor of Boston. Channing and Ware, heavily committed in other enterprises, were unavailable for the call. The choice for the post fell upon a little-known clergyman from a small town, Joseph Tuckerman.

Tuckerman was then forty-eight years old and in poor health. Having served the Liberal parish in Chelsea, Massachusetts, for twenty-five years, he found his throat would no longer stand the strain of the two sixty-minute sermons that convention demanded of a Congregational pastor each Sunday. Deciding to take on a job whose duties involved less public speaking, Tuckerman resigned his pastorate and was engaged as Boston's minister to the poor. (He soon changed the title to "minister-at-large.") What had been undertaken in the expectation that it would make few demands on his feeble body turned out to be the significant achievement of his life. Quickly caught up in his new vocation, Tuckerman burned himself out in the service of his slum parishioners.

The incoming minister-at-large saw his task in terms of implementing the principles of Unitarian moral philosophy. "Admit a moral government of the world, and that man has a moral nature," he argued, and it follows "that the moral necessities of those near and around us . . . are to be regarded as divine calls upon us."[44] To help prepare himself for his duties, Tuckerman read extensively in European social thinkers, especially in the works of Thomas Chalmers (1780–1847), a Scottish contemporary who was also engaged in applying the principles of moral philosophy to the practice of philanthropy.[45]

The conditions Tuckerman found in the shanties of the poor were hopelessly incompatible with Christian life as Unitarians understood it. Without a bare minimum of physical comfort, Tuckerman discovered, spiritual life was stifled. In such an environment people could exist only "by ceasing to feel themselves to be human beings." Tuckerman informed his fellow middle-class citizens that the slum dwellers "can be contented with their condition, and can enjoy life, only in proportion as their intellectual and moral powers shall be depressed, and as they shall live exclusively for the gratification of their merely animal propensities and passions."[46]

Was this dehumanizing poverty a necessary concomitant of urbanization? Many prophets had said so, and had warned in somber tones of the consequences of the growth of cities. Thomas Jefferson was only the most famous of those who maintained that cities would prove "great sores" upon the body politic.[47] Adam Ferguson, the Scottish moralist admired at Harvard for his work in "civil polity," had written: "If great numbers be crouded into narrow districts, or cities, they are exposed to corruption; become profligate, licentious, seditious, and incapable of public affections."[48] Some Transcendentalist intellectuals sought escape from an urbanizing society in individual or communal arcadias. But Tuckerman saw the growth of the city not as a threat, but as a challenge. His was a confident generation of Unitarians. "There can be no moral evil, either in an individual or in a city, which is inevitable. The idea of inevitable moral evil is . . . an absurdity." The evils that had attended urbanization could be eradicated and cities remain, providential instruments for human progress and "the highest moral ends of God."

The incoming minister-at-large was determined to recreate in the growing city something of the intimacy and security of the village life he had known for twenty-five years. "There the rich and the poor, or, in other words, those who had some capital and those who had none, met on terms of equality before the church door on Sunday, [and] interchanged expressions of friendly greeting," he recalled. "In every family of my flock I was at home."[49] This, of course, was the organic society idealized by Unitarian social theory. The memory of Chelsea served Tuckerman as a model for his hopes and expectations in Boston. Tuckerman did not live to see Boston's social problems vastly compounded by the Irish Potato Famine of 1845, though one may question whether even this would have dampened his faith in the potential of the urban way of life. Francis Bowen, who did live through the era of Boston's greatest social trauma, never wavered in his optimistic assessment of the city and its ability to absorb immigration.[50] Resolute acceptance of an urban civilization was one of the distinctive features of Boston-Cambridge Unitarianism in the age of the Second Awakening.

The activities Tuckerman undertook among Boston's poor were many and varied. He opened chapels where the poor could worship in their own neighborhoods without the invidious social distinctions made in meeting-houses whose pews were private property. Knowing that many of his parishioners were employed in the daytime, even on Sunday, Tuckerman scheduled services for the evening. He also started a Sunday school, where several hundred poor children could be found receiving Christian nurture on any Sabbath in the late 1830's. Adding material to spiritual bounty, the Unitarian minister would dispense clothing and sums of money when he felt it was needed—frequently in the form of loans, since he believed this would encourage frugality and diligence. Tuckerman inspired some charitably inclined Unitarian businessmen to start a Farm School in 1832, where potential juvenile delinquents (the term was used in that day) could be sent, with their parents' consent, to learn agricultural trades. The school, after being satisfied that a boy had become vocationally skilled and morally rehabilitated, would place him as a hired hand.[51]

Tuckerman achieved good relations with minority groups in Boston. He not only sympathized with the Irish, he even cooperated in a fraternal manner with their Catholic clergy. Among his projects aiding the black community was a sewing school designed to help Negro girls get jobs. Neither did the Unitarian minister neglect the people whose emissary he was. Four times in the first year of his ministry, and twice a year thereafter, Tuckerman composed lengthy reports to the Unitarian churches who paid his expenses, describing the conditions he discovered and calling for charitable interventions on a larger scale. He argued powerfully for the reform of many institutions the poor encountered—the prison, the reform school, the municipal "overseers of the poor."[52]

But the most valuable contribution of Tuckerman's was the practice of home visitations. The minister-at-large would regularly call upon troubled families and combine a program of material aid with counseling. To judge by his own accounts, Tuckerman frequently succeeded in "reforming" drunken fathers, neglectful mothers, and rebellious children. While his methods of family counseling were probably naive by twentieth-century standards, they entitle Tuckerman to be called a "pioneer in American social work."[53]

The technique of home visitation arose from Tuckerman's desire to make sure that the aid he was giving people was being put to its intended uses, and not squandered in dissipation. In all his efforts, the moral, rather than the material, purpose was primary: Tuckerman was not so much engaged in relieving suffering as in trying to make better people. The physical and intellectual needs of the poor interested him largely, if not solely, as means to satisfying their moral and spiritual needs. As his biographer has remarked, "Tuckerman, the social worker and embryonic social scientist, was [always] primarily a Protestant minister."[54]

Tuckerman regarded his mission as a witness by the community to humane values, as an attempt to bring "sympathy," "respect," and "encouragement" to people who had encountered little of these in the city. His intention was, in short, to humanize the grim, impersonal, urban environment. Tuckerman's high estimation of human nature gave him the strength for his task. The potential of man could be vindicated, even amidst the temptations of the city: "I do not believe there ever was or that there is a human being in whom there was or is no element of goodness; no element of moral recoverableness; no unextinguished spark of moral sensibility, which, with God's blessing, may not be blown into a flame." This regard for human dignity manifested no "enthusiasm" or "heated fancy," he insisted; it was grounded in "strong conviction" and "sensibility."[55]

In order to reconcile his views on the rehabilitation of the poor with the common Yankee assumption that the poor were morally corrupt, Tuckerman employed an ingenious distinction between "poverty" and "pauperism." "Poverty" he defined as simple "dependence upon alms." It was a condition carrying no moral stigma—indeed, Tuckerman went so far as to remind his contemporaries that Christ had been poor. Among those living in simple poverty might be widows and orphans, the feebleminded and the sick, and even (though Tuckerman sometimes forgot to include this group) the involuntarily unemployed. A certain amount of such destitution was inevitable and even wholesome, thought Tuckerman; it was "one of the intended conditions of man in this world." Its existence permitted the prosperous to exercise their munificence and the victims to enjoy the salutory rigors of character-building abstemiousness. "There are cases of poverty, or of dependence upon alms, of which no one of enlarged views and sensibilities would wish to free the world." The virtuous poor had a legitimate moral claim upon the rest of society for support: the right of some people to accumulate property was distinctly limited by the right of other people (who could not support themselves) to alms.[56]

On the other hand, there were the "paupers." Tuckerman defined "pauperism" as "a preference of support by alms, to support by personal labor."[57] All penury was not the result of unavoidable circumstances and the will of Providence; sometimes it was the fault of human laziness and profligacy. The paupers were the class of shirkers, the class to whom the customary middle-class moral reprobation applied. Tuckerman often employed the word "vagrant" as a synonym for "pauper." Whereas the legitimate poor should be cared for with tender charity, either in their own homes or in "almshouses," Tuckerman would confine the vagrant paupers to stern "workhouses." The Unitarian philanthropist bitterly resented the fact that paupers could not be incarcerated unless they had been convicted of some crime. He felt not the slightest concern for the fine points of civil liberties involved. "To me, indeed, it seems most absurd, to talk of the personal rights and of the constitutionally guaranteed freedom of those who not only have nothing, and who, though able, will do nothing, for self-support, but whose example is every day extending corruption to those around them."[58] Though Tuckerman admitted that the paupers might not be entirely to blame for their lack of motivation and prudence, his moralistic discussion of pauperism is basically incompatible with the environmentalist interpretation of slum depravity he offered elsewhere. By including the class of paupers in his analysis of society, Tuckerman showed his continued loyalty to traditional standards of individual moral responsibility. A Harvard Unitarian could not blame the environment for everything; sometimes the evils that befell men must represent their just deserts.[59]

The distinction between poverty and pauperism was related to the distinction Tuckerman drew between public and private philanthropy. Though an energetic and dedicated exponent of private charity, Tuckerman was an outspoken and inveterate opponent of government intervention on behalf of the poor. Moral suasion was the only means of reform he could bring himself to endorse; he was convinced that all reforms based on legal coercion were bound to entail greater evils than they were supposed to remedy. Moral suasion should be sufficient to combat prostitution, gambling, and heavy drinking; likewise it should suffice to persuade the affluent to share their surplus with the unfortunate.[60] Among the schemes for government action that Tuckerman examined and rejected were rent subsidies, public work projects for the unemployed, and public soup-kitchens. He was convinced that aiding the poor through tax monies was wastefully expensive and deadening to the moral sensibilities of all involved. Whereas private charity was morally stimulating to donor and recipient alike, public relief schemes invariably threatened to undermine individual initiative and responsibility. In short, public relief threatened to create an ever increasing number of "paupers."[61]

Tuckerman carried his devotion to voluntarism to such an extreme that he even demanded the repeal of the seventeenth-century Massachusetts statute requiring each township to make provision for its own poor. "Let not Legislatures indulge the vain imagination that it is within their province . . . to require and enforce the observance of the moral laws of God," he wrote. To support his preference for private philanthropy, Tuckerman contrasted the state of the poor in England (where there was public relief) and in Ireland (where all relief was private). The Irish poor, he acknowledged, were worse off materially, but they had stronger "domestic affections" and retained a "readiness to share their few means of comfort with each other." Furthermore, the Irish poor were inoffensive: "they are content, as our own poor are not, to live in filth, and upon food which an English or American beggar would spurn." When they received any charity, "there is no more grateful class of human beings than the Irish poor." This, in the Unitarian minister's estimation, vindicated private over public charity.[62]

Tuckerman was opposed to collective bargaining and labor unions, as well as to welfare legislation. He shared the views of Francis Bowen that labor was a commodity whose price was governed by the "natural principle" of supply and demand. Yet he could not rid himself of the older, medieval Christian, notion that there was such a thing as a "just wage." So, even though he subscribed to the commodity theory of labor, he still asked employers to pay the "full amount earned" and not to force wages down in times of "pressing necessity." Statutory minimum wages came, of course, under the interdicted category of government intervention. The minister-at-large put his faith for the improvement of labor's condition, not in such "artificial" schemes, but in "the advancement of high moral and religious principle." Tuckerman's basic conception of the good society seems to have been taken from the "civil polity" he had studied years before at Harvard College.[63]

Tuckerman the philanthropist shared the fears of class conflict expressed by Bowen the economist. If the prosperous did not recognize the just claims of the unfortunate, Tuckerman shuddered to think what would happen. The poor "look about them for the causes of their sufferings," he warned, and may well "think that they find them in the insensibility of the rich." If that happened, "discontent, envy, jealousy, and resentment" would be awakened, and the stage set for some form of class conflict.[64] The wider dissemination of democratic feelings among the working classes in the Age of Jackson made Tuckerman all the more anxious to avoid provoking their hostility. After worsening health had forced him into declining activity, he passed on to his fellow Americans this dying admonition:

No one doubts that the present is most emphatically a transition state of society. Great changes are going on with great rapidity throughout the civilized world. Nor are these merely outward changes . . . Thoughts . . . which a century ago were confined to a few minds, are now awakened . . . in the minds of the many . . . I refer particularly to prevalent thoughts, feelings, and principles of freedom, independence, and personal rights . . . The people are every day becoming more a reality; a power: and a power too which is felt, and must be respected. [But] how far is this voice the voice of wisdom? How far is vox populi also vox Dei? . . . Suppose that this multitude shall be left morally uncared for; its growing capacities receiving all their nurture . . . from appetite and passion . . . What then will be the stability either of your ecclesiastical, or republican institutions? Do you see nothing admonitory in the discontents . . . and outbreaks among those who . . . with high notions of rights, and very low notions of duties, are yet daily advancing in power? . . . The popular commentary upon liberty and rights, as they are understood by certain among us, has been written in blood by the hands of mobs. And what but an infuriated mob spirit is to be looked for in any great collisions of interests and of passions among us, from a general prevalence of insane notions of freedom, and independence, and the equal rights of man?[65]

The French Revolution had identified Christianity with social order in the minds of innumerable conservatives throughout the Western world; one of these, apparently, was the Unitarian minister-at-large. An irreligious proletariat could not be trusted.[66]

Tuckerman's efforts to reconcile social classes and bring them into a closer harmony reveal a curious mixture of Christian compassion with class-consciousness. He frequently spoke of the socioeconomic benefits of promoting organized religion among the lower orders. Religion would make the poor more honest, sober, frugal, industrious, and contented. In addition, the charitable activities of the church would help make the poor duly grateful to the rich. A "wise" minister-at-large, Tuckerman wrote, "will not fail" to remind the poor what they owe to their patrons, and will take advantage of the "daily opportunities [for] calling forth the kindly affections of the poor towards the rich." Thus the minister acted as an emissary of goodwill between the classes.[67]

It is possible that Tuckerman's writings exaggerate his dedication to class interest. Even if his own efforts were largely motivated by a desire to help the poor, he may well have found it necessary to emphasize middle-class self-interest in order to secure financial support for his activities. If a reformer were to achieve change within the existing system, he could ill-afford to propose remedies that were too drastic, ask questions that were too fundamental, or antagonize the powerful. And so Tuckerman chose to appeal to the prudence, as well as to the sentiments and conscience, of his fellow Unitarians. The Central Board of the Benevolent Fraternity of Churches, which sponsored the activities of Tuckerman and the other ministers-at-large whom he persuaded them to engage, was fond of appeals to enlightened selfishness.

Such a ministry [to Boston's poor] is greatly promotive of the interests of the wealthier classes of society . . . The political safety and security of the wealthier classes in this country, is not only greatly affected by the moral character of the poor, but rests mainly upon it. The stability of our General and State governments [and] the security of property . . . are, evidently, very much in the hands of what in Europe are called the poorer classes. They hold the votes, they wield the power; and a fearful one it will prove, unless directed by moral and religious principle. If interest, then, can bind men to each other, surely all the energies of the wealthy should be directed to affording encouragement and support to well-conducted efforts for the improvement of the moral state of the poor.[68]

His contemporaries held Tuckerman's work in great esteem, and took it for a model. To the Unitarian journal of the day, the ministry-at-large seemed "the noblest expression of that idea of moral culture which more than any other [conception] marks the age."[69] Next to his pioneering work in social welfare counseling, perhaps Tuckerman's most obvious achievement was to father a substantial interdenominational benevolent association to carry on his work. In 1834 twenty-six charitable organizations established a union in Boston, holding monthly meetings to exchange information and avoid duplications of effort. By 1838 (a dozen years after Tuckerman had begun his mission) there were at least ten ministers-at-large in Boston, of whom four were Unitarians. Reviewing the accomplishments of his own and other humanitarian undertakings, Tuckerman became fervently eloquent: "The mighty agent, by which these changes have been accomplished . . . is the power of voluntary association . . . But let all the virtuous and the wise feel its import, and faithfully avail themselves of it . . . and it will not long be doubtful to my mind, whether indeed the enterprise be feasible, of the *conversion of the world.*[70]

Tuckerman deserves to be ranked with Buckminster as an imaginative adapter of Unitarian moralism. Keeping all the while in close touch with leaders of opinion like Dr. Channing and the younger

Ware, he demonstrated how ethical theory could be put into practice. He led the Unitarian clergy into the forefront of philanthropic activity, as Buckminster had led them into literary endeavor. Even while the Unitarian Federalist ideal of a unified church-state commonwealth was dying, Tuckerman was helping to create a new institutional structure, voluntaristic rather than mercantilistic, to take its place.[71] In private benevolent association, Tuckerman forged an instrument that Unitarians would find a valuable substitute for government intervention on behalf of social morality. Like Buckminster, too, Tuckerman succeeded in bringing the merchant classes into line in support of the efforts of the moralists. Together, Liberal moralists and enlightened Boston businessmen created a tradition of Unitarian Whig philanthropy.

This philanthropy is difficult for us to assess.[72] No simple evaluation can do justice to the complexity of the motives of Tuckerman and his fellow moralists. While they welcomed America's industrial transformation, Boston's moral elite were anxious to keep its consequences under control. It was their dual intention to retain as much economic and political power as possible in the hands of the commercial classes they trusted, but at the same time to awaken these allies to an awareness of their social responsibilities. Unitarian philanthropy expressed twin commitments to capitalism and compassion, to Enlightenment reason and Christian concern, to progress and stability. From a twentieth-century standpoint, of course, it certainly looks as though Tuckerman underestimated the contribution government action could make toward social justice. But he and his co-workers came forward to help when they heard a call. Whatever their limitations may have been, they are at least entitled to respect.

EDUCATIONAL IDEALS FOR A FREE SOCIETY

The school was as important an institution as the church in the eyes of the Unitarian moralists. In fact, the church and the school had essentially the same mission, for both were basically character-building institutions, guiding people in the formation of industrious habits, religious principles, and refined sentiments. Unless the school did its part, Unitarian ministers warned, the church would not be able to carry the burden alone. The spiritual as well as the cultural aspirations of the Liberal moralists were predicated upon education: Henry Ware, Jr., listing "the means of religious improvement," included prayer, the sacrament, and hearing the preaching of the Word, but what he put first was "Reading."[73] The value of national literacy to men who hoped to foster a national awakening with literature is obvious enough, though there was much more to the Unitarians' conception of education than literacy. "Man was intended for education," was their motto; and it was the job of the moral elite to offer this opportunity to all.[74]

In Unitarian moral philosophy, education was a never ending process of self-cultivation and growth; it did not even cease with death, for Harvard Liberals thought of heaven as a place where individual self-development continued forever.[75] So conceived, education was a religious and moral duty. For men who sought their salvation through character-training, it was literally true that "life itself [was] but one long day-school" and that "education [was] the business of life."[76] It seems only appropriate that when one of the greatest graduates of antebellum Harvard set down the story of his life, he retained enough of this classic Unitarian attitude to call his autobiography *The Education of Henry Adams*.

The educational theory of the Harvard moralists was grounded in their faculty psychology. Each of man's faculties ought to be strengthened through exercise by a properly devised educational program. Such an approach to education may be broadly categorized as "mental discipline." Most theories of education held in nineteenth-century America were varieties of "mental discipline"; here as in so many other respects the Harvard Unitarians were archetypal men of their age.[77] The basic idea of mental discipline has been advocated by many famous educational theorists, and the New England Unitarians drew encouragement from a number of them. Christian Wolff (1679–1754), the German psychologist, seems to have laid the foundation for an educational theory based on the mental faculties. However, the Scottish philosopher Dugald Stewart and the Swiss educator Johann Heinrich Pestalozzi (1746–1827) were better known in New England as advocates of the "harmonious" and "balanced" development of the faculties.[78] Much earlier, of course, John Locke had proposed a varied curriculum as the basis for an education in which man's several powers could be developed. Locke's educational writings, like his works on philosophy and religion, were much admired by Yankee Liberals. Still another source of inspiration and example for Unitarian educators was none other than the English Dissenting hymnographer Isaac Watts, who wrote catechisms and religious songs for children as well as textbooks for college students and pedagogical essays for teachers. Much of Locke's influence upon New England Unitarian educational theory was actually mediated by Watts, his evangelical disciple.[79]

Unitarians distinguished three aspects of formal schooling: (1) "the development of the faculties," (2) "the acquisition of knowledge," and (3) "special fitness for the special employment on which one is to enter."[80] Of the three, the first was by far the most important, and was indeed often considered the only objective of education properly so called. The second objective was distinctly inferior, as Dr. Channing and Professor Frisbie declared: "The principal aim of a good teacher is not to fix in the memory knowledge which others have discovered, but to make the student as active as possible in discovering it for himself." "In choosing pursuits for a child, I should not so much consider what would be the most useful to know when a man, as what was best fitted to exercise the reason, and gradually unfold and invigorate the understanding; because knowledge is easily acquired at any time; but wisdom, unless it early become a habit, never will."[81] Vocational training scored a very weak third in the Unitarian list of priorities. In fact, the Harvard philosophers viewed occupational specialization with sadness. "The successful pursuit of a single art, or of the fraction of a single science, is but poor compensation for the loss of all versatility and alertness of mind. One may become a good accountant, an expert mathematician, and even a skillful lawyer, without being anything more than a fraction of a man."[82]

Education properly concerned itself with all man's faculties, including conscience and the affections. The "heart," as well as the "head," could be educated, the goal being to achieve a well-balanced total personality. Both the rational and the emotional components of man's moral nature were capable of improvement through conscious effort. To be sure, fundamental obligations were perceived alike by all normal men, but experience and training helped one apply these general rules to the complexities of human events. The rational ability to judge specific duties could be developed "by accustoming the mind to dwell on questions of casuistry . . . and to try doubtful cases rather by general rules than by particular results."[83] Perhaps even more important was the refinement of the emotional moral taste. "What is wanted," insisted President Walker, "is the education of the conscience; and this, too, not on the side of intelligence, but of sensibility."[84] In its efforts to awaken the power of conscience, Unitarian educational theory partook of the evangelical and sentimental qualities that characterized other aspects of Unitarian thought.

Harvard educational theory also gave the faculty of reason its due. One respect in which the Liberals' distinctive theological position affected their pedagogical theory was their emphasis upon open-mindedness as an educational objective. Education should "inspire a profound love of truth" and "teach the processes of investigation," William Ellery Channing insisted; one must then learn to pursue truth "no matter where it leads, what interest it opposes, [or] to what persecution or loss it lays [one] open."[85] Unitarian moralists were not guilty of confusing education with propaganda. James Walker was emphatic on this point: "It is not among the proper or legitimate objects of education, either in religion or anything else, to inculcate an implicit or blind faith, to bind down and enslave the soul to a fixed creed, or to dictate, either directly or indirectly, what the mind shall think, feel, or believe." The Harvard president claimed not to *shape* his students, so much as to help them *grow*, for "education . . . does not consist in putting things *into* the mind, but, as the name implies, in bringing things *out*." All real education was fundamentally self-education; the proper role of the teacher was limited to providing a helpful environment.[86] A Unitarian educator saw himself as a Christian humanist, promoting the fulfillment of human potential. From our own point of view, the educational ideals of the New England Unitarians may well be among their most attractive features.

Since Unitarian social theory devoted considerable attention to the role of a leadership class in creating a national culture, it is not surprising that Liberal moralists sometimes exhorted their fellow-countrymen to devote more attention to the education of an elite. Francis Bowen wrote a lengthly article for the *North American Review* exposing the defects of higher education in Jacksonian America. Local and sectarian rivalries had promoted a multiplicity of weak institutions with low academic standards. Typically, college administrators concentrated on expanding their enrollments and their physical facilities while giving little heed to the quality of instruction. As a result, Bowen complained, American colleges were not producing the intellectuals the country needed. To judge by the analyses of twentieth-century scholars, Bowen's criticisms were well founded.[87]

But the Unitarian moralists did not confine their concern to creating a patrician class of scholars; they were also deeply interested in the education of the many. "I should reluctantly part with aristocracy, if I thought the perfect gentleman was to vanish with it," Dr. Channing confessed to a friend. "But I am sure that the grace, refinement, and charm of the gentlemanly character . . . are to be diffused gradually through all classes of society." A good educational system provided the chief hope for the success of such humane aspirations; "happily for the race, the time is passing away in which intellect was thought to be the monopoly of a few, and the majority were given over to hopeless ignorance."[88] Henry Ware, Jr.'s fictional David Ellington went about telling his fellows that a liberal education was appropriate for laborers and mechanics as well as for professional men: "The common notion has been, that the mass of the people need no other culture than is necessary to fit them for their various trades. . . But the ground of a man's culture lies in his nature, not in his calling . . . He is to be educated because he is a man, not because he is to make shoes, nails, or pins. A trade is plainly not the end of his being, for his mind cannot be shut up in it."[89]

Unitarian moralists came closer to accepting truly democratic principles in their educational theory than anywhere else. They were outspoken friends of the Massachusetts common schools (which they rightly treasured as a legacy from the Puritans) , as well as of the various lyceums, endowed lectures, and other programs of adult education popular in their day. They derived their commitment to public education from two sources: (1) their faculty psychology, which taught that every man could develop his potential through mental discipline, and (2) their social theory, which stressed the importance of a cultivated elite. If the former was manifestly democratic, the latter could also be reconciled with democracy provided access to the educated classes were kept open to talent. Such was the intention of the Unitarian moralists. Despite the misgivings with which the Liberal intelligentsia often regarded social mobility, they wholeheartedly endorsed education as a means of guaranteeing equal opportunity. (Of course, they themselves had often risen by this means.) [90]

The elder Ware's Election Sermon for 1821 explained the duty of the state in keeping public education an avenue of social advancement. Though men are created equal in the sight of God, "no sooner are we born into the world, than more circumstances, than can be named or imagined, contribute to destroy this original equality." A "Christian government" is obliged to restore a measure of equality; yet it would be unjust to achieve this by expropriating the wealth of the privileged. The answer to the problem lies in "providing that the means of education shall be extended to all," thereby keeping careers open to talent.[91] Thirty-five years later President Walker declared that educators must search out talent wherever it might exist, and then place it "in the way of the highest possible culture." In this manner only could the American political experiment succeed, for only this could ensure the country a high calibre of leadership. "If this be so, gentlemen," he concluded, "it gives a new importance, a new significance, to our vocation as teachers. It is through our instrumentality that the great problem is to be solved: perfect order and perfect liberty."[92]

A good deal of the Harvard moralists' advocacy of education consisted of pleading for financial support from their fellow Americans— many of whom were not noted for their appreciation of cultural, or even spiritual, things. Eloquent phrases about enrichment of life or the development of the intellect through liberal studies must often have fallen upon deaf ears. Sometimes, therefore, evangelical Unitarian academics employed arguments based on the social utility of education. To secure governmental support, it was necessary to assure the voting public that higher education need not be an ally of political repression or reactionary exclusiveness. The Unitarian endorsement of social mobility through education may have helped here. At the same time, however, the need for private contributions to the cause of education demanded that the wealthy and influential classes be assured that education would serve conservative interests. This too could be readily maintained, and without doing violence to the pedagogical theories of Harvard moral philosophers. A well-educated population, they were sure, would be moral, law-abiding, and hard-working.[93] Without a good educational system they saw little hope for order in a free society. "When such a government as ours shall be administered [by] an immoral and uneducated people, how sure must be anarchy and ruin! " the younger Ware cried. At his inauguration as president of Harvard, James Walker declared that higher education would help the "learned professions" to "regain their supremacy" in society, so that one could justify supporting universities "even as a matter of pure conservatism." In the very same address Walker boasted of the means for advancement education had always offered the lower orders and called church-related schools "a democratic element in society."[94]

It was the ethical philosophy of the Unitarian moralists that enabled their educational theory to be humanistic, even democratic, and still conservative. Every man had within his soul a microcosmos of faculties, which, if properly developed, would enable him to rule himself. Since, of all man's powers, conscience was the highest, Unitarians found the education of the conscience at once liberating and regulating. Such an education offered the ultimate solution to the problems of society: train good men and they would freely make a good society. In this hopeful vision of human destiny, there would be no conflict between individual self-realization and the need for order.

UNITARIAN EDUCATIONAL PRACTICE

With the church sadly divided (and finally disestablished) and the state falling under the control of untrustworthy elements, the Unitarian moralists turned to alternative institutions to secure social harmony and improvement. The two most promising agencies of social control, in the evangelical Liberal view, were education and Christian moral suasion. The latter found an instrument in the benevolent organization, where the economic and moral elites of Boston united in a common cause. Education, however, seems to have proved more difficult to embody effectively in institutional form. Despite the long tradition of two centuries of schools and colleges in New England, the Boston-Cambridge intellectuals achieved only a mixed record in administering their educational institutions. The discrepancy between their exalted educational ideals and their mediocre performance is sometimes painfully sharp.

The most celebrated, as well as the most successful, of Unitarian endeavors on behalf of education was Horace Mann's campaign to reform the Massachusetts public school system. Mann, a convert to Unitariansim from Calvinism, was a close friend and associate of William Ellery Channing. Although Mann was a graduate of Brown rather than Harvard and a dabbler in the pseudoscience of phrenology, his speeches and writings on the social function of education still reveal a close affinity with the views of the Cambridge moral philosophers.[95] His efforts to organize the chaos of local school jurisdictions and his determination to restrict the teaching of religion in the common schools to "nonsectarian" Protestantism won Mann the enmity of Democrats and Calvinists, but ensured him the firm support of such Unitarian moralists as Tuckerman and Bowen.[96]

There were also private educational enterprises that attracted the endorsement of the Unitarian moralists. One of these was the famous, if short-lived, Round Hill School (1823–1834) of George Bancroft and Joseph G. Cogswell. Round Hill seemed a promising attempt to educate an elite of wealth and taste for the nation, along lines that the Harvard moralists had long advocated. Perhaps, if the rich would show the way in developing superior types of education in private schools, teaching in the common schools could later be improved. Andrews Norton contributed generously of both money and enthusiasm to the Round Hill experiment.[97] Another educational innovation that won the Liberal moralists' approval was Bronson Alcott's Temple School. William Ellery Channing overcame his misgivings at Alcott's Transcendental theological views and helped him establish the school, which a niece and a nephew of Channing attended. James Walker defended Alcott's objectives and methods of instruction at a time when the gentle mystic found more scoffers than sympathizers.[98] Yet neither Round Hill nor Temple was able to survive in Jacksonian America; probably the social climate of the country had not evolved to the point where it was ready for such institutions. When the great development of private schools took place later in the nineteenth century, it occurred largely under Episcopalian rather than Unitarian auspices.[99]

In their conception of what constituted a proper educational curriculum, Unitarian moralists generally remained within the "classical" consensus then dominant in America, best enunciated by the well-known Yale Report of 1828.[100] This standard curriculum embodied a hertiage from many past centuries. Remnants of the medieval trivium were to be found in the emphasis on logic, rhetoric, and grammar; the science taught was that of the Enlightenment; but the principal element was the Renaissance tradition of classical studies.[101] Twentieth-century commentators do not always appear to realize that Latin and Greek literature seemed liberating and broadening, not sterile and deadening, to educators of a former era. Like the Renaissance humanists, the Harvard moralists valued the study of the ancient languages as a means for individual self-development. The classics formed the staple of most formal education in America from the elementary to the college level. They were intended to provide a man with a sound basis for liberal culture, as well as with the mental discipline that came from long practice in graceful, discriminating translations from one language into another. The extensive study of moral philosophy in all its branches gave both variety and coherence to the curriculum for those youths who went on to higher learning.[102]

All too often antebellum American educational institutions fell short of achieving what they set out to accomplish, and even Harvard, where Unitarian educators enjoyed the largest library and endowment of any college in the country (still pitifully small by European standards) , left much to be desired. One trouble lay in the fact that the pedagogy was less enlightened than the curriculum. The humane educational ideals professed at Harvard contrasted strangely with the routinized, unimaginative methods of instruction that prevailed there as elsewhere. Though Unitarian educators claimed to awaken curiosity and foster a love of learning, in practice Harvard employed a "recitation system" of instruction that gave little scope to original thought and offered no introduction to research techniques. (Apparently one of the things that made "Ned" Channing's classes memorable was that he departed from this kind of rigid formality.)

Unfortunately, too much of the time and energy of the Harvard faculty was devoted to maintaining discipline. The paternalistic role of the college administration stemmed in part from their belief that intellectual training was less important than the development of "religious character."[103] But most of their preoccupation with discipline was simply a reflection of the same condition that also kept academic standards relatively low: the extreme youth of the students, many of whom were still in their early teens. Given the limitations imposed by the age level and preparation of the students, perhaps the faculty did not do too badly. The testimony of former undergraduates is mixed. Henry Adams said bitterly that Harvard "taught little, and that little ill"; yet in the last analysis he decided that "Harvard College was probably less hurtful than any other university then in existence."[104]

The Unitarian moralists who are the subjects of this study were by no means oblivious to the need for improvements at Harvard. When George Bancroft, George Ticknor, and Edward Everett returned from Europe with ideas for changing the College, they found sympathetic listeners on the faculty in Frisbie, Norton, and the elder Ware, as well as in Dr. Channing, then a Fellow of the Harvard Corporation. Ticknor, the most energetic and outspoken of the would-be reformers, seemed to have a natural ally in his brother-in-law Andrews Norton.[105] When Frisbie died in 1822, with Everett about to leave for Congress and Ware aging, Ticknor and Norton emerged as the leaders of faculty-sponsored educational reform. In July 1823 Ticknor, Norton, Ware, and other interested persons held a series of meetings at which elaborate plans for academic progress were laid: the organization of "departments," the enrichment of the standard curriculum with elective courses, modification of the "recitation system" to enable capable students to advance more rapidly, and generally higher scholarly standards combined with stricter moral discipline. The program was consistent with the humanistic objectives of Unitarian educational theory and envisioned no weakening of the core subjects of the "classical" curriculum like rhetoric, moral philosophy, and the ancient languages.[106] Unfortunately, however, the reformers soon split into two hostile camps over how to achieve their ends, Ticknor leading one group and Norton the other.

The efforts for educational improvement happened to come at the same time as a bitter controversy over the composition of the Harvard Corporation, and the two reform movements—one academic and the other structural—undercut each other tragically. As originally constituted in the seventeenth century, the President and Fellows of Harvard College had comprised the resident teaching staff of the institution. When the faculty expanded, however, not all teachers became Fellows; and as early as 1722 some clergymen who were not instructors were made Fellows. The financial troubles of the 1780's encouraged Harvard to try strengthening its position by electing Boston merchants and professional men as Fellows of the Corporation. After Eliphalet Pearson resigned to go to Andover in 1806, none of the instructors remained among the Fellows. Thus was accomplished "the evolution of the Harvard Corporation from a group of teaching fellows on an English collegiate model to a board of external trustees, connected with the living organism of the University only through the President."[107] The Immediate Government (as the Harvard faculty were then called) did not relish their loss of power, and when John Phillips died in June of 1823, they urged that one of the professors (most likely the elder Ware) be chosen to fill the vacancy created on the Corporation. Pressing even harder, they demanded that the Corporation revert to its original practice and agree to elect only resident teachers as Fellows. Receiving no satisfaction from the Corporation, the faculty took its case before the Board of Overseers. Levi Hedge, Edward Everett, and Henry Ware, Sr., were among the professors who took the lead in organizing the protest.[108]

On this institutional dispute the friends of academic reform divided. Ticknor, unwilling to jeopardize his cause by linking it with what looked like a quixotic crusade for faculty sovereignty, preferred to work through the existing structure of the governing boards. Norton, feeling that no academic changes could succeed without the support and involvement of the men who would have to implement them, wanted the cause of reform joined to the aspirations of the faculty for control of the Corporation. Reform ought to come from *within* the College, he insisted; it could not be imposed from without. Ticknor evidently had little rapport with many of his colleagues and did not see things this way. Yet any long-range program for raising the quality of education at Harvard would depend upon the quality of the faculty, and (as Norton pointed out to Justice Story) giving administrative control of the College to the Immediate Government would enhance the prestige of the faculty and facilitate the recruitment of the best teachers.[109] When the controversy between the Immediate Government and the Corporation went before the Overseers in February 1825, Norton spoke eloquently on behalf of the claims of the faculty. "The real object of the resident instructors," he declared, "was to obtain such control over the discipline and instruction of the college, as might enable them to introduce those reforms and improvements which its condition required."[110]

The outcome proved Ticknor and Norton each half right. As Ticknor had foreseen, the attempt by the faculty to recover its lost autonomy failed. The Overseers declined to sustain the historic claims of the Immediate Government; and the Corporation proceeded to elect another outsider to its vacancy—explaining that it was doing so to punish the faculty for having remonstrated![111] On June 10, 1825, the two governing boards adopted the reform proposals Ticknor had loyally deposited with them; but the atmosphere had been poisoned by too many recriminations for the faculty to accept changes forced upon them by an administration they distrusted. As Norton had feared, tutors dragged their heels and deliberately sabotaged the innovations in accustomed practices. By the time President Kirkland resigned in despair in 1828, the first wave of academic reform at Harvard had ended in failure.

Even this did not complete the chronicle of troubles. In 1823 a student riot caused the expulsion of forty-three seniors and brought much unfavorable publicity.[112] A few months later (as was related in the preceding chapter) the Democrats won control of the governorship and the lower house of the state legislature. They wasted no time in

expressing their displeasure with the heretical and evidently undisci-
plined college in Cambridge. Harvard's annual state appropriation of
$10,000 was entirely cut off, and a rival liberal arts college under Cal-
vinist auspices chartered at Amherst. The loss of financial support, in a
time of sectarian animosity and politically motivated criticism, hurt
Harvard badly. The number of students fell off alarmingly; by 1826
undergraduate enrollment was down from about 300 to about 200. In
April 1827 the University was forced to cut faculty salaries.[113] The
would-be moral and intellectual leaders of the Commonwealth had
suffered a material rebuke, as well as a blow to their prestige, from
their society.

Thus the decade of the 1820's revealed serious challenges to the preservation of institutional authority by Unitarian moralists. The demise
of the Federalist party, the "disestablishment" of Harvard College, and
the disestablishment of religion all underlined the lack of popular confidence in the Boston-Cambridge intelligentsia.[114] It was probably well
for Harvard, in these circumstances, that it retained the support of a
mercantile patrician class sympathetic to certain aristocratic values, for
if it had been at the mercy of the general public it would very likely
have enjoyed less intellectual freedom and even lower academic
standards. In 1851 the University, after a flagrant violation of its academic freedom (the Democratic politicians on the Board of Overseers
denied a professorship to Francis Bowen in reprisal for his conservative political writings) contrived to protect its integrity by securing
the removal of most of the ex-officio political members from the Overseers. By 1865 the authority of the General Court over the Harvard
governing boards had been eliminated. In this way the college, like the
church, was transformed from a public into a private institution.[115]

Yet Harvard's dependence on the Boston merchants brought other
problems, as the controversy over the composition of the Corporation
had made clear. The elite of commerce and industry could prove
almost as vexatious to the moralists as the Jacksonian populace. The
Liberal moralists, after all, had an ambiguous relationship to the business leaders of their society. On the one hand, they were the intellectual spokesmen for the economic elite—at times its retained apologists.
On the other hand, the moralists also conceived of themselves as supe-

rior to the business community and even as its critics. They expected the prosperous classes to be the instruments of the moral order, supporting and financing learning and charity in return for the privileges the social system bestowed upon them. In cultural enterprises like Buckminster's and benevolent societies like Tuckerman's this ideal was implemented. The failure of the Harvard academic reform program, by contrast, demonstrated the inability of the Immediate Government to work harmoniously with the men of affairs who dominated the Corporation.

One of those who felt most strongly that the Harvard faculty had been wrongly subjugated to the domination of unqualified outsiders was Andrews Norton. "To attempt to govern the college by gentlemen actively engaged in their own professions and in the business of the world . . . is an anomaly as great as it would be, to appoint six of our professors here to manage the affairs of an insurance company in Boston," he complained.[116] Surely, the men who were the proper intellectual and moral arbiters of society ought to be allowed to run their own institution. Yet the faculty had been "reduced to the ranks of hired instructors, overshadowed, and kept from the view of the public, and [made] accountable only to the Corporation for doing their duties according to contract."[117] Then, to succeed Kirkland in 1829, the Harvard Corporation selected as President a man who was neither a minister nor a scholar: Josiah Quincy, former mayor of Boston, chosen for his administrative ability. Thoroughly disgusted, Norton resigned his professorship the following year.

The controversy over the constitution of the Harvard Corporation was emblematic of two incipient changes in the attitudes of the Unitarian moralists. The first of these was the evolution of their concept of the intellectual. Historically, the New England intellectual had been a clergyman. Buckminster and his Anthologist circle had proposed a rival image of the intellectual: the gentleman-amateur. The gentlemanly conception of the man of letters captured the imagination of Unitarian Boston and held it for most of the nineteenth century.[118] Still, in the fight over control of Harvard College, one can discern the origins of a new professionalism, ultimately destined to displace both the clerical and the amateur ideal of scholarship. This was the vision of the scholar-educator, the professional lay academic.

The Corporation controversy was also premonitory of the disillusionment some Unitarian intellectuals came to feel with their accustomed allies among Boston businessmen. Writing in 1810, Andrews Norton had boasted, "Of the opulent men of our state, and especially of the merchants of Boston, [Harvard] has never had reason to complain."[119] After the 1820's, such expressions of trust became rarer. Though Edward Tyrell Channing and Francis Bowen remained enthusiastic friends of the business community, the admiration of other Liberal moralists waned. Soon the younger Ware was reproaching the "votaries of Mammon" for disregarding the life of the mind.[120] When Whig businessmen throughout the country denounced King Andrew's Bank War, the leading Unitarian moralist remained surprisingly aloof. "I suspect the trading community are as guilty as [Jackson]," Dr. Channing shrugged. By the 1850's even President Walker (who was most circumspect on all political and social matters) could give voice to this growing estrangement. "I cannot reconcile myself to . . . looking up to what are called the higher classes, and suing for their patronage," he confessed.[121] The acrimonious dispute over the Harvard Corporation foreshadowed the division of Boston Liberals into Cotton Whigs and Conscience Whigs.

X / The Slavery Question

THE PROBLEM OF SLAVERY was surely the most vexatious and pressing of the social issues confronting the wisdom and virtue of the Unitarian moralists. The slavery question beckoned them to exercise their function as leaders of public opinion, while simultaneously jeopardizing their relationship with their respectable, conservative constituents. Though the number of Unitarian churches in the South was negligible, many well-to-do southern families sent sons to Harvard, and the commercial ties between mill owners and cotton growers were naturally close.[1] If the service of Mammon could not, in the last analysis, be reconciled with the service of God, the social basis of Boston Unitarianism would be sorely tested. Whether Boston's economic elite would have accepted the guidance of a clerical and scholarly moral elite on a matter of such material importance as slavery is doubtful at best; however, the issue never defined itself with such clarity because, as things turned out, the intellectuals themselves could not agree on the form their leadership should take. The Harvard philosophers had prided themselves on the "moral tendencies" of their theology, but by the eve of the Civil War the practical moral consequences of Unitarian religion had come to seem doubtful in the extreme. Like many other American religious groups in the middle of the nineteenth century, the Unitarian moralists shattered themselves upon the rock of slavery.

THE AMBIGUITY OF UNITARIAN MORAL PHILOSOPHY

The problem of slavery, as it posed itself for the Unitarian moralists, was really twofold. In the first place, they asked, 'What ought one to think about slavery?' This was a moral issue, for as Dr. Channing said,

270

"the first question to be proposed by a rational being is, not what is profitable, but what is right."[2] Once this primary question had been answered, however, a second one arose, much more troublesome: 'What ought one to do about slavery?' To observe the difficulties the Liberal moralists encountered in wrestling with these issues, especially the second, is to become aware of the profound ambiguity of Harvard moral philosophy.

The slavery problem brought to the fore the basic contradiction between Unitarian ethical thought, which taught the limitless perfectibility of every person, and Harvard "civil polity," which praised a stable and hierarchical society. David Brion Davis has recently traced the emergence of Latitudinarianism and literary sentimentalism in Western civilization, showing how they fostered an ideal of human self-development that ultimately challenged the institution of slavery.[3] The moral philosophers of Harvard represented the final product, the most complete development, of this Liberal Christian impulse in the modern world. They proclaimed "every individual man a partaker of the divine image, capable of infinite progress, certain of an infinite duration." Their philosophy ascribed to every man a faculty of conscience to be cultivated—and "it is this moral power which makes all men essentially equal," a Unitarian pastor told his flock.[4] Religious liberalism in the English-speaking world was often associated with a relatively conservative social outlook, and under some circumstances a devotion to social harmony comported well with religious humanism. During the course of the American debate over slavery, however, the two became incompatible.

In their educational theory, the Unitarian moralists had successfully harmonized ethical liberalism and social mobility with community order. Since a slave was denied both educational opportunity and the hope of social mobility this resolution of the problem did not apply to him. However, there were ways in which Unitarian moralists could contrive to hide the inconsistency between their humanistic aspirations and fixed social stations. One could, for example, assume that spiritual culture was independent of material surroundings, and that a full personal development ought therefore to be possible in any station, even the lowliest. Thus Henry Ware, Jr., concluded a magnificent peroration on "the spiritual equality and immortality of all men" in this cryptic fashion: "[Christianity] would make each man perfect as an individual being; not in his relation to an accidental rank in this world, but absolutely; a thinking, self-governing, worshiping, heaven-destined creature; fitted for any position in society in this world, content with any that is allotted him."[5] Ware's admonition was no doubt principally intended to curb excessive ambition among free men, but its principles could also be employed to reconcile slaves to their lot. In keeping with this theory, Joseph S. Buckminster once preached that slaves, like other men, should accept fate and fulfill their duties in meekness and reverence. Masters, for their part, were to deal justly with their chattels, remembering that they too had a Master in Heaven.[6]

Justifications for slavery by philosophers of Liberal religion were not without precedent. In Europe, Hugo Grotius, the Renaissance humanist and Arminian theologian, had found it possible to defend the slavery interests of Dutch merchant-capitalists. The great Mr. Locke himself had made provision for slavery when drawing up the Fundamental Constitutions of Carolina.[7] Yet Buckminster's unpublished sermon of 1809 seems to be the only document among the literary remains of the twelve Harvard Unitarian moralists to accept the legitimacy of slavery. The Massachusetts Constitution of 1780 had declared "all men are born free and equal." Typically, the Harvard moralists endorsed that affirmation, though their rhetoric was no longer that of the Revolutionary era. These Liberal proponents of the Second Great Awakening were much more likely to speak of equal opportunity for moral and spiritual development than of equality per se. The degradation of slavery far exceeded the bounds within which human nature might be expected to flourish, wrote Andrews Norton in 1810. "A condition under which a human being is kept from progress is infinitely wrong," decided William Ellery Channing; "a rational, moral being" must not "be converted into a mere instrument of others' gratification."[8]

The arguments of proslavery apologists did not impress Harvard Unitarians. Liberal moralists, we have seen, rejected claims of racial superiority. Scriptural justifications for slavery fared no better at their hands. The appeal to the customs of Old Testament patriarchs was unconvincing, since the Hebrews had also practiced polygamy. New Testament injunctions on slaves to obey their masters reflected the ethic of nonresistance to evil, but did not necessarily sanction the evil. On the other hand, the whole spirit of biblical religion—especially the emphasis upon love of one's neighbor—was contrary to slavery. If the Apostolic Church had not condemned the institution outright, it was only for excusable prudential motives. Unitarian principles of biblical criticism, which allowed for a conception of "progressive revelation," were well suited to rebutting the more literal-minded of southern scriptural expositors.[9]

Private property was, perhaps, only a little less sacred than the Bible among Harvard Unitarians; yet the invocation of property rights on behalf of slavery did not move them. The rights of property formed part of the immutable moral law, deriving from "the sanction which the moral sense . . . gives to honestly earned possessions" and not from the positive law of the state. Property in people was an absurdity unknown to the rational moral sense. Though the appeal from positive law to what some Americans called a "higher law" might sound drastic, Unitarians phrased it in language of impeccable conservatism. The Liberal moralist, no doubt with relish, actually accused the proslavery writers of being the real subversives. "Of all radicals, the most dangerous, perhaps, is he who makes property the creature of the law; because what law creates it can destroy. If we of this Commonwealth have no right in our persons, houses, ships, farms, but what a vote of the legislature or the majority confers, then the same masses may strip us of them all." Government, to be sure, could tax and control property in various ways, but could not "make and unmake it at will."[10]

When the Harvard moral philosophers turned from the question of the rightness of slavery to methods for abolishing it, they came upon a much more delicate and intractable problem. At first, however, the Unitarian moralists did not take account of the magnitude of the obstacles antislavery would face. They assumed that the spread of Christian principles and a rising educational level would gradually, and more or less automatically, cause slavery to disappear. Henry Ware, Sr.'s Election Sermon of 1821, preached at the time of the second Missouri debate, illustrates their attitude. Ware's text was Acts 17:26: "God hath made of one blood all nations of men, for to dwell on all the face of the earth." The doctrine he extracted was "opposed to the subjugation of any portion of the inhabitants of a country to a state of involuntary servitude." The caste system was a disgrace to India, but the "still more horrible system of African and American slavery" fixed an "indelible stain" upon the Christians of the Western Hemisphere. Ware relied upon religious exhortation and public education to rid the world of this deep-seated social wrong. Education and Liberal religion sought "to bring men nearer together, not by impoverishing the wealthy, but by enriching the poor; . . . not by levelling the distinctions of learning and wisdom and virtue, but by enlightening the ignorant and raising men from . . . the corruptions of vice." In this vision of relatively painless progress, not only slavery, but all the "odious distinctions" based on race were destined to vanish before an awakened public conscience.[11] In the years after 1821, it would become increasingly difficult to maintain that sanguine expectation.

There was more to the Unitarian faith in the reforming power of the church and the school than simple optimism, however. By relying on rational persuasion and the refining of sentiments to eliminate evil, the Harvard moralists sought to reconcile their desire for a moral society with their desire for social stability. Change, they hoped, would be slow and peaceful. In this way the Platonic strain in Unitarianism might prove compatible with the Burkean strain; the idealistic and rationalistic component with the devotion to institutions and continuity. Conscience and prudence would work together to solve America's problems. It was a mediating viewpoint, typical of these philosophical dualists.

TEMPTATIONS TO INACTION

The Boston moralists, who closely observed all trends of opinion in the mother country, watched with fascinated approval the great crusades of English evangelicals against the international slave trade and then against the institution itself in the British West Indies.[12] Yet they did not make haste to follow the example of Wilberforce and his "Saints" in organized political action. Neither did they mount any campaign of national moral suasion to influence public opinion along the lines Ware's Election Sermon might have suggested. The clues that help explain this procrastination lie in both the moralists' social situation and the complexity of their attitudes toward moral leadership.

Some historians have theorized that antislavery efforts were prompted by the desire of genteel ex-Federalist New Englanders to recover the high prestige their families had enjoyed in an earlier generation.[13] The case of the Unitarian moralists suggests that the conception of "status anxieties," while not irrelevant to antislavery activity, must be employed with care. The twelve moralists examined in this book were not members of families whose social position had declined; on the contrary, some had risen.* Those among them who were clergymen had, however, chosen a profession whose influence was, in the long run, on the wane. Men like Buckminster and Tuckerman had found ways to mitigate this decline by cooperating with local businessmen and men of other professions in cultural and charitable enterprises. Still, the internecine Unitarian controversy over the Harvard Corporation had revealed an unwillingness on the part of the men of affairs to concede too much to the claims of the intellectuals to leadership. If the Unitarian moralists wished to cling to high social station and preserve unity within the Boston-Cambridge establishment, they would not be quick to take up arms against an institution in which commercial Massachusetts was deeply implicated. Insofar as the Harvard moralists were motivated by concern for status, they would probably tend to be inhibited from participating in antislavery agitation.

Nor would such an inhibition necessarily have reflected conscious hypocrisy. The natural inclination of the Harvard moralists, after all, would have been to identify with their own social group and be suspicious of others. A sensitive first-hand observer believed that this was an important factor in determining the Unitarian reaction to the slavery issue.

Enough account is not generally made of the purely social element in the opposition of the Unitarian ministers, as a rule, to the Abolitionists.

* *See* Appendix

They were gentlemen; they occupied a high position in the community; they belonged to a privileged order . . . With the solitary exception of Wendell Phillips, who was regarded as an aristocratic demagogue, the Abolitionists were poor, humble, despised people, of no influence; men one could not ask to dine.[14]

Significantly, William Ellery Channing met William Lloyd Garrison only once, when they saw each other by accident at a legislative committee hearing.[15]

Whatever status anxieties the Unitarian moralist felt would have been heightened by an ambiguous self-image. Ever since colonial times, there had been two rival conceptions of the ministry in New England. According to one ideal, variously called the "precise" or "zealous" type, the minister was a social critic, passing prophetic judgment upon his community. According to the "inoffensive" ideal, on the other hand, the minister was a nurturing, pastoral figure, concerned to bind up the spiritual wounds of his flock. The two ideals manifest a fundamental difficulty, which has never been resolved, in defining the function of the Protestant ministry.[16] Obviously such conflicting demands made it all the more difficult for a Unitarian moralist to decide how hard he could press an unpopular cause on his constituents. Reflecting upon the dilemma, the elder Ware mused, "It is a practical question, which the circumstances of each individual case must decide, whether the cause of truth will be better promoted . . . by the cautious reserve of an Erasmus, or the vigorous and dauntless courage of a Luther." One who thus ponders the advisability of heroics has already espoused the Erasmian outlook. Ware concluded that the prudent course was best.[17]

The Unitarian aversion to aggressive debate was nothing new. Despite the prominence of Liberal Christians in cultural and charitable enterprises, antebellum Unitarianism was always strangely lacking in the usual type of religious propaganda societies.[18] (Tuckerman's ministry-at-large might be considered an exception to the Unitarians' general reluctance to institutionalize their evangelism, but even it did not bring the Liberals into hostile territory outside Boston.) The Unitarian record on the issue of slavery reveals much the same disinclination to organize for ideological conflict. Harvard Liberals proved no more anxious to engage in controversy with southerners over the "peculiar institution" than they had been to confront fellow Yankees in theological disputations. Very likely the edge was taken off their efforts by their faith in intellectual and social progress. It was easy to procrastinate when one assumed that the ultimate victory of one's principles—whether Liberal religion or human liberty—would come about whenever the time was ripe. Ironically, the Unitarian believers in free will were afflicted with a complacent fatalism at the very time in history when many professing loyalty to predestination were girding themselves to do battle for the Lord. Lewis Tappan, the businessman-philanthropist who financed so much of the abolitionist movement in the United States, abandoned Unitarianism for Calvinist orthodoxy, complaining as he did so that the Boston Liberals lacked crusading zeal.[19]

Even when the Unitarian moralists spoke out on the slavery question, they did so in a purely individual, unorganized way. Several factors help explain this. The Harvard Liberals, like their Transcendentalist offspring, distrusted the moral effects of collective action. "Our danger is, that we shall substitute the consciences of others for our own, that we shall paralyze our faculties through dependence on foreign guides."[20] In practice Unitarians were often able to quell their doubts about organizing for worthy purposes, especially if the project were local and not too controversial. But mutual theological suspicions hindered cooperation between Unitarians and Trinitarians in any nationwide benevolent association. To Harvard moralists, participation in such activities seemed to entail the danger of compromising their distinctive religious principles. Also, the distaste for politics that the Unitarian moralists acquired after the demise of the Federalist Party deterred them from certain kinds of organized action. However, if one is to appreciate fully the difficulties encountered by the keepers of the Unitarian conscience on the slavery issue, one must take account of still another paradox in Harvard moral thought.

Despite the emphasis that Harvard civil polity gave to the organic interdependence of men in society, Unitarian Arminian theology always remained intensely individualistic. Whatever impulses toward social involvement might be prompted by the former were always in danger of being vitiated by the latter. According to Unitarian moral philosophy, "society itself was intended to be only the occasion and the theatre for the display and development of [the moral] law, in order that the virtues which it enjoins might have scope and objects on which they might be exercised."[21] By this logic, the good of the community would not be an end in itself, but only a by-product of the salvation of individuals. And salvation, for these Unitarians, had become more an individual than a corporate concern; the cultivation of a Christian character, whatever help might come from family or church, was an endeavor each man undertook for himself. "Let everyone most seriously consider, that he is bound . . . *to work out his own salvation,*" admonished the Arminian philanthropist.[22] Although Massachusetts Liberals often invoked the social affections, they did so as an aid to an essentially private enterprise. "Social life," an acute contemporary of the Unitarian moralists once remarked, they considered "a mere discipline for the nourishment of individual character."[23] As the President of Harvard put it, in society a man "has virtues and duties to acquire and practice which are necessary to his own character and final [i.e., divine] acceptance."[24] Unitarian social life was a means of personal grace.

Here, however, lurked the possibility of withdrawal as well as of social involvement. The Harvard version of Arminian theology did not teach salvation simply by works, but by character—that is, by sentiments and habits. "The life of the soul is the true life; the action of thought, sentiment, feeling, the true action. The spring is within . . . Within, therefore, is the arena on which the contest for character and immortality is to be waged." Might not too much social activity interfere with this process of self-culture? "Religion," after all, was "a delicate exotic," needing to "be sheltered from all uncongenial influences."[25] One Unitarian moralist warned that the man who "casts himself on the current of the world" risks being "seduced from the highest pursuit," that is, self-discipline. "There is no moral worth in being swept away by the crowd, even towards the best objects," another declared. "Our connection with society, as it is our greatest aid, so it is our greatest peril. We are in constant danger of being spoiled of our moral judgment, and of power over ourselves."[26]

There was much in the humanistic heritage of Liberal religion to cater to a yearning for disengagement from the community and its conflicts. The Latitudinarian impulse to nondogmatic morality could, and often did, lead to a sentimental quietism rather than an active philanthropy. Furthermore, the belletristic and cultural interests of the Harvard Unitarians provided them with a ready avenue of escape from social strife, if they chose to avail themselves of it. In Buckminster's words, Boston's literary moral elite felt like "gentle knights" surrounded by a "paynim host." Physically weak and temperamentally retiring as most of the twelve Unitarian moralists were, it would not be surprising if they often longed to retreat into a secure scholarly haven. Some of the poetry of Levi Frisbie, Andrews Norton, William Ellery Channing, and the younger Ware is either explicitly or implicitly escapist in tone and subject-matter.[27]

In the light of such strong temptations to withdrawal, it is to the credit of the Unitarian moralists that they so often recalled themselves to their public responsibilities. Fully conscious of their emotional inclination to languor and seclusion, they were forever reproaching themselves for it. "At one period of my life I was a dreamer, a castle builder," confessed Dr. Channing. Then one day he brought himself up short: "I weep over a tale of human woe. But do I ever relieve the distressed? . . . My cheeks reddened at the question; a cloud of error burst from my mind. I found that virtue did not consist in feeling, but in *acting from a sense of duty*." A strong character could only be developed in contact with society, he decided. "The revolving of elevating thoughts in our closet does little for us. We must bring them home to the mind in the midst of action and difficulty."[28] Francis Bowen and Henry Ware, Jr., condemned the "morbid" perversion of the conscience confined to the contemplation of imaginary scenes, warning young scholars that "the melody of the siren hours thus spent" would allure them "to destruction." In their classes on rhetoric and oratory, Edward Tyrell Channing at the College and Henry Ware, Jr., at the Divinity School insisted with equal vigor that the intellectual must concern himself with the relevant and the practical. "Christianity is as far as possible from being a merely solitary, sentimental, speculative faith. It is a power which overlooks all human affairs to control them."[29]

Despite the many inducements to inertia, the Unitarian moralists never lost sight of their highest vocation as the conscience of the community. "Never shrink from speaking your mind through dread of reproach," William Ellery Channing advised a colleague. "The fewer voices on the side of truth, the more distinct and strong must be your own."[30] It was not easy to heed such admonitions, not even for those who gave them. The pastor's brother, for example, never joined him in criticizing slavery; indeed, he was so ultraconservative on all political issues that (as a friend teased him) he "came near to being an English Jacobite."[31] Yet Edward Tyrell Channing phrased one of the most compelling descriptions of the role of the literary moral elite. He called them "the only true radicals." By this bold term he meant that they were "the men who aim at realizing great ideas, and who believe that much remains, and will ever remain to be learned and told." They were "true" radicals because they possessed the Platonic insight into the true Good, the immutable moral law which the institutions of society ought to implement.[32] Each in his own way, the Unitarian moralists strived to live up to that high ideal of their calling. For some of them, it took the form of speaking out on slavery. The Harvard moralists would seem to indicate there is some truth in the notion, advanced by Alfred North Whitehead a generation ago, that the ultimate origins of antislavery lie in Platonism.[33]

PATTERNS OF VACILLATION

Joseph Tuckerman had first-hand knowledge of both American and West Indian slavery from his trips to the Caribbean and the South. On a visit to Charleston in 1819, Tuckerman attended a slave auction, where he saw a shoemaker sold for $365, a carpenter for $490, a seamstress for $375, and "a very likely boy, about 12 or 13 years of age," for $400. He came away depressed.[34] As a delegate to the Constitutional Convention of 1820, Tuckerman assumed that Negroes should be barred from state office-holding. Once he turned to full-time work with the poor in 1825, however, Tuckerman came to see very clearly the incompatibility of Christian humanism and racism. Apparently a visit to England during which he met blacks on a plane of social equality with whites helped to mature his feelings on race.[35]

Alcoholism was rife in the Boston slums, and as Tuckerman worked with men who had drinking problems, trying to sustain them during their struggles to give up the habit, he came to resent the merchants who purveyed liquor to the poor. He denounced them, and thereby alienated a portion of the Boston business community. Tuckerman depended on the goodwill of the Unitarian pew-proprietors to finance his projects. An outspoken stand on slavery as well as temperance might well have put an end to the urban ministry-at-large. Consequently, though he believed in racial equality and privately encouraged others in opposition to slavery, Tuckerman felt he could not afford to make his own views public. In this way he was able to continue to serve the poor of Boston, many of whom were free blacks. Even William Lloyd Garrison found words of praise for Tuckerman's aid to the city's Negroes. So if the Unitarian social worker concentrated on helping the victims of prejudice in his own community, perhaps he should not be judged too harshly for his neglect of those farther away.

The conduct of Henry Ware, Jr., is less easily explained. Although the Harvard Divinity School disapproved of slavery in theory, for a long time it was not recognized as a social problem. One alumnus recalled that during his three years there (1830–1833), the faculty-student Philanthropic Society discussed prison reform, temperance, peace, the improvement of sailors' conditions, and other causes—but never slavery.[36] In 1834, however, the younger Professor Ware was instrumental in founding, and became president of, a Cambridge Anti-Slavery Society. "In principle" Ware considered himself an abolitionist, although his society was hostile to Garrison and hoped to induce him to moderate his appeals. When Samuel J. May, a maverick Unitarian minister who had dealings with Garrison and later took a church in the burned-over district, offered to address the society, Ware demurred, saying it was hard enough to overcome local prejudice against "the very name of [our] Society" without risking any "extraneous" speakers.[37]

Despite such caution, public reaction to the Cambridge Society was quite hostile. This, after all, was the era when well-dressed Boston mobs broke up abolitionist gatherings with violence. When Ware announced meetings of his society at church services he conducted, many took offense. The newspapers abused him; friends expostulated with him; it was even rumored that the University threatened to dismiss him if he did not resume silence. The official Harvard history insists that no such steps were taken, but Ware would have had good reason to fear that they might. The eminent German scholar, Carl Follen, had just lost his Harvard professorship of literature after becoming vocal on antislavery.[38]

However it may be, after about a year Ware ceased to play a role in antislavery activity, and his local society quietly "expired." Garrison was not interested in submitting *The Liberator* to the censorship of "six or seven gentlemen of calm and trustworthy judgment" as Ware proposed that he should, and there seemed no way to bridge the gap between his group and the Harvard one.[39] In 1835 Ware's interests turned to the Massachusetts Peace Society—a cause which, if no less worthy, was considerably less controversial, inasmuch as there were then no major wars in the Western world. The moralist's brother and memorialist felt it was unthinkable that Ware should have bowed before pressure from his critics; he attributed Ware's failure of perseverance to his dislike for the rhetoric and methods of the Garrisonians, plus a temperamental indisposition to sustained effort of any kind, especially political agitation. "He had not that kind of nerve."[40] Still, Ware never retracted his opposition to slavery. In 1839 he expressed sympathy with Dr. Channing's Conscience Whiggery and wrote a favorable review of Theodore Weld's *Slavery As It Is* for the *Christian Examiner*. During his last illness (1843) he also wrote some antislavery lyrics.[41]

Francis Bowen was another Harvard Unitarian whose political actions were not fully in keeping with his principles; indeed, the contrast in his case was even greater. Bowen disapproved of slavery on economic as well as moral grounds; like many other economists of his day he thought it kept down the growth rate of a region.[42] This is not the same as saying that slavery was unprofitable for those who owned slaves, of course; and in fact Bowen believed that both slavery and the slave trade continued to flourish primarily because they provided some men large profits. It was precisely this which gave the Harvard professor hope that slavery could be destroyed. If men were slave-owners for money, they would stop being slave-owners for money: Bowen's solution was the compensated emancipation of all minor slaves on their attaining age twenty-one. Upon liberation, the freedmen would be expatriated to Liberia or (if they would be accepted) the British West Indies—unless they went on working for their previous masters as wage earners by mutual consent. The federal government was to bear the expense of both compensation and transportation. "If the obligation . . . is national, the burden and the cost of the process should also be national," the moral philosopher observed. "Either the north has no right to meddle with the matter at all; or it is bound to do its full share of the work, and pay its proportion of the bill."[43]

Bowen was convinced that his plan was quite practical. He estimated that 96,000 slaves a year reached age twenty-one, a number that did not present insuperable obstacles to emigration. Twice that many people were exported from Ireland annually, he noted. In fact, however, Bowen expected that a large and increasing percentage of freedmen would stay where they were. The total cost of his plan he estimated at $20 million a year for the first sixteen years, and $10 million a year for the next thirty years. This did not seem prohibitively high, particularly since Bowen expected the federal government to be nagged by a financial surplus for the rest of the century. An incidental advantage of his plan, Bowen remarked, would be the creation of a strong, Christian Liberia, conversant with Western technology and able to lead Africa to economic development.[44] In retrospect, a program for peaceful gradual emancipation does indeed have its attractions, especially when compared with the way slavery was actually extinguished. However, Bowen's plan made no provision for the education of the former slaves and would have left those who remained in America an illiterate and propertyless proletariat. (Perhaps it was for this very reason that Bowen imagined the white South would accept such a program without seceding.)

Before any such scheme could be put into effect, a party dedicated to the eventual extinction of slavery would have to win control of the federal government. Yet Bowen was scarcely a zealous friend of political antislavery. During the intraparty struggles of the 1840's when Massachusetts Whigs were dividing into "Cotton" and "Conscience" wings, Bowen, insofar as scanty evidence suggests, tried to mediate between the two factions.[45] When Webster's Seventh of March Speech forced the issue, Bowen came out with a long article in the *North American Review* supporting the Compromise of 1850 and denouncing the free soil position. With a remarkable obtuseness to the importance of building an antislavery bloc in Congress, he declared the Wilmot Proviso irrelevant, because it would free no one then a slave. Like many other Cotton Whigs, Bowen rationalized his stand further by insisting that the arid Southwest was geographically unsuited to slavery anyway. The Fugitive Slave Law was indeed ticklish, but the Harvard moralist reached the peculiar conclusion that the proper course of action was to support its enactment and then try to subvert its operation by raising a fund to buy off the owners of escaped bondsmen.[46]

Andrews Norton's position on the slavery question resembles Bowen's—up until the crisis of 1850. As a young man, Norton had denounced slavery at a time when few white Americans were much exercised about the evil. Later, when Parliament freed the slaves in the British West Indies, he rejoiced.[47] But within a few years Norton's ardor for antislavery cooled; like Bowen, he drew back from political antislavery. He urged greater moderation upon politicians like Sumner and Palfrey who came into conflict with Robert Winthrop's Cotton Whigs.[48] In 1837 Norton seems to have opposed granting the use of Faneuil Hall to a committee that wanted to protest the lynching of abolitionist Elijah Lovejoy, even though the group was headed by his long-time friend Dr. Channing. Channing had not supported Norton during the fight for the rights of the Harvard faculty; one suspects this had damaged their relationship, for the proud and sensitive Norton did not easily forgive those who crossed him. Norton's annoyance with Channing was compounded by the Federal Street minister's long-suffering patience with the Transcendentalists. Apparently, Norton came to identify antislavery with the Transcendentalism he deplored.

"The violence of the abolitionists, the atheism of Kneeland and Emerson, the infidelity of Ripley and Brownson, and the ferocious jacobinism of the latter" were all lumped together in his mind.[49] Impatient to finish his massive work on the genuineness of the Gospels, Norton had no inclination to join a raucous crusade against slavery.

It was the Fugitive Slave Act that roused Norton's conscience. The aged scholar took time out from his recondite labors to offer his community one last moral exhortation: to nonviolent civil disobedience. In a long article he wrote for the *Boston Atlas* on November 26, 1850, Norton's combative spirit reappeared. Even if slave-owning might be justified under some circumstances (e.g., if the slaves would be unable to care for themselves if manumitted), slave-catching could never be moral, he insisted; for the very fact that the slave had run away proved he was being held against his capacity and will for freedom. To take freedom away from a man guilty only of aspiring to a better life was a "violation of all that is most fundamental in morality." Norton settled the matter by a straightforward appeal to empathy, such as white Americans have seldom invoked where blacks were concerned.

There can be no pretense of a right set up by any man to compel you or me to become his slave. We feel, or rather we know, that to attempt it would be an intolerable outrage, which I do not say we should have a right to resist [Unitarian moralists being always impatient of talk of "rights"], but which I do say it would be our duty to resist at all hazards.

No better example exists of the Unitarian moral sense giving solid validity to moral judgments than Norton's "we feel, *or rather we know*," that it is outrageous to enslave a man who is struggling to be free.

Norton's insistence that a law as flagrantly iniquitous as the Fugitive Slave Law need not be obeyed was controversial by any standards. No consensus existed among Harvard moralists on the legitimacy of civil disobedience. In the late eighteenth century, of course, New England Arminian intellectuals had been sure that even violent resistance to the acts of an unjust government was moral. As the memory of the Revolution faded, however, their more conservative descendants began to doubt the right or duty of civil disobedience. Not only Bowen but also both Wares denied that it existed. The privilege of the discontented, they maintained, was confined to working for changes in the law by existing procedures.[50] On the other hand, Frisbie, Walker, and William Ellery Channing had taught that civil disobedience might be justified in extreme cases. The moral authority of the law depended upon its being "an expression, not of arbitrary will, but of the public opinion of right." A wise man would choose to defer to "the collective conscience of the community" whenever possible. But if the conflict between law and conscience were unmistakable, then a man must choose the latter, for "no outward law is so sacred as the voice of God in his own breast." Still, he who broke the law for conscience's sake ought to be willing to accept whatever punishment the law prescribed.[51]

What of the clause in the Constitution requiring the return of runaway slaves? Did this not create an obligation on the part of northerners? No, replied Norton: "the compacts of men cannot annul the laws of God." When the Constitution was written, the evils of slavery "had not been brought home to men's minds" as they have since. The moral progress of civilization would be disrupted by the Fugitive Slave Act, which Norton saw as the first step toward the introduction of slavery throughout the Union, "that all free States should rest on a basis of slaves, like the republics of antiquity." The Constitutional provision for the return of escaped slaves "must lie inoperative, as something obsolete and unsuited to the times in which we live."[52] In his analysis of the Fugitive Slave Act, Norton was groping for a doctrine of progressive morality analogous to the Unitarian doctrine of progressive revelation.

A DECISION FOR CONSCIENCE

William Ellery Channing, the greatest of the Unitarian moralists, illustrates best the ambiguities of Unitarianism. Torn between Tuckerman's reform impulse and an otherworldliness comparable to John Emery Abbot's, he hesitated long. Should the moral man work for a moral society or confine his faculties to quiet self-cultivation? Given the dual values of charity and harmony, which did one choose when philanthropy disturbed social stability, as the antislavery crusade did? Only after an agonizing period of doubt did the angelic doctor of Federal Street reach a conclusion, and when he did, the answer proved no less painful than the preceding anxiety.

By birth, marriage, and temperament Channing was a member of the New England bourgeois elite. He was accustomed to dealing with the wealthy businessmen of Boston and seeking their support for the worthy causes that engaged his interest. Opposing them went against his grain. When Andrews Norton had led the Harvard faculty to fight for independence from Boston control, Channing had been on the other side.[53] Maria Weston Chapman, a member of the Federal Street congregation who joined the abolitionists against her minister's advice, felt that it was futile to hope for a forthright stand on slavery from such a man: "He had been selected by a set of money-making men as their representative for piety, as Edward Everett was their representative gentleman and scholar, Judge Story their representative jurist and companion in social life, and Daniel Webster their representative statesman and advocate."[54] There was some truth in this sarcastic description, but there was even more in the judicious summary of the biographer who wrote, "Always in Channing, and ever more pronouncedly, we have the aristocratic inclination, and the intellectual and moral criticism upon it and suppression of it."[55] Channing was a man who loved the esteem of respectable men, who feasted upon praise. ("If it be a sin to covet honor,/I am the most offending soul alive," he confided to his journal.) Yet he was also a man who, in the end, was willing to jeopardize his social gratifications for the sake of principle. In doing so, he was true to his conception of his calling. The ministry of Christ, he told a colleague, was "meant not to perpetuate what exists, but to introduce a higher condition of the church and the world."[56]

Dr. Channing had married his first cousin, Ruth Gibbs. Their family was deeply implicated in the North's complicity with slavery. Channing's own parents had possessed slaves before the Revolution. His father-in-law and uncle, George Gibbs, was a wealthy Rhode Island merchant among whose interests had been a distillery supplying the slave-traders with rum. The first antislavery opinions Channing heard came not from his family but from the rugged Calvinist theologian Samuel Hopkins who preached in Newport. Channing's two trips to slave-holding territory, to Virginia in 1798–1800 and to the Caribbean in 1830–1831, confirmed his revulsion for the institution.[57] When he returned from the West Indies he took out a subscription to *The Liberator* and began to discuss slavery privately. To take a public stand on the problem was going to be difficult. In years past the Unitarian moralist had not hesitated to denounce Jefferson's Embargo or the War of 1812, but on those issues commercial Massachusetts had applauded his views. This time it would be different. "No sect in this country has taken less interest in the slavery question, or is more inclined to conservatism than our body," Channing wrote a friend. "The slave's toil is the Northern merchant's wealth, for it produces the great staple on which all the commercial dealings of the country turn."[58]

Two important considerations that impelled Channing toward a commitment to antislavery were his dislike of greed and his love of civil liberties. Like the economist Bowen, Channing the preacher came to identify slavery with the profit motive. "What is the strength of slavery? The love of money. This makes the free States the upholders of oppression." It would be necessary to condemn avarice and revive the ideals of the Reformation and the Enlightenment. "New England has long suffered the imputation of a sordid, calculating spirit," he reflected. "Let us show that we have principles."[59] The battles led in Congress by John Quincy Adams and Joshua Giddings on behalf of the right of petition won Channing's heart. The massive smothering of freedom of expression throughout the South—and, all too often, in the North as well—acted as an incentive as well as a deterrent to the Liberal moralist. In 1835 Garrison was nearly killed by a Boston mob. The abolitionists were "sufferers for the liberty of thought" and as such entitled to Channing's respect.[60]

Even so, it was several years before Channing could bring himself to become associated in the public mind with the abolitionists. If their arguments had much intrinsic merit, they were urged in tones too strident for his sensitive ears. The abolitionists' "passionate eloquence" too easily gave way to "enthusiasm" and "fanaticism" for a Harvard Unitarian to feel comfortable. They did not work upon society from the top down, the moralist complained. Instead of approaching only men of "judiciousness" and standing, they had been willing to recruit anybody.

The abolitionists sent forth their orators, some of them transported with a fiery zeal, to sound the alarm against slavery through the land, to gather together young and old, pupils from schools, females hardly arrived at years of discretion, the ignorant, the excitable, the impetuous, and to organize these into associations for the battle against oppression. They preached their doctrine to the colored people, and collected these into their societies. To this mixed and excitable multitude, appeals were made in the piercing tones of passion; and slave-holders were held up as monsters of cruelty and crime.[61]

Such were the methods of revivalism, and they were not the means Boston Liberals sanctioned for achieving social change.

The turning point in Channing's decision for conscience may well have come one evening in the fall of 1834, when Samuel J. May visited his home to remonstrate with him about his silence. Channing explained that he could not stomach the harshness of the abolitionists' language. Surely their rhetorical excesses would alienate southern moderates. "He dwelt at length" on these stylistic objections (as May recalled the conversation) , though acknowledging agreement with the substance of the abolitionist critique of slavery. "Dr. Channing," cried May at last—for it was not easy to interrupt the flow of eloquence once his host got started—"it is not our fault that those who might have managed this great reform more prudently have left it to us to manage as we may be able." Surprised at his own temerity, May continued:

We are not to blame, Sir, that you, who, more, perhaps, than any other man, might have so raised the voice of remonstrance that it should have been heard throughout the length and breadth of the land,—we are not to blame, Sir, that you have not spoken. And now, because inferior men have begun to speak and act against what you yourself acknowledge to be an awful injustice, it is not becoming in you to complain of us, because we do it in an inferior style.[62]

May's reproof was well taken, and Channing knew it. If the moralist shirked his responsibility, others would take it up. In the next months Channing turned over in his mind the proper contents of his antislav-

ery manifesto. He spent the following summer writing at his customary rustic retreat outside Newport, and by the time a slim volume
entitled *Slavery* appeared, it was December 1835.

Channing's *Slavery* is neither a muckraking collection of data, like
Weld's *Slavery As It Is*, nor political propaganda like Helper's
Impending Crisis. It is an abstract examination of the institution of
slavery per se, in the light of the principles of Unitarian moral philosophy. The crucial chapter is the one on "Rights." This is the only
extended treatment of the subject in the literature of Harvard moralism, but one could hardly discuss the ethics of slavery without it. Even
here, Channing derives his notion of right from his notion of duty.
"The sense of duty is the fountain of human rights" because the essential rights are those which enable one to do his duty: i.e., to develop his
personal faculties, to function as a member of his community, to sustain domestic relations, and to worship God according to the dictates
of conscience. In the possession of these moral rights, all men were
"essentially equal." None of these rights was political, but all were
infringed by enslavement. To use a man as a tool "is to stunt the development which is his purpose; to subject him to a master is to prevent
his inner law from asserting its rightful sovereignty." A man had but
one true master, and that was his moral sense.[63]

Twentieth-century historians have called attention to the degrading
effects of slavery upon human personality.[64] Channing would have
agreed with those who find this the most shocking atrocity of the peculiar institution. Slavery "destroys the proper consciousness and spirit of
a man," he noted. "The slave regarded and treated as property, bought
and sold like a brute, denied the rights of humanity, unprotected
against insult, . . . and systematically subdued, that he may be a man-
ageable, useful tool, how can he help regarding himself as fallen below
his race? How must his spirit be crushed! How can he respect himself?
He becomes bowed to servility." When masters claimed their slaves
did not mind servitude they had confessed to the worst evil of the system—"the whole lot of the slave is fitted to keep his mind in childhood
and in bondage." Channing did not suppose, however, that slaves were
brutalized to the point of total insensitivity. When the well-born white
tried to enter the thought-world of the enslaved black, he decided that

"the moral nature never dies"; the slave "often feels a wrong in the violence which he cannot resist. He has often bitter hatred towards the cruel overseer . . . There are deep groans of conscious injury and revenge, which, though smothered by fear, do not less agonize the soul."[65] How successfully Channing read the mind of the slave perhaps no man today can say.

Channing also addressed himself to another problem that has interested later students of American slavery. This was the question of ethics under a slave system. "Was the 'good' Negro the one who was courteous and loyal to his master and who did his work faithfully and cheerfully?" asks Professor Kenneth Stampp. "Or was the 'good' Negro the defiant one who . . . would not submit, who fought back, ran away, faked illness, loafed, sabotaged, and never ceased longing for freedom?"[66] As a moral philosopher, Channing felt it his job to offer answers to these questions. Since a man could not fulfill his true nature as a slave, Channing (agreeing with Andrews Norton) declared that a slave was not only *entitled* to try to escape, he was morally *obliged* to try to escape. On the other hand, a slave revolt would *not* be morally justified, because it would bring utter and certain ruin on all involved. Critics of slavery must not incite slaves to rebel, and to make sure of this they ought to address themselves exclusively to the master class. Since northerners were pledged to help put down any attempt by the slaves to better their own lot through insurrection, they were under a corresponding obligation to pursue emancipation by peaceful means.

Channing never really dealt with the arguments of southern anthropologists that Negroes as a race were inferior to Caucasians and especially suited to slavery. He saw that Negroes were people and discussed them as such; their slavery was human slavery. He took issue with a leader of his own party, Henry Clay, who had insisted that slavery provided a necessary mode of race adjustment, since white and black could not co-exist unless one or the other were subjugated. He also impatiently dismissed the argument that emancipation would produce racial "amalgamation." "Can [racial] mixture go on faster or more criminally than at the present moment?" he demanded. If one wished to combat miscegenation, the only way was to "raise the colored woman to a new sense of character, to a new self-respect; and this she cannot gain but by being made free."[67]

Looking ahead to proposed solutions, Channing was willing to be flexible. He did not insist upon the classic abolitionist formula of immediate, uncompensated emancipation with no expulsion of the freedmen. He thought it would be best for the newly emancipated slaves to spend some years, perhaps a generation, under the temporary stewardship of government-appointed guardians, who would train them in literacy, household management, and those aspects of religion previously denied them. He also endorsed compensation for masters, not because they had any moral right to it, but simply for the sake of political expediency. Finally, he had little faith in schemes of colonization, which he rightly felt had too often provided an excuse for procrastination; but he was willing to entertain workable proposals for the emigration of at least some of the Negroes. His position was not far from that of Francis Bowen, except in its concern for the education of the freedmen. Not surprisingly, neither man raised the prospect of land reform. Channing did not imagine that the problems of black folk in white America would end with emancipation. He feared that "the colored man, though freed, will [still] be crushed" by white supremacy. In any contest, all the advantages of numbers, wealth, education, political influence, and military power would always rest with the whites. Among people who were quick to resort to violence and lynching, the Negro would not "enjoy that equality before the civil laws to which freedom will give him a nominal claim."[68] If racial progress was inevitable, it certainly would not be quick or easy.

Since one of Channing's major misgivings about the abolitionist cause had been the intemperate denunciation of slaveholders, he himself was careful to be fair in speaking of them. He did not accuse masters of being evil men; doubtless many were good men, but they were caught up in an evil system. A Harvard moralist might hope that men could live by reason and conscience, but he did not imagine they always did. Channing could not believe that masters never gave in to their baser impulses when dealing with helpless chattels. "I know too much of human nature, human history, [and] human passion," he insisted. "I acquit slave-holders of all peculiar depravity. I judge them by myself. I say that absolute power always corrupts human nature more or less." In any case, "I speak of the injury endured by the slave, and not of the character of the master," he pointed out. "The wrong is the same to the slave, from whatever motive or spirit it may be inflicted." Channing readily admitted the culpability of his own family and section in slavery, as well as in the other social ills with which southerners were wont to charge northern industrial society. Between North and South, he acknowledged, "God alone knows the chief offender."[69]

The Unitarian moralist's moderation in dealing with southern slave owners did not win him immunity from their angry retorts. "No book of the same number of pages in any language contains libels more foul and false" than Channing's, a southern Congressman exploded.[70] Like many another minister of what came to be called the Social Gospel, Channing found out that clergymen might preach "abstractions" safely, but were exposed to outraged condemnation when they assaulted "deep-rooted abuses, respectable vices, inhuman institutions [or] unjust means of gain." His own parishioners and colleagues in Boston shunned him. Though none ventured to offer violence to his person, the gentle minister was deeply wounded by this blow to his status in the community.[71] Now he too, like Norton after the Corporation fight, knew the taste of frustration.

Channing learned something from his bitter experience, however. For one thing, he realized at last that it was not the severe manner, but the essentially subversive matter, of the antislavery message which outraged the South.[72] For another, he came to understand and sympathize more with the vilified abolitionists. "The abolitionists deserve rebuke; but let it be proportioned to the offence," he was pleading by 1839.

Is calling the slave-holder hard names a crime of unparalleled aggravation? Is it not, at least, as great a crime to spoil a man of his rights and liberty, to make him a chattel, and trample him in the dust? And why shall the latter offender escape with so much gentler rebuke? I know, as well as the slaveholder, what it is to bear the burden of hard names, . . . and I am compelled to pronounce it a very slight [evil] not to be named in comparison with bondage.[73]

Historians inclined to indignant denunciations of the abolitionists might do well to ponder Channing's questions.

Channing always remained detached from the Garrisonian abolitionists and frequently at odds with them. Believing, as he did, that "the chief strength of a reformer lies in speaking truth from his own soul, without changing one tone for the purpose of managing or enlarging a party," he did not fit in with any of the national antislavery organizations. He regretted the rise of the Liberty Party and the turn toward political action. Though he wanted northerners to absolve themselves of complicity in slavery by ending it in the District of Columbia and repealing the fugitive slave and three-fifths clauses of the Constitution, he felt that only the voluntary action of the southern states, brought on through moral suasion, offered real hope of emancipation. Political agitation would only harden the opposition. Here, as in other contexts, the Unitarian moralist preferred to operate through other means of social influence, and avoid the coercive powers of the government.

Somewhere in the South there was "a multitude of upright, compassionate, devout minds, which, if awakened from the long insensibility of habit to the evils of slavery, would soon overpower the influences of the merely selfish slaveholder."[74] Once the message of the Second Great Awakening got through to these people, the Unitarian evangelist was confident that they would abolish human bondage of their own accord. Channing believed in progress, and he felt the tide of history was running against slavery. I have "not the smallest doubt as to the approaching fall of the institution," he told Henry Clay. "The advocates of slavery . . . cannot withstand the providence of God," he was sure. "To succeed they must roll back time to the dark ages, must send Luther back to the cell of his monastery, must extinguish the growing light of Christianity and moral science, [and] must blot out the declaration of American independence."[75] Dr. Channing died in October 1842, still secure in his benign faith in Protestant Christianity, the Enlightenment, and the ultimate victory of man's better nature.

THE DISINTEGRATION OF THE UNITARIAN CONSENSUS

By the middle of the nineteenth century, time and changing circumstances had wrought alterations in the Harvard outlook. Unitarian clergymen had been defeated in their efforts to maintain an ecclesiastical establishment and had been disappointed in the results of such traditional ecclesiastical ordinances as the Lord's Supper. To maintain their moral influence in the community, they turned to quasi-evangelical preaching techniques, to music and ritual, and most important, to sentimental literature. As first national and then state government fell under the control of untrustworthy "factions," the Unitarian moralists were forced to lay greater stress upon extrapolitical activities like education and philanthropy. But these shifts were peripheral to the central core of Harvard moral thought; they were matters of tactics and style rather than of content. The real disintegration of the Unitarian consensus was brought on by the gigantic social and intellectual upheavals of the second half of the nineteenth century.

The irrepressible conflict over slavery contributed greatly to the breakdown of the classical Harvard world view, a breakdown that occurred more or less simultaneously with the Civil War. In spite of the efforts of men like Norton and Bowen to bridge the gap, the division of Massachusetts Unitarians into Cotton Whigs and Conscience Whigs badly disrupted the cohesion of the Boston-Cambridge establishment. "One of the small side-issues" of the crusade against slavery, Henry Adams observed, was the splintering of Boston society.[76] The willingness of so many "gentlemen of property and standing" to temporize with the slave power progressively angered a number of Boston intellectuals, until the mild-mannered Dr. Channing exclaimed: "Gain is their god, and they sacrifice on this altar without compunction the rights and happiness of their fellow-creatures."[77]

With feelings running so high, it became difficult to preserve a sense of Unitarian community. The Berry Street Conferences of Liberal ministers during the 1840's and 1850's were wracked with dissension over slavery and other social issues; the American Unitarian Association was virtually paralyzed as cooperation between the antislavery minority and the Cotton Whig majority became impossible.[78] Even if Unitarianism had not been subject to these internal strains, external forces would have tended to diminish its authority. It was necessarily difficult for the old mercantile-professional-clerical elite to wield its customary influence amidst the rapid processes of urbanization and Irish immigration. By the middle of the nineteenth century, the

Boston merchant class and its clerical spokesmen had come to seem less the natural leaders of a unified commonwealth than one interest group within a pluralistic society.[79]

A man who keenly regretted the disintegration of the old order was James Walker. His activities and addresses in the two decades before the Civil War reveal a mounting fear of social change. He ceased to crusade against the Calvinists as he had in his youth, and ostentatiously refrained from supporting the humanitarian causes that engaged the energies of some of his colleagues. He refused even to vote. Walker apparently hoped that by avoiding controversy he might husband the Unitarian moralists' diminishing prestige. "I have been content to labor in my appropriate sphere as a Christian minister, making it a paramount object not to jeopardize my influence in that capacity by officiousness in other matters," he declared.[80] One cannot help wondering to what purpose Walker was storing up this influence, since he did not make use of it to resume moral leadership. When pressed by the increasing urgency of the slavery issue in the 1850's, the former moral philosopher, now president of Harvard, preferred to turn away from morality and stress prudence and conformity. "Exigencies sometimes arise," he conceded, "when each one should follow his own conscience without regard for public opinion; but in the ordinary course of things, I cannot help thinking public opinion to be a safer rule than that conceit of private judgement, that extravagance of individualism, which it is now so much the fashion to recommend."[81] Such deference to public opinion ran contrary to much of the heritage of Unitarian moralism, but it enabled Walker to excuse his abdication of responsibility. Faced with a choice of conscience or community, the conservative Unitarian moralist had chosen the latter.

Though he could not withhold some grudging recognition of the importance of their calling, President Walker could also not conceal his resentment at the antislavery men who were disturbing the peace of his commonwealth and his country.

So long as the world stands in need of agitators and reformers, there will be occasion . . . for bold and daring spirits, who are for compromising nothing . . . When such men appear, there is a touch of heroism about them, which fascinates like military glory, and causes them to be lauded much above their deserts. Be this, however, as it may, thus much is plain: they are exceptional men alike in their office and their virtues, and, when out of place, become a social pest.[82]

For generations Liberal moralists had striven to create a heightened moral sensitivity. Now, confronted with a moral issue that was actually arousing men, Walker proved unable to recognize the truest fruit of the Second Great Awakening.

In order to avoid active commitment on the overriding moral issue of his day, Walker was driven to abandon the Unitarian doctrine of conscience itself. For decades he had been a proponent of the Harvard moral philosophy, a disciple of Reid and Stewart, whose works he had lovingly edited. Then, on the eve of the Civil War, he apostatized. "Conscience belongs to our emotional, and not to our intellectual, nature," he concluded at last. "It is a *sensibility* and not a *judgement*." Since the conscience was no sovereign rational moral sense but only an affection, its dictates carried no special authority after all. Much of what was passing for public conscience was "mere persistency or obstinacy of character," he decided.[83] Walker's agonized effort to escape the conclusions of his own philosophy provides a pitiful picture of a conservative trying to evade a moral decision. Through his very attempt to recover the Unitarian consensus of an earlier era, Walker had given up its principles.

Walker, however, was not alone among Harvard Unitarians in modifying his philosophy in the years preceding the Civil War. The disputes over slavery seem to have shaken the confidence of all Unitarians, whether "Cotton" or "Conscience," in the certainty of their moral judgements. Their writings during the forties and fifties reveal an increasing awareness of the complexity of moral problems and of historical changes in moral standards. The delicate relationship between ends and means concerned them more than ever before. The dogmatic ethical formulations of Scottish common sense no longer fully contented them, and to satisfy their newer concerns, Harvard Liberals (and some Transcendental Unitarians as well) turned to a French philosopher named Théodore Simon Jouffroy (1796–1842). Walker admired Jouffroy and rendered some of his works into English; Dr. Channing also read Jouffroy with avidity during the period when the slavery question most troubled him. Soon thereafter, his Transcendentalist nephew, William Henry Channing, published a complete translation of Jouffroy's *Cours de droit naturel.*[84]

Jouffroy was a student of Reid and Stewart who translated the Scots' writings into his own language and then sought to go beyond their version of ethical intuitionism. He criticized his Scottish masters for making moral judgments seem too easy and for making insufficient allowance for moral error or disagreement. "Neither can we find in [their] system," Jouffroy complained, "an explanation of what happens when . . . a moral opinion, admitted for centuries, as for instance, the propriety of slavery, is first attacked."[85]

Jouffroy's own ethical theory is a teleological system, in which individual actions are viewed in terms of their ends, and the universe as a whole is seen as serving some yet undisclosed master end. The world of Jouffroy is not a static one, where right and wrong are fixed and knowable, but an evolving one, where men only gradually discover, through a process of struggle and growth, the means to promote their moral ends. There is a modesty, almost an agnosticism, in Jouffroy's treatment of moral issues. He stresses how often people are mistaken about the relation between an action and their purposes, how many deeds performed with good intentions turn out later to have evil consequences. Under these circumstances, only a full knowledge of the motives of an agent can entitle one to pass moral judgment on his actions.[86]

Jouffroy believed in progress, and he always retained a faith that, behind the confusion of human trial and error, there stood an ultimate moral truth. "As civilization advances, the human mind successively discovers that certain actions are conformable to absolute good," he wrote.[87] Thus Jouffroy offered Harvard Unitarians a mediating viewpoint between Platonic absolutism and Burkean conservative pragmatism. Furthermore, Jouffroy's evolutionary approach to moral issues appealed to Unitarians on both sides of the slavery dispute: one could find in it support for cautious moderation and the wisdom of experience; but, equally, one could find encouragement for an antislavery crusade invoking the "advance of civilization" against a "relic of barbarism." Consequently the Frenchman's intellectual vogue did nothing to resolve the difference of opinion among Yankee Liberals; he merely helped them to understand how such differences could exist.

The Civil War, when it finally came, reunited all Massachusetts Unitarians in defense of the northern cause, for the conservatives were just as disturbed by the prospect of disunion as the "Conscience" men were by the aggressions of the slave power. But the very fact of war went far to destroy the hopefulness which had characterized so much of antebellum Unitarian thinking and gave the Boston Brahmin mind a more somber cast. No longer was it possible to put so much faith as before in voluntary moral suasion as a means of effecting progress. Like the men of the Revolutionary generation, the Yankees of the mid-nineteenth century came to know violence at first hand. Out of their sobering experience came a kind of neo-Federalism, a turning back to institutions to accomplish what the evangelical Whiggery of the second quarter of the century had failed to secure, as well as a certain tough-mindedness that could sometimes pass over into cynicism. The social mood that had been associated with the flowering of New England Unitarianism had irrevocably gone.[88]

Of course the sectional controversy was not the only historical force hastening the classical formulation of Unitarian moral philosophy toward its demise. As early as the 1840's, Channing had sensed that the days of "Unitarian orthodoxy" were numbered, and that further intellectual progress awaited new philosophies.[89] Put simply, "mid-eighteenth-century Edinburgh could not solve the problems of mid-nineteenth-century America."[90] Numerous events helped to undermine the modern world view of which Harvard Unitarianism had been one manifestation. Perhaps the most important were the scientific discoveries in geology, biology, and (by the end of the century) physics, which dissolved the happy compromises of the Christian Enlightenment; the disturbing revelations of biblical higher criticism that quickly relegated Andrews Norton's scriptural studies to the dusty shelves of obsolete books; and the rise of a totally new conception of the university— diversified, research-oriented, and secular, where the old one had been unified, teaching-oriented, and Christian.[91]

Under Charles William Eliot, who became president of Harvard in 1869, the whole character of the institution was drastically altered.

The Unitarian liberal arts college of the early nineteenth century bore more resemblance to the Puritan Harvard of two hundred years before than it did to the Harvard created by Eliot. The new Harvard was a place of many competing philosophies. So, for that matter, was the postwar Unitarian church.[92] The old style Liberal moralist vanished with the transformation of Harvard and Unitarianism. Francis Bowen, the only one of the twelve moralists who remained active into the postwar period, defended common sense philosophy against the attacks of John Stuart Mill during the 1850's, but by the following decade even that doughty warrior was ready to relinquish the old philosophical fortress. Eventually he became a Hegelian in response to the changing intellectual currents of the time.[93] Among the prominent faculty members of Eliot's Harvard, few save Andrew Preston Peabody (1811–1893) persevered in the Unitarian outlook of the earlier era.

Moral philosophy of the Scottish variety declined faster at Harvard than it did at most other American colleges. This is, in a way, a compliment to the Harvard Unitarians of the latter part of the century. When the social environment and the new intellectual discoveries brought forth evidence against classical Unitarian thought, they obligingly, and usually graciously, gave it up. Though James Walker's reasons for abandoning it may not appear particularly admirable, the fact of the matter is that by the second half of the nineteenth century there were plenty of good reasons for doing so. Today no one maintains the Unitarian doctrines as they were once set forth by the Liberal moralists. The Harvard school of Unitarianism, like its Calvinist rivals, is now a dead philosophy.

IN RETROSPECT

There are many respects in which New England Unitarian thought of the classic era appears strangely pallid. "Blandness, mildness, equableness, and harmony" do not seem to us, as they did to William Ellery Channing, terms of superlative praise. Emerson was not unjustified in expressing impatience with the "pale negations" of Boston Unitarianism; and one of Channing's shrewdest critics once remarked that "he was kept from the highest good by the love of rectitude."[94] The Liberal moralists were frequently precious, snobbish, overrefined, softly sentimental, dealing with aspirations rather than facts. The absence of sexuality and humor from their writings only confirms the impression of thin-bloodedness they convey.[95] When they attempted to implement their ideals in the workaday world they all too often turned in disappointing performances. The gap between their promise and achievement in science, the arts, evangelism, pedagogy, and politics is too obvious to be ignored.

The judgments that Herschel Baker has passed on the European Renaissance humanists are astonishingly appropriate for these Erasmians of New England's Renaissance. "It is perhaps irrelevant to expect incisiveness or intellectual independence" from the humanists, he writes; they were "men of personal charm, of urbanity in an age of violence, of erudition, of temperate lives." But such qualities, however admirable, did not necessarily make for effectiveness. "The tone is negative; the sins are not those of commission. [Their] cautious, inhibitive strain is too basic and too persistent for an age racked with new problems demanding urgency and daring."[96] The slavery issue illustrates the Liberal moralists' weakness very well: Hamletlike, they habitually hesitated and then cursed their own inaction. "It grieves me that I am perpetually taking views of subjects which prevent co-operation with others," Dr. Channing mused.[97]

Yet, whatever their shortcomings, the Unitarian moralists expressed thoughts and feelings worthy of careful scrutiny. Though they were but a few Yankees in one small locality, their minds ranged widely. Metaphysics, ethics, theology, literature, social thought, and educational theory all came within the purview of their moral philosophy. When treating these diverse topics the Harvard moralists articulated a surprising number of the major themes in modern intellectual history. They not only formulated a remarkable synthesis of Protestantism and the Enlightenment, they also managed to anticipate many of the trends of American Victorianism. By this point it must be obvious that the conventional picture of the New England Unitarians as unalloyed optimists is a caricature. Beneath their self-assurance there often lurked apprehensions that give their attitudes complexity and foreshadow the much more agonizing doubtings of the *fin-de-siècle*. A country most observers found distressingly uniform benefited from the heterodox enclave in eastern Massachusetts. Notwithstanding their timorousness with regard to revivalism, romanticism, and democracy, the Unitarian moralists still contributed enormously to the development of American civilization.

The innovative aspect of Boston Unitarianism may be explained partly in terms of the cultural lag between the United States and Europe. More than anyone else in their time, the New England Liberals kept America in touch with currents of European thought. To be sure, with respect to the European thinkers whose ideas they borrowed, the Harvard Unitarians were derivative and seldom original. The defense of eighteenth-century Latitudinarianism in nineteenth-century America may well seem scarcely adventurous. Yet, compared to most of their fellow-countrymen and to the other American churches, the ideas of New England Unitarians were progressive. One could avoid the value-laden term "progressive" and simply state that the Boston-Cambridge Unitarians were an articulate and organized group, heading in the same direction as the rest of their culture, a little faster. By dispensing with Calvinist creeds, in promoting polite letters, and through many of their social concerns, the antebellum Unitarians laid out the paths other American intellectuals and reformers would be following later.[98] A twentieth-century American intellectual would probably find conversation easier with William Ellery Channing than with any orthodox clergyman of the same era.

What the Unitarian moralists hoped to secure by their philosophy was the legitimization of human actions and desires. Francis Bowen once wrote that there is an "impulse belonging to human nature, which impels one . . . to found every claim and action on some principle of natural right." He called this impulse "the principle of legitimacy."[99] This urge for legitimacy, or justification, formed the essential thrust behind Harvard common sense philosophy. Men believed their eyes; they accepted moral and aesthetic norms; they practiced religion. Harvard philosophers admitted that such behavior was perfectly natural, but this alone did not seem adequate justification for it. They wanted to find, in the structure of the universe itself, rational justification for doing these things.

In particular, the Harvard moralists hoped to justify their religion.

If the teachings of Christianity were sustained by the evidence, then that piety the Unitarians strove so earnestly to achieve would have unimpeachable legitimacy. Religious faith would be no mere pleasing fancy, "not a belief in dogmas or probabilities, but in facts."[100] Man's emotions would be safely and surely directed to their proper fulfillment by man's intellect. The Christianity of the Harvard Unitarians (as Francis Bowen put it in his tribute to the memory of Henry Ware, Jr.) "was founded on strong convictions and deep feeling, but [was] guided by sober judgment and excellent common sense.[101]

So the Harvard Unitarians held their religious ideas to be synthetic, empirical, and dependent upon evidence. Their views were open to rational investigation and—in the approving sense that philosophers use the term—eminently "falsifiable." And this courageous stance was their vulnerability. Before long, their fortress was undermined—to a large extent by the very biblical criticism Buckminster and Norton did so much to foster. Meanwhile advancing scientific knowledge made it difficult to accept either the sanguine natural theology of Paley or the convenient harmony of reason with Christian revelation. Yet one finds it impossible to withhold admiration from their purpose. They took their stand bravely, those old Unitarian moralists, and they had nothing to be ashamed of in their ultimate defeat. Theirs was an attractive and humane philosophy in many ways; if mankind's experience contains more uncertainty, suffering, and evil than it made room for, the more is the pity. A man with a strong sense of the harsh realities of life, Thomas Malthus, passed this apt verdict on New England Unitarianism: "It is a system which every good mind must wish to be true, but I think there are considerable difficulties from some of the texts."[102]

There was more to Harvard moral philosophy, however, than its satisfying symmetry and brave front. Insofar as the Unitarian moralists grappled with such questions as how to maintain cohesion in a democracy, how to reconcile liberty with order, and how to bring conscience and reason to bear upon the problems of society, they confronted issues that have never ceased to concern reflective Americans. Most relevant of all to our own age is their plea for a cultivated humanity, for the moral education and integration of the human personality. To the

Unitarian moralists, the concomitant of self-development was self-control. Whatever storms might roar without, the virtuous man should always maintain his inward peace. The secret to attaining this psychic security was dedication to moral principle.

Unitarian moral philosophy tried to maintain the supremacy of the individual conscience against both outside pressures and inner weaknesses. The self-sufficient, independent man surrendered neither to the blandishments of others nor to the temptations of his own lower faculties. The Unitarian moralists continued in the proud tradition of Puritan moralism that Ralph Barton Perry so well summed up: "The puritan held, incredible as it may now seem, that morals are more important than athletics, business, or art. He held that to achieve a controlling will by which to conform one's life to what one conceives to be the way of righteousness is the one thing most profoundly needful. Or rather he held that athletics, business, and art should be judged by conscience, and approved only so long as they form parts of that good life—that orderly and integral life, of the person or of the society —which must be founded on virtue."[104]

This tradition did not die with Harvard moral philosophy but lived on into the twentieth century. A ceremony held by the Boston Benevolent Fraternity of Churches in 1901, on the seventy-fifth anniversary of their founding, illustrates its persistence. Samuel J. Eliot, speaker for the occasion, led the group in a memorial service for Joseph Tuckerman.

Let us not suppose that Dr. Tuckerman was an accident . . . An original man is not an isolated fact . . . The inheritance of the New England conscience, the Puritan sense of sacred obligation, the atmosphere of Harvard College, the direct influence of William Ellery Channing, the sympathy and cooperation of Gannett and Ware and the men who founded and guided the American Unitarian Association and the Benevolent Fraternity of Churches—these all combined to make the work of Tuckerman possible.

Five other speakers then joined to praise Tuckerman and the New England moral tradition. Their remarks show the continued significance this antebellum Whig had for men of the Progressive era. Reading one of his sermons, they found it "difficult to believe that [it] was preached more than sixty years ago." To urban Americans of the early twentieth century, Tuckerman's discussion of the problems of cities seemed "a sermon for today."[105]

Sentimental religion and ethical absolutism, such as the Unitarian moralists promoted, served an important social function in nineteenth- and early twentieth-century America: they helped counterbalance the anarchy of the economic system. Disseminated through college courses, didactic fiction, and countless sermons, these attitudes encouraged people to try to mitigate the callousness of laissez-faire capitalism. A number of doctrines taught by the Harvard moralists—including the perfectibility of man, the harmony of class interests, and the influence of environment upon personal character—long continued fundamental assumptions of American humanitarianism. On the eve of the First World War, many Progressive intellectuals and reformers remained, at heart, dedicated to the values of Christianity, the Enlightenment, and universal moral order that Harvard Liberals had maintained.

By now, however, it looks as though the Protestant moral tradition has finally and irrevocably expired, and nothing has yet replaced it. The moral universe of the early nineteenth-century Unitarians has vanished. In retrospect, they appear to have been among the most attractive representatives of the modern bourgeoisie.

Biographical Appendix
Notes

Biographical Appendix

ABBOT, JOHN EMERY (1793–1817) was the son of Benjamin Abbot, principal of Phillips Exeter Academy, New Hampshire. Unless the stories of his youth have been sentimentalized beyond recognition, he had an angelic disposition even in childhood. The only one of the twelve Unitarian moralists not to take his undergraduate studies at Harvard, Abbot attended Bowdoin College, graduating in 1810. Maine in those days was an appendage of Massachusetts, and Bowdoin was in some respects a client college of Harvard, though its faculty included orthodox Congregationalists as well as Unitarians. James Bowdoin, for whom the college was named, and many of its instructors were Harvard men; Andrews Norton taught there for a time. Abbot spent five years studying divinity in Cambridge before being installed at North Church, Salem, in 1815. William Ellery Channing preached his ordination sermon. In 1817 he contracted what was apparently tuberculosis, and died two years later (in Havana, Cuba, where he had gone for his health) at the age of twenty-six.

BOWEN, FRANCIS (1811–1890) was a self-made man. By a combination of hard work and brains he put himself through Phillips Exeter Academy and Harvard College. Because he had to take time out from studies to support himself, Bowen did not graduate until he was twenty-two— quite old for those days—but he took his degree summa cum laude. He taught mathematics at Phillips Exeter and Harvard, then served as editor of the *North American Review* from 1843 to 1854. Bowen was an aggressive little man with a remarkable talent for giving offense. In 1853 an attempt to appoint him McLean Professor of History was blocked when certain state office-holders who were then ex-officio members of the Harvard Board of Overseers objected to his outspoken political conservatism. (Bowen had denounced the popular Hungarian revolutionary,

Louis Kossuth, and had supported the Compromise of 1850.) The following year, after the outcries had died down somewhat, the University was able to offer him the Alford chair of moral philosophy. As a Harvard professor Bowen continued to take stands on public issues and remain in the public eye. Although a staunch protectionist for many years, he became disillusioned with high tariff policies after the Civil War and startled the country with his ringing denunciation of the Republican platform of 1888. When President Eliot introduced the elective system at Harvard in Bowen's old age, the indefatigable professor originated and taught five new courses and published a *History of Modern Philosophy*. Six months after retiring, Francis Bowen died.

BUCKMINSTER, JOSEPH STEVENS (1784–1812) was descended, on both his mother's and father's sides, from well-to-do, slaveowning, Massachusetts families. His father, Joseph Buckminster, and both his grandfathers were ministers, men who added the prestige of piety and learning to the prestige of property. Benjamin Stevens, Buckminster's maternal grandfather, had been nominated by the Corporation to be president of Harvard College in 1769, but his well-known Tory sympathies caused the Overseers to refuse confirmation. Buckminster was a precocious child and probably a little pampered. He attended Phillips Exeter and went on to Harvard College, where he achieved an excellent academic record. After graduation, Buckminster prepared himself for the ministry, instead of reading under the direction of an older clergyman, as was the custom. His unconventional decision permitted him to engage in somewhat wider reading in contemporary European literature than might have been possible otherwise. Buckminster's affiliation with the Liberals came after he fell under the influence of James Freeman, the Anglican-turned-Unitarian minister of King's Chapel. The young man returned to Exeter to teach (among his pupils was Daniel Webster) before being called to the prestigious Brattle Street Church—a real plum for a twenty-year-old novice. Buckminster's flowery sermons there enthralled Boston's elite; after his death, George Ticknor, Samuel Dexter, and Chief Justice Parsons selected some of them for publication. (There was considerable embarrassment when it was discovered Buckminster had plagiarized many of the discourses from celebrated French divines.)

CHANNING, EDWARD TYRELL (1790–1856) was a younger brother of William Ellery Channing. Unlike those Unitarian moralists who worked their way up the social ladder through scholarship and advantageous marriages, the Channing boys were born to the New England purple. Their family belonged to the thriving merchant aristocracy of Newport, Rhode Island. The father, William, was a lawyer and a prominent Federalist; George Washington and John Jay were entertained at the Channing home when they visited the area. The Channings owned a number of slaves but manumitted them after the Revolution. After graduating from Harvard, Edward T. Channing studied law like his father, but before long he turned to a literary career. He was active in founding the *North American Review* and edited that journal for a time before becoming Boylston Professor of Rhetoric and Oratory at Harvard in 1819. Though crotchety and eccentric, he was beloved by his students; and, while no one ever called his preacher brother "Bill," Professor Channing's friends nicknamed him "Ned."

CHANNING, WILLIAM ELLERY (1780–1842) grew up in Newport, Rhode Island. He was graduated from Harvard College in 1798. Then, like many young men preparing for the ministry, Channing taught for a time: he spent two years as a schoolmaster in Richmond, Virginia. In 1803 Channing was offered his choice of the Brattle Street and Federal Street ministries; with becoming modesty, he took the less distinguished of the two positions. Under his leadership, the relatively young church on Federal Street rapidly became the most important institutional center for Unitarian religion outside of Harvard. Channing was always more of a preacher than a pastor, however; his parishioners treated him with reverence rather than intimacy, and even his friends noticed that conversations with him tended to turn into monologues. He undoubtedly came to enjoy his role as Boston's leading citizen, and the family fortune, rendered secure by a marriage to his first cousin, enabled Channing to live the part to the fullest his delicate health would permit. He traveled widely in Europe, maintained many foreign correspondences, and was everywhere acknowledged a representative of the finest culture America had yet produced. The contentment of Channing's last years was severely marred by the estrangement that developed between him and his congregation over the slavery issue. When the German scholar and antislavery spokesman Carl Follen was killed in 1840, Channing's laymen refused to permit a memorial service for their minister's close friend. This callousness provoked Channing to resign the stipend he had been receiving from the church in his semiretirement.

FRISBIE, LEVI (1784–1822) was born at Ipswich, the son of a Calvinist minister who had served as an Indian missionary in the West. He had originally intended to become a lawyer, but after an eye disorder nearly blinded him he found the more sedentary occupation of a college instructor better suited to his limitations. Appointed tutor in Latin in 1805, Frisbie was promoted to full professor in 1811. His social position was enhanced by a marriage in 1817 to Catherine Saltonstall Mellen; the same year he was installed as the first Alford professor of moral philosophy. Besides his eye ailment, Frisbie was also afflicted with periodic fits of depression that his Liberal friends blamed on his Calvinist upbringing.

HEDGE, LEVI (1766–1844) was the son of a poverty-striken country clergyman who apprenticed the boy to a stonemason. Nevertheless, Hedge managed to put himself through Harvard. In 1795 he became a tutor in philosophy there and was made professor of logic and metaphysics in 1810. Finally, in 1827, he attained the Alford chair. Three years later a paralytic stroke forced his retirement.

NORTON, ANDREWS (1786–1853) one of the most fascinating of the Unitarian moralists, was descended from a long line of New England ministers. He was born in Hingham, where the venerable Ebenezer Gay had pioneered Arminian views many years before, and attended Derby Academy, which Gay had founded. After graduating from Harvard College, he followed a customary pattern by returning to Derby to teach for a year. Norton then read divinity under the elder Henry Ware, but his only parish ministry, at the Liberal church in Augusta, Massachusetts (now Maine), ended in a few weeks. Apparently the parishioners did not find his aloofness and nervous pulpit manner to their liking. Turning then to an academic career, Norton became librarian of Harvard College in 1813. From this vantage point he pursued his interest in contemporary German scholarship with avidity. He founded and edited two magazines, the *General Repository* (1812-1813) and the *Select Journal of Foreign Periodical Literature* (1833–1834), but neither proved financially successful. For eleven years he serve as Dexter Lecturer (then Professor) in Sacred Literature, resigning in 1830 to devote his full attention to his monumental *Evidences of the Genuineness of the Gospels*. This move was made possible by Norton's marriage to Catherine

Eliot, who had inherited $130,000 from her father Samuel Eliot. The Nortons lived in a beautiful mansion, "Shady Hill," set on fifty acres of land just a mile from Harvard Yard, and invested their money in the Lowell cotton mills.

TUCKERMAN, JOSEPH (1778–1840) was as close as an American of his day could come to being a genuine aristocrat. His family had been prosperous Boston businessmen and Anglicans since the seventeenth century. His father, an ardent patriot, left the Church of England for Liberal Congregationalism and became an officer in Washington's army. The boy was reared in a spacious home on the outskirts of Boston and attended Boston Latin School. At Harvard College, he became close friends with his classmates, the future Dr. Channing and the future Justice Story. Tuckerman's father had turned over much property to him, and he gained more by each of his two marriages: the first to the daughter of a wealthy landowner, and the second to the daughter of a West Indian planter. Perhaps it was because he had been somewhat sickly as a child, and more bookish than most, that Tuckerman chose to depart from family tradition and become a minister rather than a merchant. From 1801 to 1825 he was pastor in Chelsea and something of an intellectual dilettante, but in the latter year he was called to Boston as minister-at-large. Tuckerman was a widely traveled man, who made periodic trips to the southern United States, to the Caribbean, and to Europe. He had many contacts among European social theorists, including Elizabeth Fry, the English penologist, and Baron de Gerando, the French philanthropist. He also befriended Harriet Martineau and Bronson Alcott, but his zealous preoccupation with the problems of the poor made him seem suddenly eccentric to many in polite society. "By a mysterious ordination of Providence," as a puzzled Channing put it, this good man died horribly from what may have been cancer of the throat.

WALKER, JAMES (1794–1874) came from a long line of Yankee farmers; Edward Johnson, whose *Wonder-Working Providence of Zion's Saviour in New England* bore witness to the piety of the common people of the Bay Colony, was a remote ancestor. The family began its rise to prominence with Walker's father, who became a major general in the army. Walker himself attended Harvard College, taught at Phillips Exeter (like several other Unitarian moralists), and was a member of the first class to be graduated from the new Harvard Divinity School in 1817. For the next twenty-one years he was minister at the "Harvard" Church in Charlestown, which had been formed when the Liberal faction seceded from the First Church there. He became successively a Fellow of Harvard College, Alford professor of moral philosophy, and then (in 1853) president of the University. His early fire seems to have died down as he became comfortably situated in the Yard. He experimented with the new idea of offering elective courses, but reverted to the traditional fixed curriculum. Walker spent the last fourteen years of his life in quiet retirement, a venerated relic of a bygone era.

WARE, HENRY, SR. (1764–1845) is another Unitarian moralist who illustrates upward social mobility. He was the ninth of ten children born to a simple farmer of Sherburne, Middlesex County, Massachusetts. His father was poorer than most yeomen, and he died when Henry was fifteen; but his older brothers, recognizing the boy's academic potential, sacrificed to help put him through Harvard. He was graduated first in the Class of 1785. After a year teaching school in Cambridge, Ware became a minister, succeeding the Liberal patriarch Ebenezer Gay at the First Church in Hingham. In 1805 he was chosen Hollis professor at Harvard, a position he held for the rest of his long life, though he curtailed his teaching after developing a cataract in 1839. Ware outlived three wives, who bore him nineteen children. All his grown sons became successful professional men; besides Henry Ware, Jr., they included Dr. John Ware, one of America's leading physicians, and William Ware, the author of *Zenobia* and other popular romances. The elder Ware was a benign man, who presided over his enormous family without resorting to corporal punishment—but also, one fears, a rather colorless one.

WARE, HENRY, JR. (1794–1843) had a life that was typical of the Liberal clerical elite, though fuller than most. He was born at his father's parsonage in Hingham and educated at Harvard College, graduating in 1812. He taught at Phillips Exeter for two years, and there became a close friend of the principal's son, John Emery Abbot. He married the daughter of Benjamin Waterhouse, a prominent scientist of the day. He took a seventeen-month grand tour of Europe; he edited a Unitarian magazine (the *Christian Disciple*). In 1817 Ware was ordained minister at the Second Church in Boston, a pulpit where Increase and Cotton Mather had preceded him and where Ralph Waldo Emerson followed him when he left for Cambridge in 1830. From then until his death, Ware taught at Harvard Divinity School. Cultivated, gentle, humble, and sincere, Henry Ware, Jr., was an attractive human being. Francis Bowen payed him the highest compliment in the Unitarian vocabulary when he wrote that Ware "united . . . the qualities of a cool head and a warm heart."

Notes

The following abbreviations have been used in annotation:

CD *Christian Disciple*
CE *Christian Examiner*
DAB *Dictionary of American Biography*
DNB *Dictionary of National Biography*
HCL Harvard College Library
HUA Harvard University Archives
MA *Monthly Anthology*
NAR *North American Review*
OED *Oxford English Dictionary*
WEC William Ellery Channing

INTRODUCTION

1. *The Education of Henry Adams* (Boston: Houghton Mifflin Co., 1918; reprinted 1961), pp. 33–34.

2. There are a number of books treating various aspects of American colleges before the Civil War. A good one, somewhat broader in scope than its title might suggest, is George Schmidt, *The Old Time College President* (New York: Columbia University Press, 1930). Chapter IV deals with moral philosophy.

3. The genealogy is traced by Gladys Bryson in *Man and Society: The Scottish Inquiry of the Eighteenth Century* (Princeton: Princeton University Press, 1945).

4. Francis Bowen, *The Principles of Political Economy* (Boston, 1856), p. v.

5. Quoted in full in Terence Martin, *The Instructed Vision: Scottish Common Sense Philosophy and the Origins of American Fiction* (Bloomington, Ind.: University of Indiana Press, 1961), p. 171.

6. *See* G. Stanley Hall, "On the History of American College Textbooks and Teaching in Logic, Ethics, Psychology, and Allied Subjects," Am. Antiq. Soc., *Proceedings*, n.s., 9 (1894), 137–174.

7. "Notices of Professor Frisbie," in Levi Frisbie, *Miscellaneous Writings,* ed. Andrews Norton (Boston, 1823), p. xxiv.

316

8. Undated MS letter in Andrews Norton Papers, HCL.

9. Henry F. May, *The End of American Innocence* (New York: Alfred A. Knopf, 1959) , p. 10.

10. The latest treatment of the controversy is Conrad Wright, "The Election of Henry Ware: Two Contemporary Accounts Edited with Commentary," *Harvard Library Bulletin,* 17 (1969) , 245–278.

11. Perry Miller, "From Jonathan Edwards to Emerson," *New England Quarterly,* 13 (1940), 612. *See also* Francis A. Christie, "The Beginnings of Arminianism in New England," Am. Soc. of Church History, *Papers,* 2d series, 3 (1912), 153–172.

12. *See* Conrad Wright, *The Beginnings of Unitarianism in America* (Boston: Beacon Press, 1955).

13. Harold Goddard, *Studies in New England Transcendentalism* (New York: Columbia University Press, 1908), p. 25.

14. Sydney Ahlstrom, "Theology in America: A Historical Survey," in *The Shaping of American Religion,* ed. J. W. Smith and A. L. Jamison (Princeton: Princeton University Press, 1961) , I, 253.

15. The modifications in Harvard philosophy introduced during the war years may be observed in Francis Bowen, *A Treatise on Logic* (Boston, 1864) .

16. The different "schools" within Unitarianism are well defined in George Williams, *Rethinking the Unitarian Relationship with Protestantism* (Boston: Beacon Press, 1949). The distinction between Priestley's Unitarianism and that of the Harvard moralists was particularly important; it went well beyond Arian-Socinian Christological differences. Priestley was a philosophical materialist, a determinist, and a caustic critic of the Scottish common sense philosophy admired at Harvard. Nor did Priestley's friendship with Thomas Jefferson endear him to the Federalists of eastern Massachusetts. Henry Ware, Jr., perhaps the most generous of the Harvard moralists, edited *Views of Christian Truth, Piety, and Morality* (Cambridge, 1834), a selection of Priestley's least controversial writings, on the grounds that the man had never enjoyed a fair hearing in New England; but even Ware was careful to disavow Priestley's "obnoxious" intellectual "errors" in his preface.

17. Peter Gay, in *The Enlightenment: The Rise of Modern Paganism* (New York: Alfred A. Knopf, 1967), pp. 322–335, distinguishes the "Christian component" of the Enlightenment from the secular, "pagan" component which is his own primary concern.

18. *CE,* 4 (1827) , 65.

19. James Walker in the *CE,* 9 (1830), 18.

20. George Ellis, *A Half Century of the Unitarian Controversy* (Boston, 1857) , p. xiii.

21. From a sermon by James Walker, reprinted in *Reason, Faith, and Duty* (Boston, 1892), p. 414.

22. Robert Baird, *Religion in America* (New York, 1844), p. 291.

23. David B. Tyack, *George Ticknor and the Boston Brahmins* (Cambridge: Harvard University Press, 1967), p. 3.

24. The social turmoil accompanying the Revolution is portrayed in Oscar and Mary Handlin, "Radicals and Conservatives in Massachusetts After Independence," *New England Quarterly*, 17 (1944), 343–355. For a general description of the Unitarian elite in the early national period, see *The Memorial History of Boston*, ed. Justin Winsor (Boston, 1881), esp. vol. IV.

25. Paul Goodman, *The Democratic-Republicans of Massachusetts* (Cambridge: Harvard University Press, 1964), pp. 95–96. Mark Kaplanoff has discovered another influential body of Unitarian Republicans among the bankers and lawyers of Portsmouth, N.H. *See* "The Social and Economic Bases of New Hampshire's Political Change, 1800–1805," undergraduate honors essay, Yale University, 1968.

26. *The Autobiography of Lyman Beecher,* ed. Barbara M. Cross (Cambridge: Harvard University Press, 1961), II, 81–82.

27. Baker v. Fales, 16 Mass. 487 (1820), the famous "Dedham Decision" of Chief Justice Parsons, enabled the Unitarians to take over many Congregational parishes. Parsons was himself a Unitarian, a Federalist, and a member of the Harvard Board of Overseers. The issue will be discussed more fully in Chapter VIII below.

28. Edward Buck, *Massachusetts Ecclesiastical Law* (Boston, 1865), pp. 15–23, 120–149; Levi Frisbie, *Miscellaneous Writings,* pp. 108–110; Andrew Preston Peabody, *CE,* 13 (1833), 356.

29. Samuel Eliot Morison, *Three Centuries of Harvard* (Cambridge: Harvard University Press, 1936), pp. 185, 187, 223.

30. *See* Arthur B. Darling, *Political Changes in Massachusetts, 1824–48* (New Haven: Yale University Press, 1925), p. 25; Richard Hofstadter, *Anti-Intellectualism in American Life* (New York: Alfred A. Knopf, 1963), pp. 151–54; and Goodman, *The Democratic-Republicans of Massachusetts,* pp. 166–170.

31. Untitled MS, apparently written ca. 1818, in Henry Ware, Sr., Papers, HUA. President Kirkland of Harvard had served in the force which put down Shays's Rebellion.

32. Information on costs at Harvard may be found in Josiah Quincy, *History of Harvard University* (Cambridge, 1840), II, 242, as well as in the *NAR,* 6 (1818), 426, and the *CD,* n.s., 4 (1822), 150.

33. Richard Shryock, however, disagrees; *see* "Philadelphia and the Flowering of New England," *Pennsylvania Magazine of History and Biography,* 64 (1940), 305–313.

34. *See* Lewis Simpson, "The Intercommunity of the Learned: Boston and Cambridge in 1800," *New England Quarterly,* 23 (1950), 490–503.

35. I should have devoted a chapter to the important influence Unitarian moralism exerted upon the writing of history, had not David Levin largely pre-empted the subject with his fine study, *History as Romantic Art* (Stanford: Stanford University Press, 1959).

36. Many scholars have undertaken to describe the origins of the cultural "flowering" of Boston and its vicinity. *See* especially Henry Adams, *History of the United States* (New York, 1896, reprinted 1962), IX, 201–208; Van Wyck Brooks, *The Flowering of New England* (Garden City, N.Y.: E. P. Dutton & Co., 1936, reprinted 1944), pp. 1–45; F. O. Matthiessen, *American Renaissance* (New York: Oxford University Press, 1941), p. viii; and Martin Green, *The Problem of Boston* (New York: W. W. Norton, 1966).

37. The relationship between Unitarianism and Transcendentalism is well discussed in William R. Hutchison, *The Transcendentalist Ministers* (New Haven: Yale University Press, 1959).

38. Lewis Simpson, "Introduction" to *The Federalist Literary Mind: Selections from the "Monthly Anthology"* (Baltimore: Louisiana State University Press, 1962), p. 40.

39. *See* William Charvat, *Literary Publishing in America, 1790–1850* (Philadelphia: University of Pennsylvania Press, 1959), pp. 19–37; and Kermit Vanderbilt, *Charles Eliot Norton* (Cambridge: Harvard University Press, 1959).

40. Harriet Martineau, *Society in America* (1837), ed. S. M. Lipset (Garden City, N.Y.: Doubleday Anchor Books, 1962), pp. 260–261; R. K. Webb, *Harriet Martineau* (London: William Heinemann, Ltd., 1960), p. 149.

41. May, *The End of American Innocence*, p. 52.

42. *See*, for example, Alexis de Tocqueville, *Democracy in America*, ed. Phillips Bradley (New York: Alfred A. Knopf, 1945), I, 268n; and Roland Stromberg, "Boston in the 1820's and 1830's," *History Today*, 11 (1961), 591–598.

43. George W. Cooke, *Unitarianism in America* (Boston: American Unitarian Association, 1902), pp. 321–372.

44. Thus, Joseph Tuckerman deplored the effects of the pew-proprietor system. *See Principles and Results of the Ministry-at-Large* (Boston, 1838), pp. 1–12, 47–52, 139.

45. *See* "Notices of Professor Frisbie," cited in n. 7 above. These sketches, which Norton collected, are practically the only source of knowledge we have about the life of Levi Frisbie.

46. *See* Ezra Stiles Gannett, "Obituary for Levi Hedge," *CE*, 36 (1844), 299; and Ernest Sutherland Bates, "Levi Hedge," in the *DAB*, VIII, 499.

47. Two good summaries of Walker's career are those of O. B. Frothingham, "Memoir of James Walker," Massachusetts Historical Society, *Proceedings*, 2d series, 6 (1891), 443–468; and Perry Miller, "James Walker," *DAB*, XIX, 346–347. Wilson Smith devotes a chapter to Walker in *Professors and Public*

Ethics: Studies of the Northern Moral Philosophers (Ithaca, N.Y.: Cornell University Press, 1956).

48. L. L. and Jessie Bernard, *Origins of American Sociology* (New York: Thomas Crowell, 1943), p. 820.

49. Sydney Ahlstrom justly declares Bowen "the most competent philosopher at Harvard before the coming of George Herbert Palmer, Josiah Royce, and William James." *See* "The Middle Period (1840–80)," in *Harvard Divinity School,* ed. George Williams (Boston: Beacon Press, 1949), p. 88. *See also* Joseph Dorfman, *The Economic Mind in American Civilization, 1606–1865* (New York: Viking Press, 1946), II, 835; and Benjamin Rand, "Philosophical Instruction in Harvard University from 1636 to 1906," *Harvard Graduates' Magazine,* 37 (1928), 193–199.

50. The best places to find out about the elder Ware are John Gorham Palfrey, *Discourse on the Life and Character of Henry Ware* (Cambridge, 1845); William B. Sprague, ed., *Annals of the American Pulpit* (New York, 1865), VIII, 199–206; and Joseph C. Grannis, "Henry Ware, Hollis Professor of Divinity," unpublished undergraduate honors thesis, Harvard University, 1954.

51. Dr. John Ware, the moralist's brother, wrote a *Memoir of the Life of Henry Ware, Jr.* (Boston, 1846, reprinted 1868), in two volumes, which contains much of Ware's correspondence. There is a good assessment of both Henry Wares by Conrad Wright in "The Early Period," *Harvard Divinity School,* ed. Williams. Francis Bowen's tribute to the younger Ware in the *NAR,* 62 (1846), 189–214, is the closest that gruff man ever came to tenderness in print.

52. William Charvat, *Origins of American Critical Thought* (New York: University of Pennsylvania Press, 1936, reprinted 1961), p. 186; Morison, *Three Centuries of Harvard,* p. 216.

53. *See* the "Biographical Notice" Dana prefaced to Channing's posthumously published *Lectures Read to Seniors in Harvard College* (Boston, 1856), pp. xii and xvii; also the sketch by Harris E. Starr in the *DAB,* IV, 3.

54. Norton's *Discourse on the Latest Form of Infidelity* (Cambridge, 1839) was delivered to the Harvard Divinity School Alumni Association; Ripley's rejoinder, *"The Latest Form of Infidelity" Examined* (Boston, 1839) was followed by a series of pamphlets on both sides. *See* Hutchison, *The Transcendentalist Ministers,* chap. 3.

55. The best study yet done of Norton is an unpublished undergraduate honors thesis by Allen R. Clark written at Harvard in 1942. There is an appreciative estimate of Norton's contribution to American biblical studies by Conrad Wright in *Harvard Divinity School,* ed. Williams, pp. 43–52. For contemporary eulogies to this prodigious scholar, *see* William Newall, *CE,* 55 (1853), 425–452; and *Annals of the American Pulpit,* VIII, 430–434.

56. There are innumerable short tributes to Buckminster by Unitarian writers. *Memoirs of Joseph Buckminster and His Son, Joseph Stevens Buckminster,* by the younger man's sister, Eliza Buckminster Lee (Boston, 1849), is a fascinating primary source; so is George Ticknor's review of it in the *CE,* 47 (1849), 169–195. Also see *The Federalist Literary Mind,* cited in n. 38.

57. *See* the "Memoir" by Henry Ware, Jr., prefaced to Abbot's collected *Sermons* (Boston, 1829) ; also *Annals of the American Pulpit,* VIII, 466–472.

58. Except for William Ellery Channing, Tuckerman is the only one of the twelve moralists here treated to possess a full-length twentieth-century biography. Daniel T. McColgan, *Joseph Tuckerman: Pioneer in American Social Work* (Washington: Catholic University of America Press, 1940), is laudatory and thorough. Ezra Stiles Gannett's tribute in the *Monthly Miscellany of Religion and Letters,* 3 (1840), 32–42, is also worth consulting.

59. Readers wishing a fuller portrait of the Unitarian patriarch have a number of biographies to which they can turn, including John W. Chadwick, *William Ellery Channing* (Boston: Houghton Mifflin, 1903); Arthur W. Brown, *Always Young for Liberty* (Syracuse, N.Y.: Syracuse University Press, 1956); and Madeleine Hooke Rice, *Federal Street Pastor* (New York: Bookman Associates, 1961) .

60. *See,* for example, Robert L. Patterson, *The Philosophy of William Ellery Channing* (New York: Bookman Associates, 1952) , pp. 63–65. Although he ignores both Harvard Unitarianism and Scottish common sense philosophy, Patterson's work is not without value.

61. Sydney Ahlstrom, in his article on "The Interpretation of Channing," *New England Quarterly,* 30 (1957), 99–105, called upon scholars to "reconceive Channing's milieu" through a study of the "thought-world of Boston's intellectual leaders."

62. The chief proponent of the interpretation of Channing as a neo-Hopkinsian is Herbert Schneider in "The Intellectual Background of William Ellery Channing," *Church History,* 7 (1938), 4–23. An excellent rebuttal by Conrad Wright may be found in "The Rediscovery of Channing," Unitarian Historical Society, *Proceedings,* 12:2 (1959) , 8–25. "I indeed shrink with a feeling approaching horror from some of [Hopkins'] doctrines, but I do not on that account withhold the reverence due his character," Channing wrote to Edward Park. *See Memoir of William Ellery Channing,* ed. W. H. Channing (Boston, 1851), I, 142.

63. *See* Miss Peabody's *Reminiscences of William Ellery Channing* (Boston, 1880) and the three-volume *Memoir* by Channing's nephew cited in n. 62. The principal recent advocate of Channing's essential Transcendentalism is David P. Edgell in *William Ellery Channing: An Intellectual Portrait* (Boston: Beacon Press, 1955) and elsewhere.

64. *See* Arthur Ladu, "Channing and Transcendentalism," *American Literature,* 11 (1939), 129–137.

65. WEC to Elizabeth Peabody, July 28, 1841, in her *Reminiscences,* p. 430.

66. The only authority for this oft-cited remark is Peabody, *Reminiscences,* p. 371. Too much should not be made of it; Emerson once called Edward Everett "our Cicero," but no one has ever imagined Everett a Transcendentalist.

67. Perry Miller, *The American Transcendentalists* (Garden City, N.Y.: Anchor Books, 1957), p. 4. Channing's aggrieved reaction to Parker's address may be observed in the *Memoir,* II, 441–449; and in Peabody's *Reminiscences,* p. 420.

68. Quoted in Rice, *Federal Street Pastor,* p. 300.

69. *Young Emerson Speaks: Unpublished Discourses on Many Subjects,* ed. Arthur C. McGiffert (Boston: Houghton Mifflin, 1938) gives one a good sense of Emerson's pre-Transcendental phase as a "Channing Unitarian." There is a notice of Channing's death in the *Dial,* 3 (1843), 387.

70. *CE,* 55 (1853), 445; *NAR,* 31 (1830), 46.

71. Chadwick, *William Ellery Channing,* pp. 157, 185; William C. Gannett, *Ezra Stiles Gannett* (Boston, 1875), p. 93.

72. Warner Berthoff, "Renan on W. E. Channing and American Unitarianism," *New England Quarterly,* 35 (1962), 71–92, is a convenient translation and abridgement of Ernest Renan's essay, which first appeared in 1854.

73. *Works,* I, 158; Grace Ellery Channing, "Introduction" to *Dr. Channing's Notebook: Passages from Unpublished Manuscripts* (Boston, 1887), p. 4. Some of Channing's incomplete "Principles of Moral, Religious, and Political Science" was printed in his nephew's *Memoir,* II, 402–407, and more of it in *Dr. Channing's Notebook.*

74. Since the appearance of Alan Heimert's trenchant study of eighteenth-century American religion it is by no means clear which of these the "Liberal Christians" need more (*Religion and the American Mind: From the Great Awakening to the Revolution* [Cambridge: Harvard University Press, 1966]).

75. Perry Miller, *The Life of the Mind in America: From the Revolution to the Civil War* (New York: Harcourt, Brace & World, 1965), pp. 5–6.

76. Karl Barth, *Protestant Thought from Rousseau to Ritschl,* trans. Brian Cozens from *Die Protestantische Theologie im 19. Jahrhundert* (New York: Harper & Bros., 1959), p. 54.

77. Perry Miller, *The New England Mind: From Colony to Province* (Cambridge: Harvard University Press, 1953), p. x.

78. "Review of the Life and Letters of George Ticknor," *NAR,* 123 (1876), 213.

79. Quoted by Sidney Mead in *The Lively Experiment: The Shaping of Christianity in America* (New York: Harper & Row, 1963), p. 90.

I / MIND AND MATTER

1. Edwin Arthur Burtt, *The Metaphysical Foundations of Modern Physical Science* (London: Routledge & Kegan Paul, 1924, reprinted 1959), p. 11.

2. There are, of course, many works treating the history of philosophy to which nonphilosophers can turn for aid. A great one is Sir Leslie Stephen's *History of English Thought in the Eighteenth Century,* revised ed. (New York: G. P. Putnam, 1902) ; *see esp.* I, 29–63.

3. *See* Sterling Lamprecht, *The Moral and Political Philosophy of John Locke* (New York: Russell & Russell, 1962) , pp. 49–63.

4. Berkeley, quoted by Stephen, *History of English Thought,* I, 42.

5. Hume's drastic conclusions may be found in his *Treatise of Human Nature* (1739–1740). *See also* Norman Kemp Smith, *The Philosophy of David Hume* (London: Macmillan & Co., 1941), pp. 79–88.

6. An intelligent summary of the elaboration of the Cartesian distinction between mind and matter by the British empiricists into skepticism, and of Reid's reaction, may be found in that remarkable monument to American Calvinist erudition, Samuel Miller's *A Brief Retrospect of the Eighteenth Century* (New York, 1803) , II, 1–14. A more recent treatment is A. D. Woozley, "Introduction" to Reid's *Essays on the Intellectual Powers of Man* (London: Macmillan & Co., 1941).

7. The latest study, an excellent one, is S. A. Grave, *The Scottish Philosophy of Common Sense* (Oxford: Oxford University Press, 1960) . Older works include James McCosh, *The Scottish Philosophy* (New York, 1875) ; Andrew Seth, *Scottish Philosophy* (Edinburgh, 1885); Henry Laurie, *Scottish Philosophy in its National Development* (Glasgow: Glasgow University Press, 1902); and Torgny Segerstedt, *The Problem of Knowledge in Scottish Philosophy* (Lund, Sweden: Lund University Press, 1935) .

8. McCosh, *Scottish Philosophy,* pp. 2–6; Segerstedt, *The Problem of Knowledge,* p. 16.

9. Thomas Reid, *Works,* ed. Sir William Hamilton (Edinburgh, 1863), I, 441–461.

10. Grave, *Common Sense,* p. 79.

11. Reid, *Works,* I, 101. *See also* Grave, *Common Sense,* p. 130.

12. *See* Richard Petersen, "Scottish Common Sense in America, 1768–1850," unpub. Ph.D. diss., American University, 1963, pp. 49–50; and Sydney Ahlstrom, "Scottish Philosophy and American Theology," *Church History,* 24 (1955) , 257–272.

13. *Brief Retrospect of the Eighteenth Century,* II, 3.

14. Herbert W. Schneider, *History of American Philosophy* (New York: Columbia University Press, 1946) , p. 246.

15. Stow Persons' expression in *American Minds* (New York: Holt, Rinehardt, & Winston, 1958), p. 189. American historians are gradually becoming

aware of Witherspoon's importance in philosophy, education, and politics. *See,* for example, James McAllister, "John Witherspoon," in *A Miscellany of American Christianity,* ed. Stuart Henry (Durham, N.C.: Duke University Press, 1963), pp. 183–224.

16. *See* Adrienne Koch, *The Philosophy of Thomas Jefferson* (New York: Columbia University Press, 1943).

17. Thus, Samuel Miller commented that despite his high regard for "Dr. Reid's works in general," he considered "several doctrines [of his] erroneous" (*Brief Retrospect of the Eighteenth Century,* II, 12n).

18. Benjamin Rand, "Philosophical Instruction in Harvard University from 1636 to 1906," *Harvard Graduates' Magazine,* 37 (1928), 25–46; Charles Lyttle, "A Sketch of the Theological Development of Harvard University, 1636–1805," *Church History,* 5 (1936), 301–329.

19. *See* William Charvat, *Origins of American Critical Thought* (Philadelphia: University of Pennsylvania Press, 1936), chap. 3.

20. "Editor's Notice," in Thomas Reid, *Essays on the Intellectual Powers of Man,* ed. James Walker (Cambridge, 1850), p. iii.

21. An enthusiastic response greeted it in the *NAR,* 4 (1816), 78–92.

22. John W. Chadwick, *William Ellery Channing* (Boston: Houghton Mifflin, 1903), p. 30n.

23. Francis Bowen, *Critical Essays on Speculative Philosophy* (Boston, 1842), p. 120.

24. Hedge, *Elements of Logick* (Buffalo, N.Y., 1851), p. 65. For the system as Campbell presented it, *see* McCosh, *Scottish Philosophy,* pp. 239–245.

25. Hedge, *Logick,* pp. 66–69. The statements are examples, not quotations from Hedge.

26. Bowen, in *Critical Essays,* p. 53, admits the difficulties involved more frankly than Hedge ever did.

27. Hedge, *Logick,* p. 71.

28. *See Questions Adapted to Hedge's Elements of Logic, Prepared by the Author* (Cambridge, 1823). Sample questions: "What field of knowledge is derived from consciousness?" "What is the proper province of analogy?" "Compare Locke and Reid on demonstrative reasoning." One should, of course, keep in mind the youth of antebellum Harvard undergraduates when contrasting Hedge's primitive treatment with sophisticated texts later used at Harvard College.

29. As used here, the term had nothing to do with ethical obligations. An explanation of this obsolete usage is given in the *OED,* VI, 654, definition 11 of "moral." Hedge and his contemporaries also used the word in its present sense.

30. Hedge, *Logick,* pp. 72–75. The position is philosophically unjustifiable.

31. *Ibid.,* pp. 90–95.

32. Harvard Unitarians questioned the authenticity of such favorite Trinitarian texts as 1 John 5:7, but defended the New Testament miracle stories against Transcendentalists and the Bible in general against deists. Somewhat more will be said on this topic in Chap. 3.

33. Bowen, *Critical Essays,* p. 287.

34. Henry Ware, Jr., *The Nature, Reality, and Power of the Christian Faith* (Boston, 1837), p. 6; Buckminster, *Works* (Boston, 1839), I, 184, 123.

35. *Inaugural Discourse, Delivered Before the University in Cambridge* (Cambridge, 1819), pp. 10–11.

36. "The Great Mr. Locke: America's Philosopher," *Huntington Library Bulletin,* No. 11 (1937), 107–151.

37. Reid, *Works,* I, 373; cf. Grave, *Common Sense,* pp. 11–35.

38. Bowen, *Critical Essays,* pp. 148, 50. Actually, Locke was notoriously ambiguous on this point.

39. *Ibid.,* p. 285. Elsewhere (p. 160), Bowen asserted, "[Locke] is the proper father of Reid and Stewart." *See also* Terence Martin, *The Instructed Vision: Scottish Common Sense Philosophy and the Origins of American Fiction* (Bloomington: Indiana University Press, 1961), pp. 15–18.

40. "Analysis of Locke's Essay on the Human Understanding, Sept. 1833," is the heading on the notebook. *See also* E. W. Todd, "Philosophy at Harvard, 1817–37," *New England Quarterly,* 16 (1943), 63–90.

41. William Swabey, *Being and Being Known* (New York: Dial Press, 1937), p. 2.

42. James Walker, "The Philosophy of Man's Spiritual Nature in Regard to the Foundations of Faith," (1834) in *Reason, Faith, and Duty* (Boston, 1861, reprinted 1892), p. 55.

43. *See Dr. Channing's Notebook,* ed. Grace Ellery Channing (Boston, 1887), p. 105; cf. Grave, *Common Sense,* pp. 158–159.

44. Henry Ware, Sr., Sermon on Psalm 103:1–2 (1804), MS in HUA. Scottish common sense was, of course, not the only possible philosophical basis for natural theology; Berkeley and Jonathan Edwards were idealists and great natural theologians.

45. Dugald Stewart, *Works,* ed. Sir William Hamilton (Edinburgh, 1854), III, 42. Cf. Bowen, *Critical Essays,* p. 217.

46. James Walker, "The Philosophy of Religion," *CE,* 47 (1849) 256–257; Bowen, *Critical Essays,* p. 118. Reid's list, in his own words, is reprinted in Laurie, *Scottish Philosophy,* pp. 147–149.

47. *See,* for example, Reid, *Works,* I, 489. The mode of argument may be compared with that of those twentieth-century Christians who assert that atheists must "really" believe in God.

48. *Dr. Channing's Notebook,* p. 100.

49. Locke, *Essay Concerning Human Understanding,* II.xxiii.28–31. *See also* James Gibson, *Locke's Theory of Knowledge* (New York: Cambridge University Press, 1917), pp. 169–172.

50. Reid, *Works,* I, 110. *See also* Olin McKendree Jones, *Empiricism and Intuition in Reid's Common Sense Philosophy* (Princeton: Princeton University Press, 1927), esp. p. 41.

51. Gladys Bryson, *Man and Society* (Princeton: Princeton University Press, 1945), p. 250.

52. *See,* for example, Hedge, *Logick,* p. 17; Bowen, *Critical Essays,* pp. 131–132; Buckminster, "First Forensic" (1798), MS in his Papers, Boston Athenaeum.

53. *Critical Essays,* p. 123. Cf. Locke, *Essay,* II.xxi.6. For further information on post-Lockean faculty psychology *see* Gardner Murphy, *An Historical Introduction to Modern Psychology* (New York: Harcourt, Brace & Co., 1929), p. 29.

54. *See,* for example, Andrews Norton, "Observations on the Theory of Hartley," *MA,* 5 (1808), 521–530.

55. Locke, *Essay,* II.xxiii.23; Francis Bowen, *Principles of Metaphysical and Ethical Science,* 2d. ed. (Boston, 1855), p. 51.

56. For Hume's discussion of the concept of causality, *see* his *Treatise of Human Nature* (1739–1740) and N. Kemp Smith, *Philosophy of David Hume,* pp. 88–95 and 374–410. For the Unitarians' adaptation of this to their own pious purposes, *see,* for example, Henry Ware, Sr., *Inquiry into the Foundation, Evidences, and Truths of Religion* (Cambridge, 1842), I, 241.

57. "Unitarian Christianity" (1819), *Works,* III, 74–75; "Unitarian Christianity Most Favorable to Piety" (1826), *Works,* III, 173.

58. *The Perfect Life,* ed. William Henry Channing (Boston, 1873, reprinted 1901), p. 1011.

59. Elizabeth P. Peabody, *Reminiscences of William Ellery Channing* (Boston, 1880), pp. 140, 175.

60. *See* Perry Miller, *The New England Mind: The Seventeenth Century* (Boston: Beacon Press, 1939, reprinted 1961), pp. 269–279. John H. Muirhead, *The Platonic Tradition in Anglo-Saxon Philosophy* (New York: Macmillan Co., 1931), is weak on the New England Unitarians but otherwise very valuable; Harvey Wish, "Aristotle, Plato, and the Mason-Dixon Line," *Journal of the History of Ideas,* 10 (1949), 254–266, contrasts Plato's popularity among Yankees with Aristotle's influence in the South.

61. Among a number of works, consult Rosalie Colie, *Light and Enlightenment* (Cambridge, Eng.: Cambridge University Press, 1957); Basil Willey, *The English Moralists* (London: Chatto & Windus, 1964); and F. J. Powicke, *The Cambridge Platonists* (Cambridge: Harvard University Press, 1926).

62. *Republic* VI.509–VII.521.

63. "On the Elevation of the Laboring Classes" (1840), *Works,* V, 167; WEC to an unknown friend, July 27, 1842, *Memoir of William Ellery Channing,* ed. W. H. Channing (Boston, 1851), III, 375.

64. *Works,* I, pp. vii–xx. The most detailed examination yet offered of Channing's metaphysics, that of Robert L. Patterson, confirms my opinion that he persisted in his dualism. *The Philosophy of William Ellery Channing* (New York: Bookman Associates, 1952), p. 288.

65. *The Perfect Life,* p. 981.

II / THE MORAL NATURE OF MAN

1. Two representative treatments of the response to Hobbes and Mandeville are W. E. H. Lecky, *History of European Morals,* 3d ed. (New York: D. Appleton, 1910), I, 1–160; and William Swabey, *Ethical Theory from Hobbes to Kant* (New York: The Philosophical Library, 1961). An account that is interesting both intrinsically and for its influence among Harvard Unitarians is Dugald Stewart, *The Philosophy of the Active and Moral Powers,* ed. James Walker (Cambridge, 1849), pp. 187–199. Sir Lewis Selby-Bigge, ed., *British Moralists* (Indianapolis: Bobbs Merrill, 1964), is a standard collection of primary materials.

2. Ernest Tuveson, "The Origin of 'Moral Sense,'" *Huntington Library Quarterly,* 11 (1948), 241–259; James McCosh, *The Scottish Philosophy* (New York, 1875), pp. 29–36; and Roland Stromberg, *Religious Liberalism in Eighteenth Century England* (London: Oxford University Press, 1954), pp. 84–85.

3. Translating eighteenth-century philosophical terms into twentieth-century English presents difficulties. I have chosen to render "affection" as "emotional approval"; however, the word had many meanings in the eighteenth century (*see* the *OED,* I, 153, esp. definitions 2, 3, and 6), and it is possible that our word "sensation" would capture its meaning better. In either case, the sentimentalist philosophers had in mind an involuntary, nonrational feeling.

4. Francis Hutcheson, "The Finer Powers of Perception" (posthumous, 1755), in *The Story of Scottish Philosophy,* ed. Daniel Robinson (New York: Exposition Press, 1961), pp. 31–42. *See also* William Frankena's unusual interpretation of "Hutcheson's Moral Sense Theory" in the *Journal of the History of Ideas,* 16 (1955), 356–375.

5. Selections from their writings on ethics may be found in Robinson, *Story of Scottish Philosophy.* Smith's ethical theory evinces remarkable psychological insight, and it seems a pity he should generally be remembered only for his work in economics.

6. The classification of ethical theories is explained in A. J. Ayer, *Language, Truth, and Logic,* 2d ed. (London: Victor Gollancz, 1947), chap. 6; and Wil-

liam Frankena, "Ethical Theory," *Humanistic Scholarship in America: The Princeton Studies. Philosophy* (Englewood Cliffs, N.J.: Prentice-Hall, 1964).

7. N. H. G. Robinson, *The Claim of Morality* (London: Victor Gollancz, 1952); and John Kemp, *Reason, Action, and Morality* (London: Routledge & Kegan Paul, 1964), have sections treating Cudworth's ethics. *See also* Eugene Austin, *The Ethics of the Cambridge Platonists* (Philadelphia: University of Pennsylvania Press, 1935).

8. Richard Price, *A Review of the Principal Questions in Morals,* ed. D. D. Raphael (Oxford: Oxford University Press, 1948), pp. 85–91, 111. C. D. Broad, "Some Reflections on Moral-Sense Theories in Ethics," Aristotelian Soc., *Proceedings,* 45 (1944–1945), 131–166, provides a critical yet respectful evaluation of Price's ethics. The most thorough recent study of Price is A. S. Cua, *Reason and Virtue* (Athens, Ohio: Ohio University Press, 1966).

9. *See* D. Daiches Raphael, *The Moral Sense* (London: Oxford University Press, 1947), chap. 4.

10. Thomas Reid, *Works,* ed. Sir William Hamilton (Edinburgh, 1863), II, 673.

11. *See* Torgny Segerstedt, *The Problem of Knowledge in Scottish Philosophy* (Lund, Sweden: Lund University Press, 1935), pp. 7–8, 33.

12. Reid, *Works,* I, 478–481. The best discussions of Reid's ethics are those by Raphael, *Moral Sense,* chap. 5; and S. A. Grave, *The Scottish Philosophy of Common Sense* (Oxford: Oxford University Press, 1960), chap. 7.

13. Reid, *Works,* I, 480.

14. For example, Broad's article cited in note 8 and James Bonar, *Moral Sense* (New York: Macmillan Co., 1930).

15. Jefferson became personally acquainted with Stewart while in Europe as American Minister to France, 1785–1789. The ethical theories advocated in nineteenth-century America are examined more fully than ever before in Donald Harvey Meyer, "The American Moralists: Academic Moral Philosophy in the United States, 1835–1880," unpub. Ph.D. diss., University of California, Berkeley, 1967.

16. The parallel between the two dialogues was suggested to me by McMurry S. Richey, "Jonathan Mayhew," in *A Miscellany of American Christianity,* ed. Stuart Henry (Durham, N.C.: Duke University Press, 1963), p. 317.

17. Conrad Wright, *The Beginnings of Unitarianism in America* (Boston: Beacon Press, 1955), pp. 142–145. Sentimentalism and intuitionism did have things in common, of course, particularly in their criticism of what one might call the "volitionalism" of Hobbes and Calvin. In fact, there was considerable interaction between the two schools; Cudworth and other Platonists influenced such sentimentalists as Burnet (Tuveson, "Origins of Moral Sense," p. 241), while Reid borrowed from Hutcheson.

18. *See* Jonathan Edwards, *The Nature of True Virtue* (1765), ed. William Frankena (Ann Arbor: University of Michigan Press, 1960); and Perry Miller, *The New England Mind: The Seventeenth Century* (Boston: Beacon Press, 1939, reprinted 1961), pp. 197, 271.

19. Anthony Lincoln, *Some Political and Social Ideas of English Dissent* (Cambridge, Eng.: Cambridge University Press, 1938), p. 72; Samuel Eliot Morison, *Three Centuries of Harvard* (Cambridge: Harvard University Press, 1936), p. 166.

20. Price defended free will and metaphysical dualism against the deterministic and materialistic views of Priestley. Richard Price and Joseph Priestley, *A Free Discussion of the Doctrines of Materialism and Philosophical Necessity* (London, 1778); James Walker, "The Philosophy of Religion," *CE*, 47 (1849), 267–268.

21. Joseph S. Buckminster, *Works* (Boston, 1839), II, 327; *Memoir of William Ellery Channing*, ed. W. H. Channing (Boston, 1851), I, 66; Richard Price, "On the Principle of Action in a Virtuous Agent," *MA*, 1 (1804), 456–457.

22. Ralph Waldo Emerson, *Two Unpublished Essays*, ed. Edward E. Hale (Boston, 1896), pp. 57, 76.

23. *Institutes of the Christian Religion* II.viii.5.

24. Ware's lectures were published in two volumes as *An Inquiry into the Foundation, Evidences, and Truths of Religion* (Cambridge, 1824). *See* vol. I, pp. 302–304.

25. From an MS dated 1831, among his Sermons, HUA. Ware's ethical theory could probably be described as "teleological intuitionism," though it bears some resemblance to the theory which Edward Madden has called "restricted deontology." *See* "Francis Wayland and the Limits of Moral Responsibility," American Philosophical Soc., *Proceedings*, 106 (1962), esp. 351–352.

26. Frisbie, "Synopsis of Lecture Notes" (1820), MS in HUA; Norton, *A Discourse on Religious Education* (Boston, 1818), p. 13.

27. James Walker, "Conscience" (n.d.), in his *Sermons Preached in the Chapel of Harvard College* (Boston, 1861, reprinted 1892), pp. 139–145.

28. WEC, *The Perfect Life*, ed. W. H. Channing (Boston, 1873, reprinted 1901), p. 943.

29. Levi Frisbie, *Miscellaneous Writings*, ed. Andrews Norton (Boston, 1823), pp. 127–132.

30. Bernard Bailyn, ed., *Pamphlets of the American Revolution, 1750–1776* (Cambridge: Harvard University Press, 1965), I, 242.

31. Francis Bowen, *Principles of Metaphysical and Ethical Science*, 2d ed. (Boston, 1855), p. 284; Walker, *Sermons*, p. 147.

32. Frisbie's article was reprinted in his *Miscellaneous Writings*, pp. 43–88.

33. "On Right, as a Quality of Actions," extract from lecture notes, printed *ibid.*, pp. 123–152. Frisbie acknowledged that his doctrine was the one Price had formulated (*ibid.*, p. 125).

34. "Likeness to God" (1828), *Works*, III, 234.

35. Reid, *Works*, I, 508; II, 511, and passim. When James Walker edited and annotated volumes of Reid and Stewart for use as textbooks, he chose Reid's treatment of *The Intellectural Powers of Man* (Cambridge, 1850), but preferred Stewart's work on the active powers mentioned in note 1. Walker's edition of Stewart had been reprinted nine times by 1866.

36. James Walker, *Reason, Faith, and Duty* (Boston, 1876, reprinted 1892), pp. 3–4; WEC, "Self-Culture" (1838), *Works*, II, 358.

37. A distinction pointed out by Sterling Lamprecht, in *The Moral and Political Philosophy of John Locke* (New York: Russell & Russell, 1962), pp. 60 and 72–73.

38. *Miscellaneous Writings*, p. 148.

39. John Weiss, *The Life and Correspondence of Theodore Parker* (London, 1864), I, 108–109.

40. Henry Ware, Sr., Sermon on Romans 2:14–15 (1834), MS in his Sermons, HUA.

41. James Walker, "The Philosophy of Man's Spiritual Nature in Regard to the Foundations of Faith," (1835) in *Reason, Faith, and Duty*, pp. 44–45; Henry Ware, Sr., Sermon on Romans 2:15 (1834), MS in his Sermons, HUA, pp. 7–14; Frisbie, *Miscellaneous Writings*, pp. 148–149.

42. Bowen, *Critical Essays*, p. 181; Bowen, *Principles of Metaphysical and Ethical Science*, p. 317.

43. Reid, *Works*, II, 590.

44. Walker, *Sermons*, p. 257.

45. *The New England Mind*, p. 240; Plato's *Republic*, IV.434D–441C.

46. Two classic treatments are Arthur O. Lovejoy, *The Great Chain of Being* (Cambridge: Harvard University Press, 1936); and E. M. W. Tillyard, *The Elizabethan World-Picture* (New York: Vintage Books, 1943).

47. Butler's influence on the Unitarian moralists, which was extensive, will be discussed more fully in the next chapter.

48. *Works*, II, 543, 551, and 579.

49. Frisbie, *Miscellaneous Writings*, p. 166. This is standard Christian doctrine. The Unitarian moralists very seldom mentioned sex, but there is nothing to suggest morbidity in what they did say.

50. Frisbie left only fragmentary notes on this topic, but one may compare Reid, *Works*, II, 551–566, with Bowen, *Principles of Metaphysical and Ethical Science*, p. 260–264. Of course the Unitarians had no realization of the elaborate emotional ramifications of sex which the post-Freudian world recognizes.

51. WEC, *Works*, IV, 125. Some readers will detect a similarity to Kant's principle of "ethical rigor" here.

52. Reid, *Works*, II, 558–566; Frisbie, *Miscellaneous Writings*, pp. 166–167; Stewart, *Active and Moral Powers*, p. 9.

53. *Memoir*, I, 63. His heart overflowing with noble feelings, the fifteen-year-old dashed off an impassioned letter to his sweetheart, only to realize later that he had best not mail it. Though he later married the young lady, the contents of that missive remained forever Channing's secret.

54. Frisbie, *Miscellaneous Writings*, p. 192; Bowen, *Principles of Metaphysical and Ethical Science*, pp. 264–267; Joseph Tuckerman, "Seven Discourses" (1813), in *A Memorial of Joseph Tuckerman* (Worcester, Mass., 1888), pp. 121–122.

55. Walker, "Conscience" (n.d.), in his *Sermons*, p. 137. This is a close paraphrase of Bishop Butler.

56. Reid, *Works*, II, 535; Henry Home (Lord Kames), *Essays on the Principles of Morality and Natural Religion* (Edinburgh, 1751), p. 78; Bowen, *Critical Essays*, p. 324; Bowen, *Principles*, p. 260.

57. Frisbie, *Miscellaneous Writings*, p. 194.

58. Reid, *Works*, II, 535–536; James Walker, *A Discourse on the Law of the Spiritual Life* (Boston, 1835), p. 4; Joseph S. Buckminster, Sermon on Joshua 24:15 (1810), MS in his Papers, Boston Athenaeum.

59. WEC, "Likeness to God" (1828), *Works*, III, 232; Tuckerman, *Memorial*, p. 334; Henry Ware, Jr., *Works* (Boston, 1847), III, 189.

60. WEC to Joanna Baillie, June 28, 1824. *Memoir*, II, 344.

61. Walker, *Discourse at the Induction of Frederic D. Huntington as Preacher to the University* (Cambridge, 1855), p. 3; Bowen, "Sir James Mackintosh as an Ethical Philosopher," unpublished Bowdoin Prize Essay (1833), MS in HUA.

62. Peter Gay, "The Enlightenment in the History of Political Thought," *Political Science Quarterly*, 69 (1954), 374–389; Kenneth MacLean, *John Locke and English Literature of the Eighteenth Century* (New Haven: Yale University Press, 1936), p. 48; Alexander Pope, *Moral Essays*, III.154; *The Federalist Papers*, passim.

63. Henry Ware, Sr., Sermon on Psalm 119:9 (1824), MS in his Sermons, HUA; Frisbie, *Writings*, pp. 183–184. Frisbie explained that the word "passion" was also (though rarely) used to mean any strong affection, without the derogatory connotation. *See* the *OED*, VIII, 533, definition 6c of "passion."

64. Henry Ware, Sr., Sermon on Proverbs 14:12 (1836), MS in his Sermons, HUA; WEC, "The Christian Warfare," *CE*, 1 (1824), 102–108.

65. James Walker, *Sermons*, p. 112. The "true," of course, included the "right." "Emotions" and "feelings" were used by the Unitarians in a general sense to mean both desires and affections. *See* Frisbie, *Writings*, p. 183.

66. Quoted in Elizabeth P. Peabody, *Reminiscences,* p. 154. This meaning is discussed in the *OED,* IX, 470, definition 9b of "sentiment." Reid claimed this was the only proper definition of the word (*Works,* II, 675).

67. *Sermons,* p. 253.

68. Frisbie, *Writings,* p. 200. Dr. Channing spoke of "the feeling of approbation with which we look on disinterested benevolence," while distinguishing this "emotion" from "the idea of right" which "conscience" gives (*The Perfect Life,* p. 933).

69. Price, *Review of the Principal Questions in Morals,* chap. 2, esp. p. 62; Reid, *Works,* II, 670–679.

70. Henry Ware, Jr., "On the Formation of the Christian Character" (1831), *Works,* IV, 291; E. T. Channing, *Lectures Read to Seniors in Harvard College* (Boston, 1856), p. 211.

71. Frisbie, *Writings,* p. 200.

72. Bowen, *Principles of Metaphysical and Ethical Science,* pp. 264, 317.

73. Henry Ware, Sr., Sermon on Proverbs 14:12 (1836), MS in his Sermons, HUA.

74. Bowen, "Dr. Franklin," *NAR,* 59 (1844), 472.

75. William Paley, *The Principles of Moral and Political Philosophy* (Boston, 1801), p. 48.

76. Paley has provided the perfect whipping-boy for critics ever since he wrote. One skillful recent dissection of his theory is that by N. H. G. Robinson, *The Claim of Morality* (London: Victor Gollancz, 1952), pp. 79–82. The most perceptive and devastating analysis of Paley as both man and thinker is, in my opinion, "Religion and Society: Paley and Channing," *National Review* (London), 6 (1858), 397–424.

77. Henry Ware, Jr., *Works,* II, 301.

78. Bowen, "Dr. Franklin," p. 472.

79. For example, Levi Frisbie, in his inaugural address upon becoming Alford professor of moral philosophy in 1817, sharply warned against the dangerous implications lurking in Paley's doctrines (*Miscellaneous Writings,* p. 9). The criticism leveled at Paleyan utilitarianism in class may be found among his lecture notes (*ibid.,* pp. 133–142). Donald Harvey Meyer, in his dissertation "The American Moralists," pp. 45–54, advances a number of reasons that help explain why college professors in the United States frequently employed Paley's text without endorsing his ethical theory.

80. Dugald Stewart, *Works,* ed. Sir William Hamilton (Edinburgh, 1854), III, 349–357. Stewart calls Paley's theory "specious but dangerous" (III, 353). Paley was again refuted by Stewart in *The Active and Moral Powers of Man,* printed in Boston in 1828 and republished with notes by James Walker in 1849. For Brown's views, *see* his *Philosophy of the Human Mind,* ed. Levi Hedge (Cambridge, 1827), II, 174.

81. Francis Bowen, "Sir James Mackintosh," cited in n. 61 above; Andrew Preston Peabody, *Harvard Reminiscences* (Boston, 1888), p. 5. Peabody is referring to his undergraduate days, 1823–1826.

82. Frisbie, *Miscellaneous Writings,* p. 83.

83. WEC, "Remarks on Fénelon" (1829), *Works,* I, 171; Henry Ware, Sr., Sermon on Ecclesiastes 1:17 (1834), MS in his Sermons, HUA, esp. pp. 12–13; Walker, *CE,* 13 (1832), 195. Fourteen years later Walker had come to the conclusion that Paley was not even a sound "practical" guide (*CE,* 41 [1846], 100).

My account of Paley's use at Harvard represents a departure from the one given by Wilson Smith in *Professors and Public Ethics: Studies of the Northern Moral Philosophers* (Ithaca, N.Y., Cornell University Press, 1956). Professor Smith has there presented (esp. on pp. 155–162) the Harvard moralists, and specifically James Walker, as being Paleyan theological utilitarians, at least until the mid-1830's.

84. Bowen, College Papers, 1832–1833, p. 32, MS in HUA.

85. Bowen, *Critical Essays,* p. 346. Bowen quoted Hobbes's famous adjectives in *Principles of Metaphysical and Ethical Science,* p. 326.

86. The curious failure of Edwards and his antagonists to come to grips with each other in the eighteenth century is well analyzed in Conrad Wright, "Edwards and the Arminians on the Freedom of the Will," *Harvard Theological Review,* 35 (1942), 241–261.

87. "Essay Concerning Free Agency," *NAR,* 13 (1821), 392. Cf. WEC, *Works,* I, xiii, 254.

88. James Boswell, *Life of Samuel Johnson* (London: J. M. Dent & Sons, 1913) I, 363. This dictum was taught in Harvard classrooms; *see* George Moore, "Exercises with Dr. Ware in Dogmatic Theology" (1836–1837), student notebook pp. 10–11, MS in HUA.

In 1864, more than a century after Edwards's death, a versatile New England Unitarian businessman named Rowland G. Hazard (1801–1888) published *Freedom of the Mind in Willing; or Every Human Being That Wills a Creative First Cause.* This work, however, is not a representative of the classic Harvard philosophy. It manifests the influence of Sir William Hamilton's modifications of Reid, and also foreshadows the growing sympathy for metaphysical idealism which was to appear in postwar America.

III / REASON AND REVELATION

1. *See,* for example, Gerald R. Cragg, *Reason and Authority in the Eighteenth Century* (Cambridge, Eng.: Cambridge University Press, 1963).

2. A great medievalist has explained it this way: "Since God is the author both of the truths made known by revelation and of the truths discovered by reason, there can be no conflict between them. If a conflict should appear to

exist between them, it must be no real conflict. Any such conflict must be due either to our misunderstanding of Scripture or to the vagaries of human reason which has gone astray" (Harry A. Wolfson, *Philo* [Cambridge: Harvard University Press, 1947], II, 447).

3. *An Essay Concerning Human Understanding*, IV.xix.4.

4. Samuel Eliot Morison, *Three Centuries of Harvard* (Cambridge: Harvard University Press, 1936), p. 191.

5. *See* Perry Miller's account of the history of the endowment in his own Dudleian Lecture of 1953, "The Insecurity of Nature," *Nature's Nation* (Cambridge: Harvard University Press, 1967), 120–133. John Hunt treats the Boyle Lectures in *Religious Thought in England from the Reformation to the End of the Last Century* (London, 1873), III, 97–124.

6. James Freeman Clarke, *Autobiography*, ed. Edward E. Hale (Boston, 1892), pp. 139–140.

7. Levi Frisbie, "Inaugural Address" (1817), in his *Miscellaneous Writings*, ed. Andrews Norton (Boston, 1823), pp. 8–9.

8. Henry Ware, Sr., *Inquiry into the Foundation, Evidences, and Truths of Religion* (Cambridge, 1842). The Unitarian organ printed a long and (of course) laudatory review of the work: *CE*, 32 (1842), 86–102.

9. John C. Greene, *The Death of Adam: Evolution and Its Impact on Western Thought* (New York: Mentor Books, 1959, reprinted 1961), p. 23.

10. Charles C. Gillispie, *Genesis and Geology* (Cambridge: Harvard University Press, 1951), p. 18. *See also* Conrad Wright, "The Religion of Geology," *New England Quarterly*, 14 (1940), esp. 337; and William and Mabel Smallwood, *Natural History and the American Mind* (New York: Columbia University Press, 1941), esp. p. 236.

11. WEC, "Christianity a Rational Religion" (1823), *Works* (Boston, 1848), IV, 49.

12. James Walker, "Religion and Physical Science" in *Sermons Preached in the Chapel of Harvard College* (Boston, 1861, reprinted 1892), p. 129. (The sermons, delivered in the 1840's and 1850's, are undated.) Francis Bowen, *Critical Essays on Speculative Philosophy* (Boston, 1842), p. 327; Bowen, *Principles*, pp. v, 135; and Bowen, "The Latest Form of the Development Theory," *NAR*, 90 (1860), 474–506.

13. William Paley's famous textbook, *Natural Theology* (Boston, 1802, reprinted 1866), p. 212, admitted that natural philosophy served Christian apologetic purposes less satisfactorily than natural history. On the relative importance of natural history and natural philosophy to natural theology, *see also* John Dillenberger, *Protestant Thought and Natural Science* (Garden City: Doubleday & Co., 1960), p. 150.

14. Dugald Stewart avowed natural history as the model for his study of human mental processes (*Works,* ed. Sir William Hamilton [Edinburgh, 1854],

I, 13 and 19). On natural history and natural philosophy in the United States, *see* Brooke Hindle, *The Pursuit of Science in Revolutionary America* (Chapel Hill: University of North Carolina Press, 1956); and George Daniels, *American Science in the Age of Jackson* (New York: Columbia University Press, 1968).

15. The following works were mentioned by George Moore, "Exercises with Dr. Ware in Natural and Revealed Religion," undergraduate notebook for academic year 1836–1837, MS in HUA: Edward Stillingfleet, *Originas Sacrae* (1662); Ralph Cudworth, *True Intellectual System of the Universe* (1678); Samuel Clarke, *Demonstration of the Being and Attributes of God* (1704–1705); François Fénelon, *Demonstration of the Existence, Wisdom and Omnipotence of God* (1713); William Derham, *Physico-Theology* (1713); William Wollaston, *The Religion of Nature Delineated* (1724); Joseph Butler, *The Analogy of Religion, Natural and Revealed, to the Constitution and Course of Nature* (1736); Philip Doddridge, *Lectures on Pneumatology, Ethics, and Divinity* (1763); Abraham Tucker, *The Light of Nature Pursued* (1768–1778); Joseph Priestley, *Natural and Revealed Religion* (1772–1774); Joseph Priestley, *Letters to a Philosophical Unbeliever* (1780); William Paley, *Natural Theology* (1802); Timothy Dwight, *Theology, Explained and Defended* (1818–1819); Thomas Brown, *Philosophy of the Human Mind* (1820).

16. Vol. XI (1832), 323–325.

17. Henry Ware, Jr., "How to Spend a Day," in his *Works*, I, 176.

18. The importance of Paley's text has been repeatedly remarked, and there are a number of recent analyses of it. Gillispie, *Genesis and Geology*, pp. 36–39, handles Paley rather roughly. ("The lucidity of his interpretation was not beclouded by first-hand knowledge of the subjects on which he based it.") Frederick Ferré, on the other hand, treats Paley critically, yet sympathetically. ("He shows us that it is possible to discuss theological belief without abandoning a constant concern for the relevance of empirical fact . . . We can no longer believe precisely what he believed, . . . but we can honor his goals.") "Editor's Introduction," in *Natural Theology: Selections,* by William Paley (Indianapolis: Bobbs-Merrill, 1963), p. xxxi. There is also an article by Wendell Glick on "Bishop [sic] Paley in America," *New England Quarterly,* 27 (1954), 347–354.

19. William Paley, *Natural Theology* (Boston, 1866), pp. 5–13, 39, and passim.

20. London, 1835–1839.

21. Henry Ware, Sr., "Lectures on Natural and Revealed Religion," in his Papers, HUA, may be compared with their published form, the *Inquiry* discussed above. *See also* George Moore's MS notebook.

22. Joshua Bates, quoted in Eliza B. Lee, *Memoirs of Joseph Buckminster and His Son, Joseph Stevens Buckminster* (Boston, 1849), p. 447.

23. Herbert Schneider, *A History of American Philosophy* (New York: Columbia University Press, 1946), pp. 225–227.

24. Joseph S. Buckminster, "Poem Written in November, 1799," MS in his Papers, Boston Athenaeum.

25. A. Hunter Dupree, *Asa Gray, 1810–1888* (Cambridge: Harvard University Press, 1959), pp. 120, 136, 226.

26. Lewis P. Simpson, *The Federalist Literary Mind* (Baltimore: Louisiana State University Press, 1962), p. 4.

27. WEC, *The Perfect Life,* ed. William H. Channing (1873, reprinted 1901), p. 1003.

28. Buckminster, *Works* (Boston, 1839), II, 7.

29. Henry Ware, Jr., "On Opening Our Organ" (1822), *Works,* I, 251.

30. I shall not attempt to retell the story of the dispute between conservative Unitarians and Transcendentalists; I merely wish to describe the context in which some Unitarian ideas found their fullest expression. For an understanding of the debate itself, the best place to begin is *The Transcendentalists: An Anthology,* ed. Perry Miller (Cambridge: Harvard University Press, 1950). For the events touched upon in this paragraph, *see* William R. Hutchison, *The Transcendentalist Ministers* (New Haven: Yale University Press, 1959), pp. 41–45, 55–76.

31. Even Dr. Channing was offended by Emerson's address. (Elizabeth Peabody, *Reminiscences* [Boston, 1880], pp. 378–379.) Still, few Unitarians welcomed the scandal of an open breach with the Transcendentalists; *see* Hutchison, *The Transcendentalist Ministers,* pp. 89–90. An account of the origins of Emerson's animus toward his former colleagues is given by Conrad Wright in *Harvard Divinity School,* ed. George Williams (Boston: Beacon Press, 1954), pp. 68–77.

32. Henry Ware, Jr., *Works,* III, 26–39. The *CE,* 25 (1838), 266–268, reviewed Emerson's and Ware's addresses together, distinguishing the erratic speculations of the former from the sound doctrine of the latter. Ware also sent Emerson a copy of "The Personality of the Deity," but the impossibility of drawing him into debate is manifest in the Transcendentalist's reply: "I could not give account of myself if challenged. I could not possibly give you one of the 'arguments' you cruelly hint at, on which any doctrine of mine stands. For I do not know what arguments mean, in reference to any expression of a thought. I delight in telling what I think; but, if you ask me how I dare say, or, why it is so, I am the most helpless of mortal men. I do not even see, that either of these questions admits of an answer" (quoted in John Ware, *Memoir of Henry Ware, Jr.* [Boston, 1846], II, 188).

33. Bowen's review appeared in *CE,* 21 (1837), 371–385.

34. Cited hereafter as Bowen, *Critical Essays.* This collection also includes his review of Francis Wayland's *Elements of Moral Science.* Bowen told Andrews

Norton he had intended to dedicate the book to him, but then decided dedications were old-fashioned. Bowen to Norton, May 28, 1842, Andrews Norton Papers, HCL.

35. For an exposition of several of the arguments, *see* J. J. C. Smart, "The Existence of God," in *New Essays in Philosophical Theology,* ed. Antony Flew and Alasdair MacIntyre (New York: Macmillan Co., 1955), pp. 28–46.

36. *See* Thomas Reid, *Works,* ed. Sir William Hamilton (Edinburgh, 1863), I, 458, 460.

37. Samuel Clarke, *A Demonstration of the Being and Attributes of God* (London, 1704–1705). The cosmological argument can be interpreted as an argument *a posteriori,* but Clarke treated it as an argument *a priori.* Bowen, *Critical Essays,* p. 182.

38. Bowen, *Critical Essays,* pp. 222, 192, 223.

39. Bowen, *Principles of Metaphysical and Ethical Science,* pp. 393–417.

40. Bowen, *Critical Essays,* p. xvii.

41. *Ibid.,* p. 65.

42. *Ibid.,* p. 201.

43. Henry Ware, Sr., *Inquiry,* I, 185–204; Bowen, *Principles,* p. 349.

44. Bowen, *Principles,* p. 373.

45. Walker, "Two Discourses on Immortality" (n.d.), MS in his Sermons, HUA, unpaginated.

46. *See* Jerry W. Brown, *The Rise of Biblical Criticism in America, 1800–1870* (Middletown, Conn.: Wesleyan University Press, 1969), esp. chap. 5.

47. Joseph Tuckerman, "The Theologist," *MA,* 2 (1805), 174. Tuckerman suggested that a society which knew as much about the harmonies of nature as his own enlightened one might have had little need for clarification from revelation. But in primitive times, revelation had been essential to save mankind from polytheism and idolatry.

48. Henry Ware, Sr., Sermon on Matthew 23:23 (1823), MS in his Sermons, HUA.

49. Walker, *Sermons,* p. 250; Bowen, *Principles,* p. 46; WEC, *Works,* III, 379–380.

50. WEC, "Unitarian Christianity" (1819), *Works,* III, 66.

51. Quoted in Eliza B. Lee, *Memoirs,* p. 337.

52. Locke, *Essay,* IV.xv.4.

53. Buckminster, *Works,* I, 173–174; WEC, *Works,* IV, 32.

54. Since the authoritative work of Conrad Wright, it is no longer necessary to explain that the New England Unitarians were not deists. *See The Beginnings of Unitarianism in America,* pp. 5, 147.

55. Locke's relationship to deism was an ambiguous one. Though he indignantly dissociated himself from the movement, the deists did find much use for

his principles. In the controversy between Christians and deists, Lockean doctrines were frequently invoked by both sides. *See* Franklin Baumer, *Religion and the Rise of Skepticism* (New York: Harcourt, Brace, 1960), pp. 94–95; and Roland Stromberg, *Religious Liberalism in Eighteenth-Century England* (London: Oxford University Press, 1954), p. 19. Harvard Unitarians, of course, were anxious to absolve their hero of the stigma of infidelity: *see* Walker, *Sermons*, p. 66.

56. *See* Wright, *Beginnings of Unitarianism,* pp. 242–245.

57. Henry Ware, Sr., *A Sermon Delivered at the Ordination of William Ware* (New York, 1822), p. 24; Walker, *The Deference Paid to the Scriptures by Unitarians* (Boston, 1837), p. 3.

58. *See* Thomas Paine, *The Age of Reason: Being an Investigation of True and Fabulous Theology* (London, 1794).

59. Joseph Butler, *The Analogy of Religion, Natural and Revealed, to the Constitution and Course of Nature.* An edition familiar to Harvard Unitarians would have been the one printed in Boston by Manning and Loring in 1793. Obviously Butler's argument is much less effective against atheism than against deism; nevertheless, twentieth-century commentators treat it with respect. C. D. Broad calls it "perhaps the ablest and fairest argument for theism that exists" (*Five Types of Ethical Theory* [New York: Harcourt Brace, 1930], p. 5). On the *tu quoque* argument, *see* William Warren Bartley III, *The Retreat to Commitment* (London: Chatto & Windus, 1964), passim.

60. Andrews Norton, "A Defence of Liberal Christianity" (1812), reprinted in his *Tracts Concerning Christianity* (Cambridge, 1852), p. 29; Walker, quoting Sir James Mackintosh, in *Reason, Faith, and Duty* (Boston, 1876, reprinted 1892), p. 117.

61. Henry Ware, Jr., *Works,* III, 355.

62. *Works,* I, 169; *The Perfect Life,* p. 941.

63. Paine, *The Age of Reason, Part II* (New York, 1853).

64. WEC, "Christianity a Rational Religion" (1823), *Works,* IV, 40–41.

65. Ware, *Inquiry,* II, 68–94; Buckminster, *Works,* II, 255.

66. Bowen, *Critical Essays,* pp. 321–322.

67. Conrad Wright has given this term its currency as applied to Massachusetts Arminians, though the expression was used earlier by others like Arthur C. McGiffert and Adolph von Harnack.

68. In this, as in so much else, Mayhew set the pattern for the next hundred years of New England Liberal Christianity. His views are explained in McMurry S. Richey, "Jonathan Mayhew: American Christian Rationalist," *A Miscellany of American Christianity,* ed. Stuart C. Henry (Durham, N.C.: Duke University Press, 1963), p. 318.

69. John Locke, *The Reasonableness of Christianity with a Discourse of Mir-*

acles and Part of a Third Letter Concerning Toleration, ed. Ian Ramsey (Stanford: Stanford University Press, 1958) ; Henry Ware, Sr., *Inquiry,* II, 105–106.

70. *Works,* III, 105; *The Perfect Life,* p. 1002.

71. George Moore, student notebook (1836–37), exercise no. 25, MS in HUA; Henry Ware, Jr., "Notes to a Course of Lectures Delivered before the members of the Divinity School, 1837," p. 72, MS in HUA.

72. Henry Ware, Sr., *Inquiry,* II, 22.

73. WEC, *Works,* III, 107.

74. *Ibid.,* II, 292.

75. Paine, *The Age of Reason,* p. 36. Hume's essay "On Miracles" is found in section X of his *Enquiry Concerning Human Understanding* (1748). It has been conveniently reprinted in *David Hume on Religion,* ed. Richard Wollheim (Cleveland: Meridian Books, 1963) .

76. George Ripley also challenged the use classical Unitarians made of miracles, though not because he denied their historicity. Ripley's debate with Andrews Norton is thoroughly analyzed in Hutchison, *The Transcendentalist Ministers,* chap. 3. Hildreth's open "Letter to Andrews Norton on Miracles" combined philosophical incisiveness with personal malice; it is reprinted in Martha Pingel, *An American Utilitarian: Richard Hildreth* (New York: Columbia University Press, 1948), pp. 129–152.

77. Henry Ware, Jr., *Works,* III, 49; Francis Bowen, *Principles,* p. 483.

78. *Inaugural Discourse* [as Dexter Professor of Sacred Literature] *Delivered Before the University in Cambridge* (Cambridge, 1819), p. 8.

79. *See* Clarence H. Faust, "The Background of Unitarian Opposition to Transcendentalism," *Modern Philology,* 25 (1938) , 297–334.

80. WEC, "Unitarian Christianity," *Works,* III, 61; cf. J. S. Buckminster, "Sources of Infidelity," *Works,* II, 115–129.

81. Henry Ware, Jr., *Works,* II, 238.

82. *See,* for example, Henry Ware, Jr., "Two Letters on the Genuineness of the Verse I John v. 7, and on the Scriptural Argument for Unitarianism" (1820), *Works,* II, 303–330; Henry Ware [Sr.?], *An Essay on the Use and Meaning of the Phrase, 'Holy Spirit'* (Boston, 1819) ; and Walker, "Dr. Palfrey on the Jewish Scriptures," *CE,* 25 (1838), 106–128.

83. Norton carried on a running debate with Professor Moses Stuart of Andover on the authorship of Hebrews, which begins in the *CE,* 4 (1827) , 495–520.

84. *Evidences of the Genuineness of the Gospels,* abridged edition (Boston, 1877), pp. 1, 16.

85. Three volumes of *Evidences of the Genuineness of the Gospels* (1837–1844), two volumes of his annotation and translation of the New Testament, and one volume of *Internal Evidences of the Genuineness of the Gospels,* posthumous (Boston, 1856) . In general, biblical scholarship in nineteenth-

century America lagged far behind that in Germany. *See* John H. Giltner, "Moses Stuart, 1780–1852," unpub. Ph.D. diss., Yale University, 1956; and Brown, *Rise of Biblical Criticism in America,* passim.

86. "Review of Norton's Genuineness of the Gospels," *NAR,* 59 (1844), 143.

IV / THE MORAL BASIS OF RELIGION

1. Explained by Ernst Cassirer in *The Philosophy of the Enlightenment,* trans. F. C. A. Koelin and J. P. Pettegrove (Boston: Beacon Press, 1955; first published 1932), p. 39.

2. Francis Bowen, *Critical Essays on Speculative Philosophy* (Boston, 1842), p. 190.

3. *Miscellaneous Writings of Professor Frisbie,* ed. Andrews Norton (Boston, 1823), p. 204.

4. Bowen, *Principles of Metaphysical and Ethical Science,* 2d. ed. (Boston, 1855), pp. 270–271; and Henry Ware, Sr., Sermon on Psalm 106:1–2 (1823), MS in his Sermons, HUA.

5. William Curtis Swabey, *Ethical Theory from Hobbes to Kant* (New York: The Philosophical Library, 1961), pp. 102–103. Swabey interprets Butler as a rational intuitionist in ethics, though some others have classified him with the sentimentalists. William J. Norton, Jr., seems to support Swabey in *Bishop Butler: Moralist and Divine* (New Brunswick, N.J.: Rutgers University Press, 1940), pp. 10–20. Butler's ethical doctrines are contained in *Fifteen Sermons* (1726), reprinted in his *Works,* ed. W. E. Gladstone (Oxford, 1896) ,vol. II.

6. By A. Campbell Fraser, in *Thomas Reid* (Edinburgh, 1898), p. 78.

7. Joseph Butler, *The Analogy of Religion, Natural and Revealed, to the Constitution and Course of Nature* (1736), chap. 3, in *Works,* I, 63–94, esp. 76, 79.

8. *See* Richard Price, *A Review of the Principal Questions in Morals,* ed. D. Daiches Raphael (Oxford: Oxford University Press, 1948), p. 83. For the Cambridge Platonists, *see* Roland Stromberg, *Religious Liberalism in Eighteenth Century England* (London: Oxford University Press, 1954), p. 19.

9. A favorite expression, not only of sentimental souls like James Walker, but even of the stern Bowen. *See* Walker's *Sermons Preached in the Chapel of Harvard College* (Boston, 1861, reprinted 1892), p. 147; and Bowen's *Principles,* p. 47.

10. Henry Ware, Sr., Sermon on Romans 2:15 (1823), MS in his Sermons, HUA.

11. Bowen, *Principles,* pp. 309–310, 277 (Bowen's italics). Cf. Henry, Lord Brougham, *Discourse of Natural Theology* (Philadelphia, 1835), p. 9.

12. WEC, *Works* (Boston, 1849), IV, 335. *See also* Joseph S. Buckminster, "Evidences of a Future Retribution," *Works* (Boston, 1839), II, 32–42.

13. *The Perfect Life,* ed. W. H. Channing (Boston, 1873, reprinted 1901), p. 931.

14. Henry Ware, Jr., *Works* (Boston, 1847), III, 3; Walker, "Religion Not a Science, But a Want" (1859), in *Reason, Faith and Duty* (Boston, 1876, reprinted 1892), p. 4.

15. "Religion Not a Science," p. 5.

16. Henry Ware, Sr., *Inquiry into the Foundations, Evidences, and Truths of Religion* (Cambridge, 1842), I, 45–48.

17. *Ibid.,* 51–57.

18. Frisbie, *Miscellaneous Writings,* pp. 195–196; Bowen, *Critical Essays,* pp. 232–233; Walker, *Reason, Faith, and Duty,* pp. 214–217.

19. *The Perfect Life,* p. 984.

20. Henry Ware, Jr., *Works,* III, 3 and 355. Joseph Butler had anticipated this argument: "The proper motives to religion are the proper proofs of it" (*Analogy of Religion* [1736], *Works,* I, 184).

21. WEC, *The Perfect Life,* pp. 932, 998. "Our Lord would blot out and destroy none of the native characteristics of man," Henry Ware, Jr., was careful to specify; "He seeks but to correct, renew, and exalt them" (*Works,* III, 156–157).

22. Delivered in 1834, published in the *CE,* 17 (1835), 1–5, and reprinted in *Reason, Faith and Duty,* pp. 37–61.

23. *See* George Ellis, "Remarks on the Death of Dr. Walker," Mass. Hist. Soc., *Proceedings,* 1st series, 13 (1875), 398; and O. B. Frothingham, "Memoir of James Walker," Mass. Hist. Soc., *Proceedings,* 2d series, 6 (1891),453.

24. "Evidences of Christianity" (1823), *Works,* III, 317 and 333.

25. "Religion Not a Science, But a Want," *Reason, Faith and Duty,* p. 5.

26. "Unitarian Christianity" (1819), *Works,* III, 60–61. The background of the concept of progressive revelation may be explored in Owen Chadwick, *From Bossuet to Newman: The Idea of Doctrinal Development* (Cambridge, Eng.: Cambridge University Press, 1957).

27. Joseph S. Buckminster to Joseph Buckminster, July 23, 1804; quoted in Eliza Buckminster Lee, *Memoirs* (Boston, 1849), p. 144.

28. Channing's address took an hour and half to deliver and was "well worth coming 400 miles to hear," wrote Samuel A. Eliot to Andrews Norton on May 6, 1819 (Norton Papers, HCL). The Baltimore sermon has been reprinted twice recently: in *Unitarian Christianity and Other Essays,* ed. Irving Bartlett (Indianapolis: Library of Liberal Arts, 1957); and in *Three Prophets of Religious Liberalism,* ed. Conrad Wright (Boston: Beacon Press, 1961). Both editors provide good introductions.

29. WEC, *Works,* III, 64, 83, 87.

30. For a near-contemporary account, *see* George E. Ellis, *A Half-Century of the Unitarian Controversy* (Boston, 1857). The fullest recent treatment is in

H. Shelton Smith, *Changing Conceptions of Original Sin* (New York: Charles Scribner's Sons, 1955).

31. WEC, *The Perfect Life,* p. 932.

32. WEC, "The Moral Argument Against Calvinism" (1820), *Works,* I, 236–237.

33. *Ibid.,* III, 215; cf. Henry Ware, Jr., *Works,* IV, 128.

34. *See* Bowen's review of Francis Wayland's *Moral Science,* reprinted in his *Critical Essays,* p. 320.

35. Sermon on I Corinthians 10:31 (n.d.), MS in Joseph S. Buckminster Papers, Boston Athenaeum.

36. Reading the pamphlet exchanges between Henry Ware, Sr., and Leonard Woods (the "Wood 'n Ware" Debate), one is struck by how much these two nineteenth-century American clerics held in common. Despite this, there is no doubt that passions ran high during the height of the controversy in the 1820's.

37. Leonard Woods summarized the "moral tendency" arguments invoked on both sides in *Letters to Unitarians* (Andover, 1820).

38. *See,* for example, Norton, "Thoughts on True and False Religion" (1820), reprinted in his *Tracts Concerning Christianity* (Cambridge, 1852), pp. 99–158; and Henry Ware, Sr., *Letters to Trinitarians and Calvinists* (Cambridge, 1820).

39. Henry Ware, Sr., *Letters to Trinitarians,* p. 121.

40. Walker, *Smooth Preaching* (New York, 1823), pp. 4–9.

41. Joseph Buckminster to Joseph S. Buckminster, June 25, 1804, quoted in Eliza B. Lee, *Memoirs,* pp. 141–142.

42. Joseph Haroutunian, *Piety Versus Moralism* (New York: H. Holt & Co., 1932), p. xviii. On the growth of several types of evangelical Arminianism in the United States, *see* the Rev. Timothy Smith's fascinating study of *Revivalism and Social Reform in Mid-Nineteenth-Century America* (New York: Abingdon Press, 1957).

43. WEC, "The Moral Argument Against Calvinism" (1820), *Works,* I, 240.

44. An excellent example of this tactic is Andrews Norton, "Views of Calvinism" (1822), *Tracts Concerning Christianity,* pp. 159–228.

45. Sidney Mead, *Nathaniel William Taylor* (Chicago: University of Chicago Press, 1942), p. 156. Woods, in his *Letters to Unitarians,* fluctuated between a serious defense of Calvinist principles (in Letters III, IV, and V) and apologizing for them (Letters VI, VIII, and IX).

46. Ellis, *Half-Century of Controversy,* p. 42.

47. Henry Ware, Jr., *On the formation of the Christian Character: Addressed to Those Who are Seeking to Lead a Religious Life* (1831), reprinted in his *Works,* IV, 282–391. The quotation is from p. 289.

48. Henry Ware, Jr., to Mary Pickard Ware, August 3, 1831, quoted in John

Ware, M.D., *Memoir of the Life of Henry Ware, Jr., By his Brother* (Boston, 1846, reprinted 1868), II, 114.

49. O. B. Frothingham, *Boston Unitarianism* (New York, 1890), p. 256; Ware, *Memoir,* II, 113. The sale was a large one for a Unitarian tract, which could anticipate only a narrow appeal. Orthodox religious literature catered to a much wider audience.

50. Ware to his wife, in John Ware, *Memoir of Henry Ware, Jr.,* II, 114.

51. *The Formation of the Christian Character* (1831), *Works,* IV, 296. Contemporaries often remarked on the contrast between Ware's zealous, expansive pulpit manner, and his shyness and insecurity in private life. *See* John Ware, *Memoir of Henry Ware, Jr.,* II, 255–280.

52. Frisbie, "Inaugural Address" (1817), *Miscellaneous Writings,* p. 4.

53. *CE,* 3 (1826), 408.

54. This, after all, had been Butler's chief concern as well. He was much less interested in how ethical propositions were perceived than he was in preserving the supremacy of the conscience over the other faculties. *See* D. Daiches Raphael, "Bishop Butler's View of Conscience," *Philosophy,* 24 (1949), 219–238.

55. Perhaps it will help clarify the issue to point out that many people in the post-modern era have had the opposite dilemma: they have felt emotionally attracted to religion, but could not rationally justify it.

56. "A Good Life the Best Preparation for Death" (1835), MS in James Walker Sermons, HUA.

57. Henry Ware, Jr., "Causes of Lukewarmness," *CE,* 1 (1824), 19.

58. Henry Ware, Sr., Sermon on II Kings 23:19 (1827), MS in HUA; Norton, "Address," prefaced to *Miscellaneous Writings of Professor Frisbie,* p. li.

59. Walker, "Character" (n.d.), *Sermons,* p. 175.

60. *Ibid.,* p. 177.

61. Norton, Sermon on Matthew 5:44, ca. 1810, MS in Andover-Harvard Theological Library; WEC, "The Imitableness of Christ's Character," *Works,* IV, 148.

62. Walker, "Joy Felt and Expressed at the Reformation of the Vicious" (1830), MS in his Sermons, HUA. Walker preached this sermon twenty-one times in various places, the last occasion being on March 6, 1859.

63. Henry Ware, Jr., "The Importance of Principle in Religion" (posthumous, 1847), *Works,* II, 286–287.

64. Bowen, *Critical Essays,* p. 324; George Moore, "Exercises with Dr. Ware in Natural and Revealed Religion," undergraduate notebook for academic year 1836–37, exercise #12, MS in HUA; Walker, *Reason, Faith, and Duty,* pp. 156–171; Francis Bowen, "The Importance of Industrious Habits in Youth," Perkins Prize Essay, Harvard College, 1833, MS in HUA.

65. *See* Arthur O. Lovejoy's famous article, "On the Discrimination of Romanticisms" (1928), reprinted in *Essays in the History of Ideas* (Baltimore: Johns Hopkins University Press, 1948).

66. *CE*, 20 (1836), 201.

67. Cf. Alan Heimert, *Religion and the American Mind* (Cambridge: Harvard University Press, 1966), p. 46.

68. Tuckerman, "Seven Discourses" (1813), in the *Memorial*, esp. pp. 66–91.

69. Norton, *A Discourse on Religious Education* (Boston, 1818), p. 12.

70. Walker, *Reason, Faith, and Duty*, p. 34; WEC, *The Perfect Life*, p. 931.

71. Henry Ware, Jr., "Education the Business of Life," *Works*, III, 276.

72. Buckminster, "Duty and Pleasure the Same" (n.d.), MS in his Papers, Boston Athenaeum; Henry Ware, Jr., *Works*, II, 301.

73. Walker, "The Christian Connection with the World" (1847), MS in his Sermons, HUA.

74. "Faith an Element of Power," MS in Walker's Sermons, HUA. Faith in worldly things, though properly subordinate to faith in heavenly things, was not denied or despised.

75. Henry Ware, Jr., "Education the Business of Life" (1837), *Works*, III, 271 and 276.

76. Walker, "Character" (n.d.) in his *Sermons*, p. 171. The classic exposition of the Unitarian doctrine of man's innate moral nature is Henry Ware, Sr., *Letters Addressed to Trinitarians and Calvinists.*

77. *See* Ernest Tuveson, "The Origin of 'Moral Sense,'" *Huntington Library Quarterly*, 11 (1948), 242; Gerald Cragg, *From Puritanism to the Age of Reason* (Cambridge, Eng.: Cambridge University Press, 1950), p. 43; and Basil Willey, *The English Moralists* (London: Chatto & Windus, 1964), p. 185.

78. Antinomianism, in theological terminology, is the doctrine that the moral law is not binding upon true Christian believers. It represents an extreme but logical consequence of the doctrines of predestination and salvation by faith alone. For the crisis provoked by Antinomianism in Massachusetts, the authoritative sourcebook is David D. Hall, ed., *The Antinomian Controversy, 1636–1638* (Middletown, Conn.: Wesleyan University Press, 1968).

79. Perry Miller's pioneering study "'Preparation for Salvation' in Seventeenth-Century New England" (1943), is reprinted in *Nature's Nation* (Cambridge: Harvard University Press, 1967), pp. 50–77. The definitive treatment is now Norman Pettit, *The Heart Prepared: Grace and Conversion in Puritan Spiritual Life* (New Haven: Yale University Press, 1966).

80. *See*, for example, Walker, *A Discourse on the Law of the Spiritual Life* (Boston, 1835).

81. In one of his innumerable illuminating insights, Perry Miller remarked that the Unitarians "never realized how fatally they had lost the innermost secret of Puritan expression: they made everything explicit, they propounded

the inexpressible" ("An American Language" [1958], *Nature's Nation,* p. 235).
Much of Unitarian discussion of regeneration betrays this loss.

82. WEC, *The Perfect Life,* p. 988.

83. *Ibid.,* p. 958. *See also* Walker, "Man's Competency to Know God"
(1830), *Reason, Faith, and Duty,* p. 35.

84. While a lonely young man in Richmond, Virginia, William Ellery Channing related to his uncle a story of having experienced a classic emotional conversion (*Memoir,* I, 126–127). But in later years Channing apparently decided
this early impression of his was mistaken, and he denied ever having had a conversion experience—"unless the whole of my life may be called, as it truly has
been, a *process* of conversion" (*Memoir,* I, 129). His mature view, expressed in
1815 and maintained for the rest of his life, was that such emotional traumas
were often induced by ill health, and that "an habitual regard to the will of
God" was a far better "test of piety" than one's "vicissitudes of feeling"
(*Memoir,* I, 358–359).

85. Sermon on Acts 3:9 and Sermon on I Peter 1:23 (1809?). These two sermons were delivered at the morning and afternoon service, respectively, of the
same Sunday. Two more sermons, entitled "Conversion and Regeneration,"
flesh out Buckminster's theory. All are MSS in his Papers, Boston Athenaeum.

86. WEC, Extract from a Sermon (1811), quoted in *Memoir,* I, 256.

87. Walker, *Reason, Faith, and Duty,* p. 219; WEC, *The Perfect Life,* p. 958.

88. Henry Ware, Jr., *Works,* III, 280; IV, 391; Sermon on Titus 2:6 (1825),
MS in his Sermons, HUA.

89. Herschel Baker, *The Dignity of Man: Studies in the Persistence of an
Idea* (Cambridge: Harvard University Press, 1947), p. 245.

90. *See* WEC, "First Discourse on Love to Christ," *Works,* IV, 193. As I read
him, Channing subscribed to an Arian version of what is called the *kenotic*
theory of the divinity of Christ.

91. Buckminster, *Works,* I, 95.

92. WEC, "Likeness to God: A Discourse at the Ordination of the Rev. F. A.
Farley, Providence, R.I." (1828), *Works,* III, 229.

V / MORAL MAN AND MORAL SOCIETY

1. *See* Herschel Baker on the Renaissance Christian humanists in *The Dignity of Man* (Cambridge: Harvard University Press, 1947), p. 258.

2. Alice M. Balwdin, *The New England Clergy and the American Revolution*
(Durham, N.C.: Duke University Press, 1928), pp. 24–31; Charles W. Akers,
Called Unto Liberty (Cambridge: Harvard University Press, 1964), p. 96.

3. *See* the terms of the Alford bequest, quoted in the Introduction, above.

4. Francis Bowen, *Critical Essays on Speculative Philosophy* (Boston, 1842),
p. 337.

5. Most American "conservatives" have been Lockeans. *See* W. Hardy Wickwar, "Foundations of American Conservatism," *American Political Science Quarterly,* 41 (1947), 1105–1117; and Louis Hartz, *The Liberal Tradition in America* (New York: Harcourt, Brace & Co., 1955).

6. Perry Miller, *The New England Mind: The Seventeenth Century* (Boston: Beacon Press, 1939, reprinted 1961), pp. 398–431.

7. WEC, *Works* (Boston, 1841), IV, 91–92.

8. Adam Ferguson, *Institutes of Moral Philosophy* (Edinburgh, 1773), pp. 22, 39–43, and 199–200. Gladys Bryson discusses Ferguson in *Man and Society* (Princeton: Princeton University Press, 1945). On the popularity Ferguson enjoyed at Harvard, *see* Herbert Schneider, "The Intellectual Background of William Ellery Channing," *Church History,* 6 (1938), 11.

9. *See* Daniel McColgan, *Joseph Tuckerman* (Washington, D.C.: Catholic University of America Press, 1940), p. 21; Norton's Dexter Lectures [ca. 1813] MS in HUA, esp. Lectures 10, 11, and 12.

10. Edward Tyrell Channing, *Lectures Read to Seniors in Harvard College* (Boston, 1856), pp. 81–82. The lectures were delivered from 1819 to 1851.

11. *The Recent Contest in Rhode Island* (Boston, 1844), pp. 56–57. Dr. Channing also condemned the Dorrites for carrying the principle of majority rule too far (WEC to Francis Wayland, July 3, 1842, quoted in *Memoir of William Ellery Channing,* ed. W. H. Channing [Boston, 1851], III, 252).

12. Henry Ware, Sr., Sermon on Micah 4:5 (1800), MS in his Papers, HUA (Ware gave this sermon five times between 1800 and 1832). Edward T. Channing, *Lectures,* pp. 14–15.

13. "Address Delivered Before the University in Cambridge at the Interment of Professor Frisbie, July 12, 1822," reprinted in Levi Frisbie, *Miscellaneous Writings,* ed. Andrews Norton (Boston, 1823), pp. xliii–lvi.

14. *Documents of the Constitution of England and America, from Magna Carta to the Federal Constitution of 1789,* ed. Francis Bowen (Cambridge, 1854), pp. iii–v.

15. Bowen, *Critical Essays,* pp. 334–337.

16. *Reflections on the French Revolution* (1790) and *Speech on Impeachment of Warren Hastings* (1788), both reprinted in *The Philosophy of Edmund Burke,* ed. Louis Bredvold and Ralph Ross (Ann Arbor: University of Michigan Press, 1960), pp. 14 and 18.

17. Here I follow Francis P. Canavan, S. J., *The Political Reason of Edmund Burke* (Durham, N.C.: Duke University Press, 1960). Not all commentators interpret Burke this way, but the Harvard moralists did, and that is the important fact for my purposes. A different interpretation may be found in Alfred Cobban, *Edmund Burke and the Revolt against the Eighteenth Century* (London: Allen & Unwin, 1929).

18. For the Unitarian reliance on Hooker, *see* Bowen, *Critical Essays,* p. 335; for the continuity between Burke and Hooker, *see* Charles Parkin, *The Moral Basis of Burke's Political Thought* (Cambridge, Eng.: Cambridge University Press, 1956), p. 25.

19. Basil Willey noticed it in *The Eighteenth-Century Background* (Boston: Beacon Press, 1940; reprinted 1961), p. 93.

20. Caroline Robbins, *The Eighteenth Century Commonwealthman* (Cambridge: Harvard University Press, 1959), pp. 335–353; R. K. Webb, *Harriet Martineau* (London: William Heinemann, Ltd., 1960), pp. 164 et passim.

21. Joseph S. Buckminster, *Works* (Boston, 1839), II, 298–317. Sullivan had been a Republican, but Buckminster (unlike some other Boston Federalists) was willing to forego partisan recriminations in a time of sorrow.

22. WEC, *Works,* VI, 339. Another good statement of the biological analogy is Henry Ware, Sr., "Sermon on Isaiah 9:7" (1815) MS in HUA, p. 8.

23. Thomas Reid, *Works,* ed. Sir William Hamilton (Edinburgh, 1863), II, 666.

24. Henry Ware, Sr., *Inquiry into Religion* (Cambridge, 1842), I, 221.

25. Bowen, "The Abuse of Theories: An Oration Delivered at a Student Exhibition, Oct. 16, 1832," MS in HUA.

26. Adam Ferguson, *Institutes,* p. 269; Bowen, "Abuse of Theories."

27. Joseph Tuckerman, *Principles and Results of the Ministry-at-Large in Boston* (Boston, 1838), p. 304.

28. Bowen, "The Utility and Limitations of the Science of Political Economy," *CE,* 24 (1838), 58; and WEC, "Justice to the Poor" (1817), quoted in *Memoir,* II, 67.

29. Norton, Sermon on Matthew 5:44, in his MS Sermons, 1808–12, Andover-Harvard Theological Library; Tuckerman, *Principles and Results,* p. 256; Henry Ware, Jr., *Works* (Boston, 1847), II, 210.

30. Bryson, *Man and Society,* pp. 171–172; Parkin, *Burke's Political Thought,* p. 63; William J. Norton, Jr., *Bishop Butler* (New Brunswick, N.J.: Rutgers University Press, 1940), pp. 142–148.

31. Edward T. Channing, *Lectures,* p. 141; Bowen, *Recent Contest,* p. 68.

32. Henry Ware, Jr., Sermon on Psalm 122:6 (1824), MS in HUA.

33. A didactic biography of Henry Ware, Jr.'s second wife, *Memoir of Mary Ware,* by Edward Hall (Boston, 1853), illustrates the Victorian Unitarian sentimental cult of childhood and motherhood.

34. Reid, *Works,* II, 566.

35. "Review of Henry Ware's *Sermon after the Death of John Adams,*" *CE,* 3 (1826), 319.

36. Henry Ware, Jr., *Works,* II, 211. Cf. Fred Somkin's remarkable study, *Unquiet Eagle* (Ithaca, N.Y.: Cornell University Press, 1967), which "traces an agonizing and finally unsuccessful attempt to retain the esprit of a sacred

society, a family brotherhood, within a framework of conceptual and institutional constructs based upon freedom of contract." p. 7.

37. Francis Bowen, *Principles of Political Economy* (Boston, 1856), pp. viii and 77; *Documents of the Constitution,* p. iii; "The Independence of the Judiciary," *NAR,* 57 (1843), 404.

38. Bowen, "French Ideas of Democracy and a Community of Goods," *NAR,* 69 (1849), 309; *Recent Contest in Rhode Island,* p. 9 (Bowen's italics).

39. Bowen, *Recent Contest,* p. 14; and "J. C. Calhoun on Government and the Constitution of the United States," *NAR,* 76 (1853), 473–507.

40. Levi Frisbie, "Inaugural Address" in *Miscellaneous Writings,* pp. 3–26. Andrews Norton reviewed the address for the *NAR,* 6 (1818), 224–241, calling attention to its significance. Terence Martin has noted this review (without identifying its author) in *The Instructed Vision* (Bloomington: Indiana University Press, 1961), pp. 45–53.

41. Frisbie, "Inaugural Address," pp. 13, 6, 4.

42. Bowen, *Critical Essays,* pp. iv–xiii.

43. Wilson Smith, *Professors and Public Ethics* (Ithaca: Cornell University Press, 1956), p. 170.

44. *See* Francis Bowen, "The Abuse of Theories," for one of the many Unitarian condemnations of Bentham, and James Walker's hostile review of Hildreth's *Theory of Morals* in the *CE,* 38 (1845), 125–126.

45. "Hume's Philosophical Writings," *CE,* 57 (1854), 435.

46. Bowen, Preface to *Elements of the Philosophy of the Human Mind,* by Dugald Stewart (Boston, 1864).

47. Eliza Buckminster Lee, *Memoirs* (Boston, 1849), p. 330; Henry Ware, Jr., "Duties of the Pulpit and the Pastoral Office" (1835), *Works,* II, 192; Josiah Quincy (1802–1882), *Figures of the Past from the Leaves of Old Journals* (Boston, 1883), p. 303.

48. WEC to unknown correspondent, August 28, 1828, *Memoir,* II, 257; Henry Ware, Jr., *Works,* II, 192; Walker, "Harvard Phi Beta Kappa Address, 1827," MS in HUA, p. 9.

49. John Buckingham, "Notes on Professor Henry Ware [Jr.]'s Lectures," p. 41 [ca. 1839], MS in HUA.

50. Henry Ware, Sr., *A Sermon Delivered at the Ordination of Joseph Allen* (Cambridge, 1817), pp. 3–5. Cf. William Ellery Channing's address at the dedication of Divinity Hall in Cambridge, "The Christian Ministry" (1826), *Works,* III, 281–282.

51. WEC, "The Demands of the Age on the Ministry" (1824), *Works,* III, 139; Walker, "Spiritual Discernment," *Reason, Faith, and Duty* (Boston, 1892), pp. 202–221.

52. Sidney Mead toys with the idea of Platonic sources of persuasion in *The Lively Experiment* (New York: Harper & Row, 1963), p. 96.

53. Henry Ware, Jr., *Works,* II, 194.

54. Henry Ware, Sr., *Ordination Sermon for Allen,* p. 5.

55. Tuckerman, *A Letter to the Mechanics of Boston, Respecting the Formation of a City Temperance Society* (Boston, 1831), p. 3.

56. Bowen, "The Spirit of Reform," Commencement Oration, Harvard University, Aug. 28, 1833, MS in HUA; Bowen, *Critical Essays,* p. xii.

57. *A Sermon Delivered at Hingham, Lord's-Day, May 5, 1805* (Boston, 1805), p. 9; *A Sermon Delivered on Anniversary Election* (Boston, 1821), p. 14.

58. Buckminster, Sermon on Galatians 6:9 (1808), MS in his Papers, Boston Athenaeum.

59. Norton, Dexter Lecture VIII, MS in HUA, pp. 10–11.

60. Tuckerman, *Principles and Results,* p. 302.

61. In his "Memoir" for Levi Frisbie, in Frisbie's *Miscellaneous Writings,* p. ix.

62. This opinion is based on Leonard Labaree, *Conservatism in Early American History* (Ithaca: Cornell University Press, 1948, reprinted 1959), pp. 3, 20, 28.

63. Edward T. Channing, *Lectures,* pp. 113–115; Bowen, "The Utilitarian System of Education," Commencement Address, Harvard University, Aug. 31, 1836, MS in HUA.

64. Tuckerman, *Principles and Results,* p. 237; Bowen, *Political Economy,* p. 506.

65. Buckminster, *Works,* I, 384; Henry Ware, Jr., "Education the Business of Life" (1837), *Works,* III, 286.

66. Quoted in Frank Otto Gatell, *John Gorham Palfrey and the New England Conscience* (Cambridge: Harvard University Press, 1963), p. 79.

67. Ralph Waldo Emerson, *Journals* (1846), ed. Edward Emerson and Waldo Forbes (Boston: Houghton Mifflin Co., 1909), VII, 197. Abbott Lawrence (1792–1855) was the brother of Amos Lawrence (1786–1852); both were Unitarian businessmen and philanthropists.

68. Norton, "Review of James Sabine's *Glorying in the Cross,*" *CD,* n.s., 1 (1819), 133; WEC, "The System of Exclusion and Denunciation in Religion Considered" (1815), *Works,* V, 375.

69. Buckminster, *Works,* II, 228.

70. Norton, "On the Joys and Consolations Afforded by Religion," *CE,* 2 (1825), 14; Norton, Dexter Lecture VIII, pp. 9–10; Henry Ware, Sr., MS in his Papers, HUA. During a visit to Virginia in his youth, William Ellery Channing meditated upon the notion of a "community of property," an idea that attracted him rather as a remedy for avarice than as a means of attaining economic justice. His Federalist friends and relatives laughed at the young man's dream, and he seems to have laid it aside rather quickly (*Memoir,* I, 110–119).

71. John Emery Abbot, *Sermons* (Boston, 1829), p. 113. The law of equity is discussed in William Curtis Swabey, *Ethical Theory from Hobbes to Kant* (New York: The Philosophical Library, 1961), pp. 54–55.

72. WEC, *Memoir,* II, 227.

73. *Works,* I, 384.

74. *See,* for example, Henry Ware, Jr., *Works,* III, 171; cf. Ralph Barton Perry, *Puritanism and Democracy* (New York: The Vanguard Press, 1944), p. 315.

75. Walker, *Reason, Faith, and Duty,* p. 253.

76. Tuckerman, *Principles and Results,* p. 257; and *Gleams of Truth, or, Scenes from Real Life* (Boston, 1852), pp. 106–107.

77. *See* Norton, "On the Punishment of Sin," *CE,* 2 (1825), 169–178.

78. Henry Ware, Sr., *Inquiry into Religion,* I, 6; Francis Bowen, *Principles of Metaphysical and Ethical Science* (Boston, 1855), p. 333.

79. Henry Ware, Sr., *Inquiry into Religion,* I, 208.

80. This complacent remark by the Anglican natural theologian Abraham Tucker was repeated approvingly by Francis Bowen in *Principles of Metaphysical and Ethical Science,* p. 357.

81. Quoted in Elizabeth Peabody, *Reminiscences of William Ellery Channing* (Boston, 1880), p. 415. Orestes Brownson's two great essays on "The Laboring Classes" were published in the *Boston Quarterly Review,* 3 (1840), 358–395 and 420–512.

82. *See* "A Good Life the Best Preparation for Death" (1835), MS in Walker's Sermons, HUA; Bowen, "Industrious Habits," p. 9; Henry Ware, Jr., "How to Spend a Day," *Works,* I, 166 and 183; and WEC, "On the Elevation of the Laboring Classes" (1840), *Works,* V, 161.

83. A glance at the biographical sketches in the Appendix will show that a number of the Unitarian moralists themselves were self-made men. There is an interesting discussion of the intellectual defenses of the Boston bourgeoisie in Norman Jacobson, "Class and Ideology in the American Revolution," *Class, Status, and Power,* ed. R. Bendix and S. M. Lipset (Glencoe, Ill.: Free Press, 1953), pp. 547–554.

84. *The Select Journal,* 1 (1834), 95.

85. Walker, Harvard Phi Beta Kappa Address, 1827, MS in HUA, p. 16.

VI / THE RELIGION OF THE HEART

1. WEC, Election Sermon for 1830, *Works* (Boston, 1841), IV, 85.

2. William G. McLoughlin, *Modern Revivalism* (New York: Ronald Press Co., 1959), p. 8.

3. Jeremy Belknap, *Memoirs of Two Useful Ministers of Christ* (Boston, 1793), testifies to the admiration felt in New England for Doddridge and

Watts. *See also* Arthur Davis, *Isaac Watts* (New York: Dryden Press, 1943). Geoffrey Nuttal has written *Richard Baxter and Philip Doddridge* (London: Oxford University Press, 1951).

4. Perry Miller, *Jonathan Edwards* (New York: Meridian Books, 1949, reprinted 1959), p. 19.

5. *See* Clayton Chapman, "Benjamin Colman," unpub. Th.D. diss., Boston University, 1947.

6. Charles Chauncy, *Seasonable Thoughts on the State of Religion in New England* (Boston, 1743), p. 327.

7. WEC, "Discourse at the Ordination of John Emery Abbot" (1815), *Works*, III, 21; and John Emery Abbot, *Sermons* (Boston, 1829), p. 177.

8. *See* the *OED*, IX, 461, definition 6 of "sensibility."

9. Henry Ware, Jr., "Memoir" of Abbot, prefaced to Abbot's *Sermons*, p. xxiii.

10. Alvan Lamson, quoted in John Ware, *Memoir of Henry Ware, Jr.* (Boston, 1846), I, 75. Besides the published *Sermons* already cited, there is a collection of Abbot Sermon MSS in the Saltonstall Papers at the Mass. Historical Society.

11. Abbot, *Sermons*, pp. 264 and xxiv.

12. Abbot, "The Right Hand of Fellowship," in Henry Ware, Sr., *Ordination Sermon for Joseph Allen* (Cambridge, 1817), p. 30.

13. Abbot, *Sermons*, pp. 30–31.

14. *Sermons*, pp. 57, 331, 14.

15. *See*, for example, Joseph Buckminster, "The Religious Affections" (n.d.), *Works* (Boston, 1839), I, 269–270; Henry Ware, Jr., *Works* (Boston, 1847), IV, 254.

16. James Walker, "Evidences of Christianity," *CE*, 14 (1833), 188; Henry Ware, Sr., *Sermon Delivered at the Ordination of Alvan Lamson* (Boston, 1818), pp. 15–16.

17. *See* Norton's articles on the poetry of Richard Crashaw and Thomas Ken, in the *CD*, n.s., 5 (1823), 81–92 and 127. O. B. Frothingham described Norton as "a man of the warmest affections [and] evangelical feelings" (*Boston Unitarianism* [New York, 1890], p. 245).

18. Buckminster in the *MA*, 2 (1805), 413.

19. Walker, *Sermons Preached in the Chapel of Harvard College* (Boston, 1861, reprinted 1892), p. 252.

20. François de Salignac de la Mothe Fénelon (1651–1715), was Archbishop of Cambrai. A translation into English of *Selections from Fénelon with an Introduction by Mrs. Follen* (who was the wife of the Professor of German at Harvard) went through four editions between 1829 and 1841. William Ellery Channing wrote a celebrated character study of him in 1829 (*Works*, I, 167–215). The vogue Fénelon enjoyed among Boston Unitarians has been

described in Austen Warren's charming *New England Saints* (Ann Arbor: University of Michigan Press, 1956), pp. 58–74.

21. Quoted in Eliza Buckminster Lee, *Memoirs* (Boston, 1849), p. 336.

22. Henry Ware, Jr., *Works*, III, 355.

23. On this, *see* Walter E. Houghton, *The Victorian Frame of Mind* (New Haven: Yale University Press, 1957).

24. Buckminster, "Prayers and Addresses from the Communion Table," MS in his Papers, Boston Athenaeum.

25. Abbot, *Sermons*, pp. 345 and 297.

26. Sermon on Luke 6:12, MS in Andrews Norton Sermons (1808–1812), Andover-Harvard Theological Library; Norton, "On Prayer," *CD*, n.s., 3 (1821), 401–407.

27. Walker, "Providence" (1843; revised 1856), in *Reason, Faith, and Duty* (Boston, 1892), p. 85.

28. Norton, Sermon on Luke 6:12, MS in Andover-Harvard Theological Library. The most extensive collection of the moralists' prayers is that among the Joseph S. Buckminster Papers in the Boston Athenaeum.

29. Levi Frisbie, *Miscellaneous Writings* (Boston, 1823), p. 208.

30. Abbot, *Sermons*, pp. 353, 356–357.

31. *Miscellaneous Writings of Professor Frisbie*, p. 188. Other moralists also treated suffering and disease as a "school of religious discipline." *See* Buckminster, *Works*, I, 96–112; Henry Ware, Sr., Sermon on Psalm 102:23 (1826), MS in HUA. At one point in his youth, William Ellery Channing subjected himself to a severe ascetic regimen, which did lasting damage to his health. He later repented this misguided zeal, and frequently cautioned others against such excesses (*Memoir,* ed. W. H. Channing [Boston, 1851], I, 199; II, 14).

32. Henry Ware, Jr., "Memoir," p. xix.

33. For further information, consult Seymour Katz, "The Unitarian Ministers of Boston, 1790–1860," unpub. Ph.D. diss., Harvard University, 1960.

34. Stow Persons, *Free Religion: An American Faith* (New Haven: Yale University Press, 1947), p. 8.

35. Timothy Smith, who has a chapter on "Evangelical Unitarianism" in the 1850's (focusing on the career of Frederick D. Huntington), suggests that the Harvard Unitarians of that period felt attracted to evangelicalism because they had been chastened by the Transcendentalist controversy (*Revivalism and Social Reform in Mid-Nineteenth-Century America* [New York: Abingdon Press, 1957], pp. 95–102). While I agree, I would add that evangelical Unitarianism can be traced through the younger Ware back to Buckminster at the beginning of the century.

36. Edward Tyrell Channing, *Lectures Read to Seniors in Harvard College* (Boston, 1856), p. 13; Henry Ware, Jr., "Notes to a Course of Lectures Deliv-

ered Before the Members of the Divinity School, Commencing Sat., Ap. 29, 1837," MS in HUA, p. 53.

37. Henry Ware, Jr., praising the eloquence of a colleague ("Memoir of Nathan Parker," Ware's *Works*, II, 34).

38. *See* Richard Niebuhr, *The Kingdom of God in America* (Chicago: Willet, Clark, & Co., 1937), p. 108. John Locke, interestingly enough, had detested rhetoric as an academic subject because he felt it illegitimate to freight ideas with emotional connotations (*Essay Concerning Human Understanding*, III.x.34).

39. Alan Heimert, *Religion and the American Mind* (Cambridge: Harvard University Press, 1966), p. 44.

40. E. T. Channing, *Lectures*, pp. 80–81.

41. WEC, *Works*, V, 95. Cf. the *OED*, III, 215–216, definition 2 of "enthusiasm." Charles Abbey and John Overton, *The English Church in the Eighteenth Century* (London, 1878), I, 530–535, have a good discussion of the meaning of "enthusiasm" in religious discourse.

42. Henry Ware, Jr., "Extracts from a Journal," in *David Ellington, With Other Writings* (Boston, 1846).

43. Walker, "The Oneida and Troy Revivals," *CE*, 4 (1827), 249–250. In a sequel article, "Dissentions Among the Revivalists," *CE*, 6 (1829) 101–130, Walker gloated over the split between Finney and Lyman Beecher.

44. *See* James Walker, "The Revival Under Whitefield," *CE*, 4 (1827), 464–495; and Edward T. Channing, "George Whitefield," *NAR*, 48 (1839), 478–500.

45. Henry Ware, Sr., *Sermon Delivered at the Ordination of Joseph Allen* (Cambridge, 1817), p. 13; *Sermon Delivered Before the Convention of Congregational Ministers of Massachusetts* (Boston, 1818), p. 5.

46. Abbot, *Sermons*, p. 229; Walker, *Sermons*, p. 252.

47. Blair's work, first published in 1783, has been edited by Harold Harding (Carbondale, Ill.: Southern Illinois University Press, 1965). It will be discussed further in the next chapter.

48. Buckminster, *Works*, I, 269–270; II, 86.

49. *The Perfect Life*, ed. W. H. Channing (Boston, 1873, reprinted 1901), p. 936.

50. John Ware, *Memoir of Henry Ware, Jr.*, I, 101–104; James Freeman Clarke, *Autobiography* (Boston, 1892), p. 89.

51. *Sermons*, pp. 354–355, 110–111.

52. Henry Ware, Jr., "Notes to a Course of Lectures," p. 80.

53. *Ibid.*, p. 81.

54. *Sober Thoughts* is reprinted in Henry Ware, Jr., *Works*, II, 99–144. See esp. pp. 107 and 125.

55. Walker, "Spiritual Death" (1837; revised 1858), in *Reason, Faith, and Duty*, esp. p. 98.

56. Tuckerman, *Memorial,* pp. 93–94; Abbot, *Sermons,* pp. 55 and 300; Buckminster, *Hints on the Neglect of the Lord's Supper* (Boston, 1825).

57. *See* Robert Baird, *Religion in America* (New York, 1844), p. 277; and Samuel Gilman, *Contributions to Religion* (Charleston, 1860), p. 415.

58. John Buckingham, "Notes on Ware's [i.e., Henry Ware, Jr.'s] Lectures" (ca. 1839), student notebook in HUA, pp. 55–56. Henry Ware, Sr., pointed out another stumbling block to a wider use of the communion: the ingrained Puritan feeling that participation in the sacrament demanded an extraordinary degree of holiness (Sermon on Luke 22:19–20 [1824], MS in HUA).

59. When one Unitarian parish abandoned the Lord's Supper for a simple rite commemorating Christ's death, Dr. Channing dismissed the change as one of mere "form" (WEC to N. L. Frothingham, May 11, 1842, quoted in W. H. Channing, *Memoir,* II, 401).

60. Henry Ware, Jr., *Formation of the Christian Character* (1831) in his *Works,* IV, 373. This is an extreme form of the doctrine known in sacramental theology as "receptionism."

61. Henry Ware, Jr., Sermon on I Kings 19:8 (1823), MS in his Sermons, HUA.

62. *Lectures on Revivals* (1835), p. 12; quoted in McLoughlin, *Modern Revivalism,* p. 11.

63. Henry Ware, Jr., "Hints on Extemporaneous Preaching" (1824, revised 1830), in his *Works,* II, 376. *See also* John Ware, *Memoir of Henry Ware, Jr.,* I, 72–74.

64. Henry Ware, Jr., felt the clergy had a lot to learn about effective public speaking from the other professions: "Is it not mortifying," he wrote, "to observe a sensible man, who, if he had been a lawyer, would have spoken sensibly, as a man speaks to men,—now, because he is a theologian, talk solemnly to his bewildered and yawning congregation on some subject in which they have no concern, and in some phraseology which he himself would not dream of employing on any other occasion of real life?" (*Works,* IV, 273).

65. WEC, *Works,* III, 146; II, 267.

66. Abbot, *Sermons,* p. 290.

67. Henry Ware, Jr., "Notes," p. 59.

68. There is an extensive literature dealing with English hymnody, Harry Escott, *Isaac Watts: Hymnographer* (London: Independent Press, 1962), being especially thorough. J. H. Colligan, *Eighteenth-Century Nonconformity* (London: Longmans, Green & Co., 1915); and J. Laird, *Philosophical Incursions into English Literature* (Cambridge, Eng.: Cambridge University Press, 1946), help relate evangelical hymns to other aspects of culture. The American developments are covered in Henry Wilder Foote, *Three Centuries of American Hymnody* (Cambridge: Harvard University Press, 1940), esp. pp. 196–202. Two interesting Unitarian hymnals are *Singers and Songs of the Liberal Faith,*

ed. Alfred Putnam (Boston, 1875) ; and *Hymns for Public Worship,* ed. J. S. Buckminster (Boston, 1808).

69. Henry Ware, Jr., "Sacred Music," *CE,* 3 (1826), 489–498, continued *ibid.* 4 (1827), 67–77 and 300–309; and Samuel Eliot Morison, *Three Centuries of Harvard* (Cambridge: Harvard University Press, 1936) , p. 268.

70. Dr. Channing thought it foolish to maintain "that Christianity has an intrinsic glory, a native beauty, which no art or talent of man can heighten," and expressed admiration for the way Catholics stimulated the religious affections with images (WEC, *Works,* III, 141, and VI, 202) .

71. The Transcendentalist Unitarians as well as the more conservative Harvard moralists displayed considerable interest in liturgics. *See* William R. Hutchison, *The Transcendentalist Ministers* (New Haven: Yale University Press, 1959) , p. 176.

72. *See* Smith, *Revivalism and Social Reform,* pp. 95–102; and Jane Johnson, "Through Change and Through Storm: Federalist-Unitarian Thought, 1800–1860," unpub. Ph.D. diss., Radcliffe College, 1958, pp. 73–76.

73. John Ware, *Memoir of Henry Ware, Jr.,* I, 219–225.

74. *Ibid.,* I, 228; Whitney Cross, *The Burned-Over District* (Ithaca: Cornell University Press, 1950), p. 15.

75. Historians of the denomination seem agreed on this. *See,* for example, Earl M. Wilbur, *History of Unitarianism* (Cambridge: Harvard University Press, 1952), pp. 463–467. Emerson Davis' remarkable *Half-Century: A History of Changes in the United States Between 1800 and 1850* (Boston, 1851) gives the following statistics for Massachusetts (p. 351):

	Liberal ministers	Orthodox ministers
1812	138	179
1846	124	417

76. Henry Ware, Jr., *Works,* II, 409; Henry Ware, Sr., *Ordination Sermon for Alvan Lamson,* p. 14; WEC, *Works,* III, 146–147.

77. WEC, quoted in *Memoir,* II, 158.

78. *See* William Hutchison, *The Transcendentalist Ministers,* and, of course, Perry Miller's famous article "From Jonathan Edwards to Emerson" (1940) , reprinted in *Errand into the Wilderness* (Cambridge: Harvard University Press, 1956) , pp. 184–203.

VII / GENTEEL LETTERS

1. For a sophisticated discussion of the relationship between Unitarianism and the literary flowering of New England, *see* Lawrence Buell, "Unitarian Aesthetics and Emerson's Poet-priest," *American Quarterly,* 20 (1968) , 3–20.

2. Francis Bowen, "Review of Mrs. Lee's *Memoirs of the Buckminsters,*" *NAR,* 69 (1849), 354, 357.

3. Thacher, "Memoir" (1815), prefaced to Joseph S. Buckminster, *Works* (Boston, 1839); Ticknor, "Memoirs of the Buckminsters," *CE*, 47 (1849), 169–195; Norton, "Character of Rev. Joseph Stevens Buckminster," *General Repository*, 2 (1812), 309.

4. Joseph Allen, *Our Liberal Movement in Theology* (Boston, 1882), pp. 36–37.

5. Presumably the emerging political awareness of the yeoman farmers in the Connecticut Valley was the sort of thing that troubled Buckminster; on this, *see* Robert J. Taylor, *Western Massachusetts in the Revolution* (Providence, R.I.: Brown University Press, 1954). Actually, the problems of ministers in maintaining their status antedated the Revolution.

6. "The Character of Dr. Cooper" (n.d.), MS in Joseph Stevens Buckminster Papers, Boston Athenaeum.

7. Samuel Eliot Morison, *Three Centuries of Harvard* (Cambridge: Harvard University Press, 1936), p. 241.

8. Joseph Tuckerman was a charter member of this club. *The Journal of the Proceedings of the Anthology Society,* ed. M. A. DeWolfe Howe, was published by the Boston Athenaeum in 1910.

9. *See* Josiah Quincy, *History of the Boston Athenaeum* (Cambridge, 1851), esp. pp. 1–22; and Charles K. Bolton, ed., *The Influence and History of the Boston Athenaeum* (Boston, 1907). The *Catalogue of the Library of the Late Rev. J. S. Buckminster,* printed when the books were put up for auction after their owner's death in 1812, may still be seen in the Harvard College Library. Beside one impressive list of calfbound gilt volumes, some contemporary hand wrote in the margin: "These are too splendid for the quotidian use of our young Goths!"

10. For the importance of the magazine in American cultural history *see* George Willis Cooke, *Unitarianism in America* (Boston, 1902), chap. 5; Frank Luther Mott, *History of American Magazines* (Cambridge: Harvard University Press, 1930, reprinted 1957), I, 253–259; and especially Lewis P. Simpson, ed., *The Federalist Literary Mind: Selections from the "Monthly Anthology and Boston Review" 1803–1811* (Baltimore: Louisiana State University Press, 1962).

11. August, 1804, pp. 456–457.

12. Edward Tyrell Channing related the story of the founding of the *NAR* in a letter to Willard Phillips, August 14, 1852, Phillips Papers, Mass. Historical Society.

13. It may be found in his *Works*, II, 339–364, or in the Unitarian organ of the period, the *MA*, 7 (1809), 145–158. Some of the address has been reprinted by Simpson in *The Federalist Literary Mind,* pp. 95–102.

14. Quoted in Eliza Buckminister Lee, *Memoirs* (Boston, 1851), pp. 396–397.

15. Buckminster, *Works*, II, 340.

16. *Ibid.,* II, 350.

17. The debate is described in Robert Middlekauff, *Ancients and Axioms* (New Haven: Yale University Press, 1963), pp. 128–130, 194–195.

18. Buckminster, *Works,* II, 348.

19. Another American who linked his hopes for a national literature to political conservatism was the Episcopalian Fisher Ames. See his essay "American Literature," *Works* (Boston, 1854), II, 428–442.

20. Buckminster, *Works,* II, 344.

21. James Walker, "Address Delivered Before the Phi Beta Kappa Society at Cambridge. Aug. 30th, 1827," MS in HUA.

22. *See* Wilson Smith, *Professors and Public Ethics* (Ithaca: Cornell University Press, 1956), pp. 167–169.

23. *MA,* 2 (1805), 170–174; *MA,* 4 (1807), 43–44.

24. Andrews Norton, *Review of Professor Frisbie's Address* (Cambridge, 1823), p. 33. First published in the *NAR,* 6 (1818), 224–242.

25. Henry Ware, Jr., *Works* (Boston, 1847), III, 264–266.

26. The three essays are found together in his *Works,* I, 3–215. Robert E. Spiller discusses Channing's literary reputation in "A Case for W. E. Channing," *New England Quarterly,* 3 (1930), 55–81.

27. "Remarks on National Literature" (*Works,* I, 243–280) has been reprinted several times, lately in *The Achievement of American Criticism,* ed. Clarence A. Brown (New York: Ronald Press, 1954), pp. 126–145.

28. *Works,* I, 254, 257–258.

29. Anthology Society, *Journal,* pp. 125, 131. "Ned" Channing's ideal arbiter of community taste was the *Tatler; see* his article on it in the *NAR,* 46 (1838), 341–366.

30. The similarity is noted in Verle Dennis Flood, "A Study in the Aesthetics of Taste in America: The Role of Common Sense Philosophy in the Literary Criticism of the Boston Anthologists," unpub. Ph.D. diss., State University of Iowa, 1959, p. 7.

31. Bowen, "College Education," *NAR,* 55 (1842), 303–304.

32. Buckminster in the *MA,* 5 (1808), 57.

33. Bowen, *Principles of Political Economy* (Boston, 1856), p. ix.

34. Bowen, "College Education." Cf. E. T. Channing in the *NAR,* 9 (1819), 66–67. When pressed for examples of great American intellects, Liberals found scarcely any to point to save Franklin and Edwards—and the latter was an embarassment to say the least (WEC, *Works,* I, 254).

35. "Review of Ripley's *Specimens of Foreign Standard Literature*" in the *Boston Quarterly Review,* 1 (1838), 433–444; *The Education of Henry Adams* (Boston: Houghton Mifflin Co., 1961), p. 19. One recent scholar, pointing out the Unitarians' infatuation with English literary fashions, has concluded that notwithstanding all their striving for cultural enrichment, the Unitarians ended up sterile, "cut off . . . from the perpetually verdant American mainstem"

(Donald B. Meyer, "The Dissolution of Calvinism," *Paths of American Thought*, ed. A. M. Schlesinger, Jr., and Morton White [Boston: Houghton Mifflin Co., 1963], p. 82).

36. Cf. Bernard Bailyn and John Clive with regard to an earlier period: "England's Cultural Provinces: Scotland and America," *William and Mary Quarterly*, 3d series, 11 (1954), 212–213.

37. Henry Ware, Jr., *Works*, II, 216.

38. *See* William Charvat, *The Origins of American Critical Thought* (Philadelphia: University of Pennsylvania Press, 1936, reprinted 1961), pp. 1 and 3.

39. E. T. Channing, *Lectures Delivered to Seniors in Harvard College* (Boston, 1856), pp. 177–178.

40. *See* the anonymous article "On Taste" in the first volume of the *MA* (1804), pp. 435–439, laying down the canons of literary criticism the journal was to follow.

41. Thomas Reid, *Works* (Edinburgh, 1863), I, 492, 499. Reid's treatment of aesthetics was included in the annotated edition of his *Intellectual Powers,* which James Walker prepared (Cambridge, 1850).

42. For secondary treatments, *see* Walter J. Hipple, Jr., *The Beautiful, the Sublime, and the Picturesque in Eighteenth-Century British Aesthetic Theory* (Carbondale, Ill.: Southern Illinois University Press, 1957), pp. 149–157; and Henry Laurie, *Scottish Philosophy in its National Development* (Glasgow: Glasgow University Press, 1902), pp. 312–318.

45. Edward Tyrell Channing, *Lectures,* p. 164.

46. Thomas Reid, *Works,* I, 492.

47. Walker explained the dual meaning of the term in "Spiritual Discernment," *Reason, Faith, and Duty* (Boston, 1892), p. 207.

48. Rev. Samuel Gilman, study journal (May 14, 1815) in his Papers, 1807–1858, HUA.

49. Bowen, *Critical Essays,* p. 233.

50. Readers wishing further discussion of the influences on Harvard Unitarian aesthetic theory are referred to the fine work of Verle Flood, "A Study in the Aesthetics of Taste in America."

51. Dugald Stewart, quoted in Terence Martin, *The Instructed Vision* (Bloomington, Ind.: Indiana University Press, 1961), p. 123.

52. Samuel Holt Monk, *The Sublime: A Study of Critical Theories in XVIII Century England* (New York: Modern Language Association of America, 1935), p. 234.

53. Norton, "Sir Walter Scott," *Select Journal,* 1 (1833), 75.

54. *See* Robert McLean's careful study of *George Tucker: Moral Philosopher and Man of Letters* (Chapel Hill: University of North Carolina Press, 1961), esp. pp. 139–143.

55. Frisbie, *Miscellaneous Writings*, p. 198; and Norton, in the *CE*, 3 (1826), 404.

56. Norton, "Introduction" to *Miscellaneous Writings of Professor Frisbie*, p. lii.

57. Norton, *CE*, 19 (1836), 331–334; cf. *Republic* X.595–604.

58. Plato would have considered Unitarian willingness to invoke the affections foolhardy. See *Republic* X. 602–604.

59. Among the eighteenth-century British aestheticians whom the Harvard Unitarians read were Archibald Alison and Lord Monboddo, both avowed Platonists. Some sharp insights into the continuing Platonism of the genteel tradition in American letters may be found in George Santayana, *The Genteel Tradition at Bay* (New York: Charles Scribner's Sons, 1931), pp. 18–21.

60. Norton, *Review of Frisbie's Address*, p. 25; *Select Journal*, 2 (1834), 107; and Frisbie, "On Tacitus," *Miscellaneous Writings*, p. 32.

61. *The League of the Alps, and Other Poems* (Boston, 1826); *The Forest Sanctuary, and Other Poems* (Boston, 1827).

62. Henry Ware, Jr., *David Ellington, With Other Writings* (Boston, 1846), pp. 184–188.

63. For sample Unitarian reviews, *see* James Walker in the *CE*, 16 (1834), 248–251; and Francis Bowen in the NAR, 56 (1843), 109–137.

64. *The Poets and Poetry of America*, ed. Rufus Griswold (Philadelphia, 1842), contains an ample selection of Unitarian writing, including a number of the moralists here discussed. It was a very popular collection, going through sixteen editions by 1856.

65. Henry Ware, Jr., did comment that "The Waverly novels . . . may be read with less danger than the plays of Shakespeare, and . . . with equal intellectual pleasure and improvement." *CE*, 4 (1827), 332.

66. *See* Norton, *CD*, n.s., 3 (1821), 479–480; and E. T. Channing, *Lectures*, p. 286.

67. WEC's "Remarks on the Character and Writings of John Milton" (1826) was an important document of the struggle to legitimize creative literature in America. Milton's poetry was not mere entertainment, Channing insisted; it was written "with something of the conscious dignity of a prophet" and intended as a public blessing (*Works*, I, 7).

68. Henry Ware, Jr., *Works*, III, 161–162.

69. Samuel Miller, *A Brief Retrospect of the Eighteenth Century* (New York, 1803), II, 179; Henry Ware, Jr., "Review of Miller's *Clerical Manners and Habits*," *CE*, 4 (1827), 324–333; Josiah Quincy (1802–1882), *Figures of the Past: From Leaves of Old Journals* (Boston, 1833), p. 36. On the positive effects of didacticism (and the particularly important role of Unitarian moralists) in legitimizing American art, *see* further in William Charvat, *Origins of*

American Critical Thought, pp. 13–17; and Neil Harris, *The Artist in American Society, 1790–1860* (New York: George Braziller, 1966), pp. 300–316.

70. *See* "The Unitarian Conscience as an Active Power" in chap. II above.

71. Andrews Norton was puzzled by the occasional perversity of artists who could not see "that in all religious and moral conceptions, the noblest materials of poetry, the philosophers are far in advance of the poets." *CE,* 19 (1836), 331.

72. Norton, *MA,* 2 (1805), 511.

73. E. T. Channing, *Lectures,* p. 125.

74. WEC, "The Character and Writings of John Milton," *Works,* I, 9.

75. Robert M. Schmitz, *Hugh Blair* (New York: King's Crown Press, 1948), p. 1; Harold Harding has edited Blair's *Lectures* in two volumes (Carbondale, Ill.: Southern Illinois University Press, 1965).

76. *CE,* 9 (1830), 304. For a general discussion of the place of sentiment in neoclassical taste, *see* James Sutherland, *A Preface to Eighteenth Century Poetry* (Oxford: Oxford University Press, 1948).

77. E. T. Channing, *Lectures,* pp. 17 and 244; Henry Ware, Jr., "Notes to a Course of Lectures Delivered Before the Members of the Divinity School" (1837), MS in HUA, p. 67.

78. On seventeenth-century Puritan rules of rhetoric, *see* Perry Miller, *The New England Mind: The Seventeenth Century* (Boston: Beacon Press, 1939, reprinted 1961), pp. 300–330.

79. E. T. Channing, *Lectures,* p. 21; Norton, *CE,* 3 (1826), 403; WEC, *Works,* I, 9–10.

80. There is a most illuminating treatment of the development of literary sentimentalism, relating it to Latitudinarian religion and "Whiggish" civilization in general, in Hoxie N. Fairchild, *Religious Trends in English Poetry* (New York: Columbia University Press, 1939), I, 535–576.

81. "The Poetry of Mathematics: A Lecture for the Boston Lyceum" (n.d.), *Works,* I, 137.

82. WEC, *The Perfect Life* (Boston, 1873, reprinted 1901), pp. 1003–1004.

83. Henry Ware, Jr., "The Existence of the Deity," *Works,* III, 7.

84. Norton in the *CE,* 19 (1836), 351; Buckminster, Sermon on Psalm 104:30, MS in his Papers, Boston Athenaeum.

85. Buckminster, *MA,* 4 (1807), 592–593.

86. *See* the *OED,* X, 31, definition 7 of "sublime": "affecting the mind with a sense of overwhelming grandeur or irresistible power; calculated to inspire awe, deep reverence, or lofty emotion."

87. Ernest Tuveson has unraveled for us the tangled intellectual processes that led to the use of aesthetic experience as a "means of grace." Prompted by Lockean epistemology and eighteenth-century natural theology, many Christians

took to "substituting communion with nature for communion in the sacrament" (*The Imagination as a Means of Grace* [Berkeley: University of California Press, 1960], p. 57). On the interrelationships of philosophy, science, and aesthetics, *see also* F. E. L. Priestley, "Newton and the Romantic Concept of Nature," *University of Toronto Quarterly,* 17 (1948), 323–336.

88. WEC, "Self-Culture" (1838), *Works,* II, 366–367.

89. Buckminster, *Works,* I, 283–284.

90. See the *MA,* 5 (1808), 367–372. J. S. J. Gardiner, ex-Tory, High Federalist, and Episcopal rector of Trinity Church, as reactionary in literary taste as he was in politics and religion, objected to Buckminster's defense of Gray. Any departure from the strictest classical style of Pope was anathema to Gardiner. The Buckminster-Gardiner literary debate, illustrating the state of critical tastes in Boston, has been partially reprinted by Lewis Simpson in *The Federalist Literary Mind,* pp. 196–207.

91. Norton, *Review of Professor Frisbie's Address,* pp. 19–22.

92. Frisbie, *Writings,* p. 20; Norton, *Select Journal,* 1 (1833), 250–293.

93. WEC to Joanna Baillie, April 2, 1831, quoted in *Memoir,* II, 348. Upon receiving news of Byron's death, he blurted out, "Such examples of perverted talent should reconcile the less gifted to their obscure lot" (*ibid.,* II, 343).

94. Andrews Norton, "The New York Edition of Lord Byron's Works," *CD,* n.s., 2 (1820), 415. Norton's bitterness was increased because New York retailers who were willing to sell Byron boycotted Unitarian tracts as corrupting.

95. Walker in the *CE,* 7, 234.

96. The *MA* proudly proclaimed on its title-page, "Edited by a Society of Gentlemen." This topic may be pursued further in Edwin H. Cady, *The Gentleman in America* (Syracuse: Syracuse University Press, 1949), esp. chap. 3.

97. Walter Jackson Bate, *From Classic to Romantic: Premises of Taste in Eighteenth-Century England* (New York: Harper Torchbooks, 1946), p. 172.

98. Howard Mumford Jones has recalled our attention to the importance of Renaissance ideas in America in *O Strange New World* (New York: Viking Press, 1964).

99. *See,* for example, Joseph S. Buckminster, *Works,* II, 358; and George E. Ellis, *A Half-Century of the Unitarian Controversy* (Boston, 1857), p. 15.

100. WEC, *Works,* II, 323.

101. William Emerson's "Preface" to the first issue of the journal (November 1803), stated that it aspired to nothing less than to be "versed in almost every art and science."

102. J. S. Buckminster in the *MA,* 3 (1806), 22.

103. Van Wyck Brooks captured the mood of Unitarian literature quite well. His method in *The Flowering of New England* (New York: E. P. Dutton, 1938) was notably less successful in treating Yankee radicals like Thoreau.

104. Richard Henry Dana's *Two Years Before the Mast* (Boston, 1840) and a few lines from the Brahmin poets might qualify. E. T. Channing's correspondence with Dana, in the Mass. Historical Society, and his review of Dana's book, *NAR,* 52 (1841), 56–75, are interesting.

105. Martin Green has recently provided us with an interesting discussion of the virtues and weaknesses of the Unitarian cultural establishment in *The Problem of Boston* (New York: W. W. Norton & Co., 1966).

VIII / UNITARIAN WHIGGERY

1. George Fredrickson, *The Inner Civil War: Northern Intellectuals and the Crisis of the Union* (New York: Harper and Row, 1965), p. 9. Cf. Rowland Berthoff, "The American Social Order: A Conservative Hypothesis," *American Historical Review,* 65 (1960), 495–514.

2. WEC to Lucy Aikin, June 22, 1835, in their *Correspondence,* ed. Anna Le Breton (London, 1874), p. 251.

3. "Historians and the Problem of Early American History," *American Historical Review,* 67 (1962), 626–646.

4. Edward Tyrell Channing, *Lectures Read to Seniors in Harvard College* (Boston, 1856), pp. 72–73.

5. "Public Opinion" (1856), in *Reason, Faith, and Duty* (Boston, 1892), pp. 234–235.

6. E. T. Channing, *Lectures,* p. 83; Henry Ware, Sr., *Sermon Delivered at the Ordination of Alvan Lamson* (Boston, 1818), p. 18.

7. WEC, "Spiritual Freedom" (1830), *Works,* IV, 22.

8. Henry Ware, Sr., *Sermon at the Ordination of William Peabody* (Springfield, Mass., 1820), p. 12.

9. Levi Frisbie, *Miscellaneous Writings* (Boston, 1823), p. 99.

10. W. H. Channing, *Memoir of William Ellery Channing* (Boston, 1851), I, 92.

11. MS headed "Article Devoir" (n.d.), HUA.

12. Bowen, *The Recent Contest in Rhode Island* (Boston, 1844), pp. 54–55.

13. *Critical Essays on Speculative Philosophy* (Boston, 1842), pp. 335–338.

14. WEC, *Works* (Boston, 1849), IV, 96; *The Federalist,* no. 51.

15. Alice Baldwin, *The New England Clergy and the American Revolution* (Durham, N.C.: Duke University Press, 1928), pp. 49–50; E. T. Channing, *Lectures,* pp. 73–74.

16. Bowen, *NAR,* 56 (1843), 405.

17. WEC, *Works,* VI, 345–348; WEC, "Dangers of Free Institutions" (1814), quoted in *Memoir,* II, 65; James Walker, "On Moral Temperance," *Liberal Preacher,* n.s. 2 (1832), 161–169; Walker, "Compromises," *Sermons* (Boston, 1892), pp. 282–283.

18. John Adams, "A Government of Laws and Not of Men," *MA,* 10 (1811), 243–245. As a representative of the revolutionary generation, Adams possessed a different perspective from the postrevolutionary moralists here discussed. Still, some of the concern he felt for social order found echoes in their writings. See John Howe, *The Changing Political Thought of John Adams* (Princeton: Princeton University Press, 1966).

19. Joseph S. Buckminster, *Discourse Preached in the Church in Brattle Square, Boston, 1811* (Albany, N.Y., 1848).

20. The first one of which we have record is John Cotton's of 1634. An anachronistic relic of the union between church and state in the Puritan Commonwealth, the Election Sermon was finally abolished by statute in 1884. Lindsay Swift, "The Massachusetts Election Sermon," Mass. Colonial Soc. *Publications,* 1 (1895), 388–451. The proceedings in the late eighteenth century have been described by Harry Kerr in "The Election Sermon: Primer for Revolutionaries," *Speech Monographs,* 29 (1962), 13–22. They do not seem to have been much different in the early nineteenth century.

21. The text used by James Walker in *A Sermon Delivered on the Day of General Election* (Boston, 1828).

22. These injunctions are taken from Henry Ware, Sr., *A Sermon Delivered on the Anniversary Election* (Boston, 1821), pp. 9–14.

23. *Ibid.,* p. 4; Henry Ware, Sr., *Inquiry into Religion* (Cambridge, 1842), I, 235–236.

24. "Spiritual Freedom: Discourse Preached at the Annual Election," *Works,* IV, 67–103.

25. From Article III of the "Declaration of Rights" in the Constitution of 1780.

26. *See* their complaints in Oscar and Mary Handlin, eds., *The Popular Sources of Political Authority: Documents on the Massachusetts Constitution of 1780* (Cambridge: Harvard University Press, 1966), esp. pp. 26, 30–33, 475–506.

27. Edward Buck, *Massachusetts Ecclesiastical Law* (Boston, 1865), p. 43. *See also* Paul Lauer, *Church and State in New England* (Baltimore, 1892); and William G. McLoughlin, *Isaac Backus and the American Pietistic Tradition* (Boston: Little, Brown and Co., 1967).

28. Henry Ware, Sr., "Dudleian Lecture delivered in the Chapel of HC, May 8, 1811," MS in HUA, p. 18.

29. E. T. Channing, *Lectures,* p. 122; Frisbie, "Remarks on the Right and Duty of Government to Provide for the Support of Religion by Law" (1821), *Miscellaneous Writings,* pp. 89–120.

30. WEC, *Works,* VI, 285.

31. Frisbie, *Miscellaneous Writings,* p. 90.

32. Walker, *CE,* 13 (1833), 348.

33. Walker, "Difficulties in Parishes," *CE,* 9 (1836), 6.

34. William Paley's views are best found in his *Principles of Moral and Political Philosophy* (1785); Edmund Burke's in his *Speech on the Petition of the Unitarians* (1792).

35. Joseph Tuckerman, "Funeral Oration for Washington" (1799), in *A Memorial of Joseph Tuckerman* (Worcester, Mass., 1888), p. 23. The first President's opinions on this subject have been examined by Paul Boller in *George Washington and Religion* (Dallas: Southern Methodist University Press, 1963).

36. Frisbie, *Miscellaneous Writings*, pp. 101–104. For the "confusion" in the minds of dissenters on this subject, *see* Alan Heimert, *Religion and the American Mind* (Cambridge: Harvard University Press, 1966), p. 524n.

37. Gerald R. Cragg, *Reason and Authority in the Eighteenth Century* (Cambridge, Eng.: Cambridge University Press, 1963), esp. pp. 182–183, provides a good discussion of the Latitudinarian ideal of a comprehensive church. As Arians, the New England Unitarians considered Christ God's Son, although inferior in dignity to the Father.

38. Walker, "Power Less Likely to be Abused by Unitarians than by the Orthodox," *CE,* 7 (1829), 229–240.

39. Ware, *Inquiry into Religion,* II, 310.

40. The career of this shrewd ecclesiastical politician, who forged an alliance between Old Lights and New Lights against the Liberals, is traced in James K. Morse, *Jedidiah Morse* (New York: Columbia University Press, 1939). A vast bibliography of polemical pamphlets may be found in E. H. Gillett, "History and Literature of the Unitarian Controversy," *Historical Magazine,* 2d series, 9 (1871), 221–324. *See also* William Wallace Fenn, "How the Schism Came," Unitarian Hist. Soc. *Proceedings* I:I (1925), 3–21.

41. The Unitarians were in fact subjected to much personal abuse. John M. Mason, *The Evangelical Ministry Exemplified* (New York, 1822), is an example of Calvinist argument at its most intemperate; Moses Stuart's "Letter to Dr. Channing on Religious Liberty," *Miscellanies* (Andover, Mass., 1846), is an example of Calvinist argument at its best.

42. WEC, "The System of Exclusion and Denunciation in Religion Considered" (1815), *Works,* V, 373–392.

43. Walker, "Difficulties in Parishes," *CE,* 9 (1830), 8.

44. E. T. Channing, *Lectures,* p. 135.

45. WEC, *Works,* VI, 199.

46. *CE,* 13 (1833), 351–363; Frisbie, *Miscellaneous Writings,* p. 115.

47. Daniel H. Calhoun, *Professional Lives in America, 1750–1850* (Cambridge: Harvard University Press, 1965), contains a fascinating discussion of the problems facing the New England clergy on pp. 88–117.

48. William A. Robinson, *Jeffersonian Democracy in New England* (New Haven: Yale University Press, 1913), esp. pp. 128–150.

49. *See* the *Journal of Debates and Proceedings in the Convention of Delegates Chosen to Revise the Constitution of Massachusetts* (Boston, 1821); Shaw Livermore, *The Twilight of Federalism* (Princeton: Princeton University Press, 1962), pp. 117–125; and Daniel McColgan, *Joseph Tuckerman* (Washington, D.C.: Catholic University of America Press, 1940), pp. 54–59.

50. Frank Otto Gatell, *John Gorham Palfrey and the New England Conscience* (Cambridge: Harvard University Press, 1963), p. 49.

51. Tuckerman in the *Journal of Debates,* p. 165.

52. Henry Ware, Jr., to [Joseph] Allen, Dec. 30, 1820, in John Ware, *Memoir of Henry Ware, Jr.* (Boston, 1846), I, 144. The machinations of the Unitarian Federalists in submitting a conglomerate amendment they had designed to be defeated are laid bare in Jacob Meyer, *Church and State in Massachusetts from 1740 to 1833* (Cleveland: Western Reserve University Press, 1930), pp. 192–200. Alone among Unitarians in favoring disestablishment was Joseph Story, who having left the Federalist Party to support Jefferson had been rewarded with a place on the United States Supreme Court.

53. Among those who refused on principle to take the test oath were not only the nonreligious, but prominent and devout dissenters. *Journal of Debates,* pp. 85, 87.

54. Henry Ware, Sr., *A Sermon Delivered on the Anniversary Election* (Boston, 1821).

55. Eliphalet Baker v. Samuel Fales, 16 Mass. 488 (1820).

56. Customarily, a minister had been chosen who was acceptable to both the church and the wider parish, but agreement often became impossible after the Unitarian-Trinitarian controversy came into the open. *See* the *Result of the Ecclesiastical Council Convened at Dedham* (Dedham, 1818).

57. Nathaniel Ames, the Jeffersonian physician of Dedham (and brother of arch-Federalist Fisher Ames), described the controversy there with sardonic detachment. Following Jonathan Swift, Dr. Ames dubbed the two parties of Federalist Congregationalists "Big Endians" and "Little Endians." *See* Charles Warren, *Jacobin and Junto, or Early American Politics as Viewed in the Diary of Dr. Nathaniel Ames* (Cambridge: Harvard University Press, 1931), pp. 286–311.

58. The most careful twentieth-century student of the issue concludes that the law was on the side of the orthodox and the court was swayed by "denominational partisanship" (Leonard W. Levy, *The Law of the Commonwealth and Chief Justice Shaw* [New York: Harper Torchbooks, 1957, reprinted 1967], p. 38).

59. *Ibid.,* p. 41.

60. *See* Samuel E. Morison, *Harrison Gray Otis: The Urbane Federalist* (Boston: Houghton Mifflin, 1969), pp. 437–442; and Arthur B. Darling, *Political*

Changes in Massachusetts, 1824–1848 (New Haven: Yale University Press, 1925), pp. 39–42.

61. Orthodox Congregationalists had some readjustments to make, too; *see* Samuel Pearson, Jr., "From Church to Denomination: American Congregationalism in the Nineteenth Century," *Church History,* 38 (1969), 67–87.

62. George Ellis, *A Half-Century of the Unitarian Controversy* (Boston, 1857), p. 45; George Cooke, *Unitarianism in America* (Boston: American Unitarian Association, 1902), p. 159.

63. Donald B. Meyer, "The Dissolution of Calvinism" in *Paths of American Thought,* ed. A. M. Schlesinger, Jr., and Morton White (Boston: Houghton Mifflin Co., 1963), p. 80.

64. WEC, *Works,* VI, 150–151, 154, 164, 166, 168.

65. WEC, "Remarks on Napoleon Bonaparte" (1827–28), *Works,* I, 163, Cf. Richard Power, "A Crusade to Extend Yankee Culture, 1820–65," *New England Quarterly,* 13 (1940), 638–653.

66. WEC, *Works,* I, 159.

67. WEC, *Works,* VI, 331. *See also* his address "On the Education of the People, and Especially of the Laboring Class" (1837), quoted in William Henry Channing, *Memoir,* III, 64–65.

68. Edmund Burke, "Letters on a Regicide Peace," quoted in Charles Parkin, *The Moral Basis of Burke's Political Thought* (Cambridge, Eng.: Cambridge University Press, 1956), p. 101.

69. Bowen in the *NAR,* 56 (1843), 383–384; WEC, quoted in *Memoir,* II, 63 and III, 279.

70. Bowen, *Political Economy,* p. 95. Cf. Hobbes, "solitary, poor, nasty, brutish, and short" (*Leviathan,* I.xiii.9).

71. Thomas Brown, *Philosophy of the Human Mind,* ed. Levi Hedge (Cambridge, 1827), II, 4.

72. Cf. the activities of Calvinist evangelists described in such books as Charles R. Keller, *The Second Great Awakening in Connecticut* (New Haven: Yale University Press, 1942); Charles C. Cole, *The Social Ideas of the Northern Evangelists* (New York: Columbia University Press, 1954); and John R. Bodo, *The Protestant Clergy and Public Issues, 1812–1848* (Princeton: Princeton University Press, 1954).

73. George W. Pierson, *Tocqueville and Beaumont in America* (New York: Oxford University Press, 1938), pp. 393–396, 448.

74. Quoted *ibid.,* pp. 421–423.

75. *Dr. Channing's Notebook,* ed. Grace Channing (Boston, 1887), p. 8; "Election Sermon for 1830," *Works,* IV, 95.

76. *Democracy in America,* by Alexis de Tocqueville, trans. Henry Reeve, "Edited, with notes, the translation revised and in great part rewritten, and the additions made to the recent Paris editions now first translated, by Francis

Bowen, Alford Professor of Moral Philosophy in Harvard University" (Cambridge, 1862), two volumes. Bowen's text went through eight editions in the nineteenth century and served as the basis for Phillips Bradley's revision of 1945, which is now standard.

77. One of William Ellery Channing's most widely read essays, "On Napoleon" (1827–28), was written to teach Americans the dangers of this passion. Channing warned that the passion for power was "confined to no form of government," but "agitates our own country, and still throws an uncertainty over the great experiment we are making here in behalf of liberty" (*Works*, I, 154).

78. James Walker, *Sermon Delivered on the Day of General Election* (Boston, 1828), p. 14.

79. *Works*, I, 333–334, and IV, 103. WEC to Lucy Aikin, April, 1834, in their *Correspondence*, pp. 203–204.

80. Reported in the Boston *Statesman*, Jan. 12, 1828, and quoted in Arthur Darling, *Political Changes in Massachusetts, 1824–1848*, p. 57.

81. Even the pro-Democratic Arthur Schlesinger, Jr., finds Henshaw somewhat repugnant. *The Age of Jackson* (Boston: Houghton Mifflin, 1945), pp. 147, 165–175, 434.

82. Bowen, *The Principles of Political Economy Applied to the Condition, the Resources, and the Institutions of the American People* (Boston, 1856), p. 2.

83. *See* the *OED*, III, 35, definitions 3, 4, and 5 of "economy"; *see also* Joseph Flubacher, *The Concept of Ethics in the History of Economics* (New York: Vantage Press, 1950), esp. pp. 327–331.

84. WEC, *Works*, I, 246.

85. Michael O'Connor, *Origins of Academic Economics in the United States* (New York: Columbia University Press, 1944), pp. 60, 100. William Ellery Channing defended free trade as late as 1829 (*Works*, I, 350).

86. Joseph Dorfman has provided a good summary of Bowen's views in his comprehensive history of American economic thought. I am concentrating here on the relationship of Bowen's economic ideas to the other concerns of Harvard moral philosophy. *See* Joseph Dorfman, *The Economic Mind in American Civilization, 1606–1865* (New York: Viking Press, 1946), II, 835–844.

87. Bowen, *Political Economy*, pp. vi and vii.

88. *Ibid.*, pp. 214–215.

89. *Ibid.*, pp. 65, 107–115. Joseph Tuckerman promoted the development of savings banks as a means to encourage thrift among the poor.

90. *Ibid.*, pp. 18–19. Bowen's article, "French Ideas of Democracy and Community of Goods," *NAR*, 69 (1849), esp. 324, pursues this subject further.

91. "Self-Culture" (1838), *Works*, II, 389–390.

92. Bowen, *Principles of Metaphysical and Ethical Science* (Boston, 1855), p. 315.

93. *Political Economy,* p. 27.

94. *Political Economy,* pp. 53, 89, 91.

95. WEC, *Works,* I, 255.

96. Walker, "Difficulty, Struggle, Progress," *Sermons* (Boston, 1892), pp. 199, 202. *See also* Octavius B. Frothingham, *Boston Unitarianism, 1820–1850* (New York, 1890), p. 115.

97. Buckminster, *Works* (Boston, 1839), I, 384; Tuckerman, "Letter to the Benevolent Fraternity of Churches," *CE,* 17 (1834), 246; Bowen, "The Jurisprudence of Insanity," *NAR,* 60 (1845), 3.

98. Tuckerman, *Principles and Results of the Ministry-at-Large* (Boston, 1838), p. 236; WEC, *Works,* II, 391.

99. *See* Richard Bushman, *From Puritan to Yankee* (Cambridge: Harvard University Press, 1967), pp. 54–72.

100. WEC, *Works,* I, 351–353; Bowen, *Political Economy,* pp. ix, 95–103; Bowen, "The Oregon Question," *NAR,* 62 (1846), 214–252. *See also* Rush Welter's fine article, "The Frontier West as Image of America's Society," *Mississippi Valley Historical Review,* 46 (1960), 593–614.

101. *Works,* II, 181–261.

102. W. H. Channing, *Memoir of William Ellery Channing,* III, 261–270.

103. WEC to James F. Clarke, April 22, 1837, quoted in Clarke's *Autobiography* (Boston, 1899), pp. 118–119; Joseph Tuckerman, *Principles and Results,* p. 156. *See* further Samuel Reznick, "The Depression of 1819–22," *American Historical Review,* 39 (1933), 28–47; and William Charvat, "American Romanticism and the Depression of 1837," *Science and Society,* 2 (1937), 67–82.

104. Two thought-provoking treatments of the doubts Americans entertained about their rapidly developing society are Marvin Meyers, *The Jacksonian Persuasion* (Stanford: Stanford University Press, 1957); and Fred Somkin, *Unquiet Eagle* (Ithaca: Cornell University Press, 1967).

105. WEC, "The Duty of the Free States" (1842), *Works,* VI, 370–371; WEC, "A Letter to the Editor of the 'Western Messenger,' Louisville, Kentucky," *ibid.,* II, 284.

106. WEC, "The Present Age" (1841), *ibid.,* VI, 168.

IX / PROBLEMS OF MORAL LEADERSHIP

1. Donald Mathews, "The Second Great Awakening as an Organizing Process," *American Quarterly,* 31 (1969), 23–43, calls attention to the importance of institutions outside New England.

2. Henry Ware, Sr., *A Sermon Delivered Before the Evangelical Missionary Society* (Boston, 1820), p. 4.

3. Henry Ware, Jr., "The Duty of Usefulness," (1828), *Works* (Boston, 1847), III, 167. Scholars have taught us much in the past few years about the

connection between the Second Great Awakening of religion and antebellum social reform. *See* Gilbert Barnes, *The Anti-Slavery Impulse* (New York: Appleton-Century, 1933); Alice F. Tyler, *Freedom's Ferment* (Minneapolis: University of Minnesota Press, 1944); Timothy Smith, *Revivalism and Social Reform in Mid-Nineteenth Century America* (New York: Abingdon Press, 1957); and Frank Thistlethwaite, *The Anglo-American Connection in the Early Nineteenth Century* (Philadelphia: University of Pennsylvania Press, 1959).

Conflicting sociological accounts of the origins of the Protestant reform thrust are offered in David Donald, *Lincoln Reconsidered* (New York: Alfred A. Knopf, 1956); Louis Filler, *The Crusade Against Slavery* (New York: Harper & Bros., 1960); and Joseph R. Gusfield, *Symbolic Crusade: Status Politics and the American Temperance Movement* (Urbana, Ill.: University of Illinois Press, 1963).

Remarkable for its broad scope, as well as for its interesting interpretation, is Charles I. Foster, *An Errand of Mercy: The Evangelical United Front, 1790–1837* (Chapel Hill: University of North Carolina Press, 1960). Perhaps the most stimulating overview of the subject is John L. Thomas, "Romantic Reform in America," *American Quarterly,* 17 (1965), 656–681.

4. James Walker, *Reason, Faith and Duty* (Boston, 1876, reprinted 1892), p. 353.

5. Henry Ware, Jr., "Eminent Philanthropists," *CE,* 2 (1825), 23; Francis Bowen, "Sir James Mackintosh," unpublished Bowdoin Prize Essay, Harvard College, 1833, MS in HUA.

6. Foster's *Errand of Mercy* is excellent on the connection between the means and objectives of British and American reformers. Another provocative exploration of the origins of moralistic reform is Richard A. Soloway, "The Onslaught of Respectability: A Study of English Moral Thought During the French Revolution, 1789–1802," unpub. Ph.D. diss., Univerity of Wisconsin, 1960.

7. Henry Ware, Jr., "Memoir of Nathan Parker, D.D.," *Works,* II, 47–50. For the adoption of the Parker plan in Boston, see John Ware, *Memoir of Henry Ware, Jr.* (Boston, 1846), I, 179.

8. Joseph Tuckerman, *The Principles and Results of the Ministry-at-Large in Boston* (Boston, 1838), p. 81.

9. Tuckerman, *On the Elevation of the Poor: A Selection from His Reports As Minister-at-Large in Boston,* intro. Edward Everett Hale, (Boston, 1874), p. 139.

10. Henry Ware, Sr., *Sermon Delivered Before the Convention of Congregational Ministers* (Boston, 1818), p. 10 (cf. other sermons in his Papers, HUA); Joseph S. Buckminster, *Works* (Boston, 1839), II, 410.

11. Levi Frisbie, *Miscellaneous Writings* (Boston, 1823), pp. 88 and 200.

12. John Emery Abbot, *Sermons* (Boston, 1829), p. 114.

13. Walker, *CE,* 13 (1833), 399; and Walker, *CE,* 2 (1825), 248.

14. *See* Charles C. Cole, *The Social Ideas of the Northern Evangelists, 1826–1860* (New York: Columbia University Press, 1954), pp. 110–111.

15. Henry Ware, Jr., *The Combination Against Intemperance Explained and Justified* (Cambridge, 1832); Bowen, "Prison Discipline," *NAR,* 66 (1848), 145–190.

16. Henry Ware, Jr., "Sermon Given to the Roxbury Charitable Society, Sept. 16, 1818," MS in his Sermons, HUA; Buckminster, Sermon on Deuteronomy 33:29 (1807), MS in his Papers, Boston Athenaeum.

17. Joseph Tuckerman, *First Annual Report of the Association of Delegates from the Benevolent Societies of Boston* (Boston, 1835), pp. 7–8.

18. Tuckerman, *On the Elevation of the Poor,* pp. 56–58. According to George Fredrickson, Tuckerman's philanthropic techniques were more compassionate than those of later American charitable organizations (*The Inner Civil War* [New York: Harper & Row, 1965], p. 213).

19. Bowen, "The Abuse of Theories: An Oration Delivered at a Student Exhibition, Harvard University, Oct. 16, 1832," MS in HUA.

20. Bowen, *Political Economy* (Boston, 1856), pp. 131–155. When Joseph Tuckerman visited the famous author of the *Essay on Population* at his home in London, he made similar objections to Malthusianism. The episode is related by Tuckerman's biographer, Daniel T. McColgan. *Joseph Tuckerman: Pioneer in American Social Work* (Washington, D.C.: Catholic University of America Press, 1940), pp. 216–218.

21. WEC, "Ministry for the Poor" (1835), *Works,* IV, 266.

22. Tuckerman, *The Principles and Results of the Ministry-at-Large,* p. 231.

23. *Ibid.,* pp. 228, 244, 246.

24. *Ibid.,* pp. 88–89, 106. Dr. Channing was also convinced that the ministry-at-large was a distinctive product of Unitarian moral philosophy, and, in a rare expression of exclusiveness, opposed co-operating with other denominations in it. *See* John W. Chadwick, *William Ellery Channing* (Boston: Houghton Mifflin, 1903), pp. 326–327.

25. William H. Channing, *Memoir of William Ellery Channing* (Boston, 1851), I, 192 and III, 245–250; Walker, *CE,* 19 (1835), 54–82; *CE,* 23 (1837), 1–29; Walker, *Reason, Faith, and Duty,* p. 275.

26. Quoted in McColgan, *Joseph Tuckerman,* p. 223.

27. WEC, *Memoir,* ed. W. H. Channing, I, 201 and 234.

28. Henry Ware, Jr., *Works,* III, 307.

29. *See* esp., Tuckerman, *Gleams of Truth, or, Scenes from Real Life* (Boston, 1852).

30. Tuckerman, *Principles and Results,* p. 232.

31. A selective bibliography of their writings on these subjects:

BIBLE SOCIETY: Joseph Stevens Buckminster, *Circular Address from the Bible Society of Massachusetts* (Boston, 1809).

TEMPERANCE: WEC, "Address on Temperance" (1837), *Works,* II, 299–346; Henry Ware, Jr., *The Criminality of Intemperance* (Boston, 1823), and *The Combination Against Intemperance Explained and Justified* (Cambridge, 1832); Joseph Tuckerman, *A Letter to the Mechanics of Boston Respecting the Formation of a City Temperance Society* (Boston, 1831); Andrews Norton, "Review," in the *CD,* n.s. 5 (1823), 446–457.

PEACE: Henry Ware, Jr., "The Promise of Universal Peace" (1833) *Works,* III, 122–140, and "The Progress of Peace Principles" *CE,* 33 (1843), 291–306; WEC, "War" (1835), *Works,* IV, 237–263.

ANTI-DUELING: Henry Ware, Jr., "The Law of Honor," *Works,* III, 141–155.

ORPHANAGES: Joseph Stevens Buckminster, "Discourse Before the Female Asylum for Orphans," *Works,* II, 411–412.

PRISON REFORM: Francis Bowen, "Prison Discipline," *NAR,* 66 (1848), 145–190.

LEGAL REFORM: Francis Bowen, "The Jurisprudence of Insanity," *NAR,* 60 (1845), 1–37.

JUVENILE DELINQUENCY REFORM: Joseph Tuckerman, *Eighth Semi-Annual Report of the Fifth Year as Minister-at-Large* (Boston, 1831).

32. A convenient summary of Unitarian efforts in many humanitarian organizations is available in George Willis Cooke, *Unitarianism in America* (Boston: American Unitarian Association, 1902), pp. 321–372.

33. Tuckerman, *Principles and Results of the Ministry-at-Large,* pp. 65–71.

34. The population grew from 25,000 in 1800 to 100,000 in 1840. Some sober reflections on the problems of urbanization in Boston were offered by George Ticknor in his review of Eliza Lee's *Memoirs of the Buckminsters, CE,* 47 (1849), 169–195.

35. The best study of antebellum Boston poverty is in Oscar Handlin, *Boston's Immigrants: A Study in Acculturation,* revised ed. (Cambridge: Harvard University Press, 1959), though it concentrates on the period after 1845. *See also* W. H. Fish, "Unitarianism and Philanthropy," *Meadville Theological School Bulletin,* 3 (1909), 3–14; and William Charvat, "American Romanticism and the Depression of 1837," *Science and Society,* 2 (1937), 67–82.

36. Henry Ware, Jr., *Works,* III, 436.

37. McColgan, *Joseph Tuckerman,* pp. 171–172; Tuckerman, *Principles and Results,* p. 282.

38. Henry Ware, Jr., *Discourse Preached at the Ordination of Robert Waterson as Minister-At-Large* (Boston, 1840), p. 5. The Rev. Charles Lowell, Liberal pastor of West Church, succeeded in adopting a system for families to

share the ownership of pews, thereby enabling working-class families to participate fully in the life of his parish. Though this gained him the largest congregation of any Unitarian church in the city, his example was not followed elsewhere. *See* Frank Otto Gatell, *John Gorham Palfrey and the New England Conscience* (Cambridge: Harvard University Press, 1963), pp. 41–42.

39. A statistic arrived at through a survey of church records conducted by the Unitarian ministers-at-large in 1835, using data from the 1830 census (Tuckerman, *Principles and Results,* pp. 19–26).

40. Buckminster, Sermon on Galatians 6:9 (June, 1808), MS in his Papers, Boston Athenaeum; Henry Ware, Jr., *Discourse for Waterson's Ordination,* p. 17.

41. Andrew Norton, *Review of Professor Frisbie's Address* (Cambridge, 1823, first published 1818), p. 26.

42. WEC, "Discourse on Dr. Tuckerman" (1841), *Works,* VI, 97.

43. Henry Ware, Jr., *Works,* III, 307.

44. Tuckerman, *Principles and Results,* pp. 32–33.

45. For Chalmers' influence on Tuckerman, *see* McColgan, *Joseph Tuckerman,* pp. 99–116. McColgan compiled a list of "works much perused by Joseph Tuckerman," which he appended to his biography. Among the authors are John Quincy Adams, Francis Bacon, Edmund Burke, Letitia Barbould (English Dissenter, reformer, and hymn-writer), Charles Dickens, Thomas à Kempis, Johann Pestalozzi, Nassau Senior, and Jeremy Taylor (Anglican metaphysical poet), as well as standard writers on moral philosophy, natural theology, and political economy.

46. Tuckerman, *Principles and Results,* p. 68.

47. *See* Morton and Lucia White, *The Intellectual Versus the City* (Cambridge: Harvard University Press, 1962).

48. Adam Ferguson, *Institutes of Moral Philosophy,* 2d. ed. (Edinburgh, 1773), p. 244.

49. Quoted in William B. Sprague, *Annals of the American Pulpit* (New York, 1865), VIII, 346.

50. Much of Bowen's faith was predicated upon his belief in the adaptability and inherent equality of the newcomers: "Even the Irish immigrant here soon loses his careless, lazy, and turbulent disposition, and becomes as sober, prudent, industrious, and frugal as his neighbors," he declared in 1856. The confidence of antebellum Unitarians can be contrasted with the pessimism and racism which overcame many postwar Brahmins. *See,* for example, the introduction which Edward Everett Hale wrote for an 1874 edition of Tuckerman's writings, expressing Hale's misgivings about the prospects for a cohesive urban society (*On the Elevation of the Poor,* cited in note 9).

51. In 1837 there were 110 boys at the Farm School (Tuckerman, *Principles and Results,* p. 137).

52. Tuckerman's quarterly reports of 1837, and his semiannual reports for the next four years, were all published in Boston by Isaac R. Butts.

53. The title of McColgan's biography. For a thorough discription of Tuckerman's methods of operation, *see* Cooke, *Unitarianism in America,* pp. 247–261, and McColgan, *Joseph Tuckerman,* pp. 117–122.

54. McColgan, *Joseph Tuckerman,* p. 123.

55. Joseph Tuckerman, *Principles and Results,* p. 8; *American Unitarian Biography,* ed. William Ware (Boston, 1851), II, 52–54.

56. Tuckerman, *Principles and Results,* pp. 286, 64, 311. Tuckerman added, however, that only the propertied person himself could be the judge of how much of his goods he should turn over to the poor, and how much he should keep.

57. *Ibid.,* pp. 291–292.

58. Tuckerman, *An Essay on the Wages Paid to Females for Their Labour* (Philadelphia, 1830), pp. 46–47.

59. For a further discussion of Tuckerman's classification of paupers and the poor, and of his method of treating them, *see* Christopher Eliot, "Joseph Tuckerman," Unitarian Hist. Soc., *Proceedings,* 4:1 (1935), esp. 27–29.

60. Tuckerman, *On the Elevation of the Poor,* pp. 105–106.

61. *Ibid.,* pp. 84–89.

62. Tuckerman, *Principles and Results,* pp. 283 and 275.

63. *Ibid.,* pp. 300–301; cf. Francis Bowen, *Political Economy,* pp. 228–229. Tuckerman had won the traditional Harvard award for academic excellence, the *detur digniori,* in 1797, and received as a prize a copy of Adam Ferguson's *Civil Society.*

64. Tuckerman, *On the Wages Paid to Females,* p. 17.

65. Tuckerman, *Principles and Results,* pp. 55–58.

66. William Ellery Channing added a further twist to Tuckerman's warning: if the middle class remained "comfortable" and "insensible" of the moral claims of the poor, it would *deserve* the revolution which would eventually ensue ("Ministry for the Poor," [1835], *Works,* IV, 299–300).

67. Tuckerman, "Letter to Executive Committee," p. 236; and *On the Elevation of the Poor,* p. 27.

68. *Second Annual Report of the Central Board of the Benevolent Fraternity of Churches* (Boston, 1836), p. 7.

69. Cyrus Bartol, "Review of Tuckerman's *Principles and Results of the Ministry at Large,*" CE, 25 (1838), 220. Tuckerman's influence extended to many Europeans; *see* the "Memoir" (1848) written by the Englishwoman Mary Carpenter in *American Unitarian Biography,* II, 29–136.

70. Tuckerman, *A Letter on the Principles of the Missionary Enterprise* (Boston, 1827), p. 40. Tuckerman's italics.

71. Cf. Clifford S. Griffin's hypothesis, "Religious Benevolence as Social Control, 1800–1865," *Miss. Valley Hist. Review,* 44 (1957), 423–444.

72. The judgments of historians vary. Father McColgan found Tuckerman's religious motivations highly praiseworthy (*Joseph Tuckerman,* p. xiii); while Christopher Eliot welcomed the nineteenth-century philanthropist as an ally against the welfare state ("Joseph Tuckerman," p. 31). More recently, others have evaluated Tuckerman less favorably. Arthur M. Schlesinger, Jr., regards his brand of reform as largely a sop to the guilt-feelings of the employing class (*The Age of Jackson* [Boston: Little, Brown & Co., 1945], p. 273). Robert H. Bremner finds Tuckerman "obsessed by a fear of pauperism . . . The only commodity [he] dared offer [the poor] was advice" (*American Philanthropy* [Chicago: University of Chicago Press, 1960], p. 60).

73. Henry Ware, Jr., *On the Formation of a Christian Character* (1831), *Works,* IV, 314. A similar enumeration by Buckminster is headed by "education." MS in his Papers, Boston Athenaeum.

74. Walker, "Balance of Character," *Liberal Preacher,* 1 (1828), 170. WEC's "Remarks on Education" (1833), *Works,* I, 369–387, is a noble presentation of Liberal ideals.

75. Two citations of many possible: Norton, "The Duty of Continual Improvement," *CE,* 2 (1825), 412–419; Walker, "The End Not Yet," *Sermons* (Boston, 1861, reprinted 1892), p. 327.

76. Henry Ware, Jr., "Education the Business of Life," (1837), *Works,* III, 271–296.

77. *See* Walter B. Kolesnick, *Mental Discipline in Modern Education* (Madison: University of Wisconsin Press, 1958), pp. 10–29; and Laurence R. Veysey, *The Emergence of the American University* (Chicago: University of Chicago Press, 1965), pp. 22–25.

78. *See* Will Monroe, *The Pestalozzian Movement in the United States* (Syracuse, N.Y.: C. W. Bardeen, 1907); Dugald Stewart, *Elements of the Philosophy of the Human Mind* (Boston, 1818), I, 20; and the *MA,* 7 (1809), 264–271.

79. *See* Paul J. Fay, "Isaac Watts: An Unsung Singer of Education," *School and Society,* 28 (1928), 217–224; also *CD,* n.s., 2 (1820), 461.

80. Henry Ware, Jr., *Works,* III, 272–273.

81. WEC, quoted in W. H. Channing, *Memoir* (Boston, 1851), II, 131; Frisbie to Levi Frisbie, Sr., July 31, 1803, *Miscellaneous Writings,* p. xiv.

82. Bowen, *Political Economy* (Boston, 1856), p. 68.

83. Bowen, *Critical Essays on Speculative Philosophy* (Boston, 1842), p. 311.

84. Walker, "The Heart More than the Head," *Sermons,* p. 269.

85. "Remarks on Education" (1833), *Works,* I, 382; "Self-Culture" (1838), *Works,* II, 360–361.

86. James Walker, *CE,* 14 (1833), 191; and Walker, *Sermons,* pp. 204 and 295.

87. "College Education," *NAR*, 55 (1842), 302–343; Richard Hofstadter and Walter Metzger, *The Development of Academic Freedom in the United States* (New York: Columbia University Press, 1955), pp. 209–212.

88. WEC to Lucy Aiken, Aug. 26, 1832, in their *Correspondence*, ed. Anna Le Breton (London, 1874), p. 146; "Likeness to God" (1828), *Works*, III, 249.

89. Henry Ware, Jr., "How to Spend a Day," *Works*, I, 173–174; WEC, "Self-Culture," *Works*, II, 368–369.

90. The reader is referred to the biographical sketches in the appendix.

91. Henry Ware, Sr., *A Sermon Delivered on the Anniversary Election* (Boston, 1821), pp. 15–16.

92. Walker, *Introductory Lecture Delivered Before the American Institute of Instruction* (Boston, 1856), p. 19.

93. There is a considerable secondary literature describing this attitude, which was typical of orthodox as well as Liberal academics in the early national period. *See,* for example, Merle Curti, *The Social Ideas of American Educators* (New York: Charles Scribner's, 1935, reprinted 1965), pp. 86–87.

94. Henry Ware, Jr., Sermon on Psalm 122:6 (for a fast day), 1824, MS in HUA; Walker, *Inaugural Address as President of Harvard College* (Cambridge, 1853), pp. 34–46.

95. "The Necessity of Education in a Republican Government" (1838), *Life and Works of Horace Mann*, ed. Mary Mann (Cambridge, 1867), II, 143–188. Rush Welter, *Popular Education and Democratic Thought* (New York: Columbia University Press, 1962), chaps. 5 and 6, helps relate Mann to his Unitarian Whig intellectual context. Mann's correspondence with Dr. Channing may be found in the Horace Mann Papers, Mass. Historical Society. Their relationship is also discussed in Jonathan Messerli's excellent dissertation, "Horace Mann: The Early Years," Harvard Graduate School of Education, 1963.

96. Raymond Culver, *Horace Mann and Religion in the Massachusetts Public Schools* (New Haven: Yale University Press, 1929); Joseph Tuckerman, *On the Elevation of the Poor*, pp. 126–127; Francis Bowen, "Horace Mann," *NAR*, 60 (1845), 224–246.

97. WEC, "Remarks on Education" (1833), *Works*, I, 387; George Bancroft to Andrews Norton, April 24, 1825; Joseph G. Cogswell to same, January 1, 1831, and December 11, 1832, MSS in Andrews Norton Papers, HCL.

98. Madeleine H. Rice, *Federal Street Pastor* (New York: Bookman Associates, 1961), pp. 195–196; James Walker, "Review of Bronson Alcott's Conversations with Children," *CE*, 23 (1837), 252–261.

99. The development of private academies and preparatory schools in the United States will be traced in James S. McLachlan's forthcoming book, *American Boarding Schools* (New York: Charles Scribner's Sons, 1970). It explores the connection between Round Hill and Unitarian educational ideals in some detail.

100. *See* George P. Schmidt, "Intellectual Crosscurrents in American Colleges, 1825–1855," *American Historical Review,* 42 (1936), 46–67. The Yale Report has been partially reprinted in *American Higher Education: A Documentary History,* ed. Richard Hofstadter and Wilson Smith (Chicago: Chicago University Press, 1961), I, 275–291.

101. For the background of classical learning in America, *see* Richard M. Gummere, *The American Colonial Mind and the Classical Tradition* (Cambridge: Harvard University Press, 1963). George P. Schmidt, *The Liberal Arts College* (New Brunswick, N.J.: Rutgers University Press, 1957), contains a good description of the usual curriculum in chap. 3.

102. Two Unitarian defenses of the "classical" curriculum are Frisbie's "On Tacitus" (1818), *Miscellaneous Writings,* pp. 27–41; and Bowen's "Classical Studies at Cambridge," *NAR,* 54 (1842), 35–73.

103. WEC, Extract from his Papers as a Fellow of Harvard College (1813–1826), quoted in *Memoir,* II, 130.

104. *The Education of Henry Adams* (Boston: Houghton Mifflin, 1961), p. 55. Joseph Story remembered the old Harvard system fondly; he is quoted in Channing's *Memoir,* I, 45–50. James Freeman Clarke, on the other hand, complained about its shortcomings in his *Autobiography,* ed. Edward E. Hale (Boston, 1899), pp. 34–42.

105. George Bancroft to Andrews Norton, April 24, 1825, Norton Papers, HCL; George Ticknor, *Life, Letters, and Journals* (Boston, 1880), I, 355; WEC, quoted in *Memoir,* II, 132–137 and III, 77–81. Norton married Catherine Eliot; Ticknor, her sister Anna. The two women were daughters of Samuel Eliot, who had endowed the Eliot Professorship of Greek held by Edward Everett.

106. The story of this reform movement is related at length by David Tyack in *George Ticknor and the Boston Brahmins* (Cambridge: Harvard University Press, 1967), pp. 85–128. Some of Ticknor's proposals are reprinted in Hofstadter and Smith, *American Higher Education,* I, 269–273.

107. Samuel E. Morison, *Three Centuries of Harvard* (Cambridge: Harvard University Press, 1936), pp. 158–160. *See also* John Kirkpatrick, "The Rise of Non-Resident Government in Harvard University," *Harvard Graduates' Magazine,* 31 (1922), 186–193.

108. *Memorial to the Reverend and Honourable the Overseers of Harvard University* (Cambridge, 1824), signed by Henry Ware, Levi Hedge and Edward Everett.

109. Andrews Norton to Joseph Story, August 2, 1823, Norton Papers, HCL. This letter explains Norton's position thoroughly.

110. Norton, *Speech Delivered before the Overseers of Harvard College* (Boston, 1825), p. 7.

111. Josiah Quincy, *History of Harvard University* (Cambridge, 1840), II, 344.

112. *See* Samuel E. Morison, "The Great Rebellion in Harvard College and the Resignation of President Kirkland," Colonial Soc. of Mass., *Transactions,* 27 (1928), 54–112.

113. Quincy, *History of Harvard University,* II, 365.

114. Such developments were all perceived as parts of a whole by James Walker in *On the Exclusive System* (Boston, 1830) ; and *CE,* 13 (1833) , 346.

115. *See* Samuel E. Morison, "Francis Bowen, an Early Test of Academic Freedom in Massachusetts," Mass. Hist. Soc., *Proceedings,* 65 (1936), 507–511; and Hofstadter and Metzger, *Academic Freedom in the United States,* pp. 247, 253.

116. Norton to Joseph Story, Aug. 2, 1823, MS in Andrews Norton Papers, HCL.

117. Norton to John Gorham Palfrey, June 8, 1840, Norton Papers, HCL. The trend which Norton deplored was, of course, widespread in American colleges; *see* Earl J. McGrath, "The Control of Higher Education in America," *Educational Record,* 17 (1936) , 259–272.

118. Of the twelve moralists treated here, only seven were ordained ministers: Dr. Channing, the Wares, Abbot, Tuckerman, Buckminster, and Walker.

119. *MA,* 9 (1810) , 350.

120. Henry Ware, Jr., "The Principles That Should Govern a Young Man in the Choice of a Profession" (n.d., but between 1830 and 1843), *Works,* III, 265.

121. WEC to Jonathan Phillips, Dec. 28, 1833, MS in Phillips Papers, Mass. Historical Society, Boston; Walker, *Discourse at the Induction of Frederick D. Huntington, as Preacher to the University* (Cambridge, 1855) , p. 17.

X / THE SLAVERY QUESTION

1. Harvard's reputation for religious heterodoxy kept southern students away for much of the antebellum period, but when Jared Sparks became president he made use of his southern contacts to recruit extensively. Between 1849 and 1853 almost one third of the undergraduates in Harvard College were southerners. *See* Samuel E. Morison, *Three Centuries of Harvard* (Cambridge: Harvard University Press, 1936) , p. 281. No less than seventeen Confederate generals were Harvard alumni.

2. WEC, *Works* (Boston, 1848), II, 7.

3. David Brion Davis, *The Problem of Slavery in Western Culture* (Ithaca, N.Y.: Cornell University Press, 1966) , esp. pp. 348–364.

4. Henry Ware, Jr., *Works* (Boston, 1847), IV, 244; WEC, *Works,* III, 305.

5. "The Object and Means of the Christian Ministry" (1837), *Works,* IV, 245.

6. Joseph S. Buckminster, Sermon on Joshua (1809), MS in Houghton Library, HCL.

7. Davis, *The Problem of Slavery*, pp. 114–118.

8. Andrews Norton in the *MA*, 8 (1810), 397–419. WEC, *Notebook*, ed. Grace Ellery Channing (Boston, 1887), p. 23; WEC, *Works*, II, 369.

9. WEC, *Slavery* (1835), *Works*, II, 99–106.

10. WEC, "Remarks on the Slavery Question, in a Letter to Jonathan Phillips" (1839), *Works*, V, 49. Adam Ferguson, the Scot often treated as an authority on civil polity by Harvard Unitarians, had held that "the supposed property of the master in the slave is a matter of usurpation, not of right" (*Institutes of Moral Philosophy*, 2d ed. [Edinburgh, 1773], p. 202).

11. Henry Ware, Sr., *A Sermon Delivered on the Anniversary Election* (Boston, 1821), pp. 14–18.

12. For example, WEC to Lucy Aikin, Aug. 30, 1833, *Correspondence* (London, 1874), p. 181. Even J. S. Buckminster had a copy of Wilberforce's antislavery writings, as the printed *Catalogue* of his library (Boston, 1812) shows.

13. *See* esp. David Donald, "Toward a Reconsideration of Abolitionists," reprinted in Donald's *Lincoln Reconsidered* (New York: Alfred A. Knopf, 1961), pp. 19–36.

14. Octavius B. Frothingham, *Boston Unitarianism, 1820–1850* (New York, 1890), pp. 196–197.

15. John W. Chadwick, *William Ellery Channing* (Boston: Houghton Mifflin, 1903), pp. 287–289. Chadwick calls his persistent refusal to have any personal relations with Garrison "the most inexplicable feature of his antislavery career, and the most unfortunate."

16. Here I am indebted to conversation with David D. Hall, as well as to his unpublished dissertation, "The Faithful Shepherd: The Puritan Ministry in Old and New England, 1570–1660," Yale University, 1963.

17. Henry Ware, Sr., *A Sermon Delivered at the Ordination of Charles Brooks* (Boston, 1821), p. 3.

18. *See* John R. Bodo, *Protestant Clergy and Public Issues* (Princeton: Princeton University Press, 1954), pp. 23–28. A contemporary observer who reached much the same conclusions was Robert Baird; *see* his *Religion in America* (New York, 1844), p. 278.

19. Tappan's parting shot upon leaving New England and the American Unitarian Association was published under the title *Letter from a Gentleman in Boston to a Unitarian Clergyman of that City* (Boston, 1828). His line of argument (that Liberal religion had a feeble "moral tendency"!) angered Unitarians and provoked Henry Ware, Jr., to issue a *Reply of a Unitarian Clergyman to the "Letter of a Gentleman in Boston"* (Boston, 1828).

20. WEC, "Remarks on Associations" (1829), *Works*, I, 290.

21. Francis Bowen, *Principles of Metaphysical and Ethical Science,* 2d ed. (Boston, 1855), p. 327.

22. Joseph Tuckerman in *A Memorial of Joseph Tuckerman* (Worcester, Mass., 1888), p. 262.

23. This is from the brillant anonymous essay on "Paley and Channing" in the London *National Review,* 6 (1858), 398.

24. James Walker, *Sermons Preached in the Chapel of Harvard College* (Boston, 1861, reprinted 1892), p. 273.

25. Henry Ware, Jr., *Works,* III, 292; Walker, *Sermons,* p. 363.

26. Henry Ware, Jr., *Works,* III, 293; WEC, "Remarks on Associations" (1829), *Works,* I, 291.

27. On the escapist tendencies within Unitarianism and Transcendentalism, *see* Jane Johnson, "Through Change and Through Storm: Federalist-Unitarian Thought, 1800–1860," unpub. Ph.D. diss., Radcliffe College, 1958.

28. WEC, quoted in his newphew's *Memoir,* I, 104–108 and 180.

29. Bowen, *Critical Essays on Speculative Philosophy* (Boston, 1842), p. 233; Henry Ware, Jr., "Facilities and Hinderances to a Religious Life on the Part of the Scholar" (n.d.), *Works,* III, 339; and "Sources of Moral Weakness and Moral Strength," *Works,* III, 178–186; Edward T. Channing, *Lectures Read to Seniors in Harvard College* (Boston, 1856), pp. 126, 203, and 262.

30. WEC, "Charge at the Ordination of John Sullivan Dwight" (1840), *Works,* V, 310.

31. George Ticknor, *Life, Letters, and Journals* (Boston, 1876, reprinted 1880), I, 183.

32. E. T. Channing, *Lectures,* p. 160.

33. Alfred North Whitehead, *Adventures of Ideas* (New York: Macmillan Co., 1933), esp. pp. 17–32.

34. Daniel McColgan, *Joseph Tuckerman* (Washington, D.C.: Catholic University of American Press, 1940), p. 50.

35. Mass. Constitutional Convention of 1820, *Journal of Debates* (Boston, 1821), p. 87; McColgan, *Tuckerman,* p. 223.

36. James Freeman Clarke, *Autobiography,* ed. Edward E. Hale (Boston, 1891), pp. 213–214.

37. John Ware, *Memoir of Henry Ware, Jr.,* II, 146–155. Since May was a Puritan descendant and a Harvard alumnus (a former pupil of the elder Ware, in fact), it is especially interesting that he should have been regarded as an outside agitator.

38. *See* Morison, *Three Centuries of Harvard,* pp. 254–255; and Henry A. Pochmann, *German Culture in America* (Madison: University of Wisconsin Press, 1957), p. 115.

39. Henry Ware, Jr., to Samuel J. May, October 15, 1834, and to "a friend," October 23, 1835, quoted in Ware's *Memoir,* II, 152–155.

40. John Ware, *Memoir of Henry Ware, Jr.,* II, 150.

41. *See* the *CE,* 26 (1839), 272; *CE,* 27 (1839), 284; and Ware's "Anti-Slavery Song" (Tune: "Wild Hunt of Lutzow"), *Works,* I, 244–245.

42. *Political Economy* (Boston, 1856), pp. 116–117.

43. "Review of *Captain Canot, or Twenty Years of an African Slaver,* by Brantz Mayer," *NAR,* 80 (1855), 153–170; quotation from p. 160.

44. *Ibid.,* pp. 155–158.

45. Charles Sumner to Francis Bowen, August 10, 1847; Bowen to John G. Palfrey, December 28, 1847, MSS in Houghton Library, HCL. Massachusetts Whig politics in this period is treated in Kinley Brauer, *Cotton Versus Conscience* (Lexington, Ky.: University of Kentucky Press, 1967).

46. Francis Bowen, "The California and Territorial Question," *NAR,* 71 (1850), 221–268.

47. *MA,* 8 (1810), 397–419; *Select Journal,* 1 (1834), 98, and 2 (1834), 48.

48. Andrews Norton to John G. Palfrey, October 29, 1846, Norton Papers, HCL; Norton to Nathan Appleton, November 4, 1846, Appleton Papers, Mass. Historical Society.

49. [Andrews Norton?], newspaper clippings from *Boston Atlas* and *Boston Daily Advertiser,* December 1837, among Andrews Norton Papers, HCL; Norton to William Ware, n.d. (ca. 1840), MS in Norton Papers.

50. Francis Bowen, *Critical Essays,* pp. 336–337; Henry Ware, Sr., Sermon on Psalm 103:1–2 (1804) and Sermon on Psalm 85:8 (1831), MS in HUA; Henry Ware, Jr., "The Duties of Young Men in Respect to the Dangers of the Country" (ca. 1842), *Works,* II, 211–212.

51. Frisbie, "The Right and Duty of Government to Provide for the Support of Religion by Law" (1821), *Miscellaneous Writings,* pp. 99–100; Walker, "Our Duty in Respect to Other Men's Consciences" (1860), *Reason, Faith and Duty* (Boston, 1892), 433–435; Channing, "Spiritual Freedom" (1830) and "Lecture on War" (1838), *Works,* IV, 78–79, and V, 138–140. The quotations are from Walker and Channing, respectively.

52. [Andrews Norton] "Remarks on the Fugitive Slave Law," *Boston Atlas,* Nov. 26, 1850.

53. WEC to unknown correspondent, Sept. 27, 1824, MS in HUA. Dr. Channing's brother Edward was the only professor, other than Ticknor, not to sign the statement asserting the right of resident instructors to be Fellows of Harvard College.

54. Quoted in Chadwick, *William Ellery Channing,* p. 265.

55. *Ibid.,* p. 189.

56. Journal entry in 1810, printed in W. H. Channing's *Memoir,* I, 223. He is quoting from *Henry V,* IV.iii. "Charge at the Ordination of John S. Dwight" (1840), *Works,* V, 315.

57. *Memoir,* I, 32 and 85; WEC to Andrews Norton, Jan. 24, 1831, Norton Papers, HCL.

58. Chadwick, *William Ellery Channing,* pp. 318–319; WEC, *Works,* V, 29.

59. Clarke, *Autobiography,* p. 119; WEC, *Works,* II, 142.

60. WEC, *Works,* II, 121, 144.

61. *Ibid.,* 128.

62. Quoted in W. H. Channing, *Memoir,* III, 156–158.

63. *Slavery* occupies pp. 5–153 of vol. II of the collected *Works.*

64. Slavery "was in its essence a process of infantilization," writes Kenneth Stampp in *The Peculiar Institution* (New York: Alfred A. Knopf, 1956), p. 327. Among other treatments of this controversial topic, the most widely read has been Stanley Elkins, *Slavery* (Chicago: University of Chicago Press, 1959), chap. 3.

65. *Works,* II, 60, 67, 70; and V, 38.

66. "The Historian and Southern Negro Slavery," *American Historical Review,* 57 (1952), 613–624.

67. *Slavery* (1835), *Works,* II, 116; *see also* WEC, "Remarks on the Slavery Question" (1839), *Works,* V, 7–106.

68. WEC, *Works,* V, 58.

69. WEC, *Works,* II, 75, 51, and V, 84.

70. Waddy Thompson of South Carolina, quoted in Madeleine Rice, *Federal Street Pastor* (New York: Bookman Associates, 1961), p. 223.

71. WEC to Ferris Pell, May 14, 1842, quoted in *Memoir,* II, 324–325; WEC to George Ellis, February 27, 1837, Ellis Papers, Mass. Historical Soc.

72. WEC to a Virginian, September 16, 1841, quoted in *Memoir,* III, 238.

73. WEC, "Remarks," *Works,* V, 96–97.

74. WEC, "Emancipation," *ibid.,* VI, 61.

75. WEC, "Letter to the Hon. Henry Clay on the Annexation of Texas" (1837), *ibid.,* II, 229.

76. Henry Adams, "Review of Ticknor's *Life, Letters, and Journals,*" *NAR,* 123 (1876), 214.

77. David Van Tassel, "Gentlemen of Property and Standing: Compromise Sentiment in Boston in 1850," *New England Quarterly,* 23 (1950), 307–319; WEC to James G. Birney, Nov. 1, 1836, *Works,* II, 172.

78. *See* Charles Lyttle, "Tentative History of the Ministerial Conference in Berry Street," *Meadville Theol. School Quart. Bull.,* 24 (1930), 15–25.

79. *See* Oscar and Mary Handlin, *Commonwealth: Massachusetts, 1774–1861* (New York: New York University Press, 1947), pp. 195–217; *See also* Oscar Handlin, *Boston's Immigrants,* revised ed. (Cambridge: Harvard University Press, 1959).

80. James Walker, *Discourse Delivered in Harvard Church, Charlestown, on Taking Leave of His Society* (Cambridge, 1839), p. 24. *See also* Wilson Smith, *Professors and Public Ethics* (Ithaca: Cornell University Press, 1956), chap. 8.

81. Walker, "Public Opinion" (1856), *Reason, Faith, and Duty,* p. 224.

82. Walker, "Our Duty in Respect to Other Men's Consciences" (1860), *ibid.,* p. 436.

83. *Ibid.,* pp. 429 and 427.

84. Orestes Brownson, "Jouffroy," *CE,* 22 (1837), 181–217; Walker in the *CE,* 24 (1838), 273; Dugald Stewart, *Active and Moral Powers of Man,* ed. James Walker (Cambridge, 1849), Appendix; WEC to Jonathan Phillips, November 5, 1834, Mass. Historical Soc.; WEC to Andrews Norton, n.d. [1836], Norton Papers, HCL; Théodore Simon Jouffroy, *Introduction to Ethics,* trans. W. H. Channing (Boston, 1840).

85. Jouffroy, *Introduction to Ethics,* p. 313.

86. *Ibid.,* pp. 315–321.

87. *Ibid.,* p. 292.

88. George Fredrickson, *The Inner Civil War* (New York: Harper & Row, 1965), pp. 27, 70, and passim.

89. WEC to James Martineau, September 10, 1841, quoted in *Memoir,* II, 399.

90. Sydney Ahlstrom, "Theology in America: A Historical Survey," in *The Shaping of American Religion,* ed. A. L. Smith and J. W. Jamison (Princeton: Princeton University Press, 1961), I, 260.

91. *See* Laurence R. Veysey, *The Emergence of the American University* (Chicago: University of Chicago Press, 1965).

92. *See* Stow Persons, *Free Religion: An American Faith* (New Haven: Yale University Press, 1947); *see also* John W. Chadwick, *Old and New Unitarian Belief* (Boston, 1894).

93. Bowen, "J. S. Mill on the Theory of Causation," *NAR,* 78 (1854), 82–105.

94. WEC, "Notices of Samuel Cooper Thacher," (1818), *Works,* V, 435; Ralph Waldo Emerson, *Works* (Boston, 1903), X, 204 and 552; anonymous article in London *National Review,* 6 (1858), 416.

95. WEC once confessed that he did not find *Don Quixote* funny: "I sympathize with and venerate the knight too much to laugh at him, and wish to join him in discomfiting his assailants" (quoted in *Memoir,* III, 363).

96. Herschel Baker, *The Dignity of Man: Studies in the Persistence of an Idea* (Cambridge: Harvard University Press, 1947), p. 274.

97. WEC, quoted in *Memoir,* III, 98.

98. James S. McLachlan has found that, out of a sample of 450 prominent late nineteenth-century "mugwump" reformers, over one third (33.9 percent) had been reared Unitarians. This was more than were identified with any other

denomination. *See* "The Genteel Reformers," unpub. Master's thesis, Columbia University, 1960.

99. Bowen, *Critical Essays,* p. 333.

100. Frederick T. Gray, *Sermon Occasioned by the Death of Henry Ware, Jr.* (Boston, 1843), p. 11.

101. Bowen, *NAR,* 62 (1846), 196.

102. Quoted in David Edgell, *William Ellery Channing: An Intellectual Portrait* (Boston: Beacon Press, 1955), p. 97.

104. Ralph Barton Perry, *Puritanism and Democracy* (New York: Vanguard Press, 1944), p. 158.

105. Christopher R. Eliot, *et al., The Seventy-Fifth Anniversary of the Founding of the Ministry-at-Large* (Boston, 1901), pp. 21, 28.

Index

Index